CHILDREN OF THE WHALES

Story and Art by Abi Umeda

Volume

17

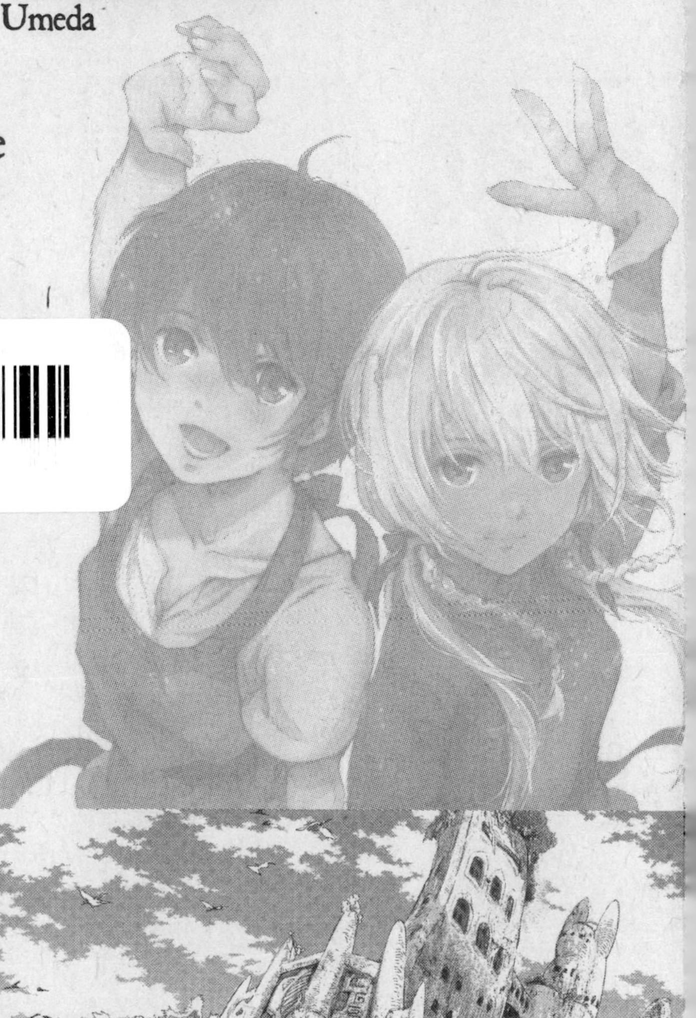

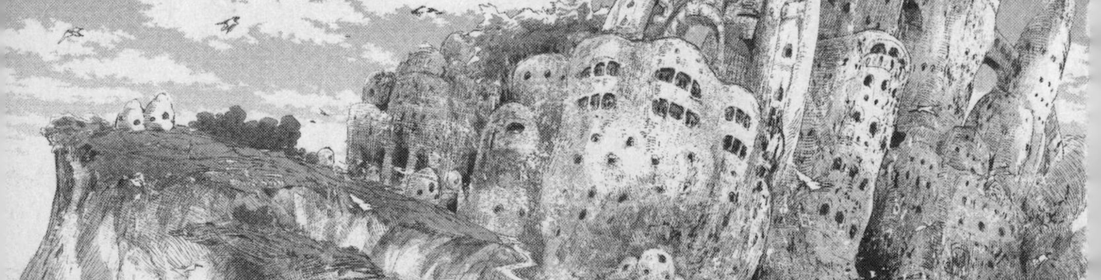

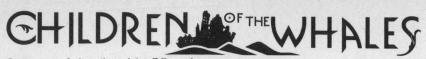

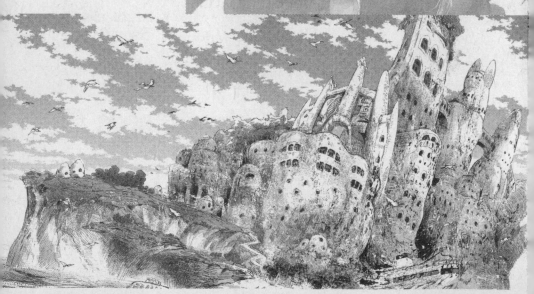

Characters

On the Mud Whale

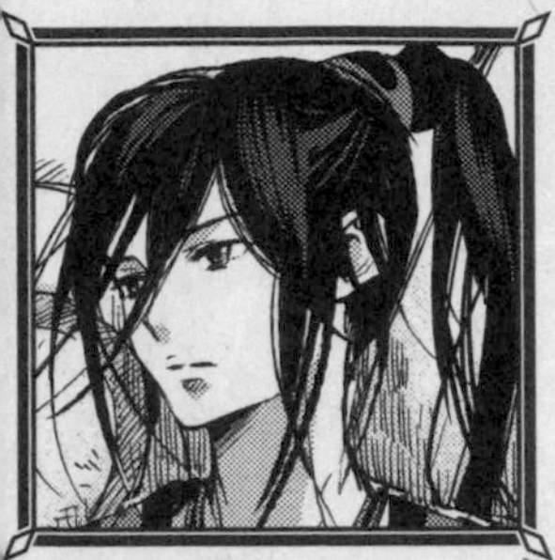

Ouni
(Marked, 16 years old)

A very powerful thymia user who possesses the strength of a daimona. He was being held by Orca but Chakuro and the others rescue him.

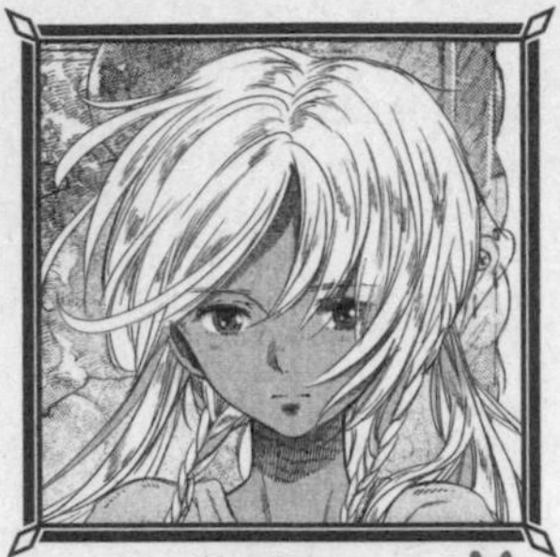

Lykos
(Marked, 14 years old)

A girl from the Allied Empire who comes aboard the Mud Whale. She is captured by Orca but is saved by Chakuro and others.

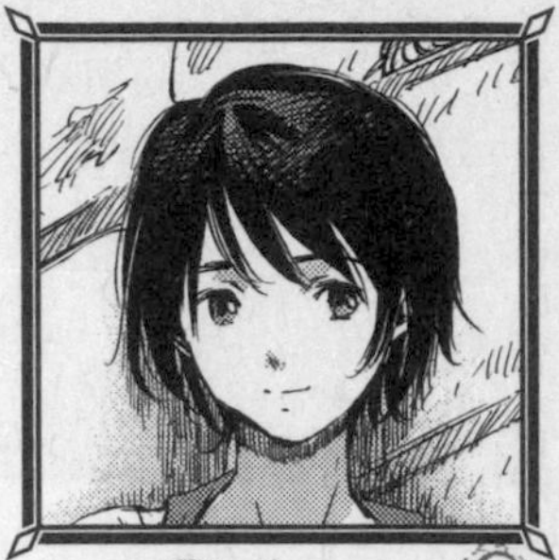

Chakuro
(Marked, 14 years old)

The young archivist of the Mud Whale. He sneaks onto Karcharías to save Lykos and Ouni. He and Orca have a confrontation.

Former Allied Empire

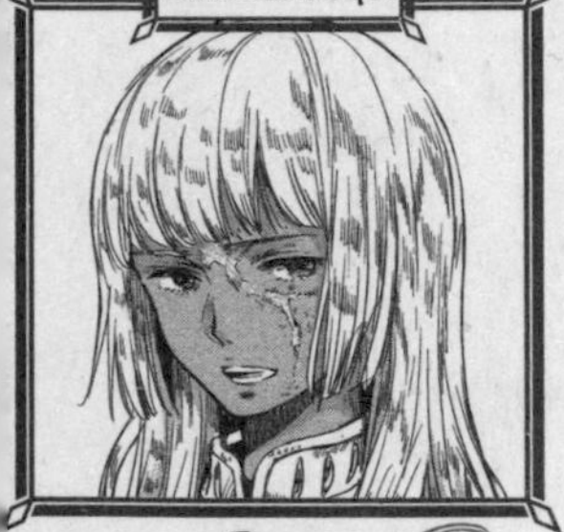

Orca
(Marked)

powerful thymia user and Lykos's brother. He as seized the battleship Karcharías and declared his independence from the empire.

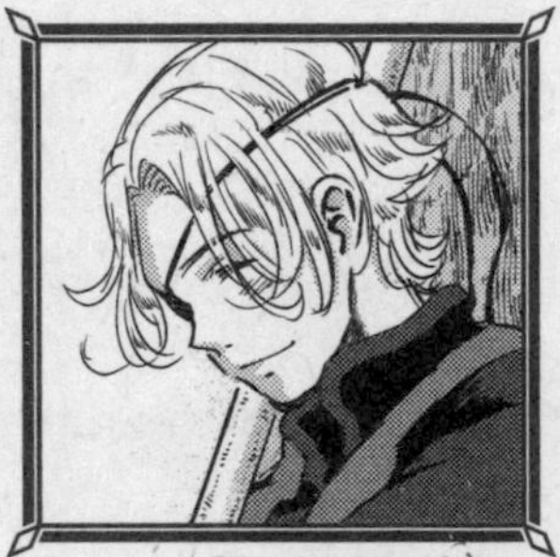

Shuan
(Marked, 26 years old)

Former commander of the Vigilante Corps. He accompanies Suou to Karcharías as his bodyguard after Suou asks him for help.

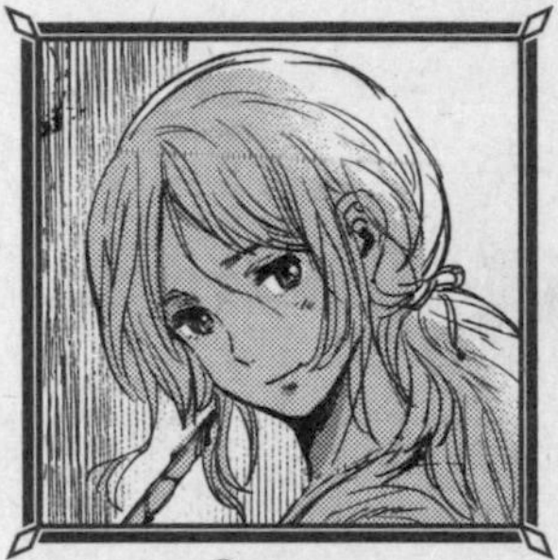

Suou
(Unmarked, 17 years old)

Mayor of the Mud Whale. He secretly goes to Karcharías to rescue his friends and attempts to negotiate with Orca.

Allied Empire

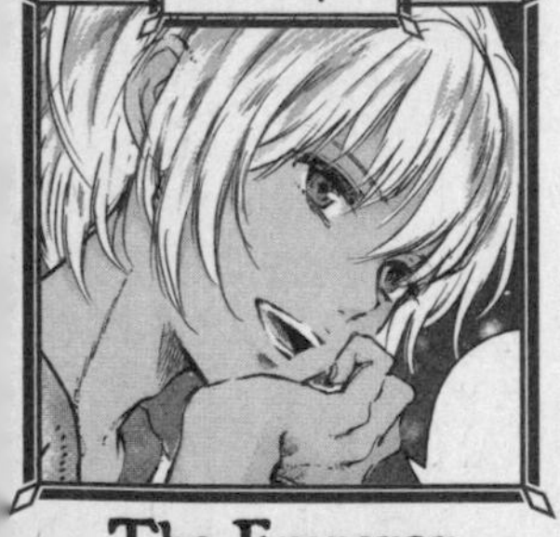

The Emperor

The most powerful man in the empire bears an uncanny resemblance to Chakuro. He seeks Faláina and plans to crush Orca's insurrection.

Allied Empire

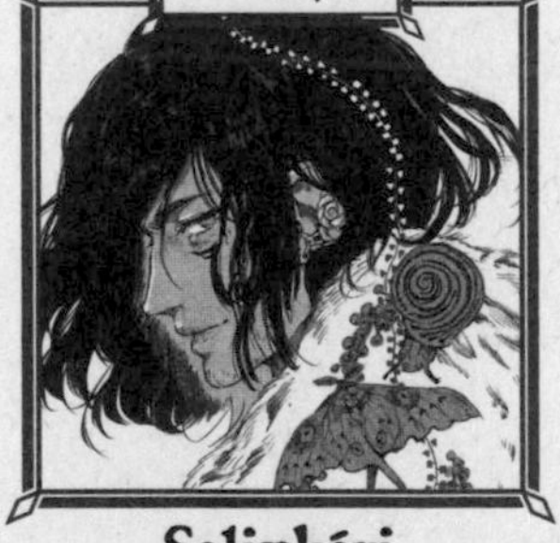

Salinkári

Commander of the battleship Geráki. He brainwashed Orca when he was younger and made him destroy the island of Kítrino.

Former Allied Empire

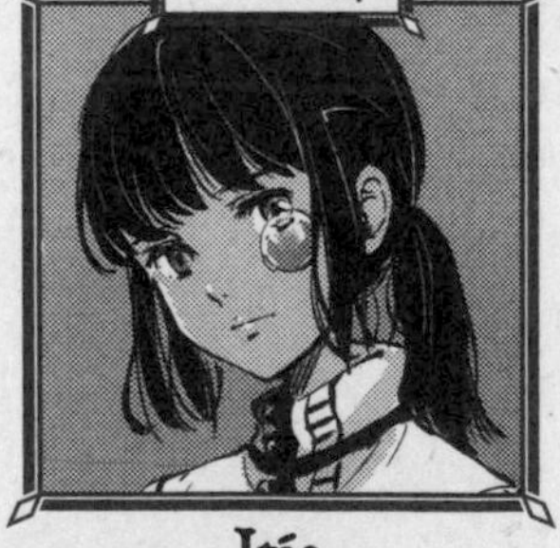

Itía

The archivist on the battleship Skyros before it sank. Although she is Orca's wife, she sympathizes with Chakuro and agrees to help him.

Glossary of the Sea of Sand

The Mud Whale — A huge, drifting island-ship. Those in the empire who resisted giving up their emotions were exiled here, along with all their descendants.

Thymia — Telekinetic power derived from emotions.

The Marked — The 90 percent of the Mud Whale population who are thymia users. They are all short-lived.

The Unmarked — The members of the Mud Whale population who cannot use thymia. Unlike the Marked, they are long-lived.

Nous — A unique organism that obtains energy from peoples' emotions and gives people the power of thymia in return.

Nous Fálaina — A Nous that dwells deep within the Belly of the Mud Whale. Unlike other Nouses, it consumes the life force of humans rather than their emotions.

The Allied Empire — A large nation on the Sea of Sand that controls its citizenry through the Nouses and their absorption of emotions.

Daímonas — A legend from the empire. A being said to be able to destroy a Nous.

 A Record of the Mud Whale and the Sea of Sand

Year 93 of the Sand Exile.

The Mud Whale drifts endlessly through the Sea of Sand, home to about 500 people who know nothing of the outside world.

Under the influence of Orca's sasa, Chakuro and the others have a vision the truth buried in the God of Death's heart. Chakuro is able to persuade Orca to come to the Mud Whale, where he protects the island from the battleship Geráki's attack and confronts Salinkári.

At the same time, a mysterious predator has been set loose from the battleship Geráki to menace the Mud Whale and turn its citizens into zombies one by one!

"The Mud Whale was our entire world."

Table of Contents

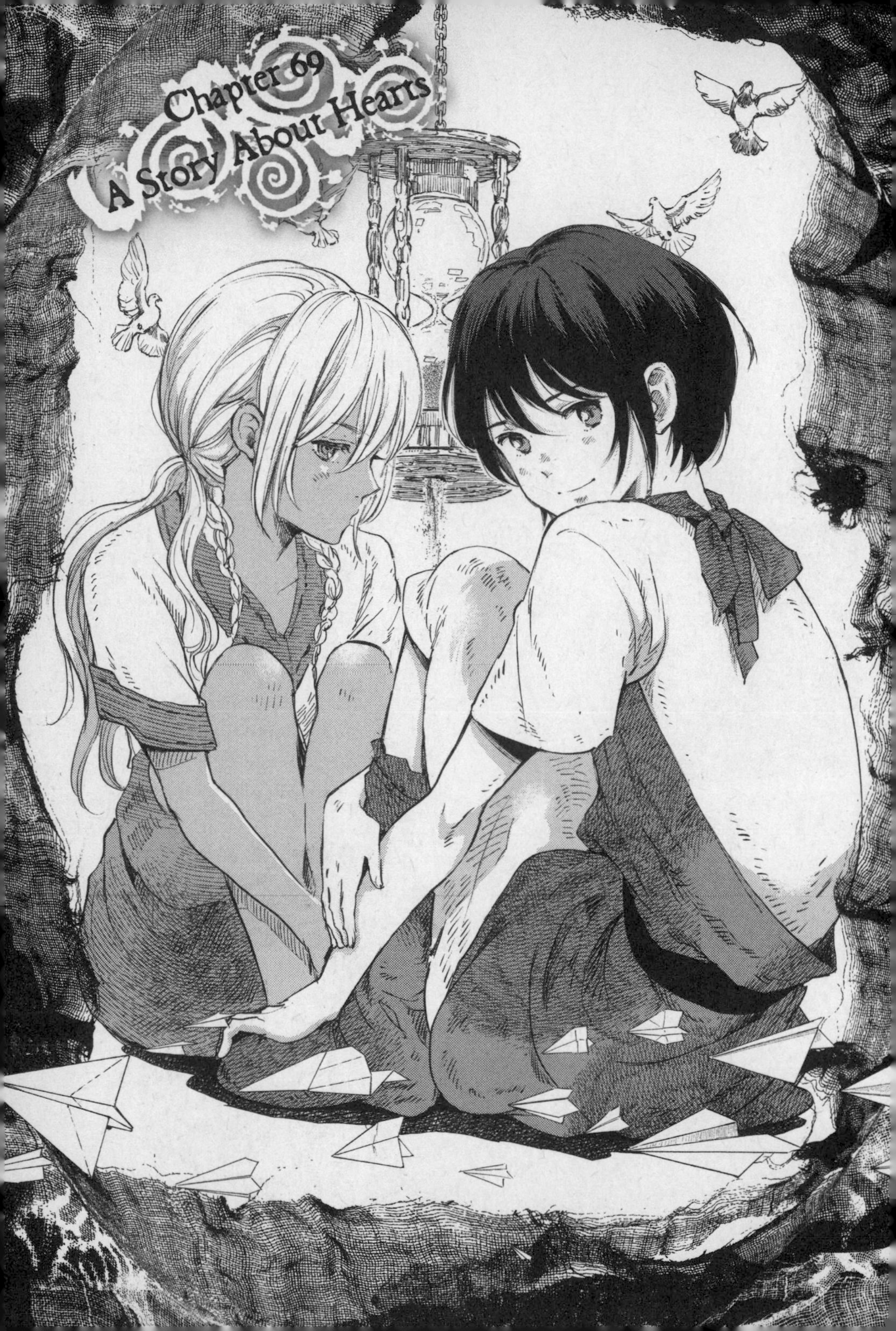
Chapter 69
A Story About Hearts

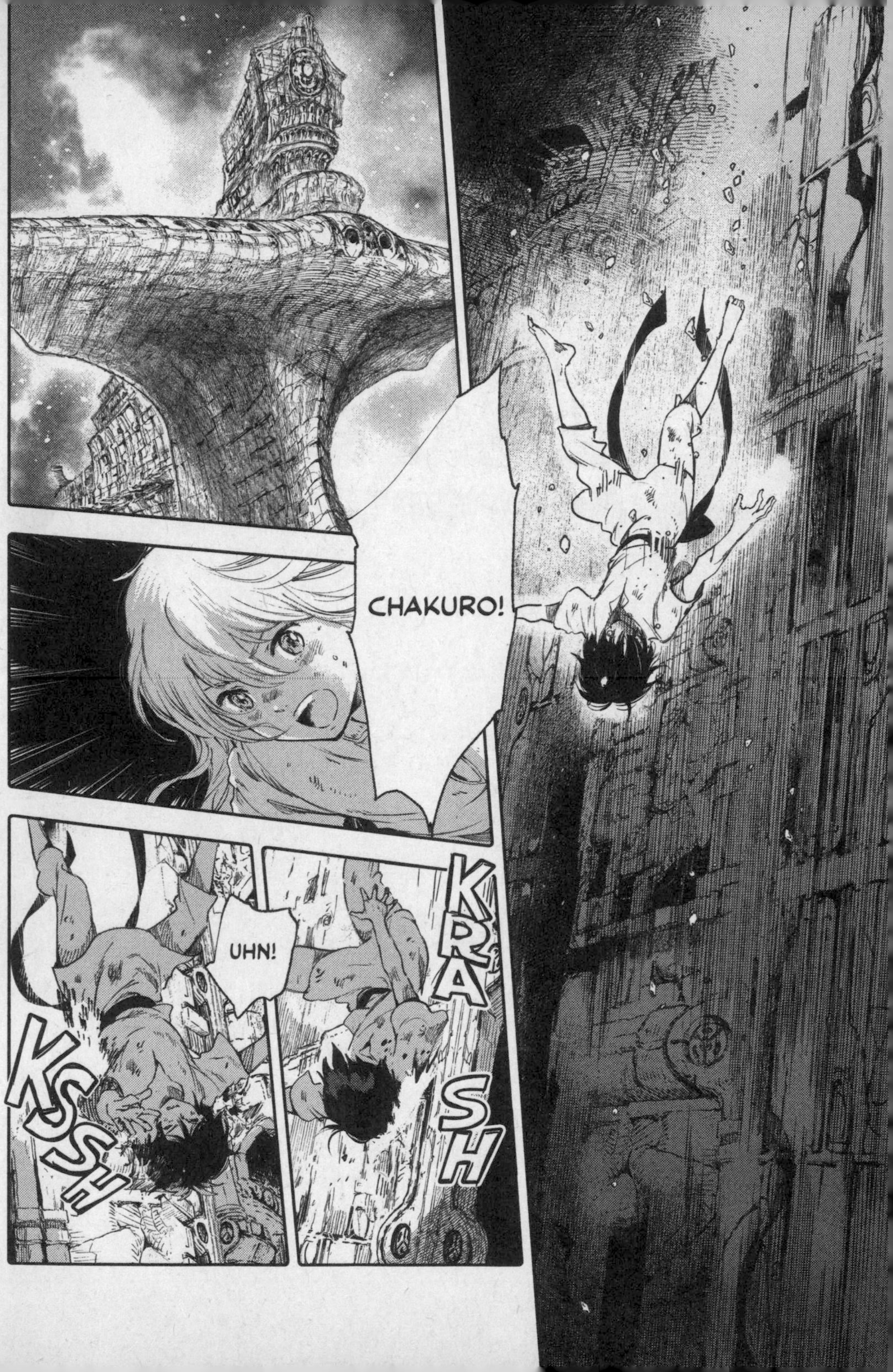
CHAKURO!
KRASH
UHN!
KSSH

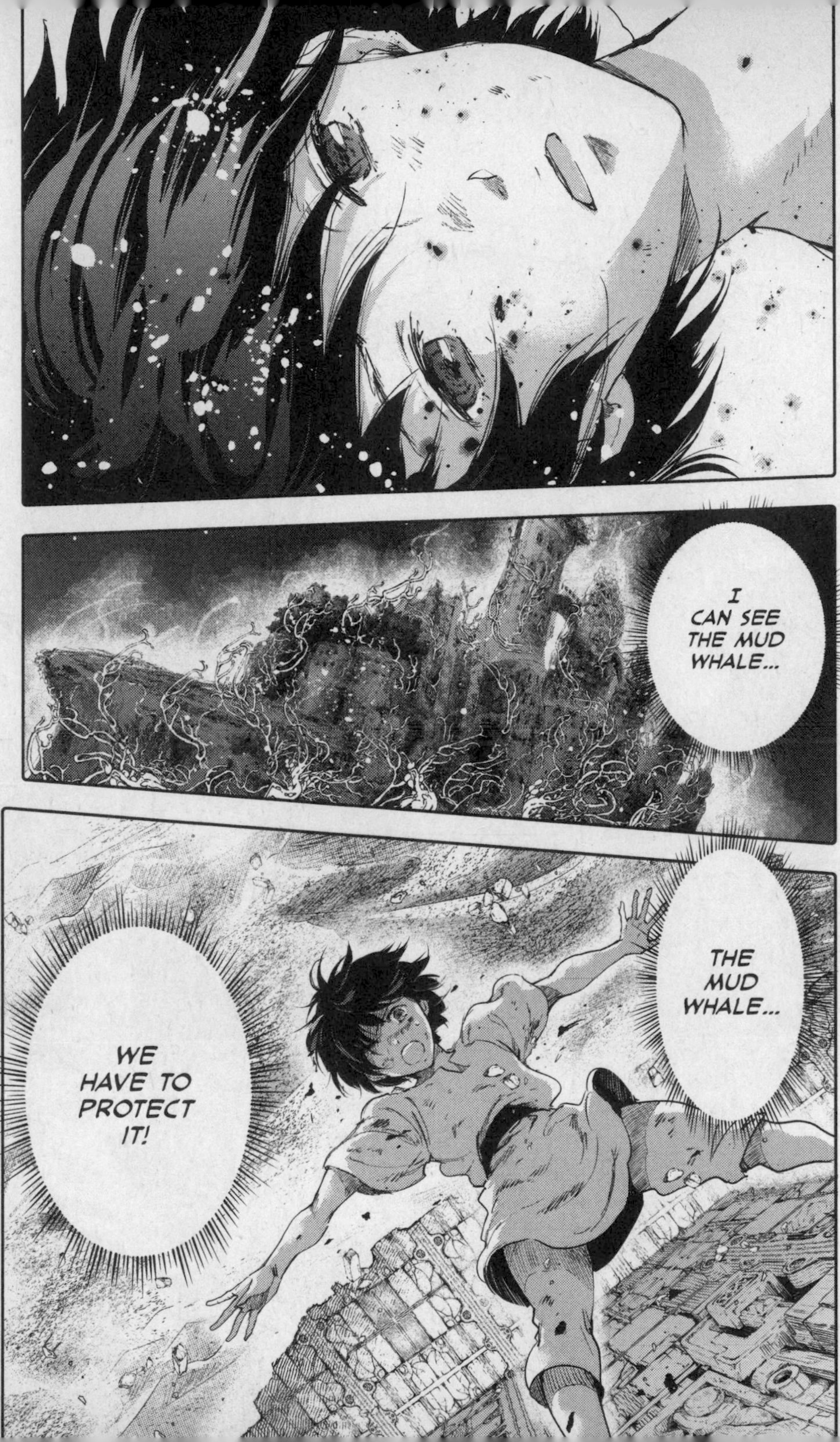
I CAN SEE THE MUD WHALE...
THE MUD WHALE...
WE HAVE TO PROTECT IT!

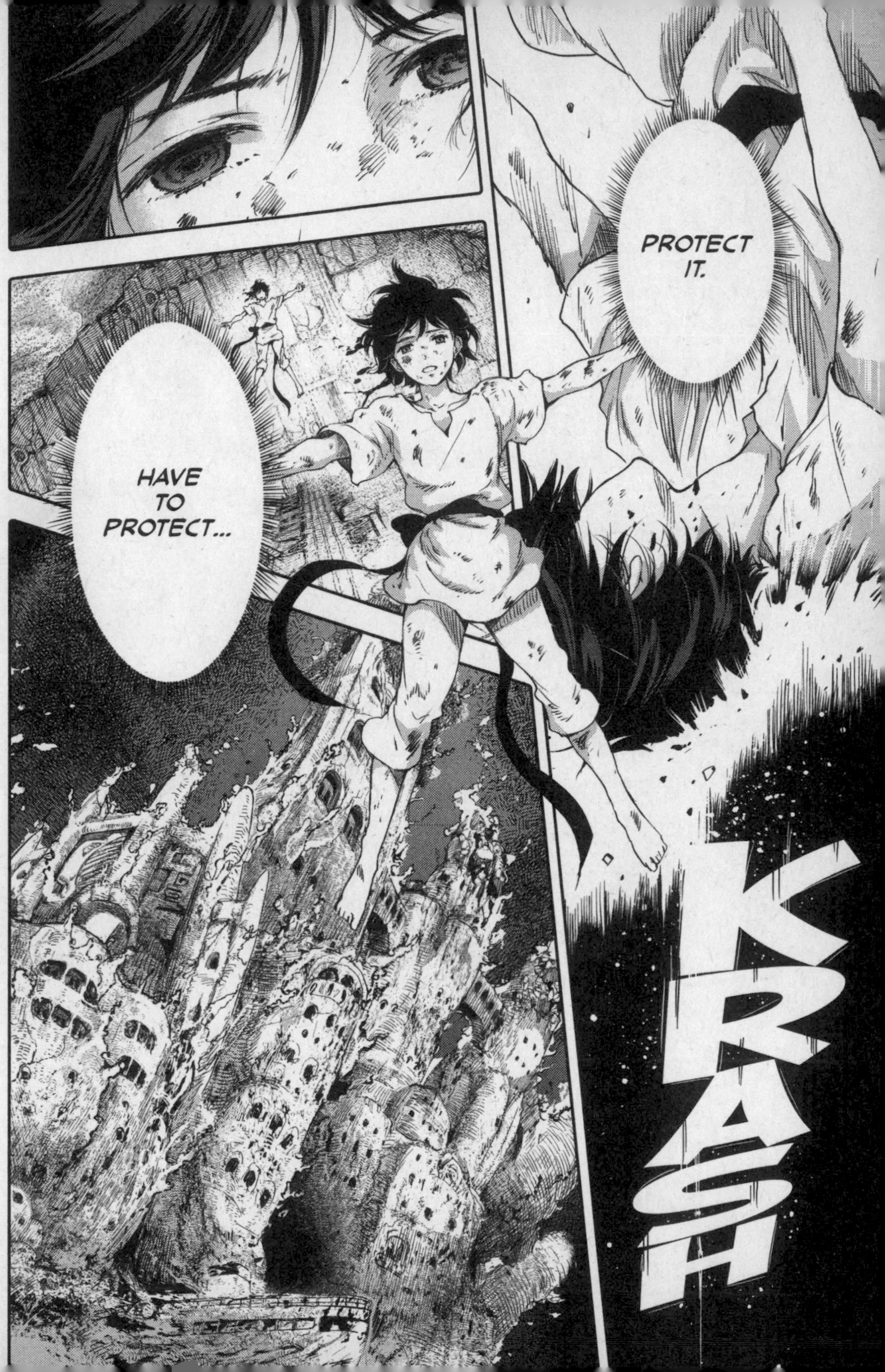
PROTECT IT.
HAVE TO PROTECT...
KRASH

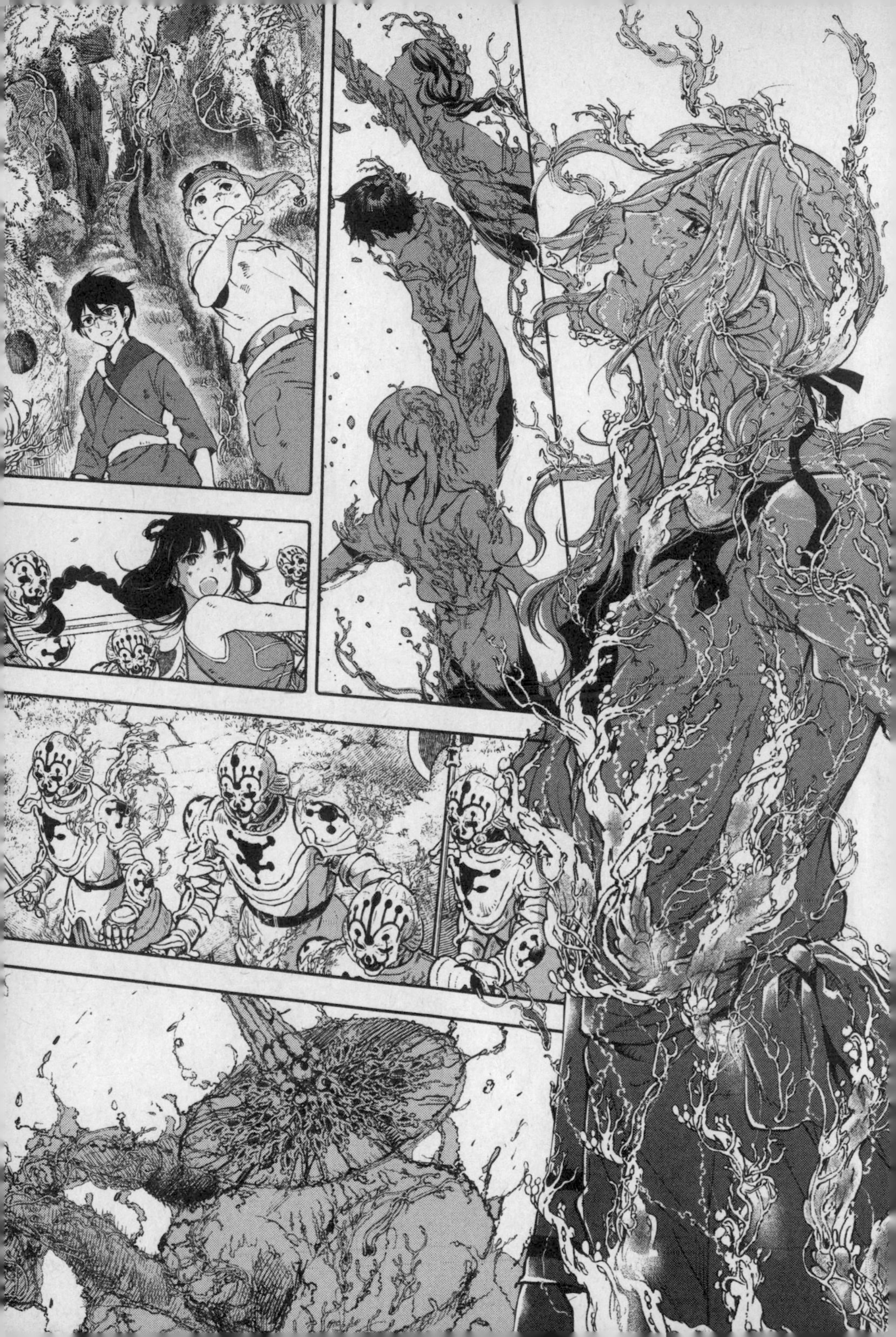

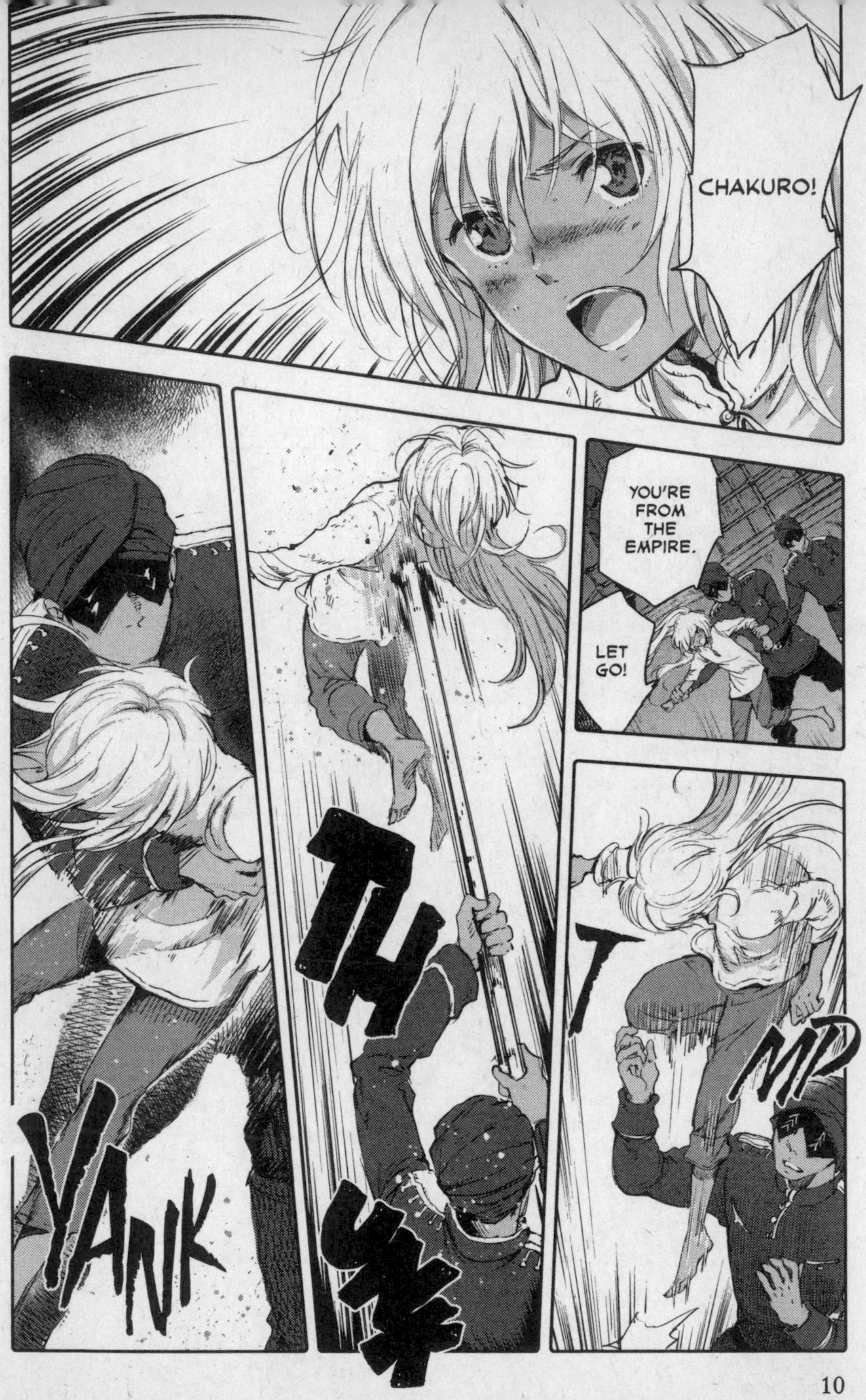
CHAKURO!
YOU'RE FROM THE EMPIRE.
LET GO!
YANK

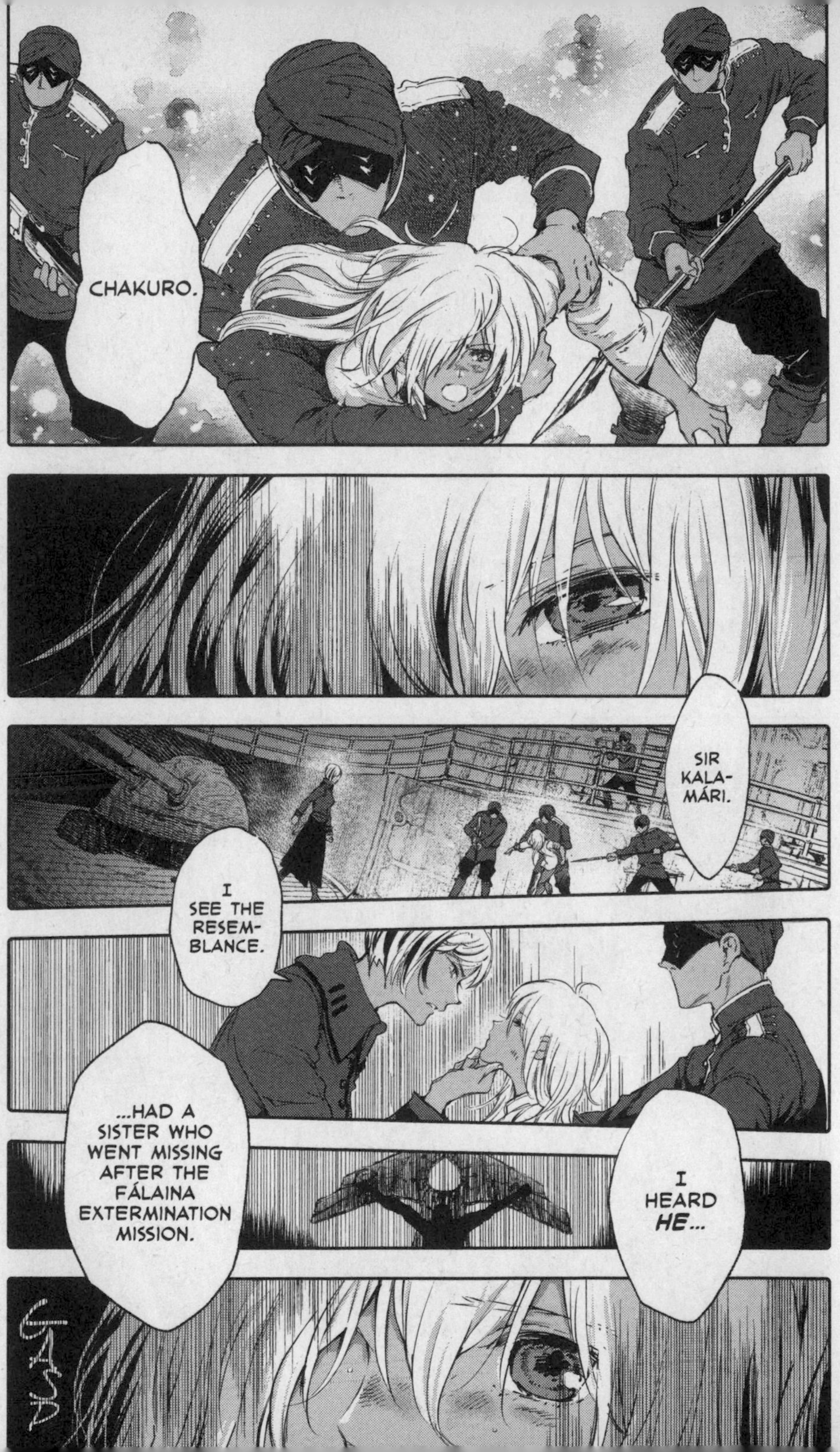
CHAKURO.
SIR KALA-MÁRI.
I SEE THE RESEM-BLANCE.
I HEARD HE...
...HAD A SISTER WHO WENT MISSING AFTER THE FÁLAINA EXTERMINATION MISSION.

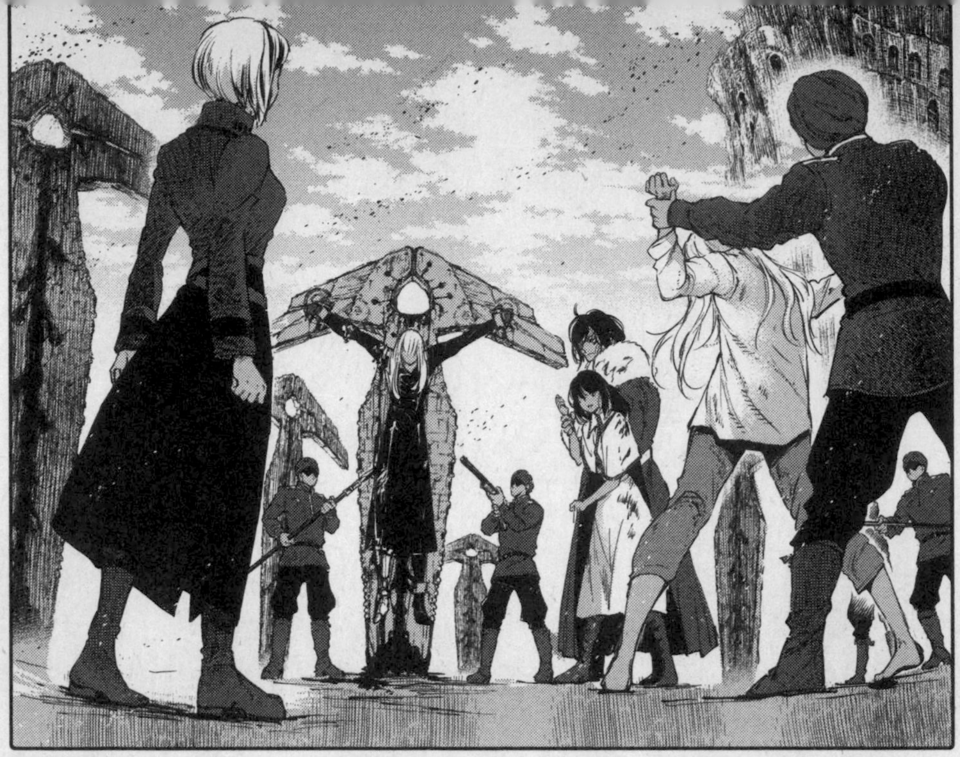

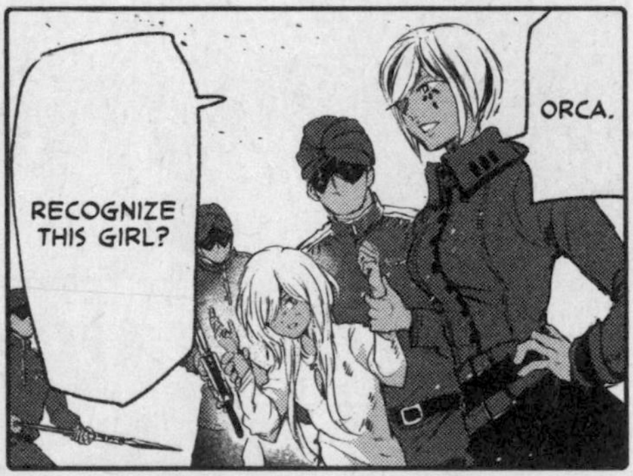
ORCA.
RECOGNIZE THIS GIRL?

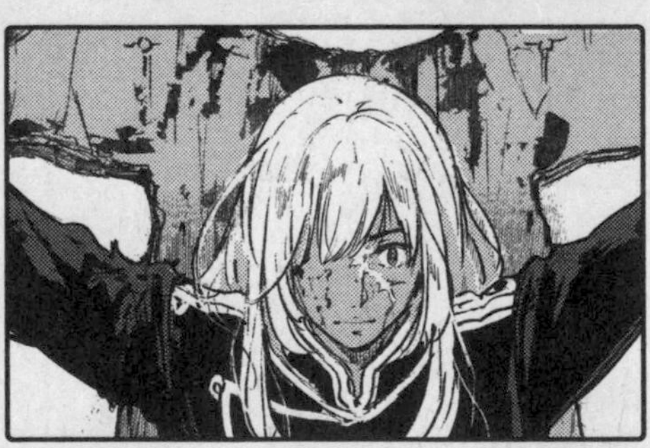

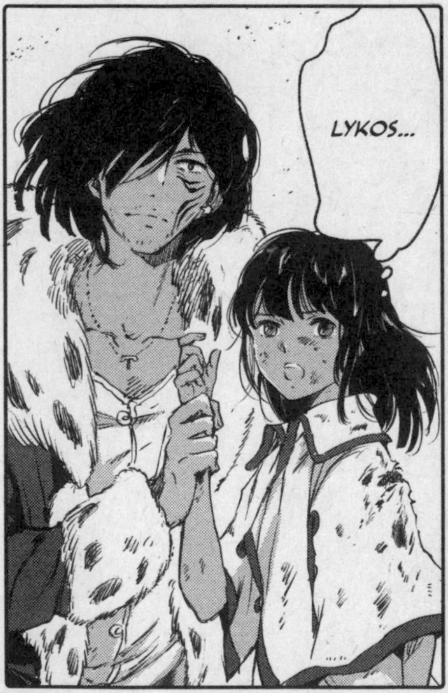
LYKOS...

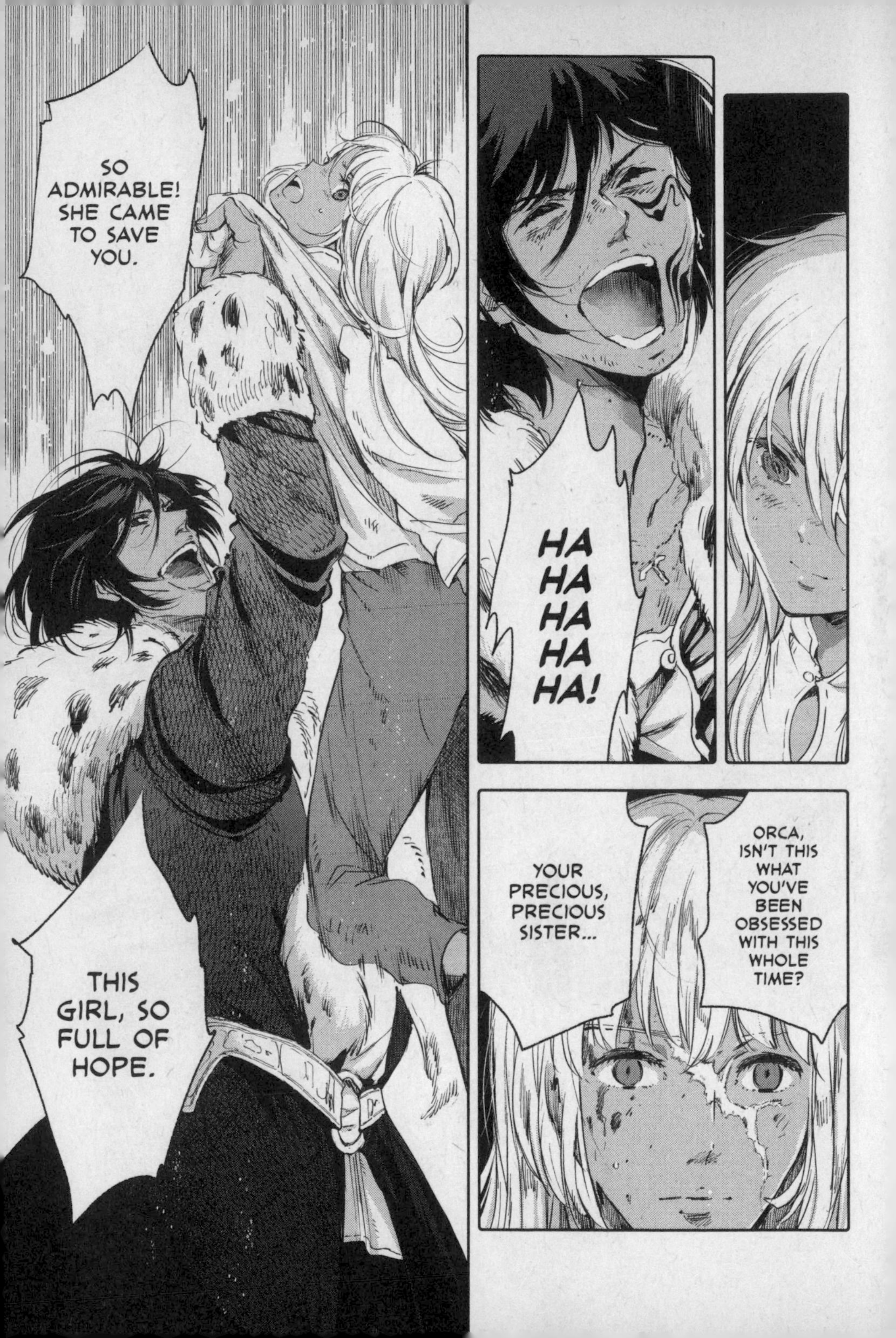
HA HA HA HA HA HA!
ORCA, ISN'T THIS WHAT YOU'VE BEEN OBSESSED WITH THIS WHOLE TIME?
YOUR PRECIOUS, PRECIOUS SISTER...
SO ADMIRABLE! SHE CAME TO SAVE YOU.
THIS GIRL, SO FULL OF HOPE.

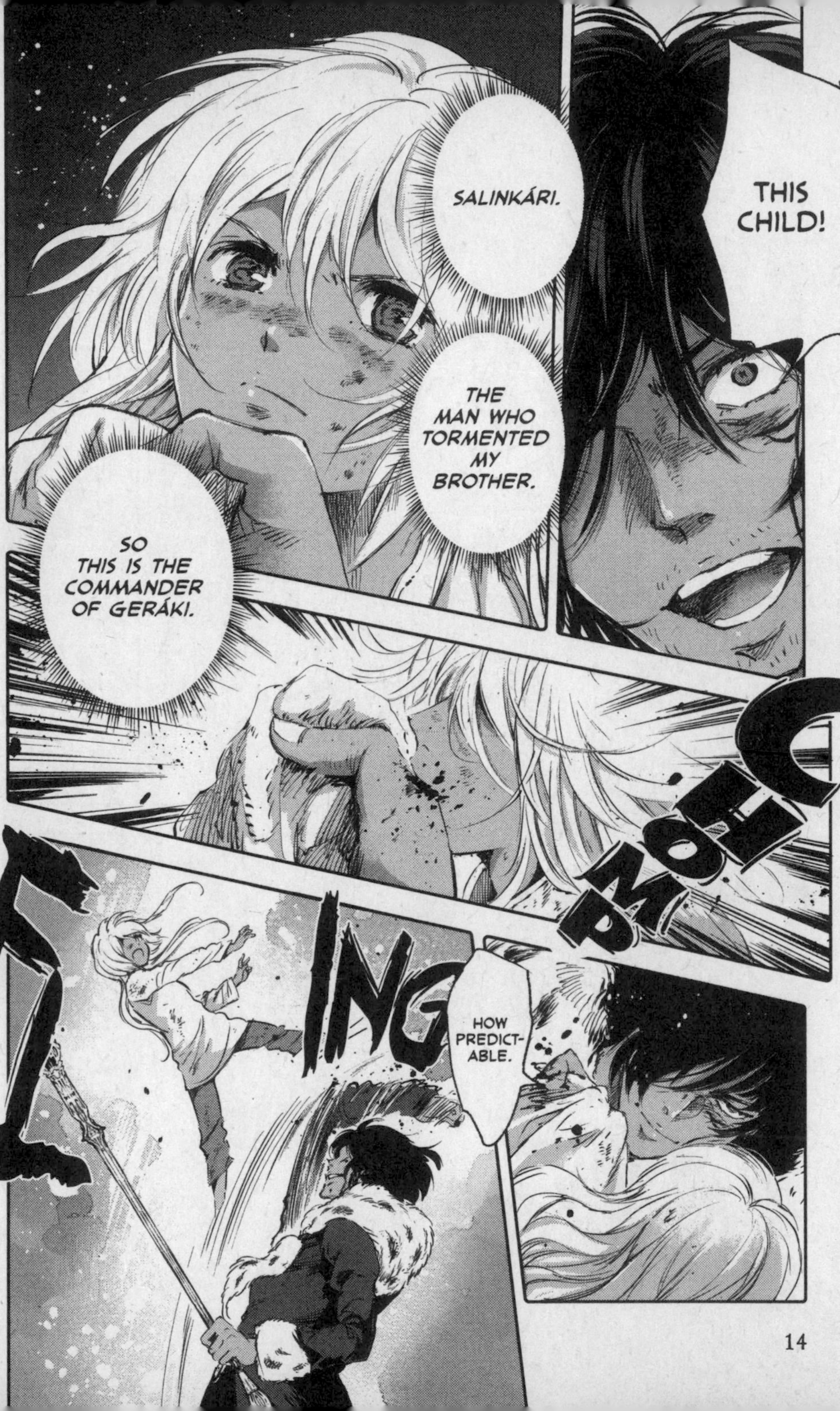
THIS CHILD!
SALINKÁRI.
THE MAN WHO TORMENTED MY BROTHER.
SO THIS IS THE COMMANDER OF GERÁKI.
CHOMP
HOW PREDICT-ABLE.
TING

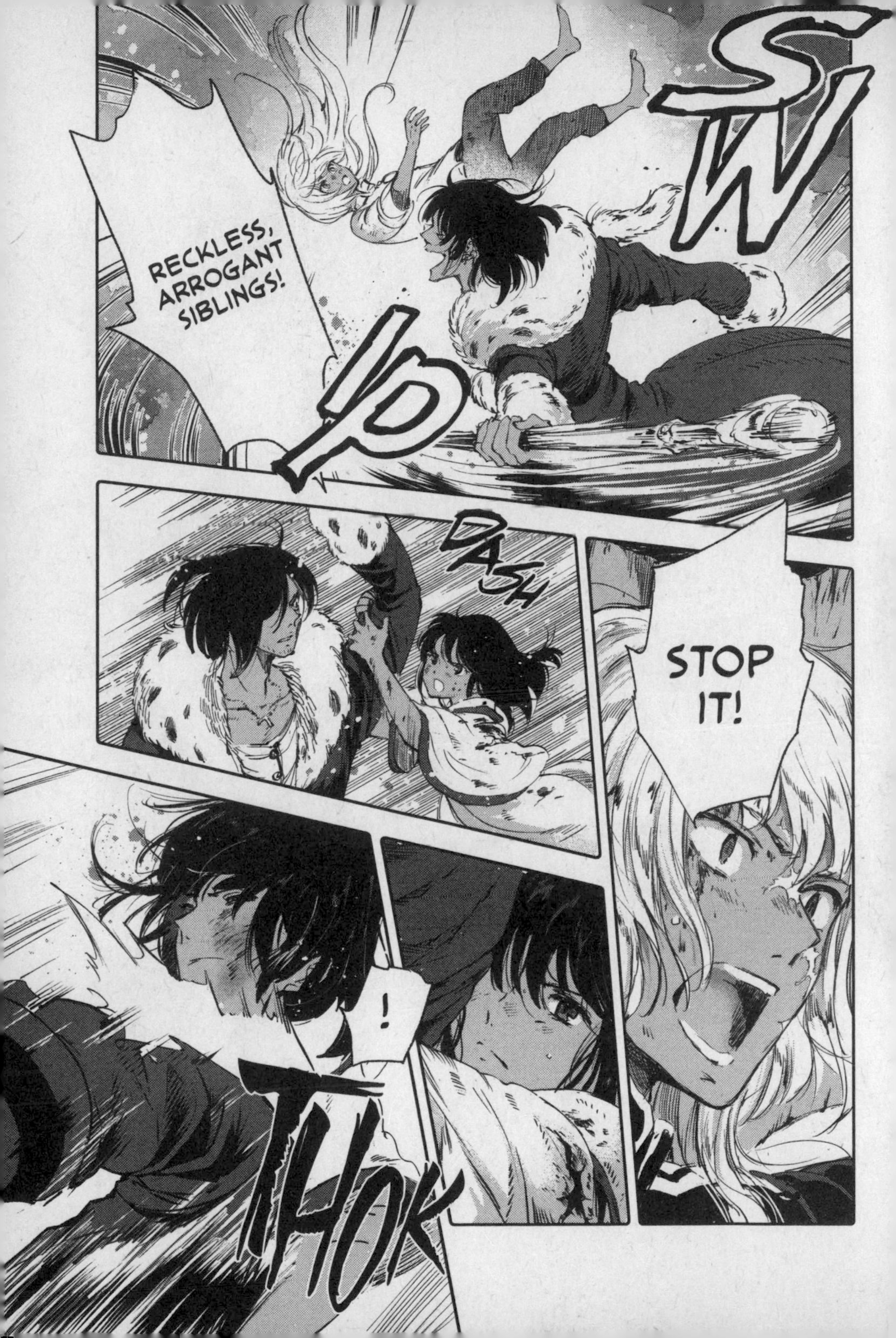
SW
RECKLESS, ARROGANT SIBLINGS!
IP
DASH
STOP IT!
!
THOK

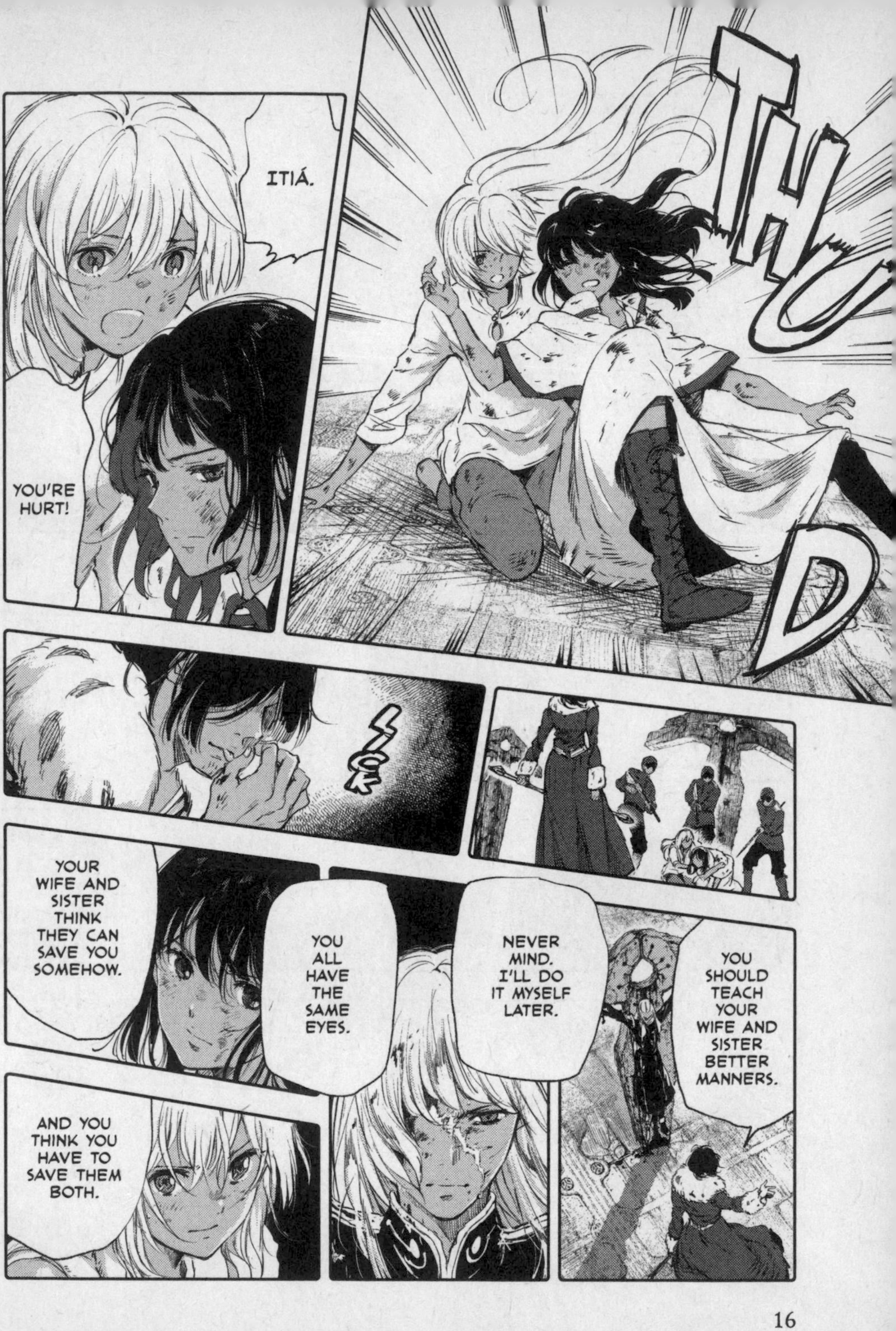
THUD
ITIÁ.
YOU'RE HURT!
LICK
YOU SHOULD TEACH YOUR WIFE AND SISTER BETTER MANNERS.
NEVER MIND. I'LL DO IT MYSELF LATER.
YOU ALL HAVE THE SAME EYES.
YOUR WIFE AND SISTER THINK THEY CAN SAVE YOU SOMEHOW.
AND YOU THINK YOU HAVE TO SAVE THEM BOTH.

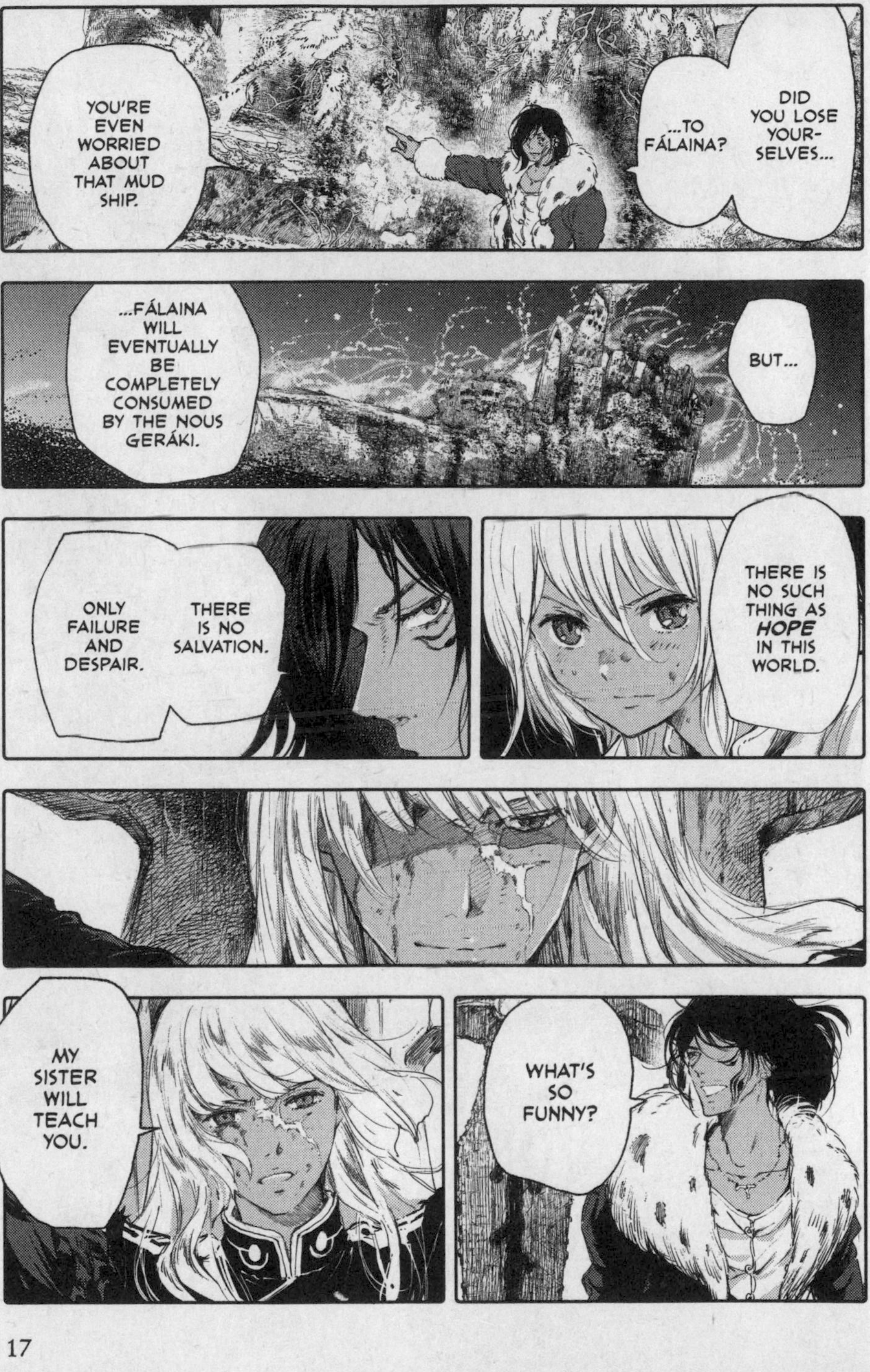
DID YOU LOSE YOURSELVES...
...TO FÁLAINA?
YOU'RE EVEN WORRIED ABOUT THAT MUD SHIP.
BUT...
...FÁLAINA WILL EVENTUALLY BE COMPLETELY CONSUMED BY THE NOUS GERÁKI.
THERE IS NO SUCH THING AS *HOPE* IN THIS WORLD.
THERE IS NO SALVATION.
ONLY FAILURE AND DESPAIR.
WHAT'S SO FUNNY?
MY SISTER WILL TEACH YOU.

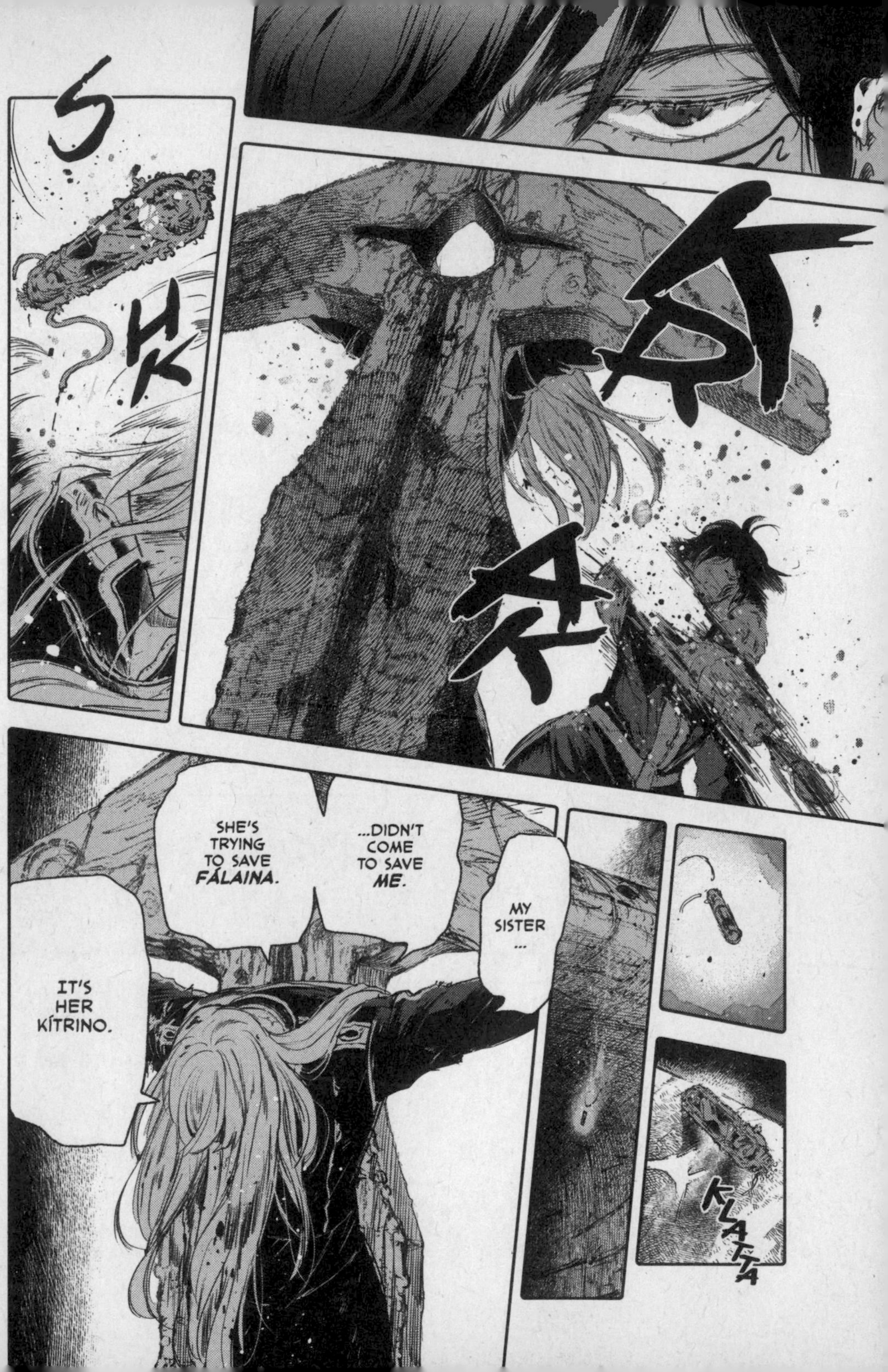
SHK
KLATTA
MY SISTER ...
...DIDN'T COME TO SAVE *ME*.
SHE'S TRYING TO SAVE *FÁLAINA*.
IT'S HER KÍTRINO.

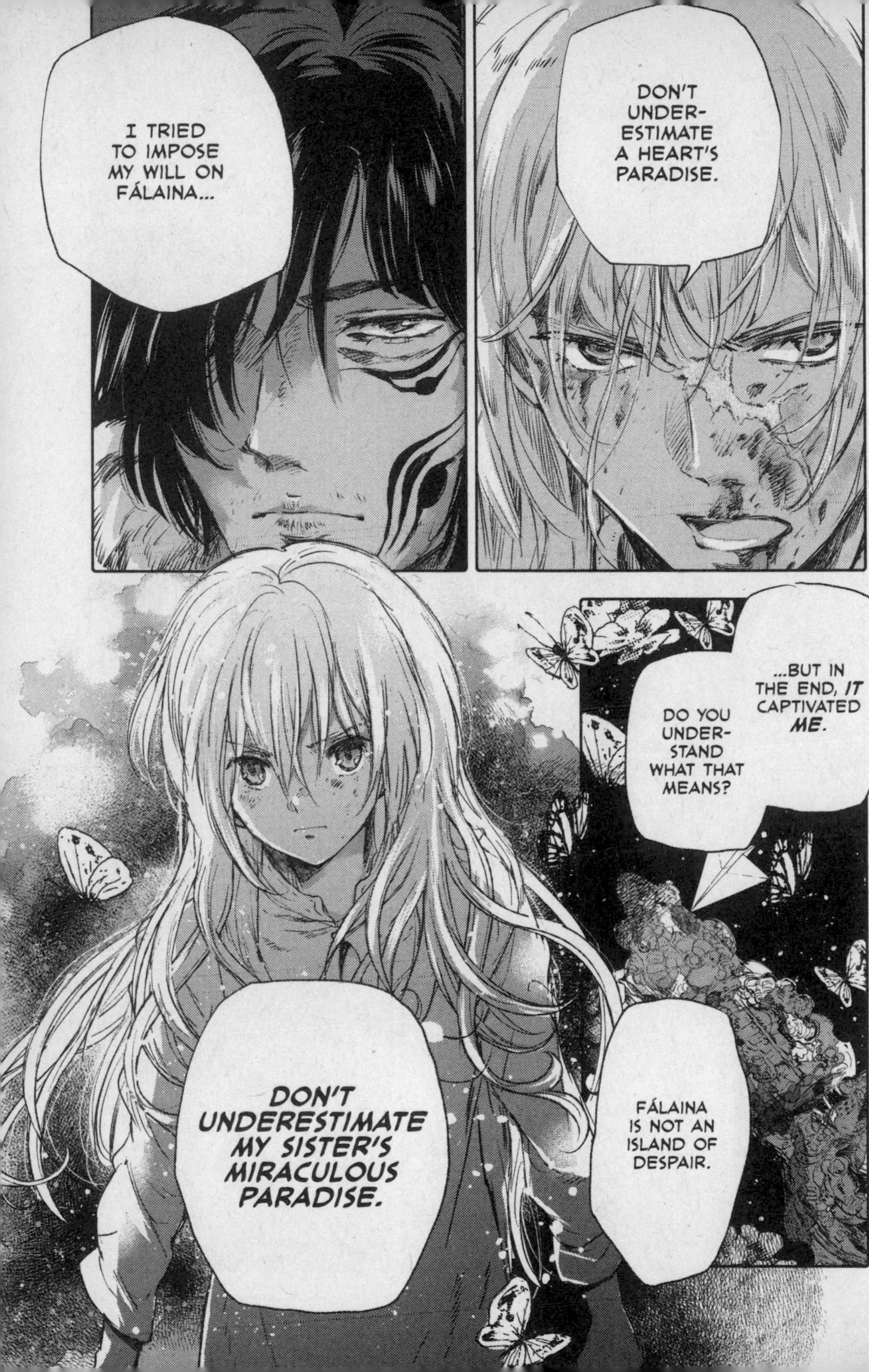
DON'T UNDER-ESTIMATE A HEART'S PARADISE.
I TRIED TO IMPOSE MY WILL ON FÁLAINA...
...BUT IN THE END, *IT* CAPTIVATED *ME*.
DO YOU UNDER-STAND WHAT THAT MEANS?
FÁLAINA IS NOT AN ISLAND OF DESPAIR.
DON'T UNDERESTIMATE MY SISTER'S MIRACULOUS PARADISE.

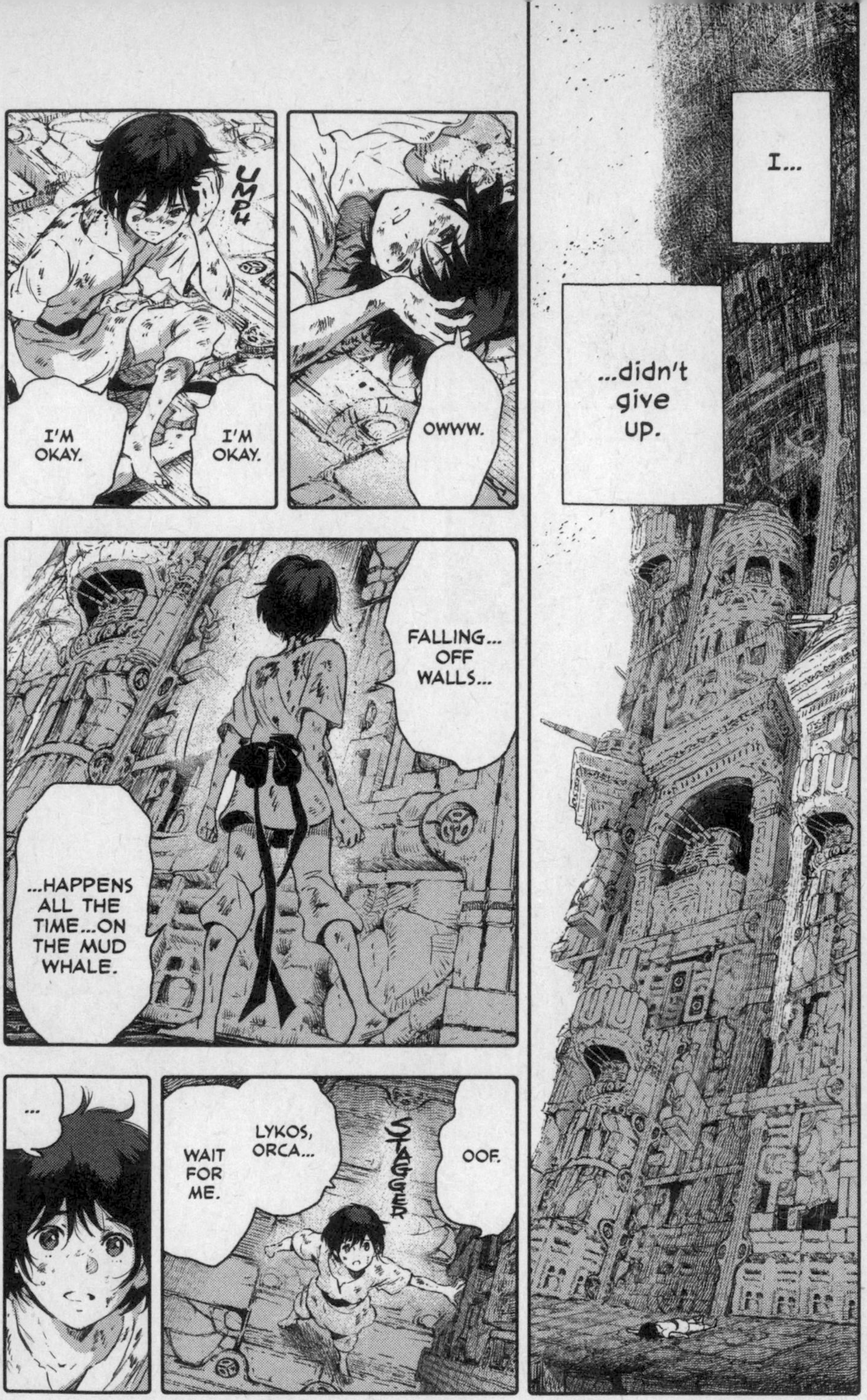
I...
...didn't give up.
OWWW.
UMPH
I'M OKAY.
I'M OKAY.
FALLING... OFF WALLS...
...HAPPENS ALL THE TIME...ON THE MUD WHALE.
OOF.
STAGGER
LYKOS, ORCA...
WAIT FOR ME.
...

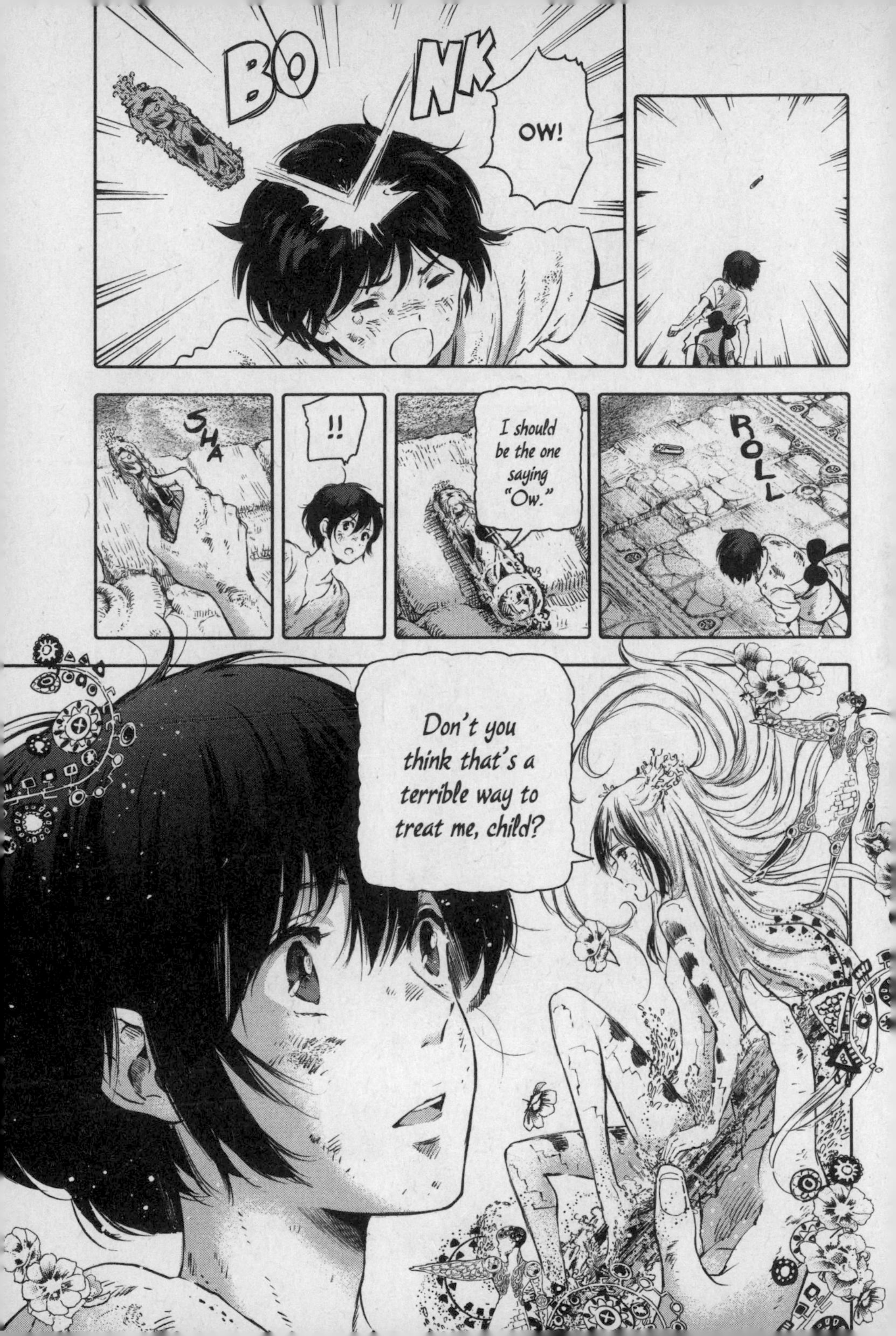
BONK
OW!
ROLL
I should be the one saying "Ow."
!!
SHA
Don't you think that's a terrible way to treat me, child?

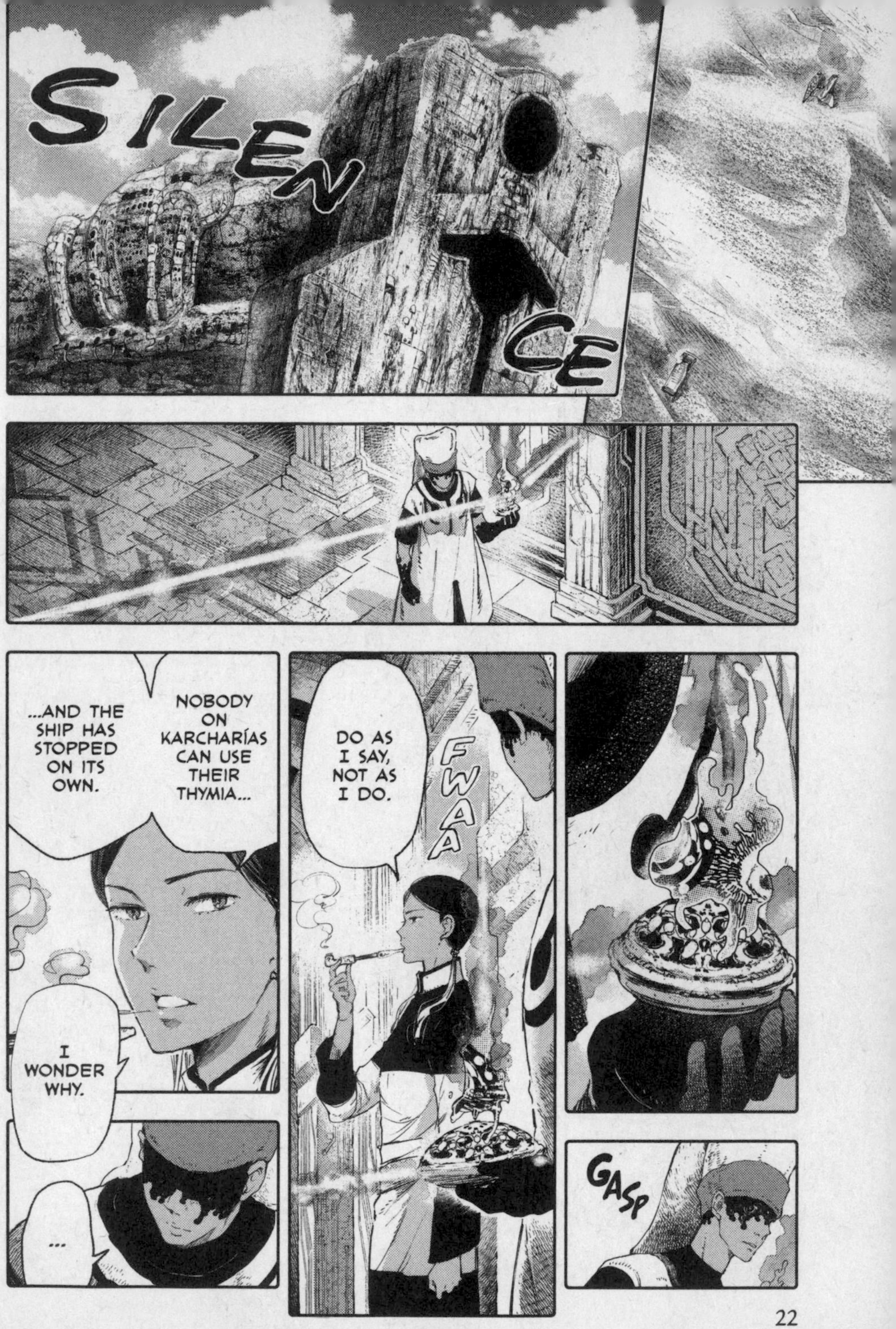
SILENCE
GASP
FWAA
DO AS I SAY, NOT AS I DO.
NOBODY ON KARCHARÍAS CAN USE THEIR THYMIA...
...AND THE SHIP HAS STOPPED ON ITS OWN.
I WONDER WHY.
...

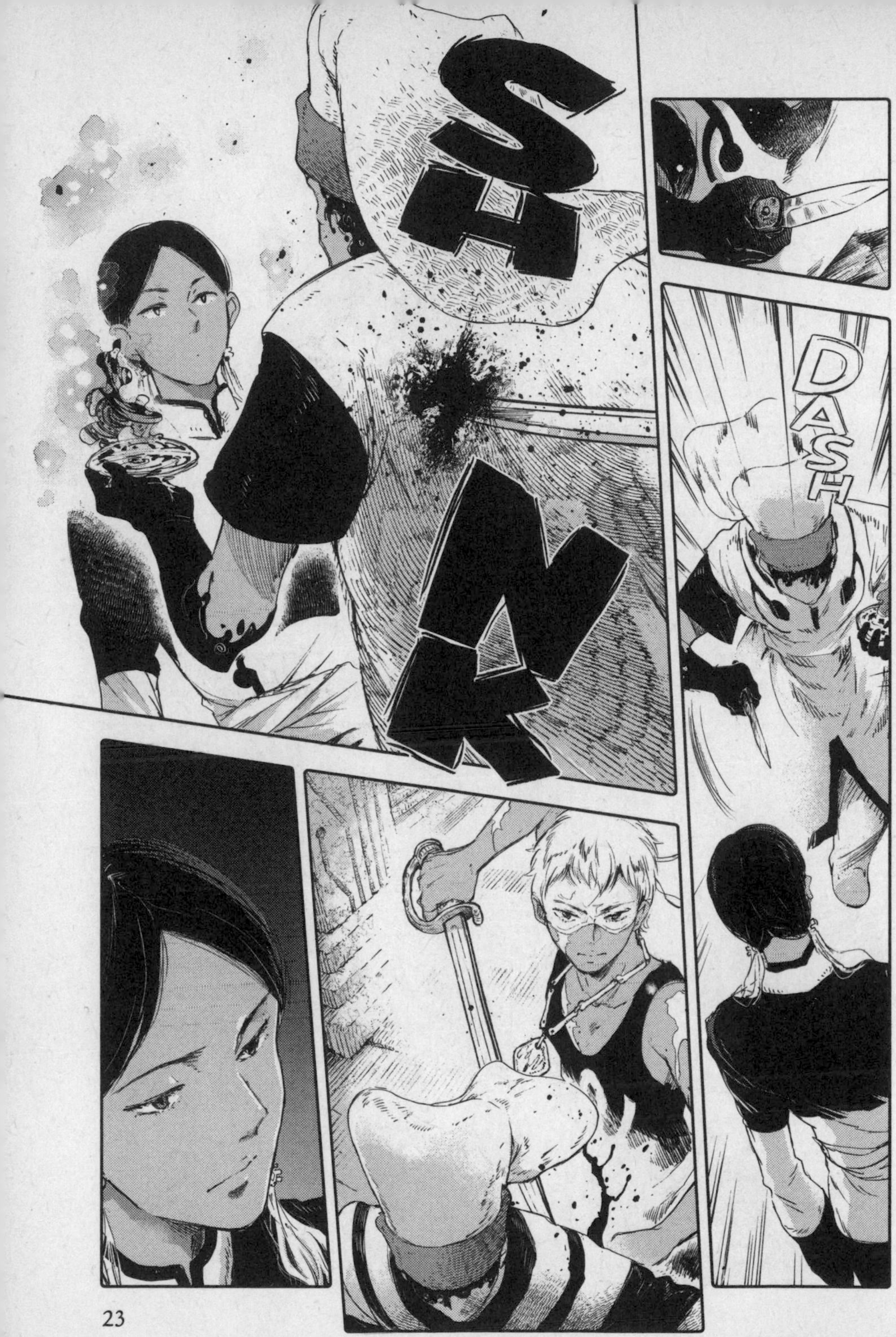
DASH
SHANK

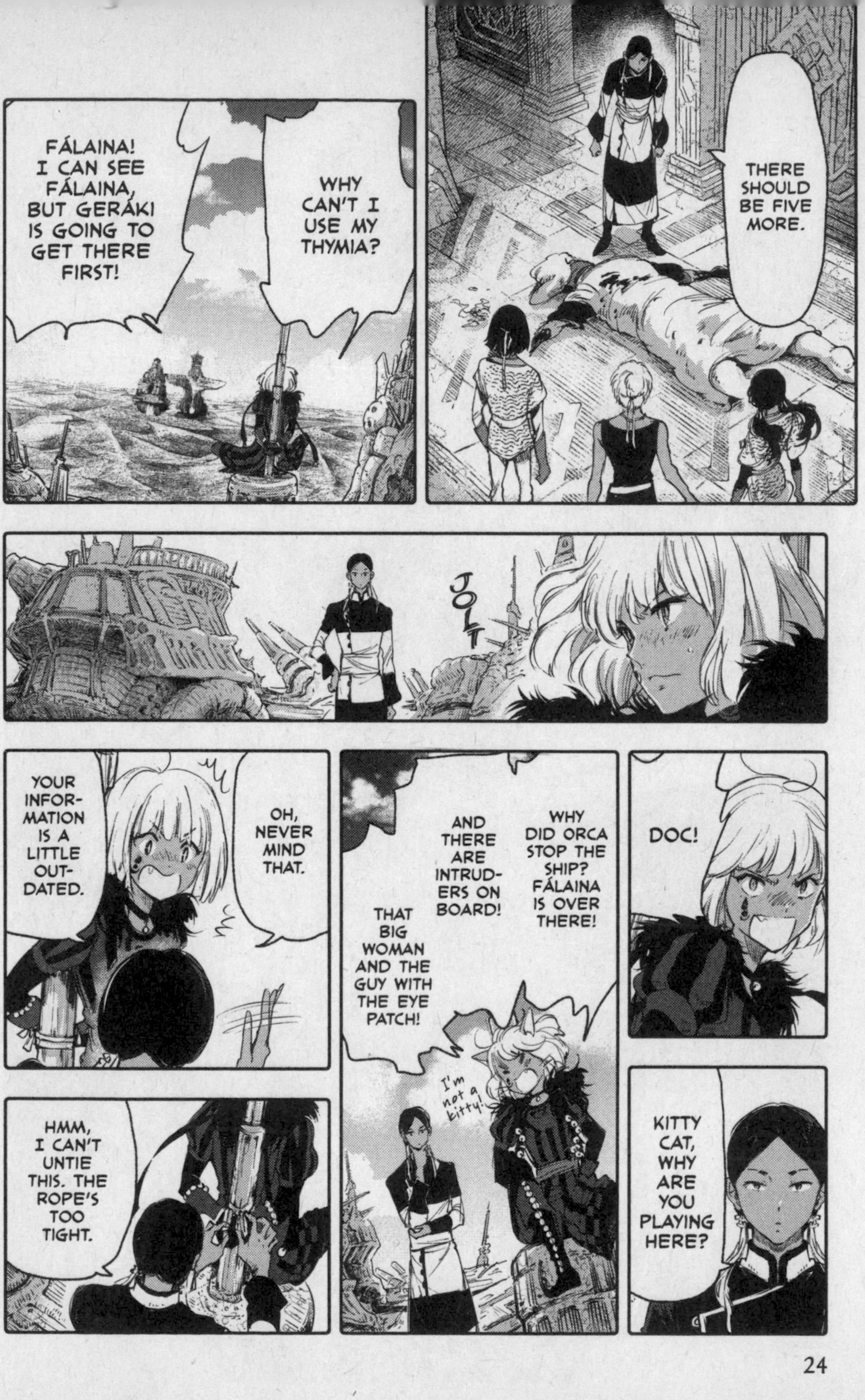
THERE SHOULD BE FIVE MORE.
WHY CAN'T I USE MY THYMIA?
FÁLAINA! I CAN SEE FÁLAINA, BUT GERÁKI IS GOING TO GET THERE FIRST!
JOLT
DOC!
KITTY CAT, WHY ARE YOU PLAYING HERE?
I'm not a kitty!
WHY DID ORCA STOP THE SHIP? FÁLAINA IS OVER THERE!
AND THERE ARE INTRUDERS ON BOARD!
THAT BIG WOMAN AND THE GUY WITH THE EYE PATCH!
OH, NEVER MIND THAT.
YOUR INFORMATION IS A LITTLE OUTDATED.
HMM, I CAN'T UNTIE THIS. THE ROPE'S TOO TIGHT.

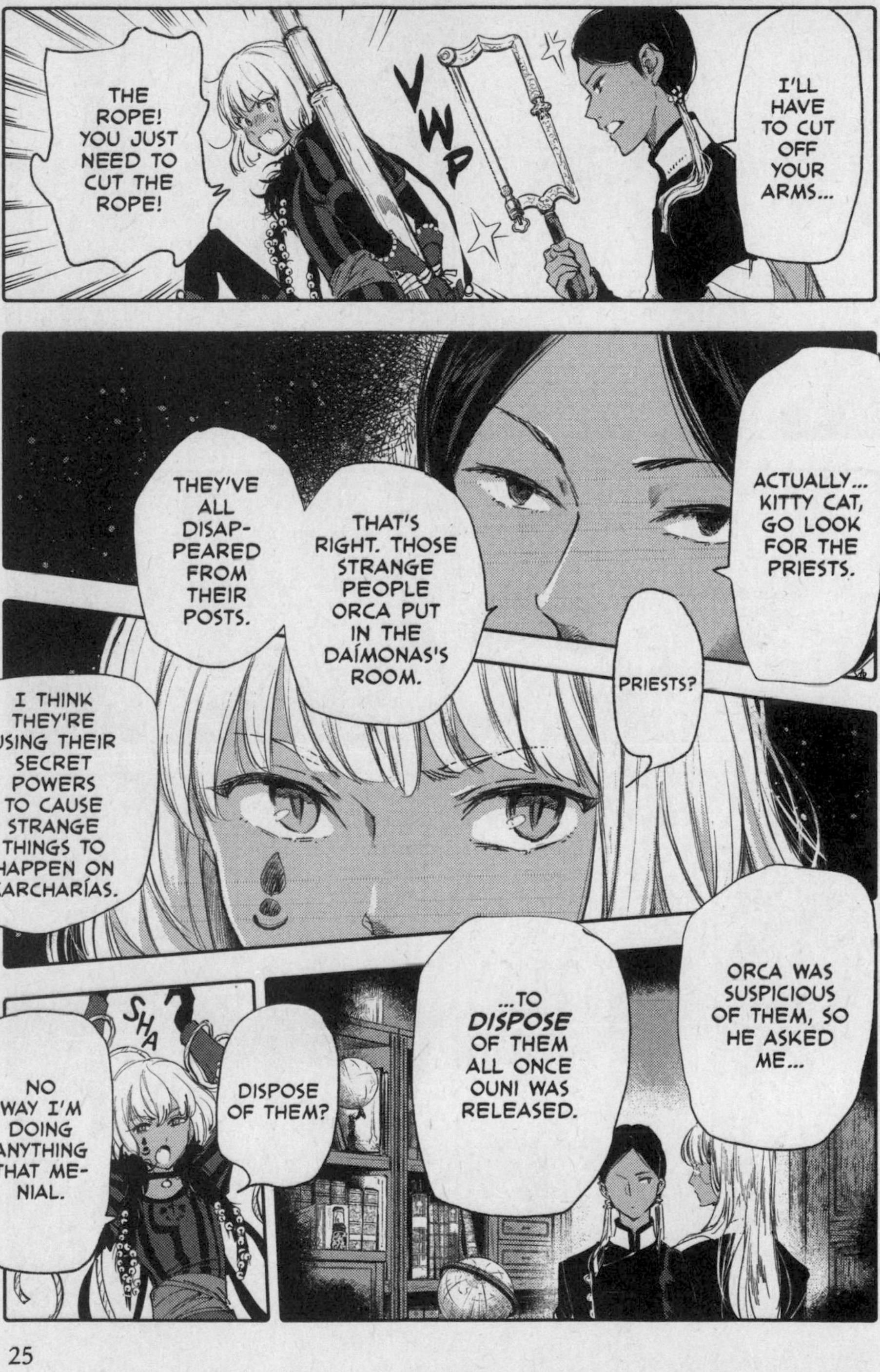
I'LL HAVE TO CUT OFF YOUR ARMS...
VWP
THE ROPE! YOU JUST NEED TO CUT THE ROPE!
ACTUALLY... KITTY CAT, GO LOOK FOR THE PRIESTS.
PRIESTS?
THAT'S RIGHT. THOSE STRANGE PEOPLE ORCA PUT IN THE DAÍMONAS'S ROOM.
THEY'VE ALL DISAP-PEARED FROM THEIR POSTS.
I THINK THEY'RE USING THEIR SECRET POWERS TO CAUSE STRANGE THINGS TO HAPPEN ON KARCHARÍAS.
ORCA WAS SUSPICIOUS OF THEM, SO HE ASKED ME...
...TO *DISPOSE* OF THEM ALL ONCE OUNI WAS RELEASED.
DISPOSE OF THEM?
SHA
NO WAY I'M DOING ANYTHING THAT ME-NIAL.

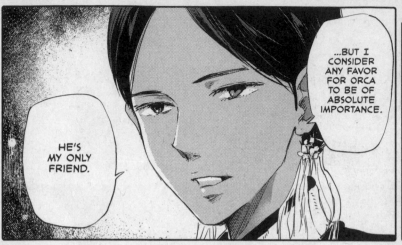

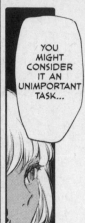

YOU MIGHT CONSIDER IT AN UNIMPORTANT TASK...
...BUT I CONSIDER ANY FAVOR FOR ORCA TO BE OF ABSOLUTE IMPORTANCE.
HE'S MY ONLY FRIEND.
...
NEVER MIND.
I'LL JUST ASK THE INSECT CAGE.
THEY'RE LOYAL, GOOD KIDS...
...AND ORCA PREFERS THEM ANYWAY.
THEY'VE ALREADY DISPOSED OF ONE PRIEST.
TRMBL
COME, INSECT KIDS, IT'S TIME TO GO TO WORK.
YOU'RE ALL BRILLIANT, ORCA'S FAVORITES.
TRMBL

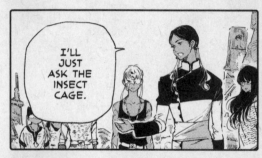

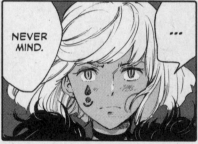

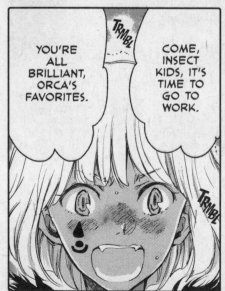

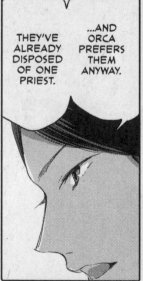

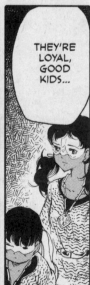

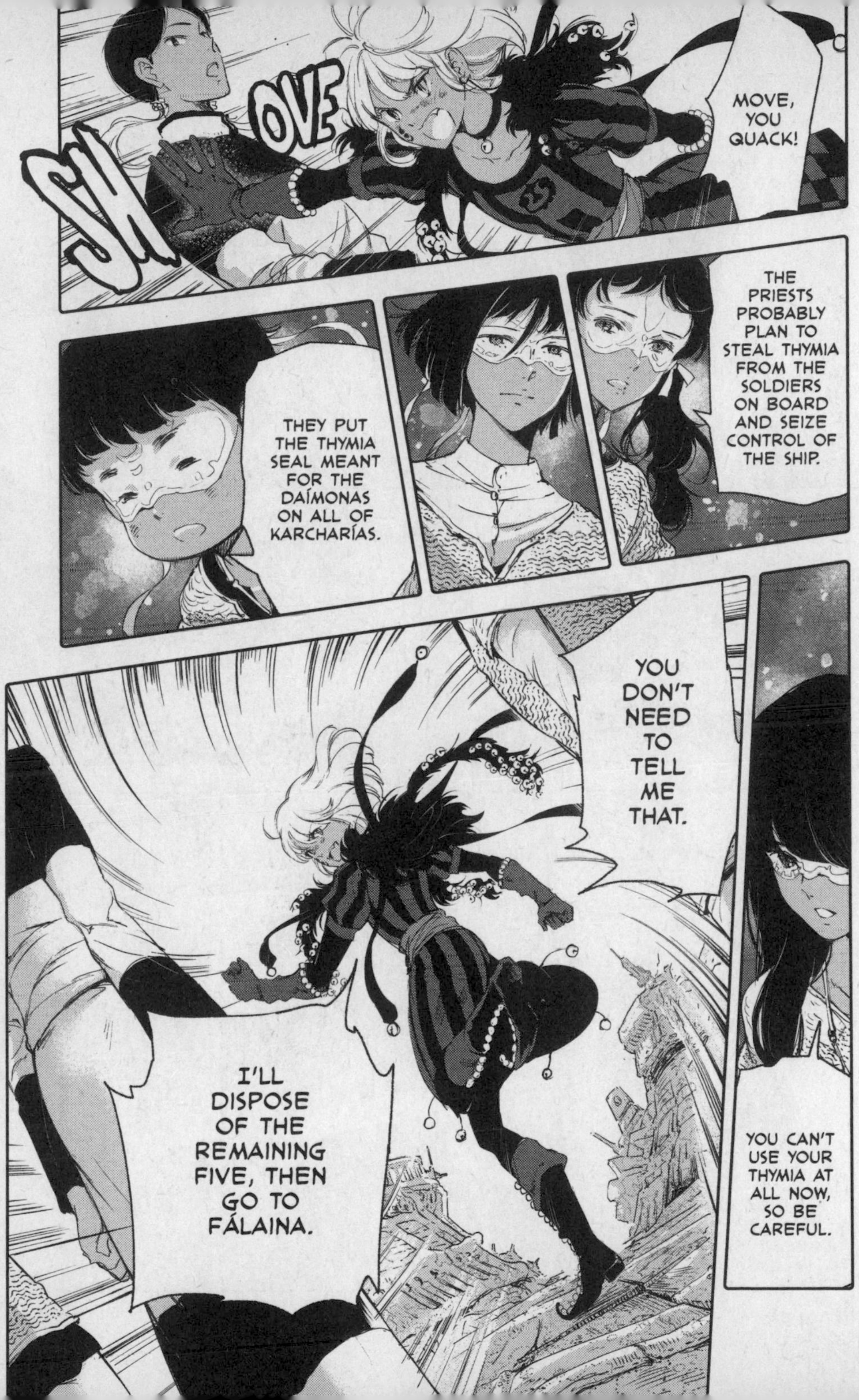
MOVE, YOU QUACK!
SHOVE
THE PRIESTS PROBABLY PLAN TO STEAL THYMIA FROM THE SOLDIERS ON BOARD AND SEIZE CONTROL OF THE SHIP.
THEY PUT THE THYMIA SEAL MEANT FOR THE DAÍMONAS ON ALL OF KARCHARÍAS.
YOU CAN'T USE YOUR THYMIA AT ALL NOW, SO BE CAREFUL.
YOU DON'T NEED TO TELL ME THAT.
I'LL DISPOSE OF THE REMAINING FIVE, THEN GO TO FÁLAINA.

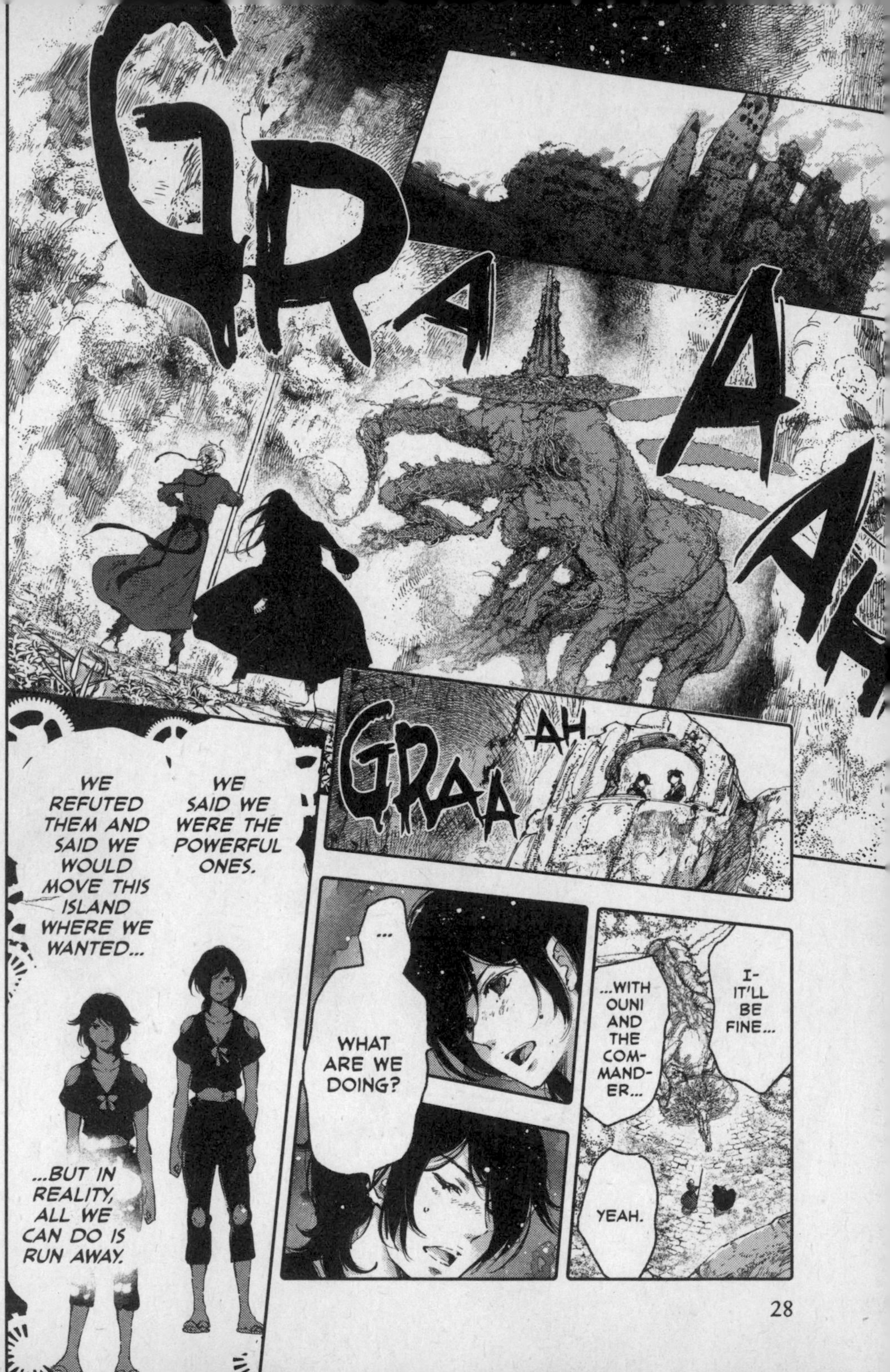
GRAAAAH
GRAA AH
I- IT'LL BE FINE...
...WITH OUNI AND THE COM-MANDER...
YEAH.
...
WHAT ARE WE DOING?
WE SAID WE WERE THE POWERFUL ONES.
WE REFUTED THEM AND SAID WE WOULD MOVE THIS ISLAND WHERE WE WANTED...
...BUT IN REALITY, ALL WE CAN DO IS RUN AWAY.

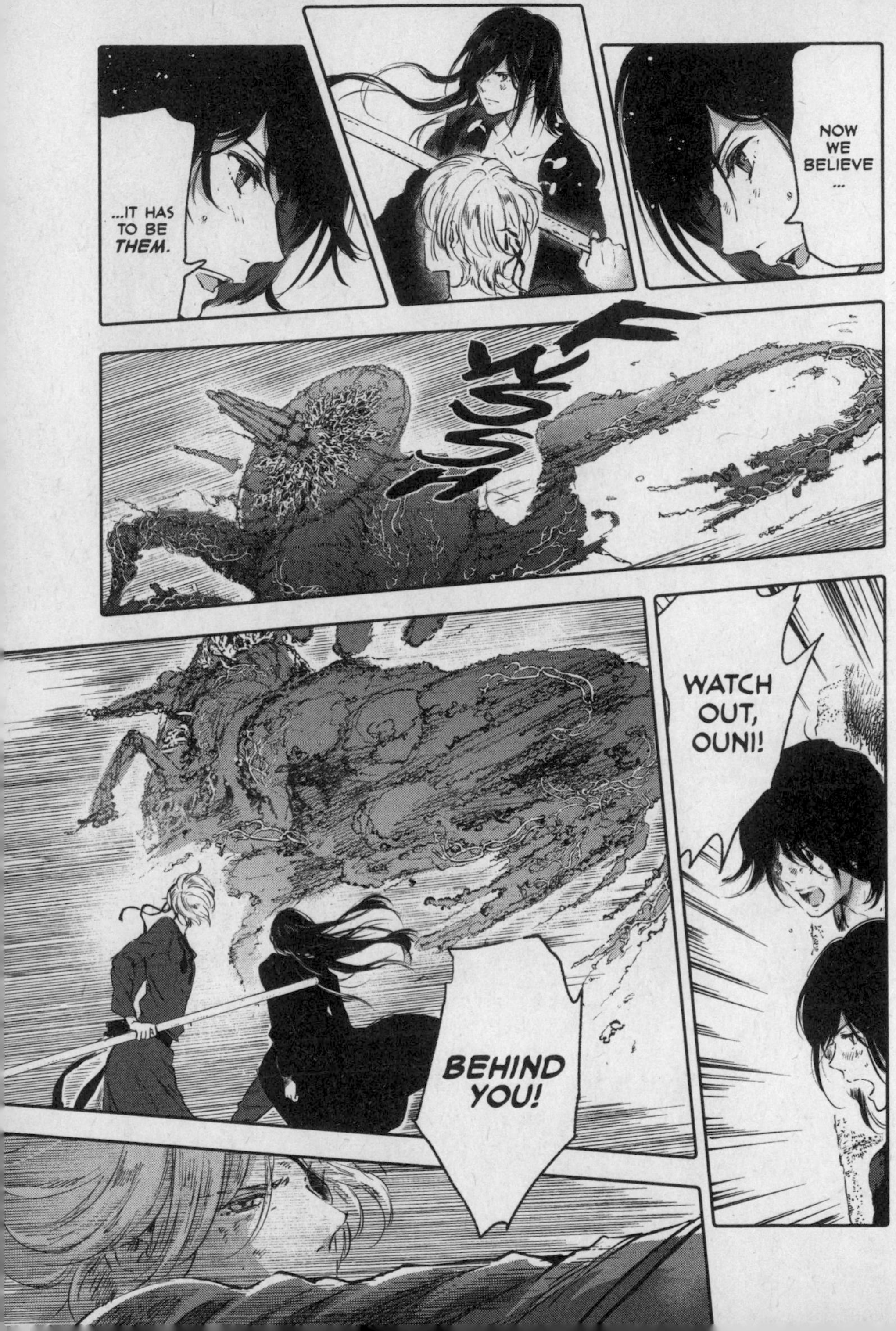
NOW WE BELIEVE ...
...IT HAS TO BE *THEM*.
WATCH OUT, OUNI!
BEHIND YOU!

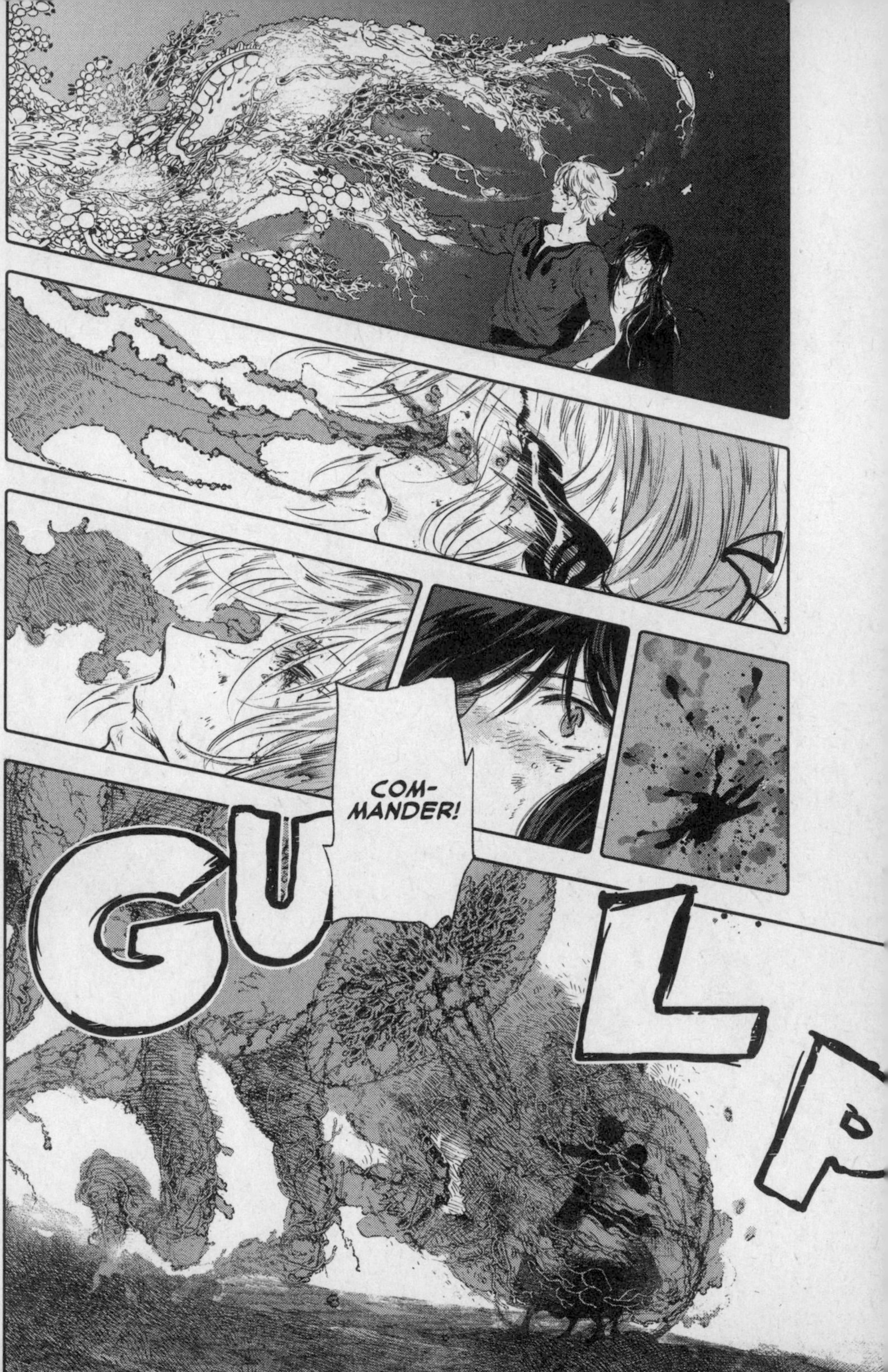
COM-MANDER!
GULP

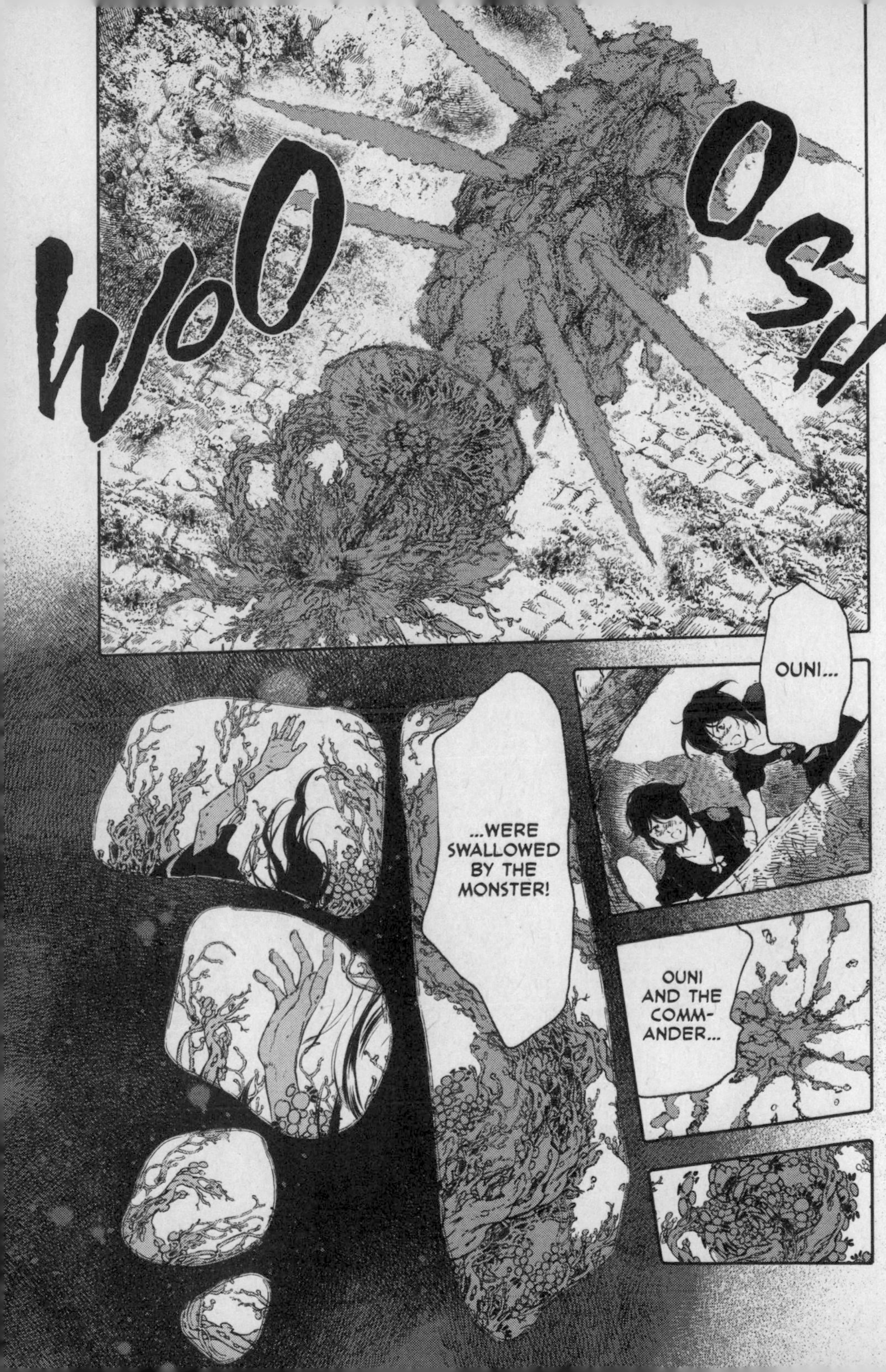
WOOSH
OUNI...
OUNI AND THE COMMANDER...
...WERE SWALLOWED BY THE MONSTER!

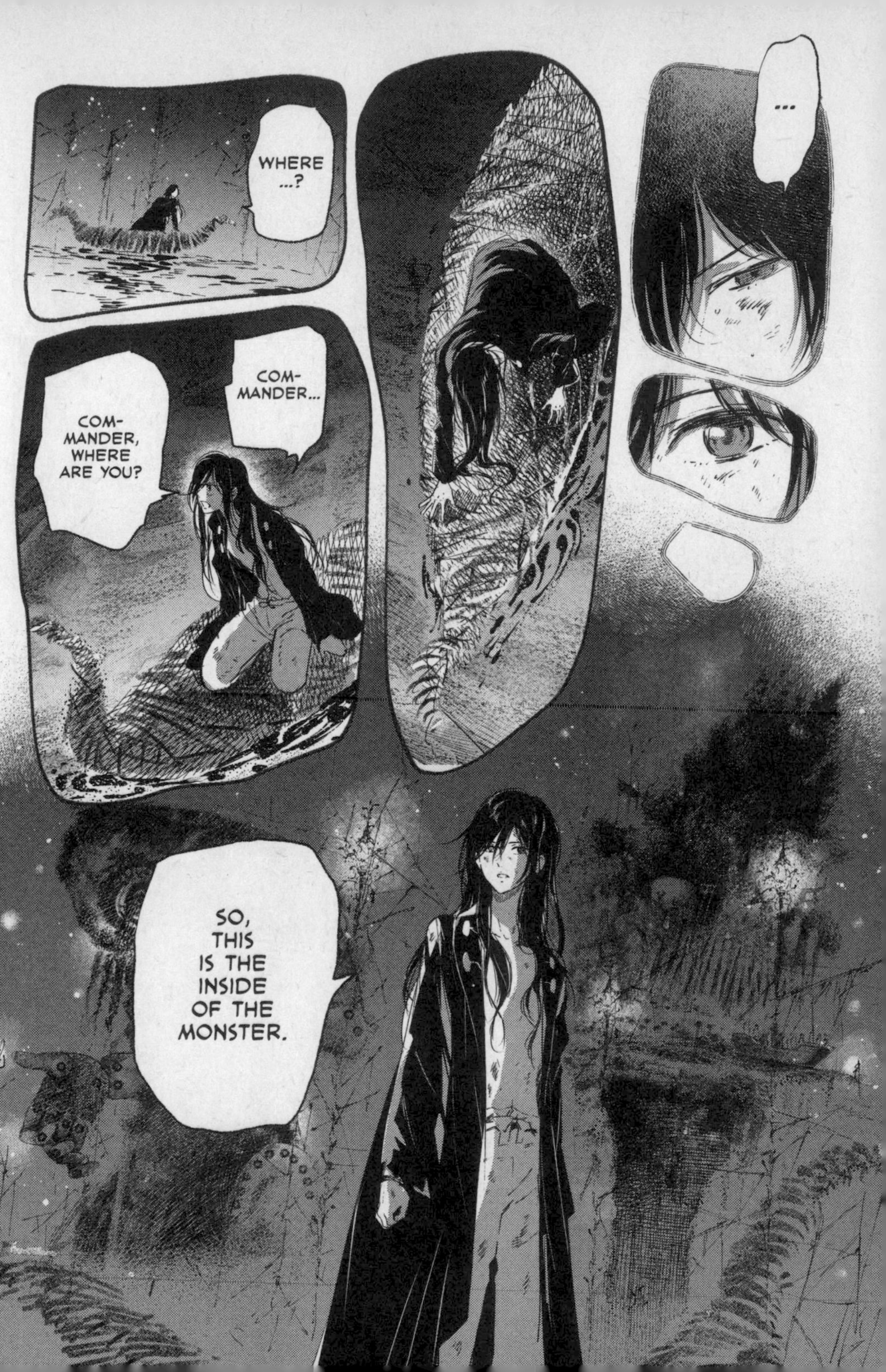
...
WHERE ...?
COM-MANDER...
COM-MANDER, WHERE ARE YOU?
SO, THIS IS THE INSIDE OF THE MONSTER.

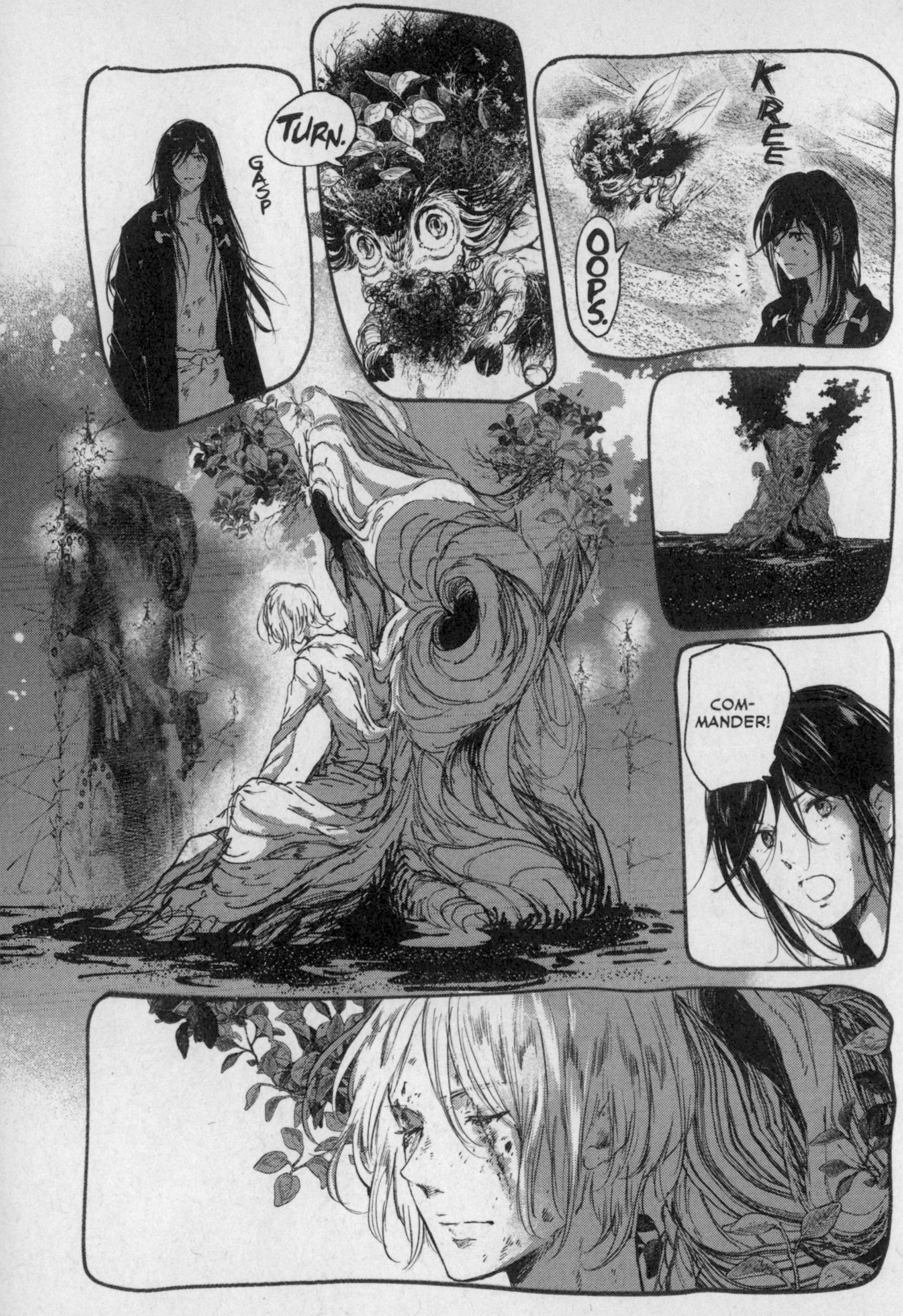
KREE
OOPS.
TURN.
GASP
COM-MANDER!

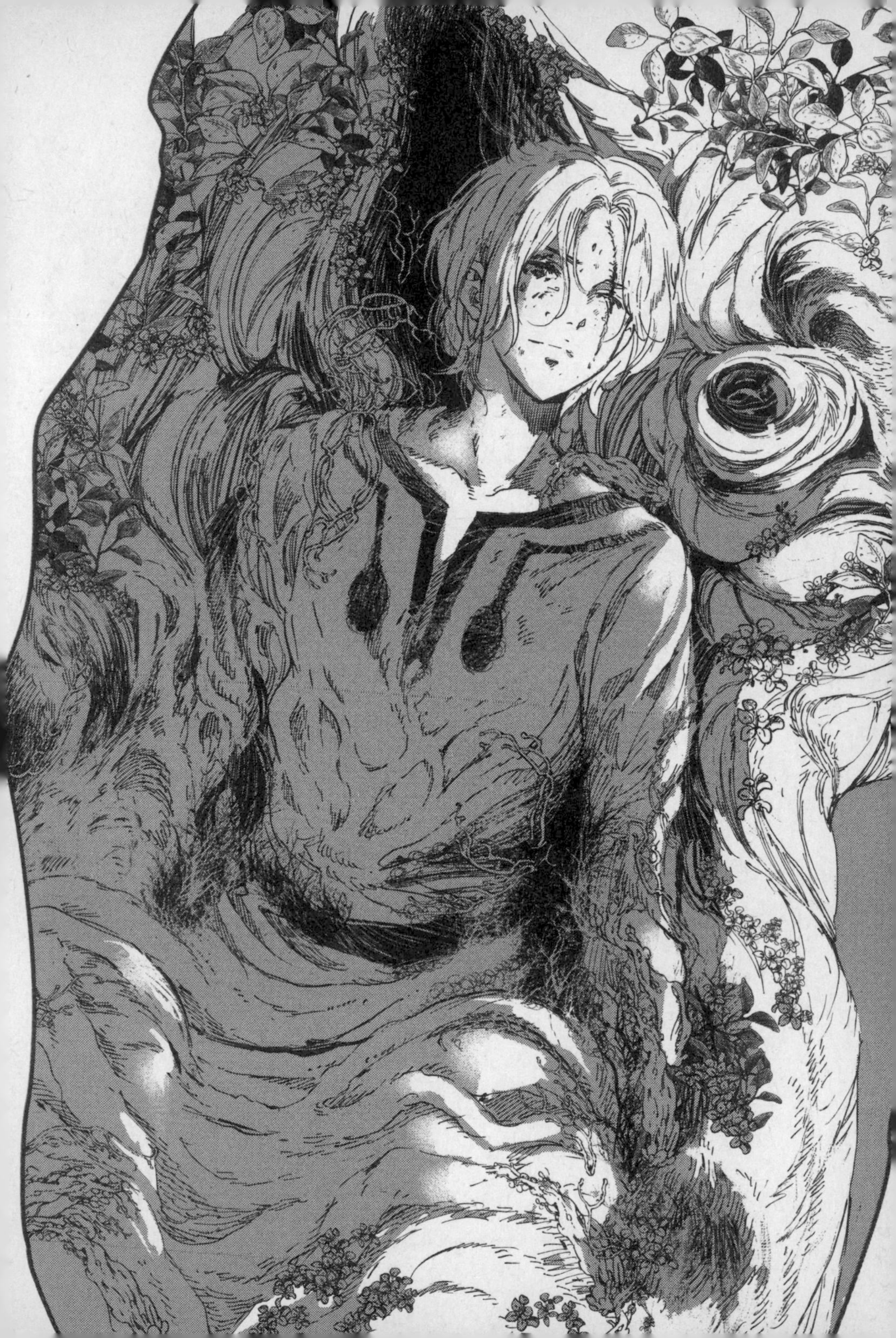

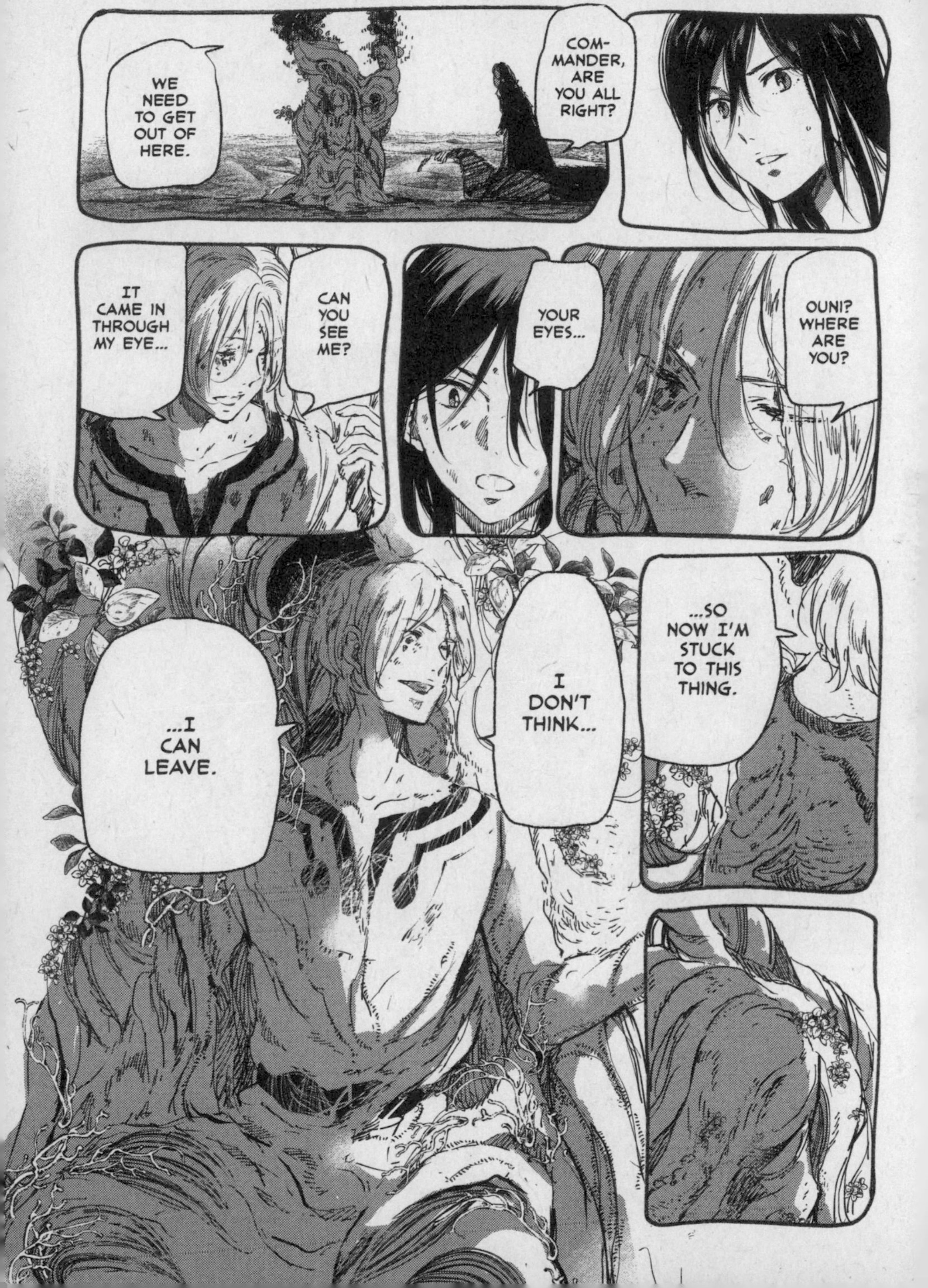
COM-MANDER, ARE YOU ALL RIGHT?
WE NEED TO GET OUT OF HERE.
OUNI? WHERE ARE YOU?
YOUR EYES...
CAN YOU SEE ME?
IT CAME IN THROUGH MY EYE...
...SO NOW I'M STUCK TO THIS THING.
I DON'T THINK...
...I CAN LEAVE.

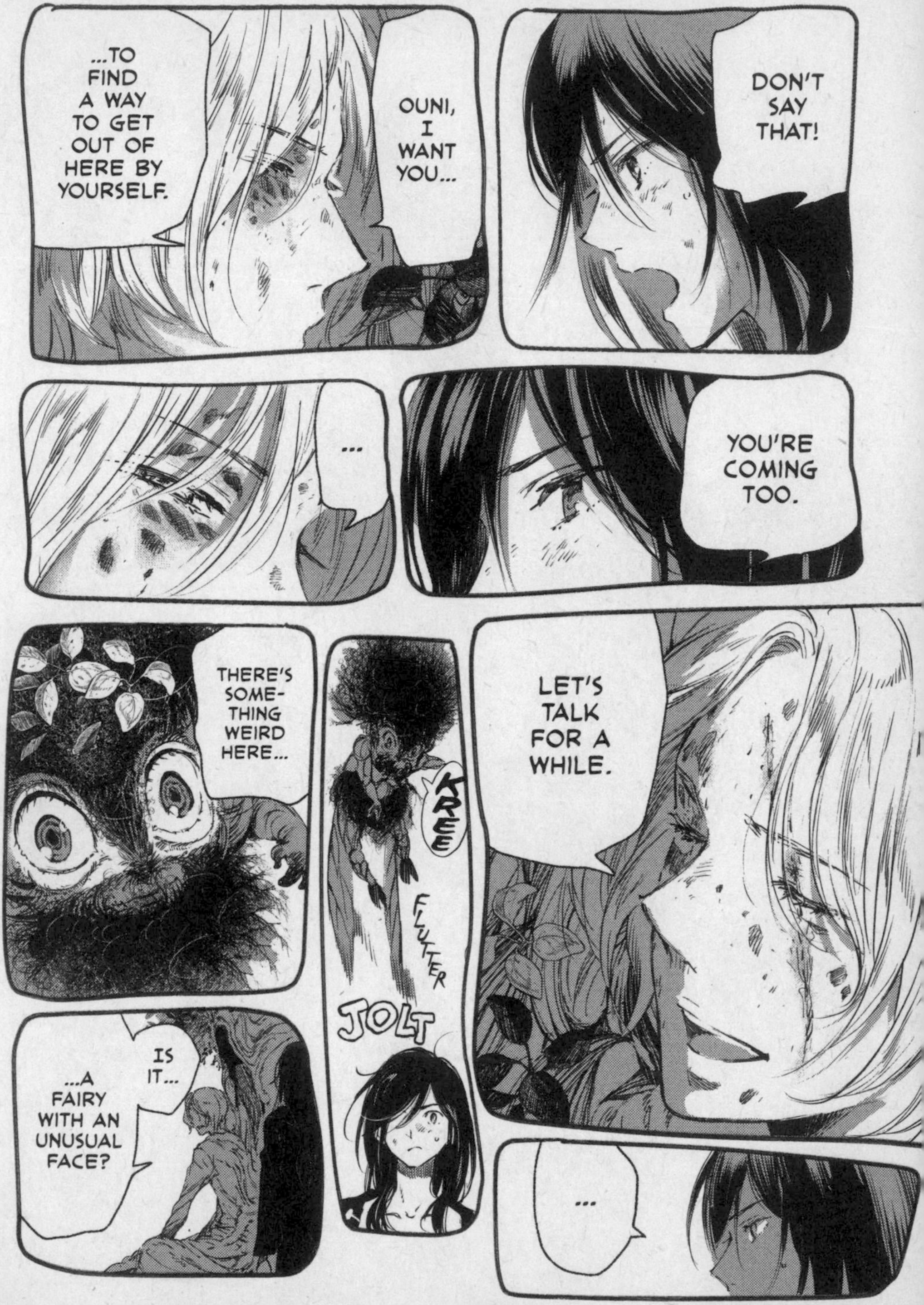
DON'T SAY THAT!
OUNI, I WANT YOU...
...TO FIND A WAY TO GET OUT OF HERE BY YOURSELF.
YOU'RE COMING TOO.
...
LET'S TALK FOR A WHILE.
...
KREE
FLUTTER
JOLT
THERE'S SOME-THING WEIRD HERE...
IS IT...
...A FAIRY WITH AN UNUSUAL FACE?

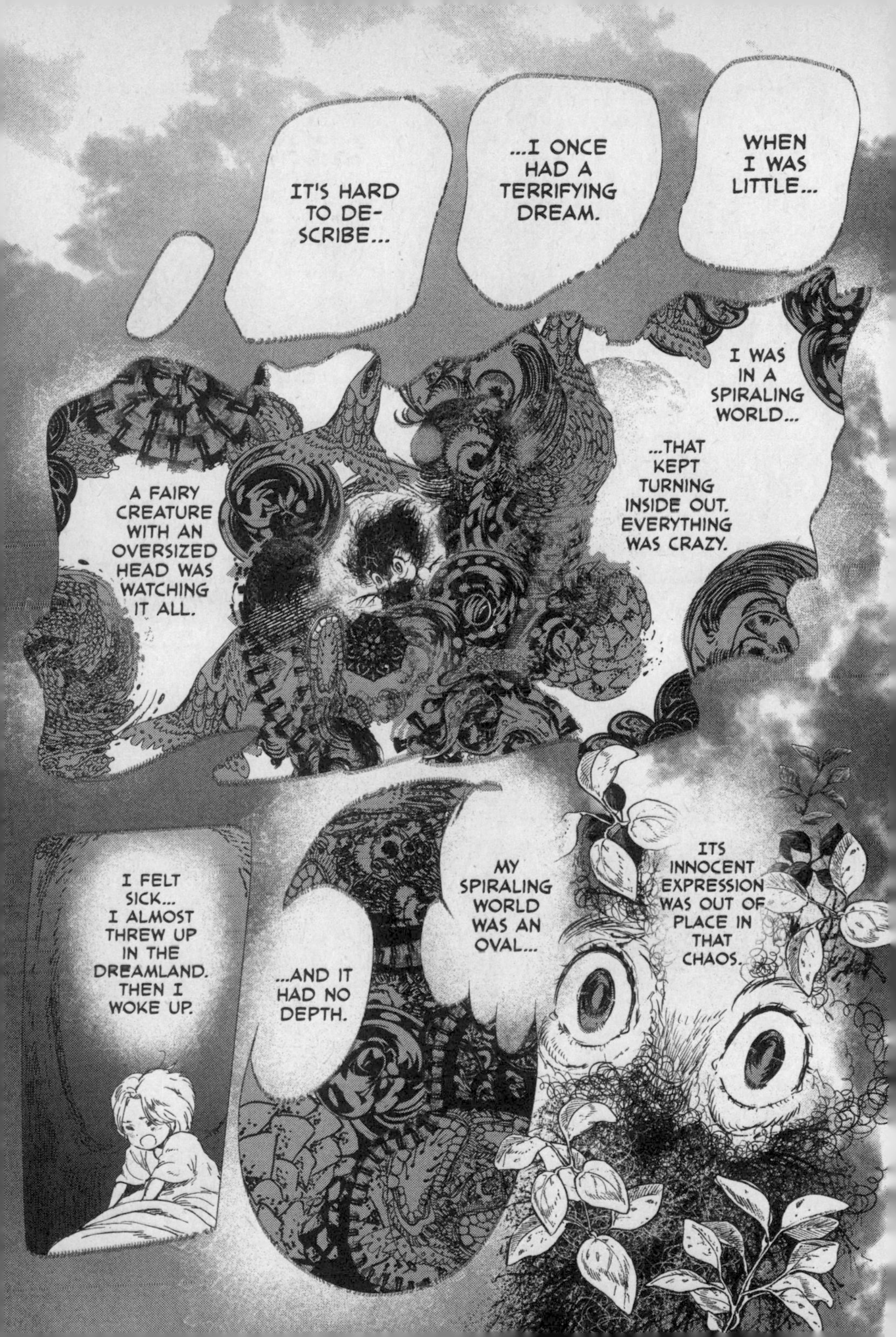
WHEN I WAS LITTLE...
...I ONCE HAD A TERRIFYING DREAM.
IT'S HARD TO DE-SCRIBE...
I WAS IN A SPIRALING WORLD...
...THAT KEPT TURNING INSIDE OUT. EVERYTHING WAS CRAZY.
A FAIRY CREATURE WITH AN OVERSIZED HEAD WAS WATCHING IT ALL.
ITS INNOCENT EXPRESSION WAS OUT OF PLACE IN THAT CHAOS.
MY SPIRALING WORLD WAS AN OVAL...
...AND IT HAD NO DEPTH.
I FELT SICK... I ALMOST THREW UP IN THE DREAMLAND. THEN I WOKE UP.

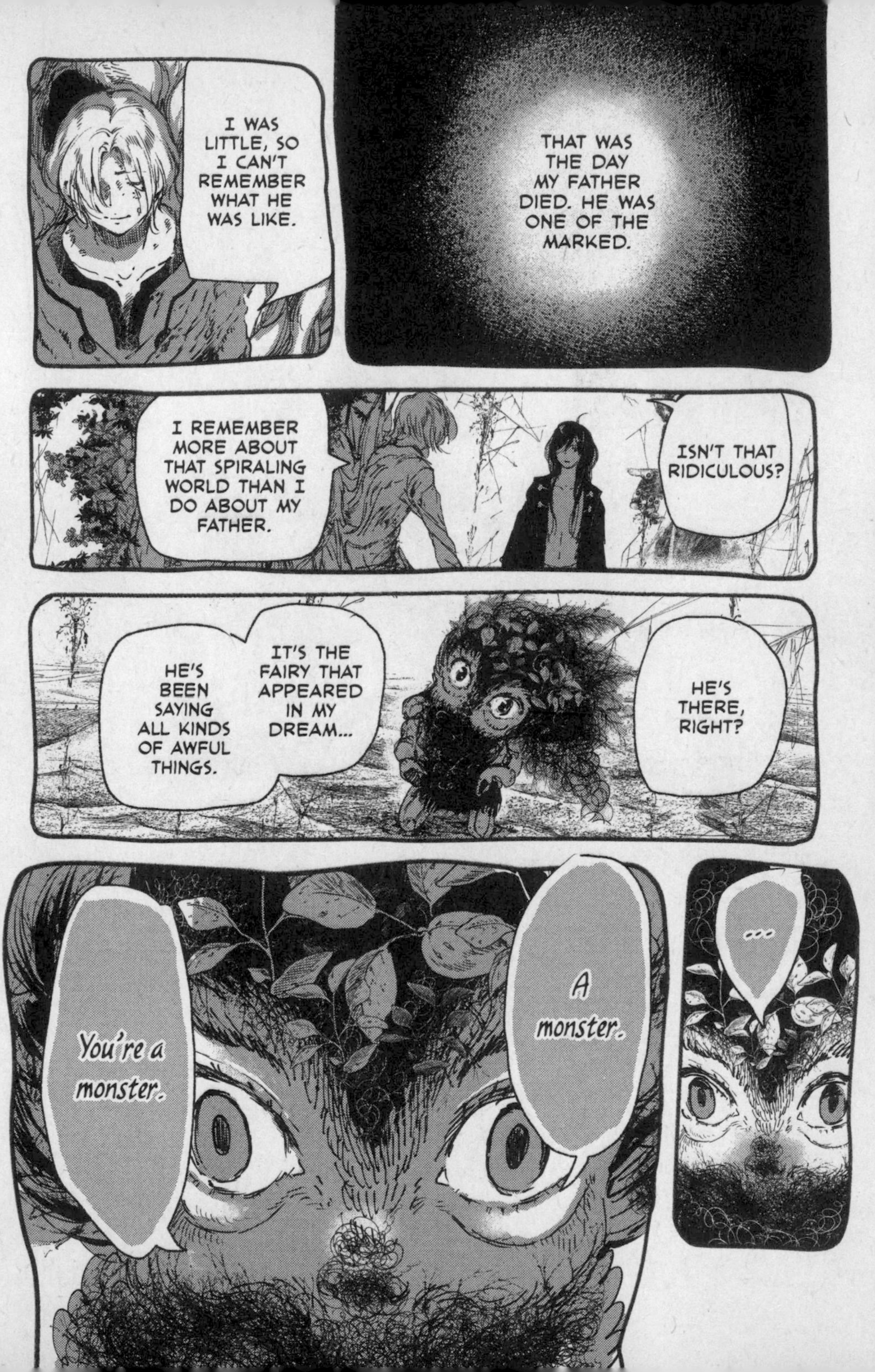
THAT WAS THE DAY MY FATHER DIED. HE WAS ONE OF THE MARKED.
I WAS LITTLE, SO I CAN'T REMEMBER WHAT HE WAS LIKE.
ISN'T THAT RIDICULOUS?
I REMEMBER MORE ABOUT THAT SPIRALING WORLD THAN I DO ABOUT MY FATHER.
HE'S THERE, RIGHT?
IT'S THE FAIRY THAT APPEARED IN MY DREAM...
HE'S BEEN SAYING ALL KINDS OF AWFUL THINGS.
...
A monster.
You're a monster.

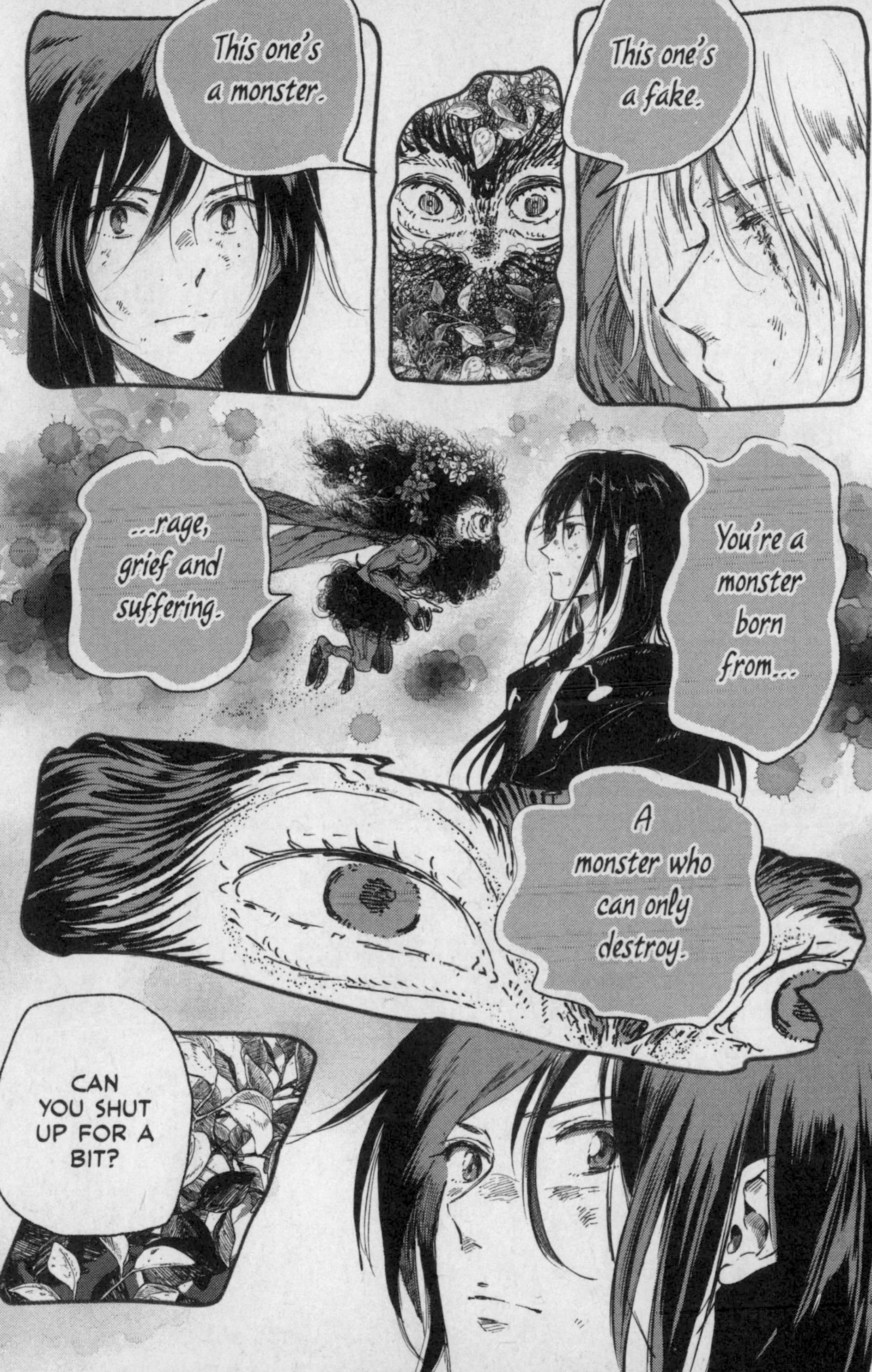
This one's a fake.
This one's a monster.
You're a monster born from...
...rage, grief and suffering.
A monster who can only destroy.
CAN YOU SHUT UP FOR A BIT?

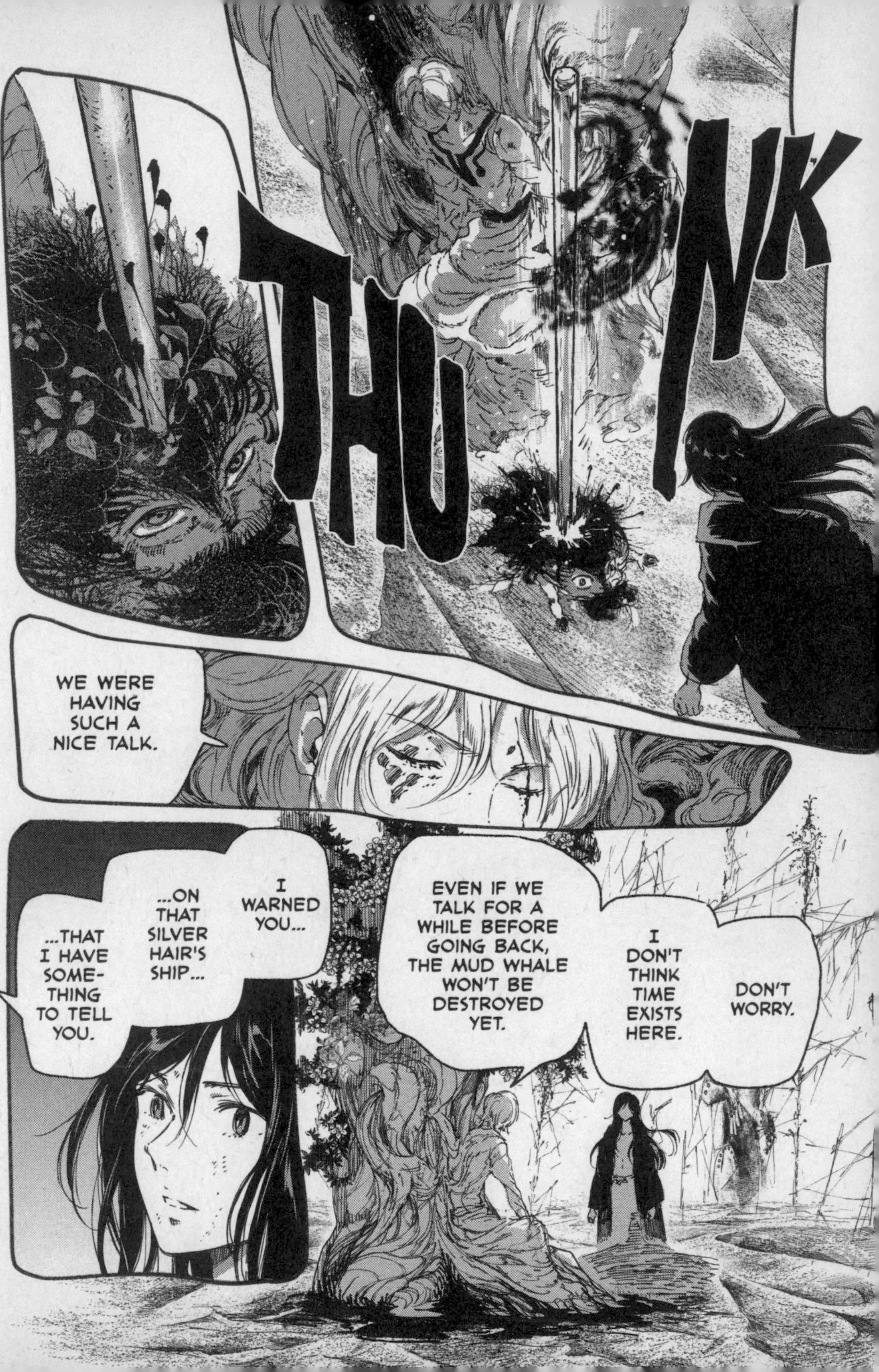
THUNK
WE WERE HAVING SUCH A NICE TALK.
DON'T WORRY.
I DON'T THINK TIME EXISTS HERE.
EVEN IF WE TALK FOR A WHILE BEFORE GOING BACK, THE MUD WHALE WON'T BE DESTROYED YET.
I WARNED YOU...
...ON THAT SILVER HAIR'S SHIP...
...THAT I HAVE SOME-THING TO TELL YOU.

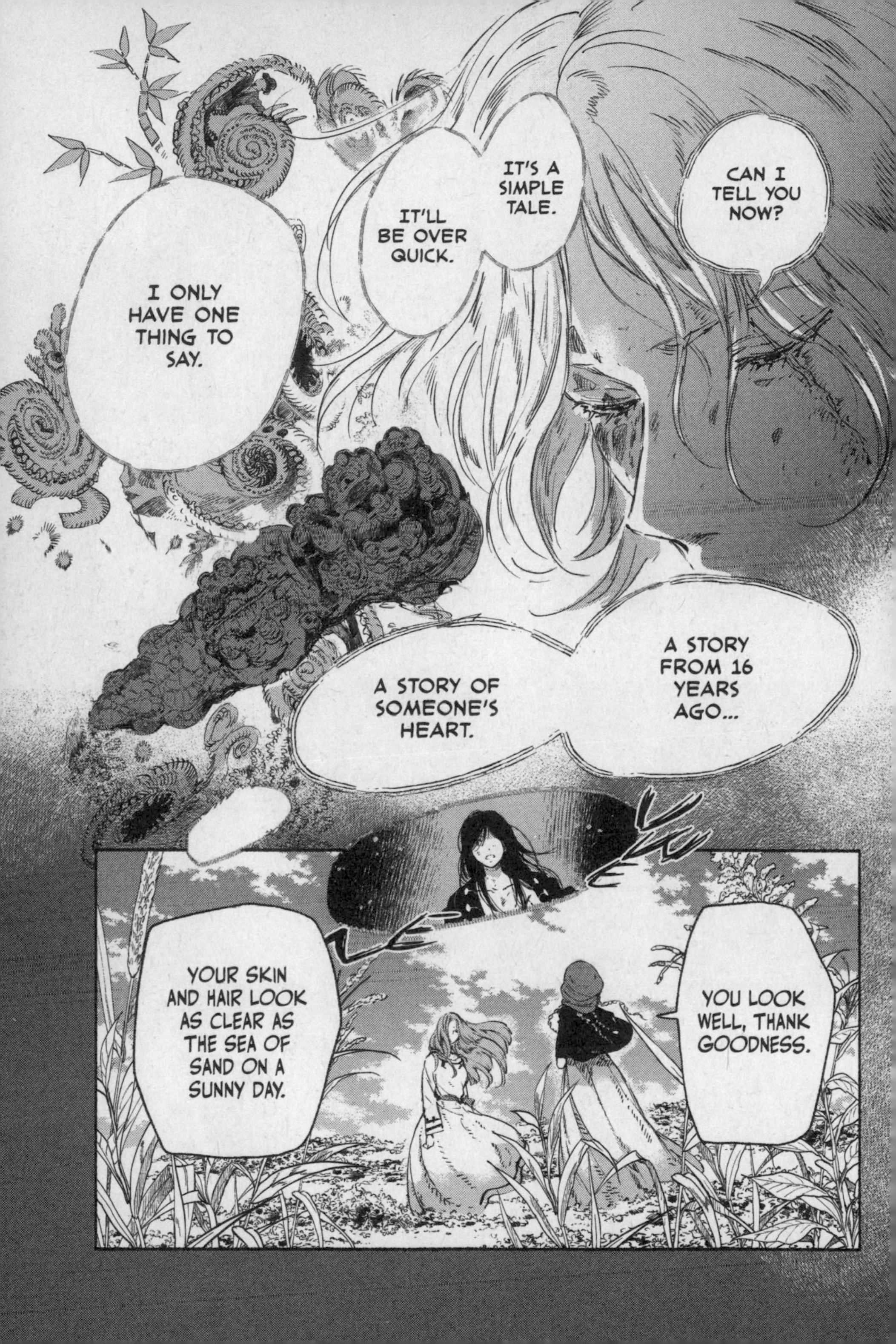
CAN I TELL YOU NOW?
IT'S A SIMPLE TALE.
IT'LL BE OVER QUICK.
I ONLY HAVE ONE THING TO SAY.
A STORY FROM 16 YEARS AGO...
A STORY OF SOMEONE'S HEART.
YOU LOOK WELL, THANK GOODNESS.
YOUR SKIN AND HAIR LOOK AS CLEAR AS THE SEA OF SAND ON A SUNNY DAY.

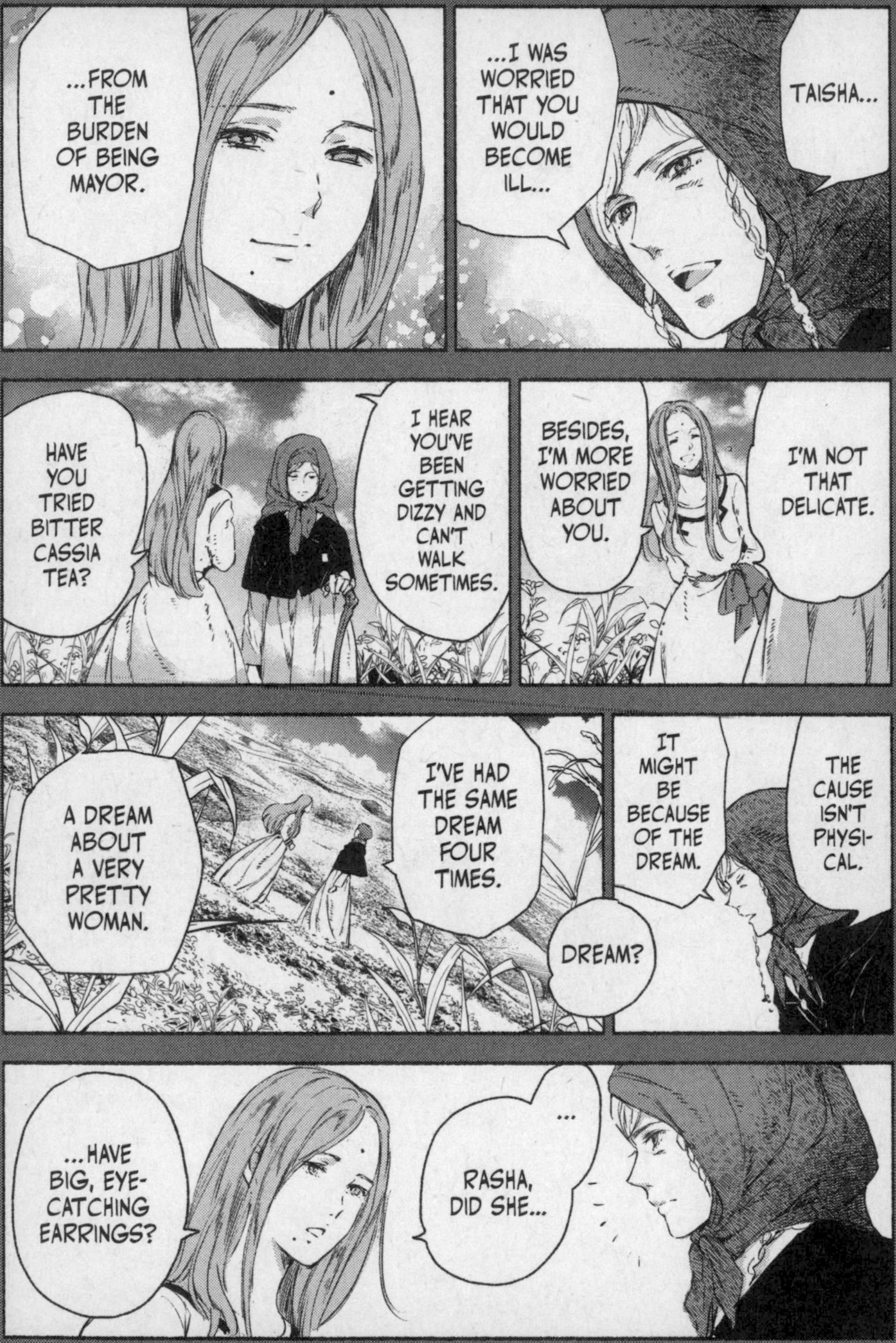
TAISHA...
...I WAS WORRIED THAT YOU WOULD BECOME ILL...
...FROM THE BURDEN OF BEING MAYOR.
I'M NOT THAT DELICATE.
BESIDES, I'M MORE WORRIED ABOUT YOU.
I HEAR YOU'VE BEEN GETTING DIZZY AND CAN'T WALK SOMETIMES.
HAVE YOU TRIED BITTER CASSIA TEA?
THE CAUSE ISN'T PHYSI-CAL.
IT MIGHT BE BECAUSE OF THE DREAM.
DREAM?
I'VE HAD THE SAME DREAM FOUR TIMES.
A DREAM ABOUT A VERY PRETTY WOMAN.
...
RASHA, DID SHE...
...HAVE BIG, EYE-CATCHING EARRINGS?

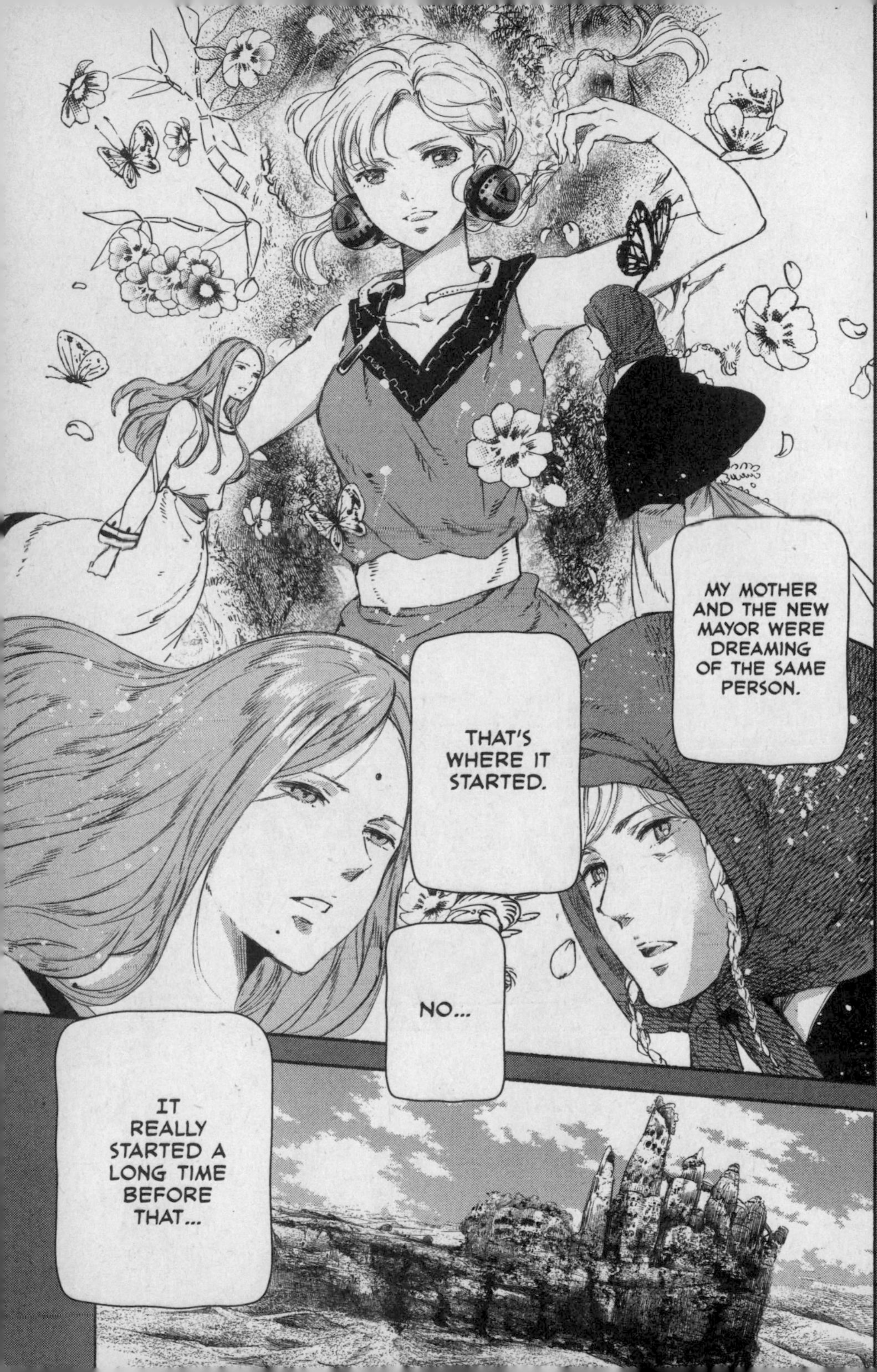
MY MOTHER AND THE NEW MAYOR WERE DREAMING OF THE SAME PERSON.
THAT'S WHERE IT STARTED.
NO...
IT REALLY STARTED A LONG TIME BEFORE THAT...

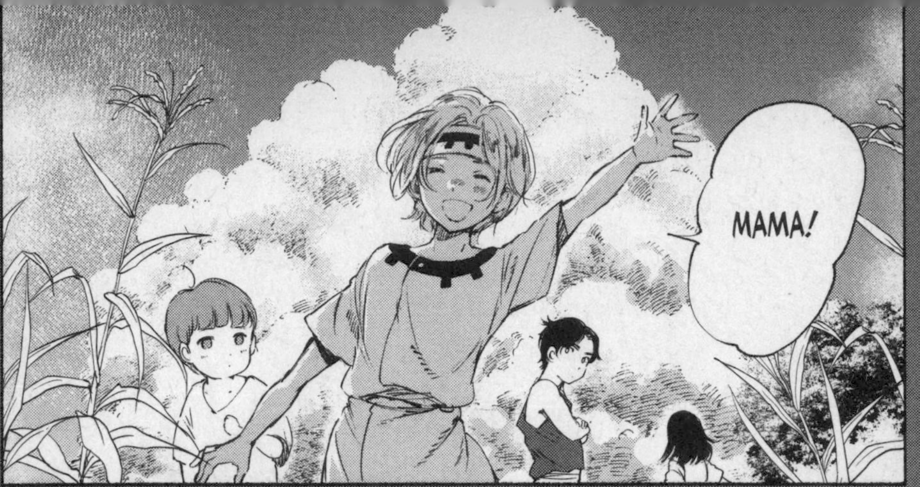
MAMA!

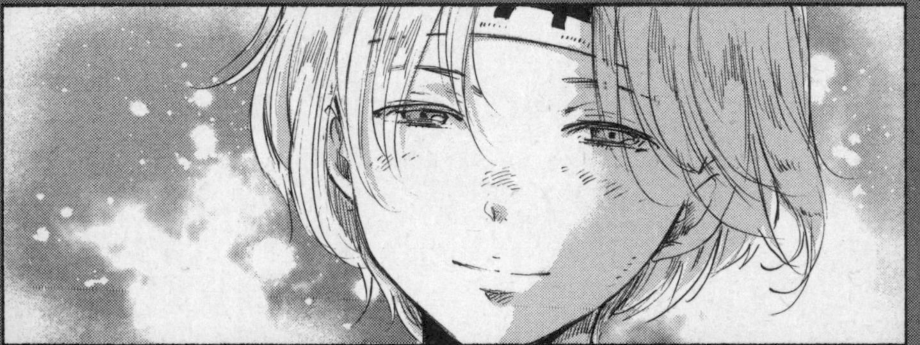

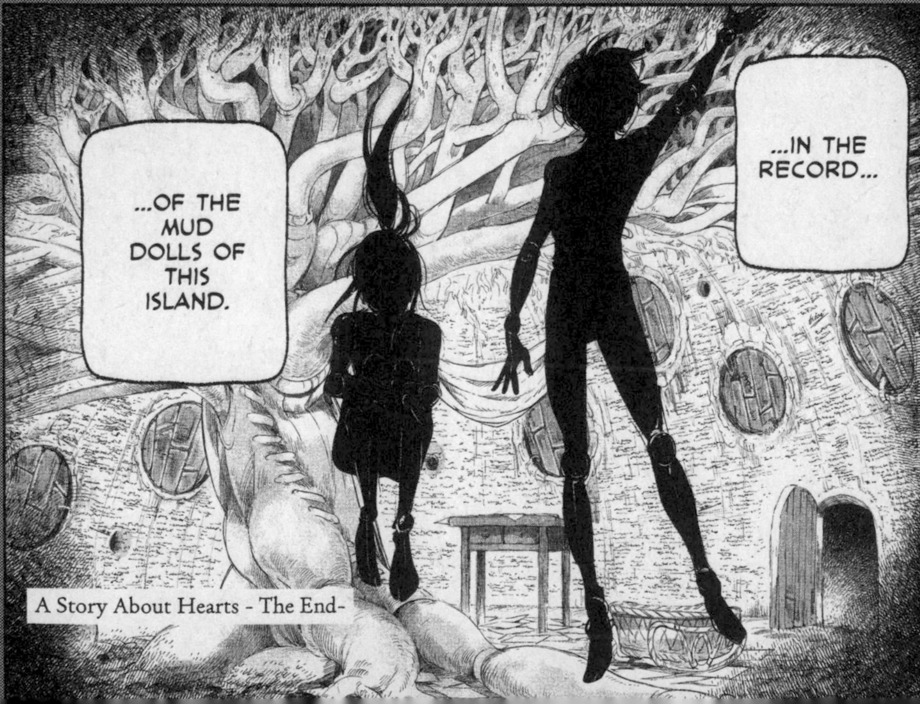
...IN THE RECORD...
...OF THE MUD DOLLS OF THIS ISLAND.

A Story About Hearts - The End-

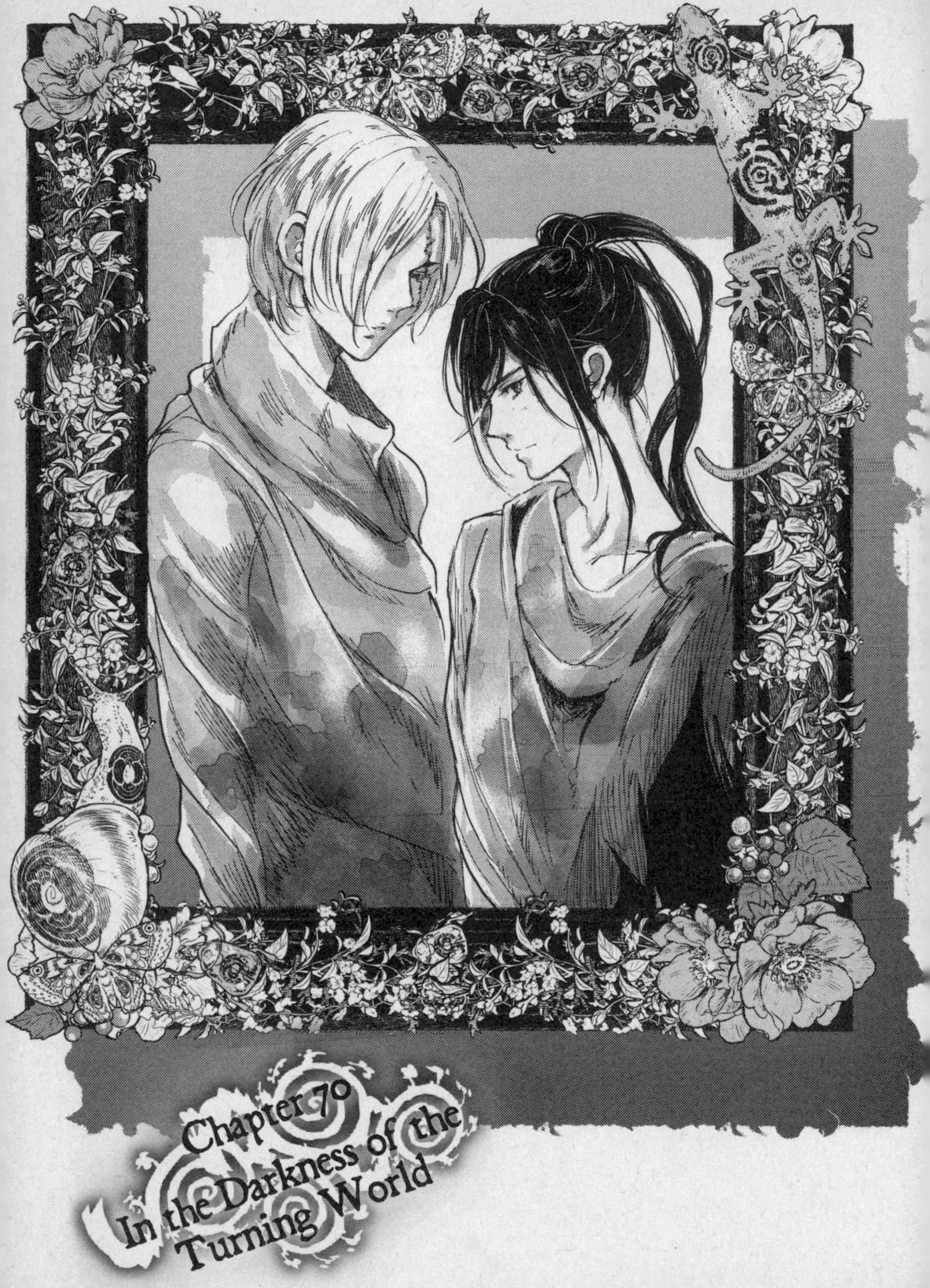

Chapter 70
In the Darkness of the Turning World

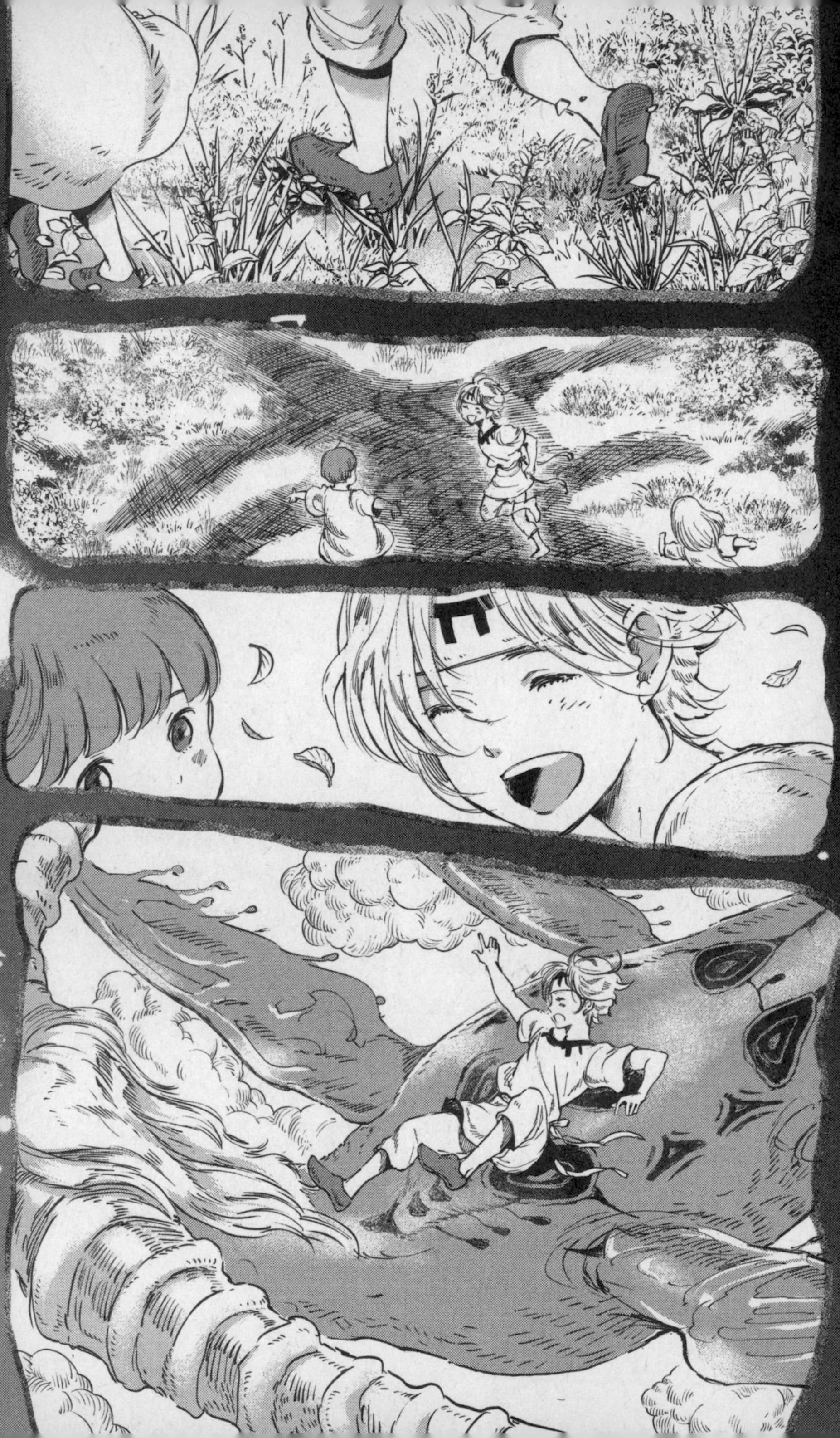

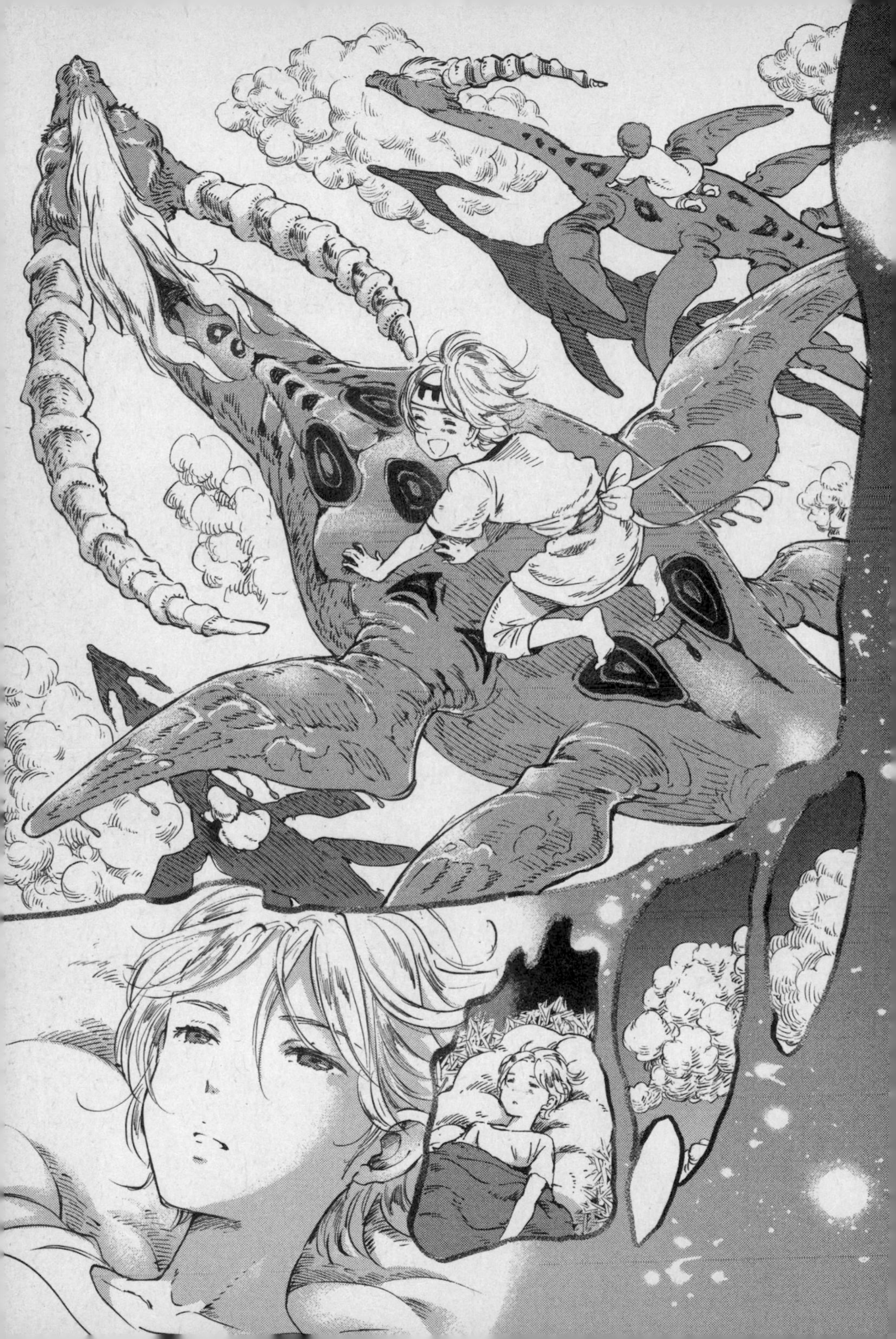

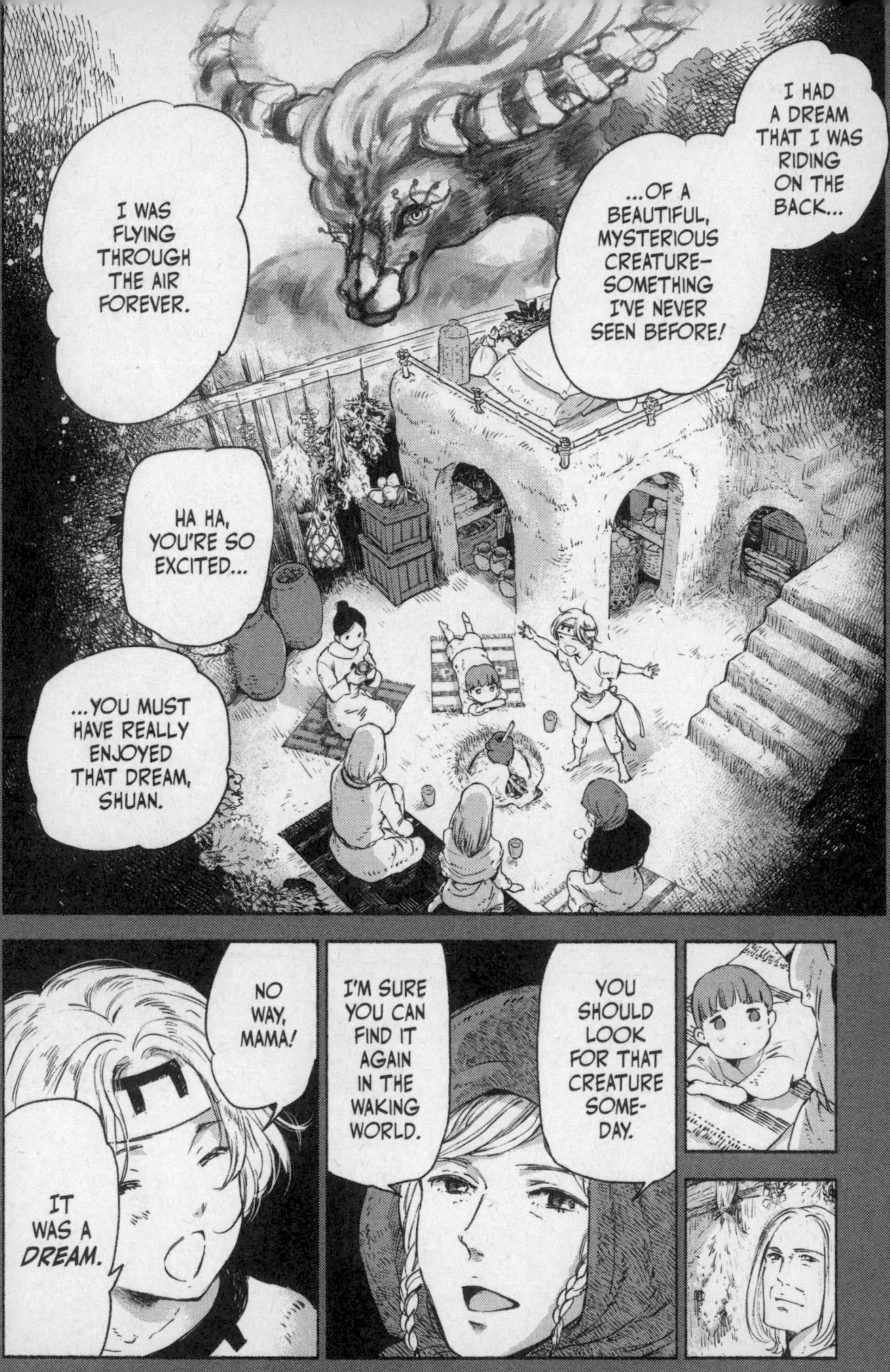
I HAD A DREAM THAT I WAS RIDING ON THE BACK...
...OF A BEAUTIFUL, MYSTERIOUS CREATURE—SOMETHING I'VE NEVER SEEN BEFORE!
I WAS FLYING THROUGH THE AIR FOREVER.
HA HA, YOU'RE SO EXCITED...
...YOU MUST HAVE REALLY ENJOYED THAT DREAM, SHUAN.
YOU SHOULD LOOK FOR THAT CREATURE SOME-DAY.
I'M SURE YOU CAN FIND IT AGAIN IN THE WAKING WORLD.
NO WAY, MAMA!
IT WAS A *DREAM*.

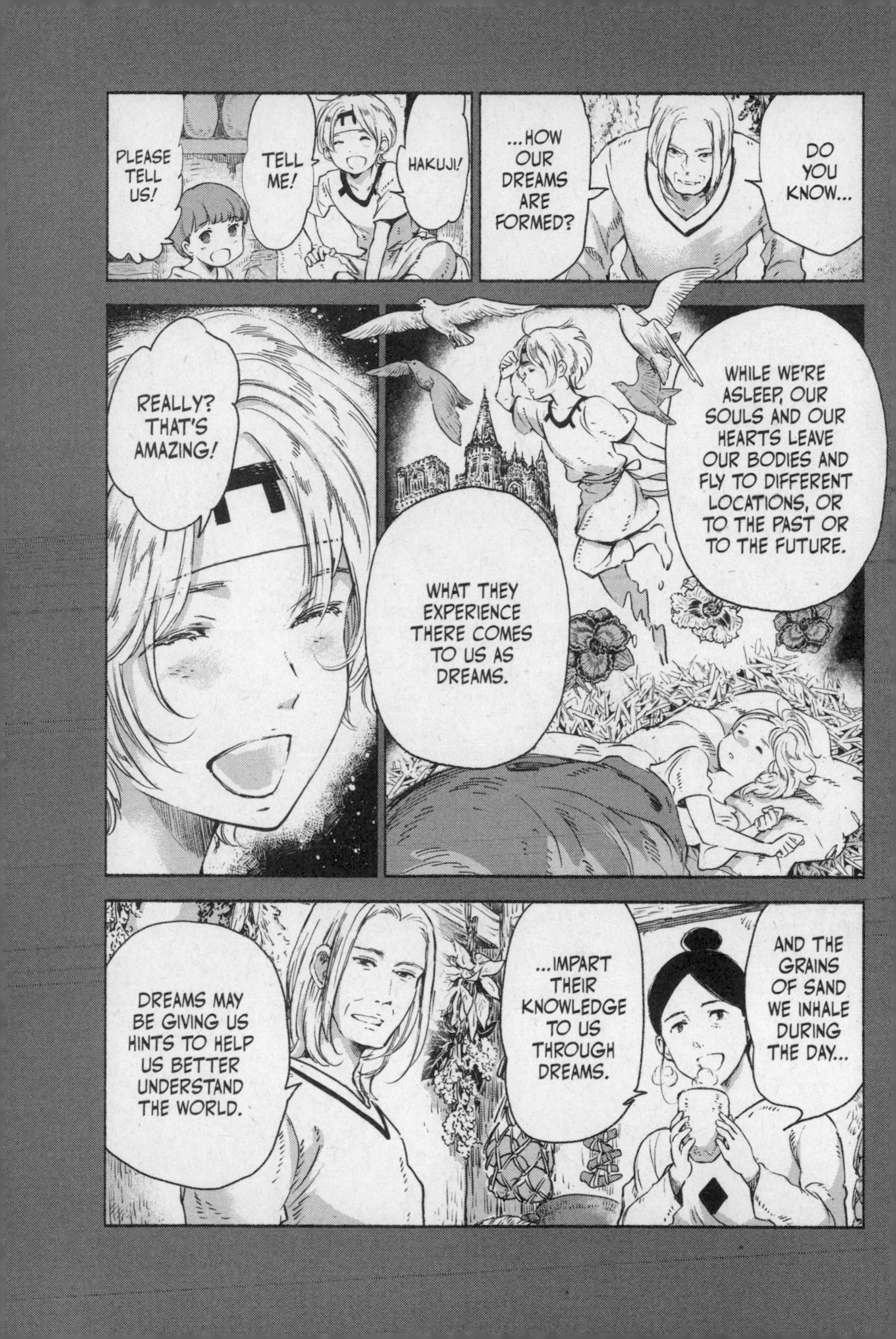
DO YOU KNOW...
...HOW OUR DREAMS ARE FORMED?
HAKUJI!
TELL ME!
PLEASE TELL US!
WHILE WE'RE ASLEEP, OUR SOULS AND OUR HEARTS LEAVE OUR BODIES AND FLY TO DIFFERENT LOCATIONS, OR TO THE PAST OR TO THE FUTURE.
WHAT THEY EXPERIENCE THERE COMES TO US AS DREAMS.
REALLY? THAT'S AMAZING!
AND THE GRAINS OF SAND WE INHALE DURING THE DAY...
...IMPART THEIR KNOWLEDGE TO US THROUGH DREAMS.
DREAMS MAY BE GIVING US HINTS TO HELP US BETTER UNDERSTAND THE WORLD.

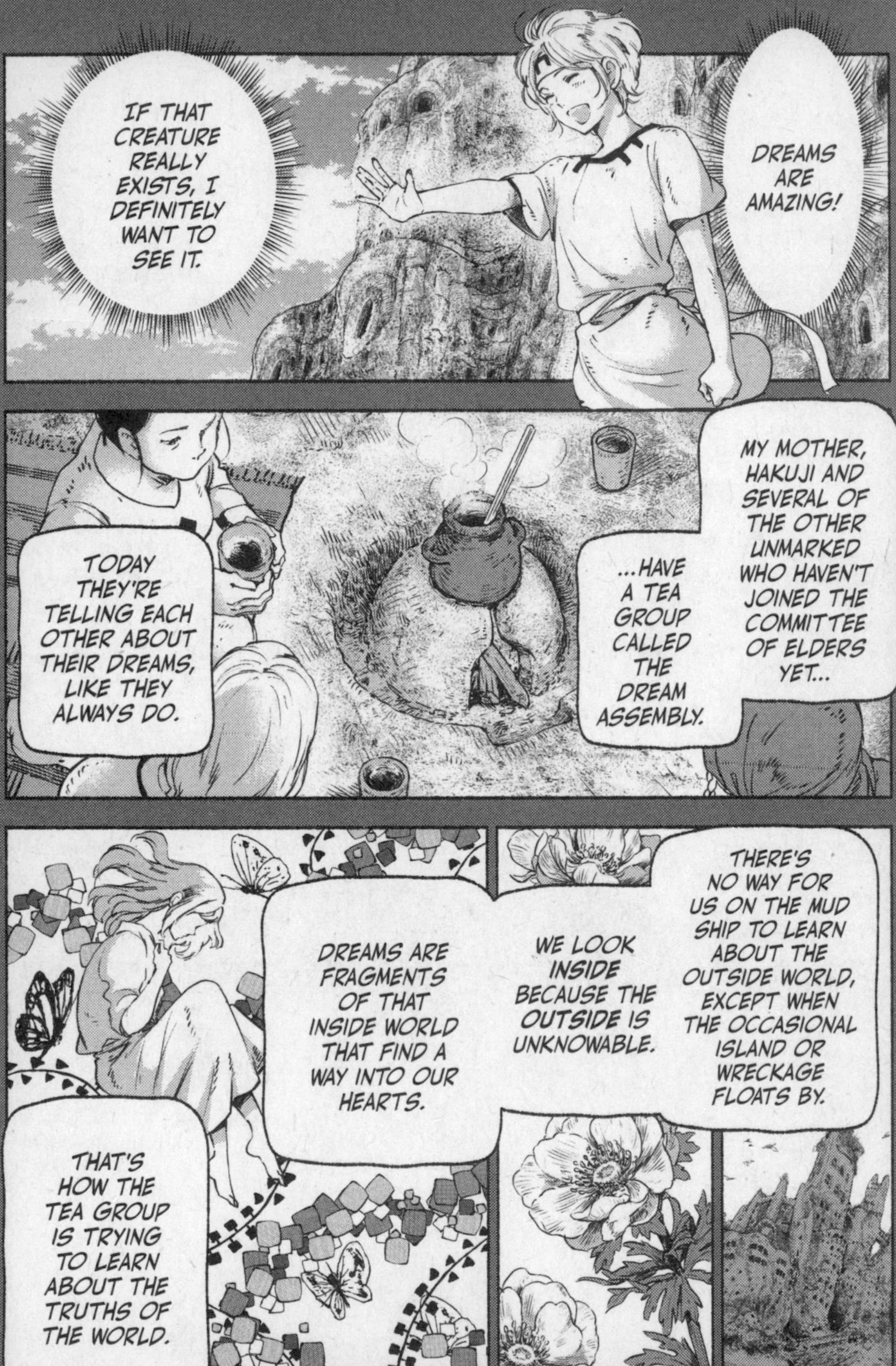
DREAMS ARE AMAZING!
IF THAT CREATURE REALLY EXISTS, I DEFINITELY WANT TO SEE IT.
MY MOTHER, HAKUJI AND SEVERAL OF THE OTHER UNMARKED WHO HAVEN'T JOINED THE COMMITTEE OF ELDERS YET...
...HAVE A TEA GROUP CALLED THE DREAM ASSEMBLY.
TODAY THEY'RE TELLING EACH OTHER ABOUT THEIR DREAMS, LIKE THEY ALWAYS DO.
THERE'S NO WAY FOR US ON THE MUD SHIP TO LEARN ABOUT THE OUTSIDE WORLD, EXCEPT WHEN THE OCCASIONAL ISLAND OR WRECKAGE FLOATS BY.
WE LOOK INSIDE BECAUSE THE OUTSIDE IS UNKNOWABLE.
DREAMS ARE FRAGMENTS OF THAT INSIDE WORLD THAT FIND A WAY INTO OUR HEARTS.
THAT'S HOW THE TEA GROUP IS TRYING TO LEARN ABOUT THE TRUTHS OF THE WORLD.

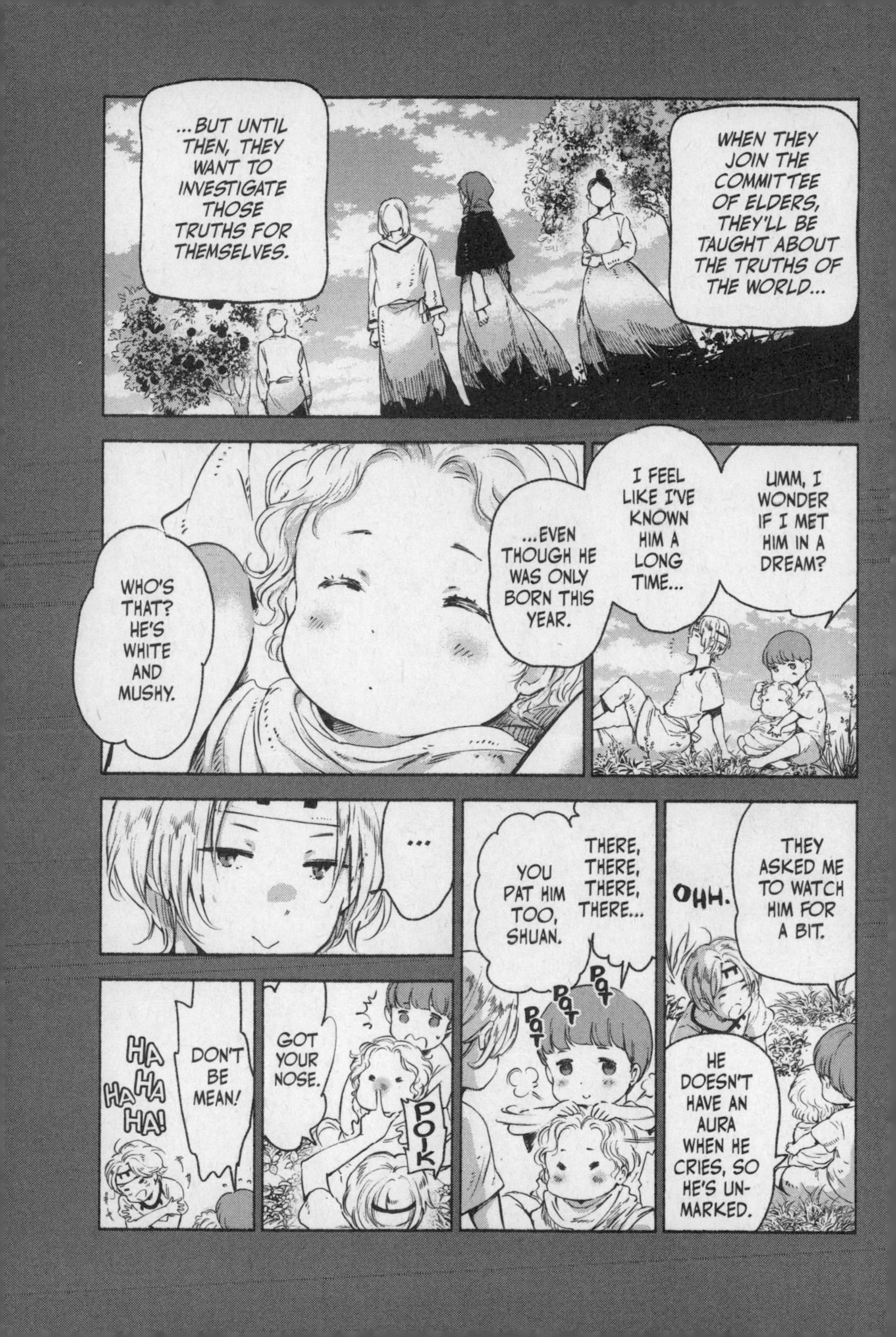
WHEN THEY JOIN THE COMMITTEE OF ELDERS, THEY'LL BE TAUGHT ABOUT THE TRUTHS OF THE WORLD...
...BUT UNTIL THEN, THEY WANT TO INVESTIGATE THOSE TRUTHS FOR THEMSELVES.
UMM, I WONDER IF I MET HIM IN A DREAM?
I FEEL LIKE I'VE KNOWN HIM A LONG TIME...
...EVEN THOUGH HE WAS ONLY BORN THIS YEAR.
WHO'S THAT? HE'S WHITE AND MUSHY.
THEY ASKED ME TO WATCH HIM FOR A BIT.
OHH.
HE DOESN'T HAVE AN AURA WHEN HE CRIES, SO HE'S UN-MARKED.
THERE, THERE, THERE, THERE...
YOU PAT HIM TOO, SHUAN.
PAT PAT PAT
...
GOT YOUR NOSE.
POIK
DON'T BE MEAN!
HA HA HA HA!

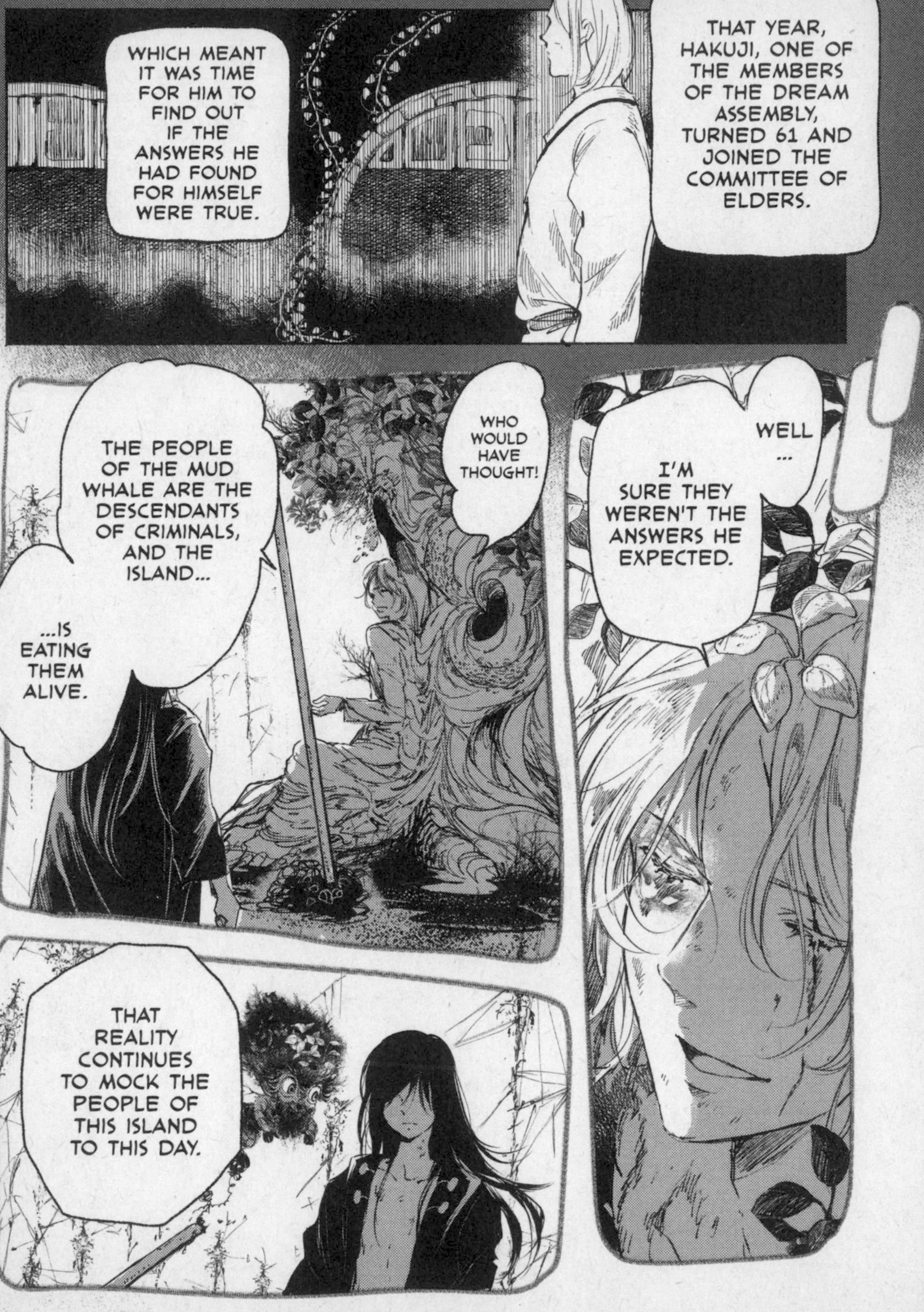
THAT YEAR, HAKUJI, ONE OF THE MEMBERS OF THE DREAM ASSEMBLY, TURNED 61 AND JOINED THE COMMITTEE OF ELDERS.
WHICH MEANT IT WAS TIME FOR HIM TO FIND OUT IF THE ANSWERS HE HAD FOUND FOR HIMSELF WERE TRUE.
THE PEOPLE OF THE MUD WHALE ARE THE DESCENDANTS OF CRIMINALS, AND THE ISLAND...
...IS EATING THEM ALIVE.
WHO WOULD HAVE THOUGHT!
WELL ...
I'M SURE THEY WEREN'T THE ANSWERS HE EXPECTED.
THAT REALITY CONTINUES TO MOCK THE PEOPLE OF THIS ISLAND TO THIS DAY.

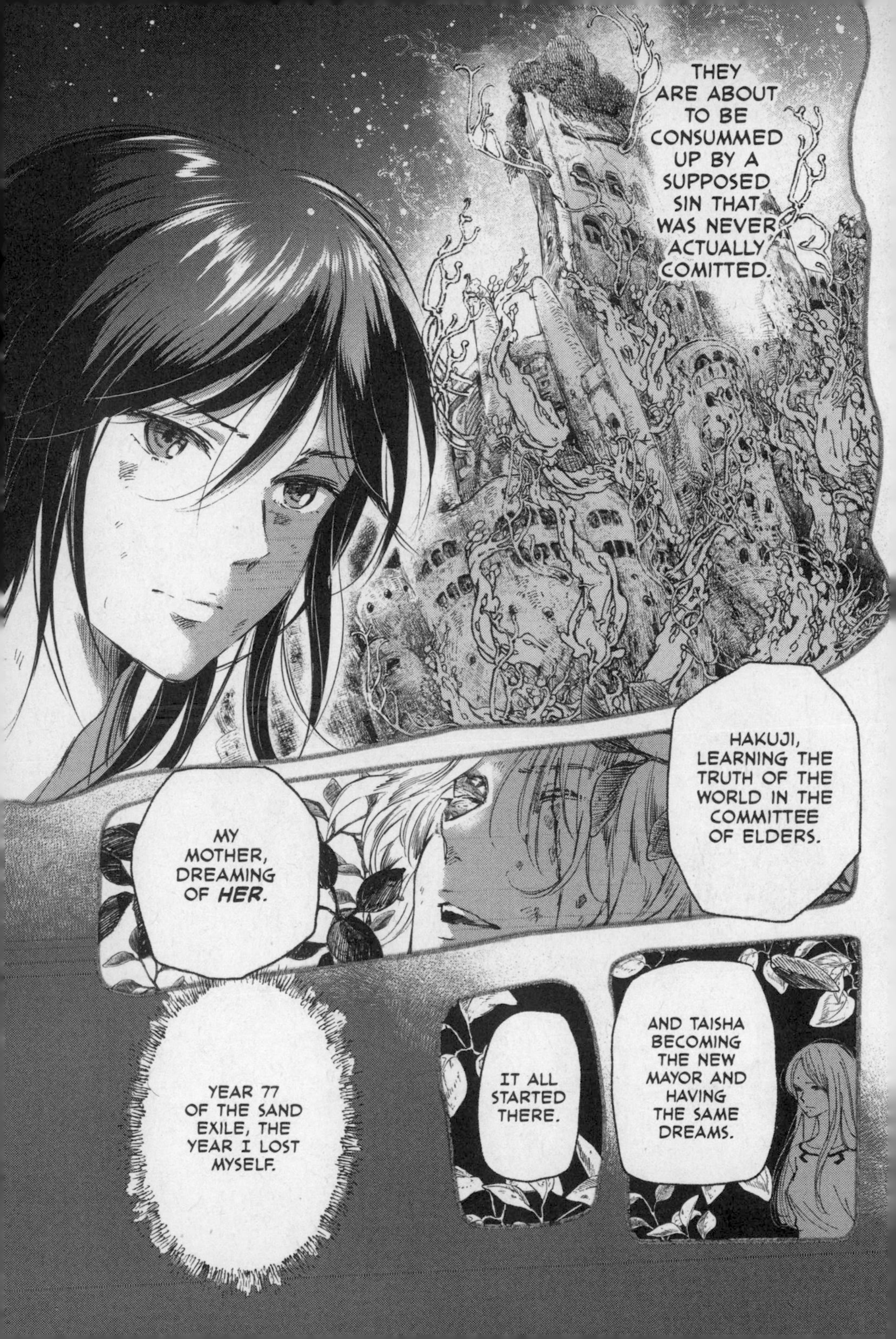
THEY ARE ABOUT TO BE CONSUMMED UP BY A SUPPOSED SIN THAT WAS NEVER ACTUALLY COMITTED.
HAKUJI, LEARNING THE TRUTH OF THE WORLD IN THE COMMITTEE OF ELDERS.
MY MOTHER, DREAMING OF *HER*.
AND TAISHA BECOMING THE NEW MAYOR AND HAVING THE SAME DREAMS.
IT ALL STARTED THERE.
YEAR 77 OF THE SAND EXILE, THE YEAR I LOST MYSELF.

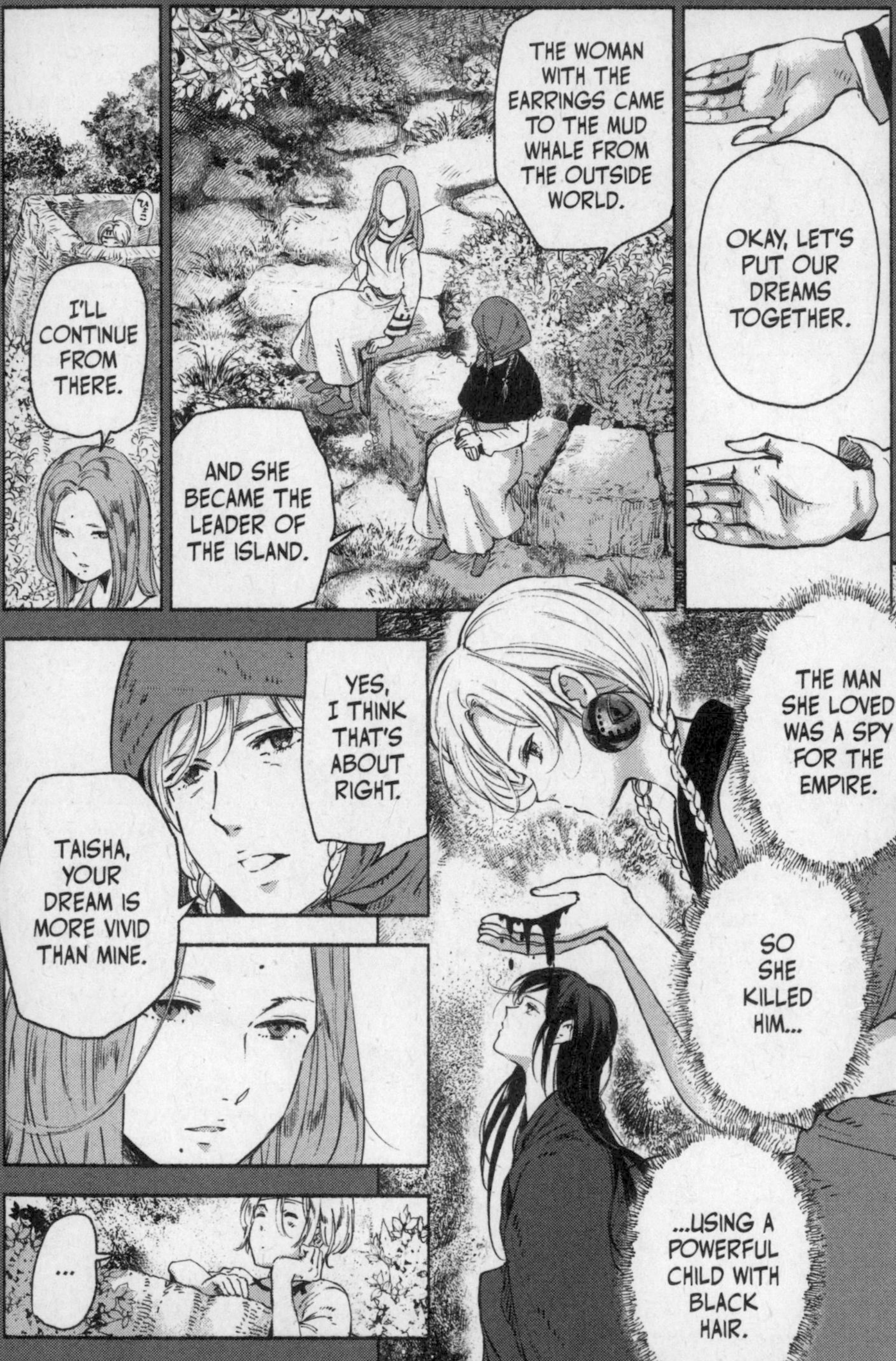
OKAY, LET'S PUT OUR DREAMS TOGETHER.
THE WOMAN WITH THE EARRINGS CAME TO THE MUD WHALE FROM THE OUTSIDE WORLD.
AND SHE BECAME THE LEADER OF THE ISLAND.
I'LL CONTINUE FROM THERE.
THE MAN SHE LOVED WAS A SPY FOR THE EMPIRE.
SO SHE KILLED HIM...
...USING A POWERFUL CHILD WITH BLACK HAIR.
YES, I THINK THAT'S ABOUT RIGHT.
TAISHA, YOUR DREAM IS MORE VIVID THAN MINE.
...

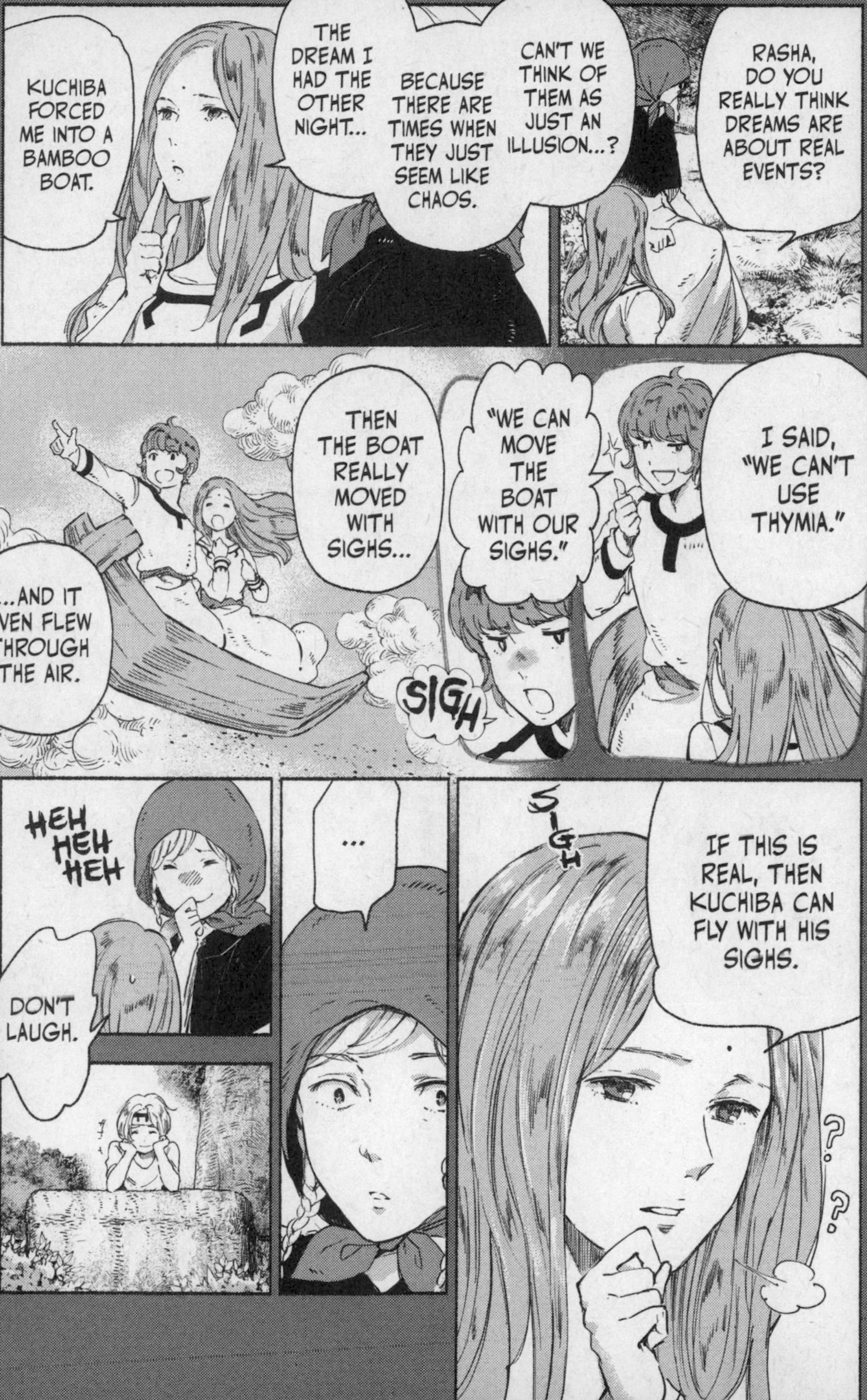
RASHA, DO YOU REALLY THINK DREAMS ARE ABOUT REAL EVENTS?
CAN'T WE THINK OF THEM AS JUST AN ILLUSION...?
BECAUSE THERE ARE TIMES WHEN THEY JUST SEEM LIKE CHAOS.
THE DREAM I HAD THE OTHER NIGHT...
KUCHIBA FORCED ME INTO A BAMBOO BOAT.
I SAID, "WE CAN'T USE THYMIA."
SIGH
"WE CAN MOVE THE BOAT WITH OUR SIGHS."
THEN THE BOAT REALLY MOVED WITH SIGHS...
...AND IT EVEN FLEW THROUGH THE AIR.
SIGH
IF THIS IS REAL, THEN KUCHIBA CAN FLY WITH HIS SIGHS.
...
HEH HEH HEH
DON'T LAUGH.

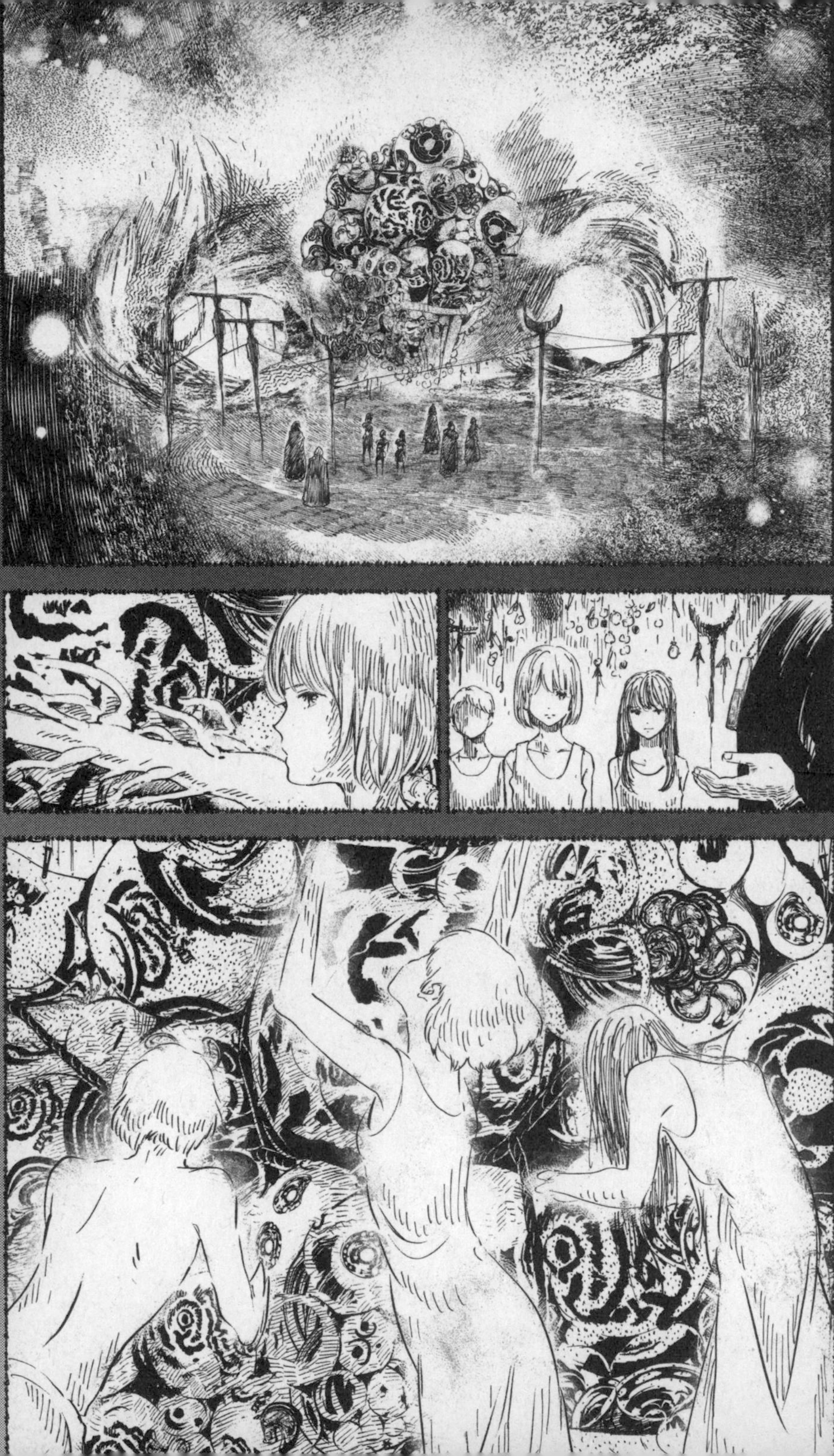

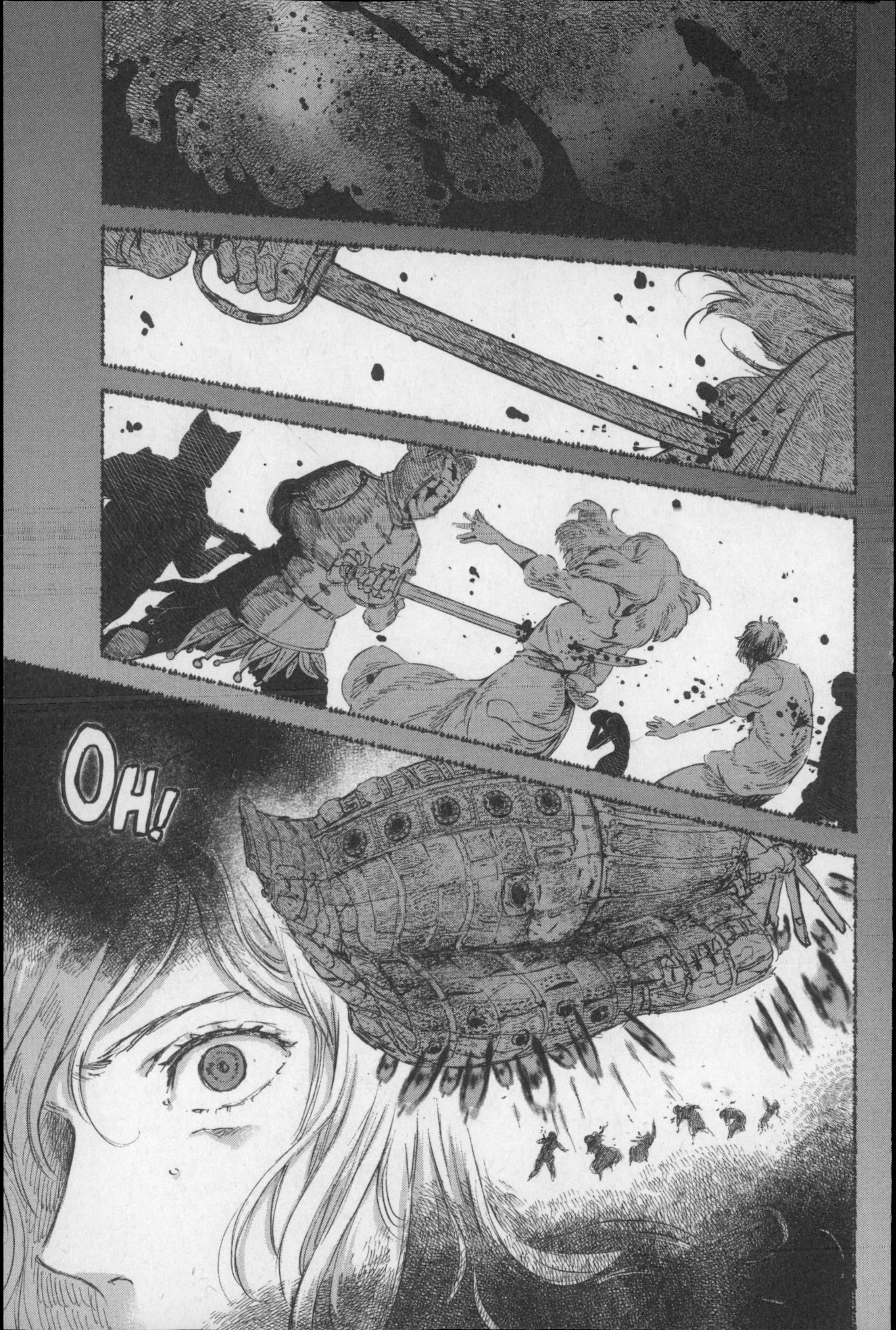
OH!

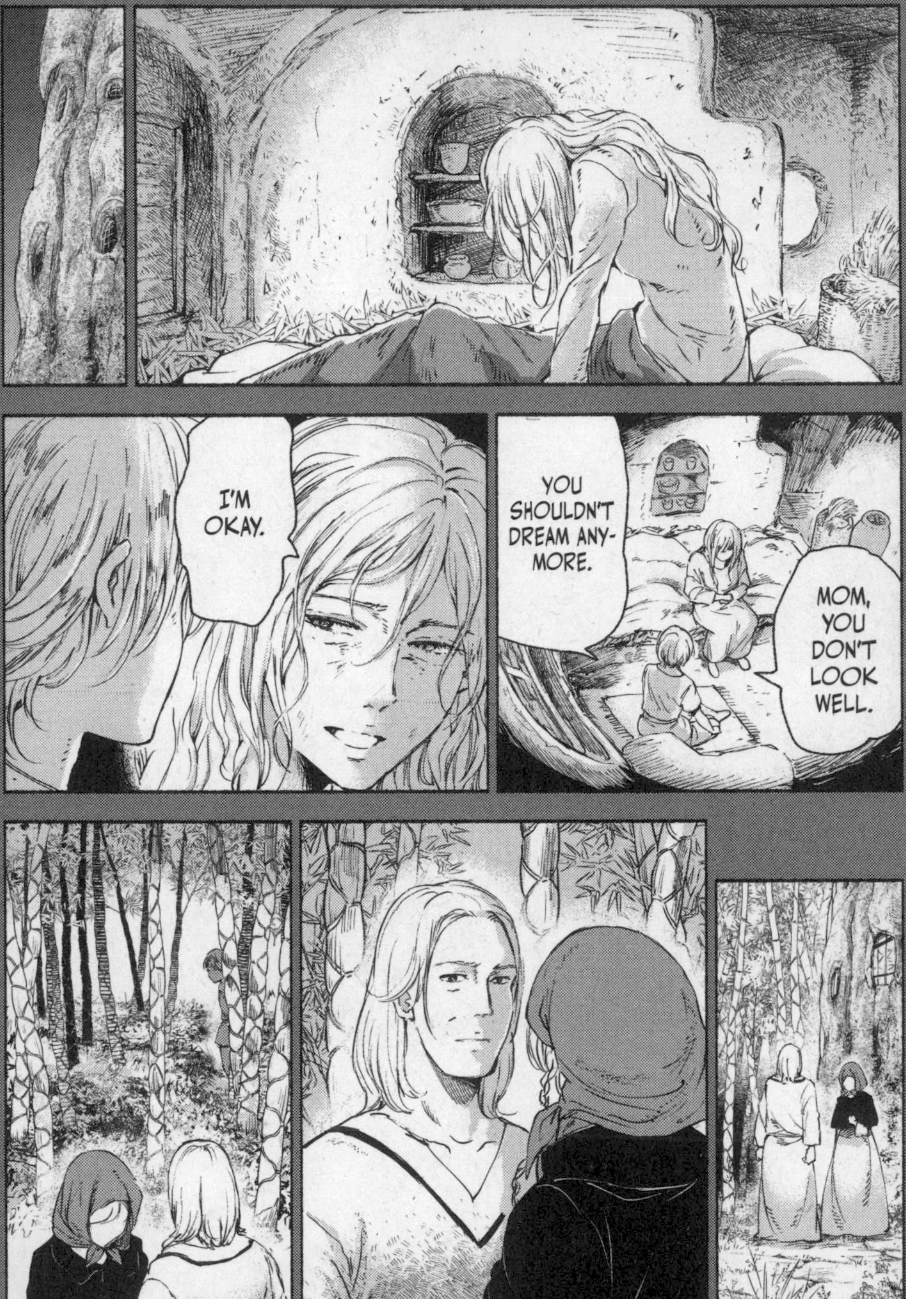
MOM, YOU DON'T LOOK WELL.
YOU SHOULDN'T DREAM ANY-MORE.
I'M OKAY.

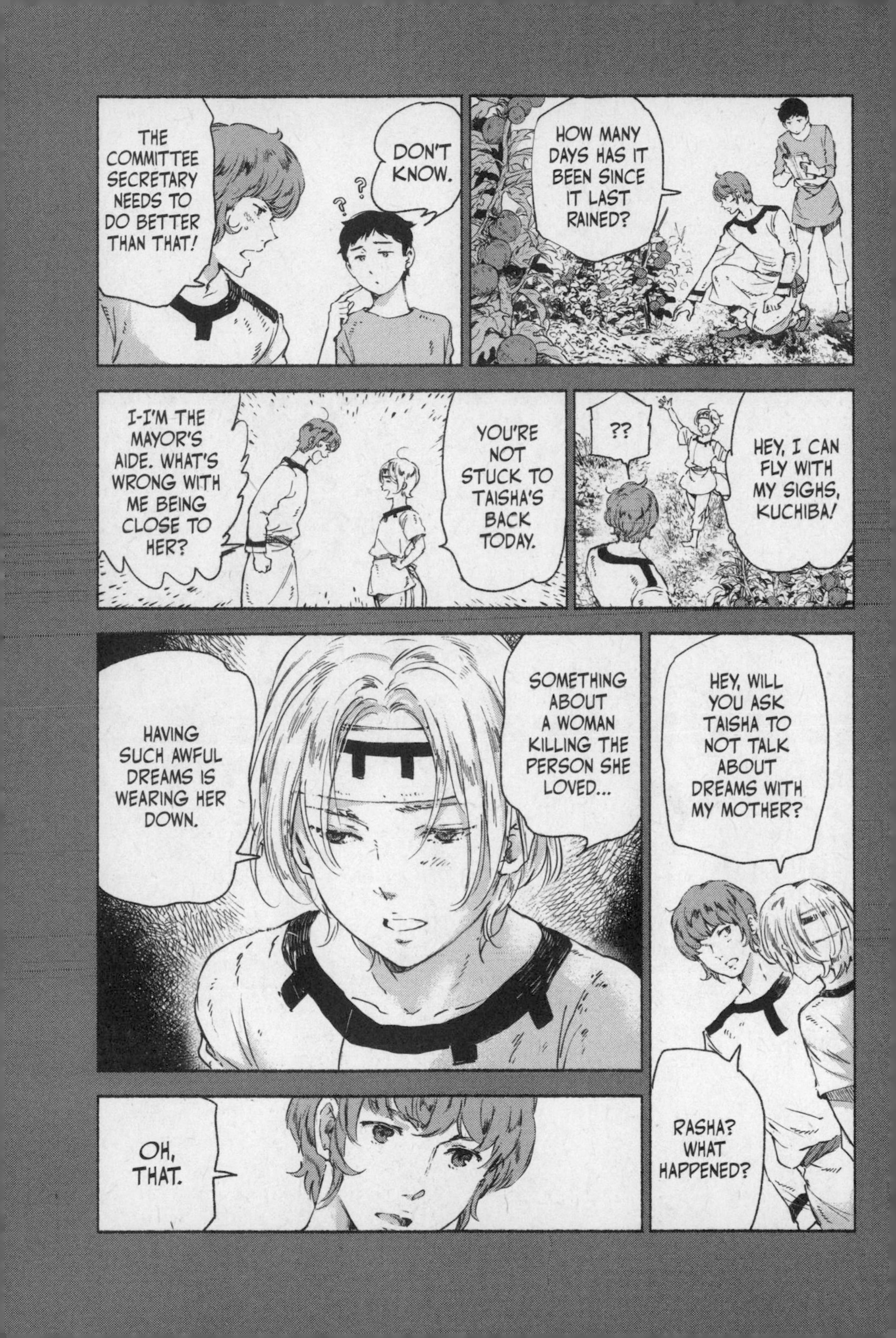
HOW MANY DAYS HAS IT BEEN SINCE IT LAST RAINED?
DON'T KNOW.
THE COMMITTEE SECRETARY NEEDS TO DO BETTER THAN THAT!
HEY, I CAN FLY WITH MY SIGHS, KUCHIBA!
??
YOU'RE NOT STUCK TO TAISHA'S BACK TODAY.
I-I'M THE MAYOR'S AIDE. WHAT'S WRONG WITH ME BEING CLOSE TO HER?
HEY, WILL YOU ASK TAISHA TO NOT TALK ABOUT DREAMS WITH MY MOTHER?
RASHA? WHAT HAPPENED?
SOMETHING ABOUT A WOMAN KILLING THE PERSON SHE LOVED...
HAVING SUCH AWFUL DREAMS IS WEARING HER DOWN.
OH, THAT.

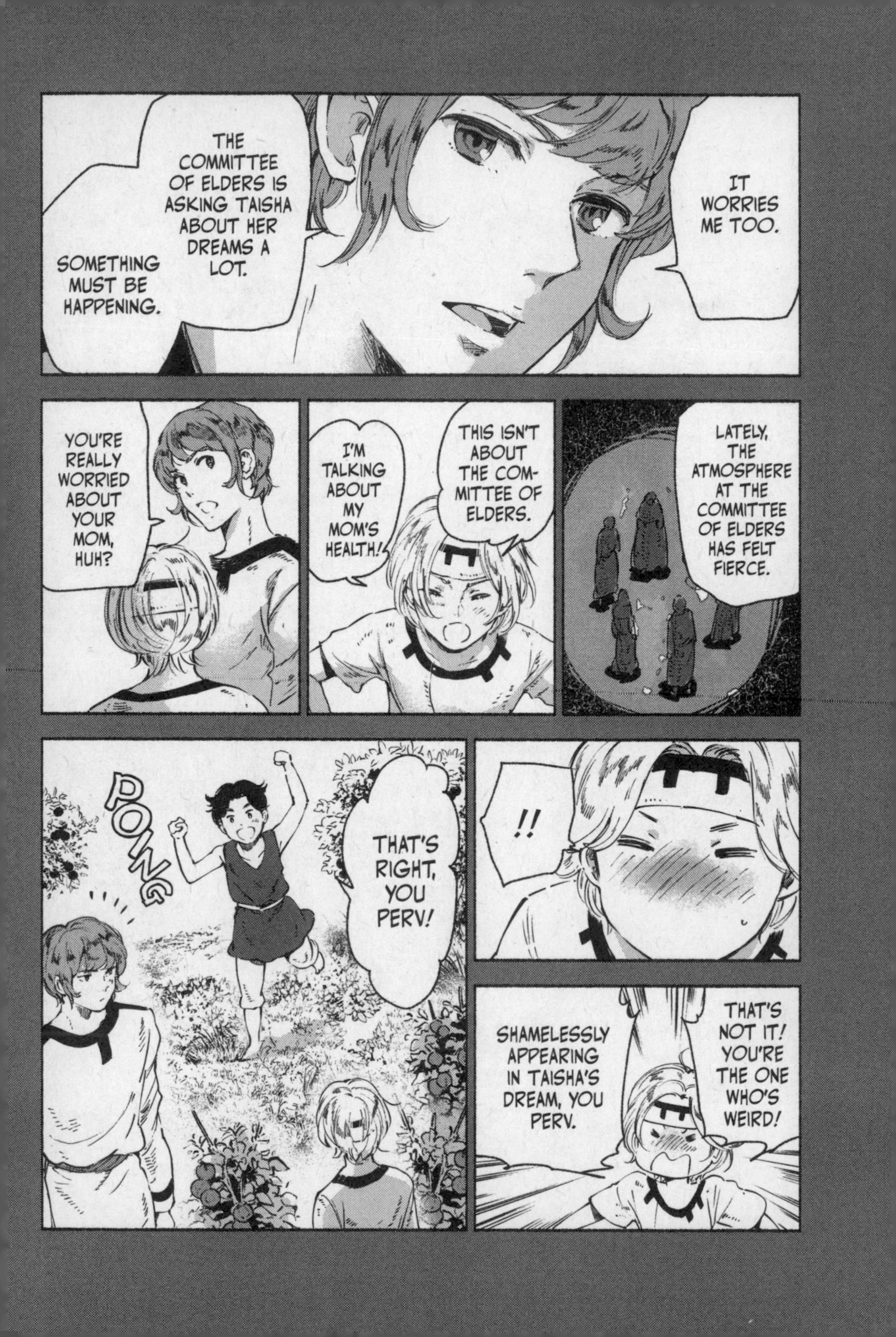
THE COMMITTEE OF ELDERS IS ASKING TAISHA ABOUT HER DREAMS A LOT.
SOMETHING MUST BE HAPPENING.
IT WORRIES ME TOO.
YOU'RE REALLY WORRIED ABOUT YOUR MOM, HUH?
THIS ISN'T ABOUT THE COM-MITTEE OF ELDERS.
I'M TALKING ABOUT MY MOM'S HEALTH!
LATELY, THE ATMOSPHERE AT THE COMMITTEE OF ELDERS HAS FELT FIERCE.
POING
THAT'S RIGHT, YOU PERV!
!!
SHAMELESSLY APPEARING IN TAISHA'S DREAM, YOU PERV.
THAT'S NOT IT! YOU'RE THE ONE WHO'S WEIRD!

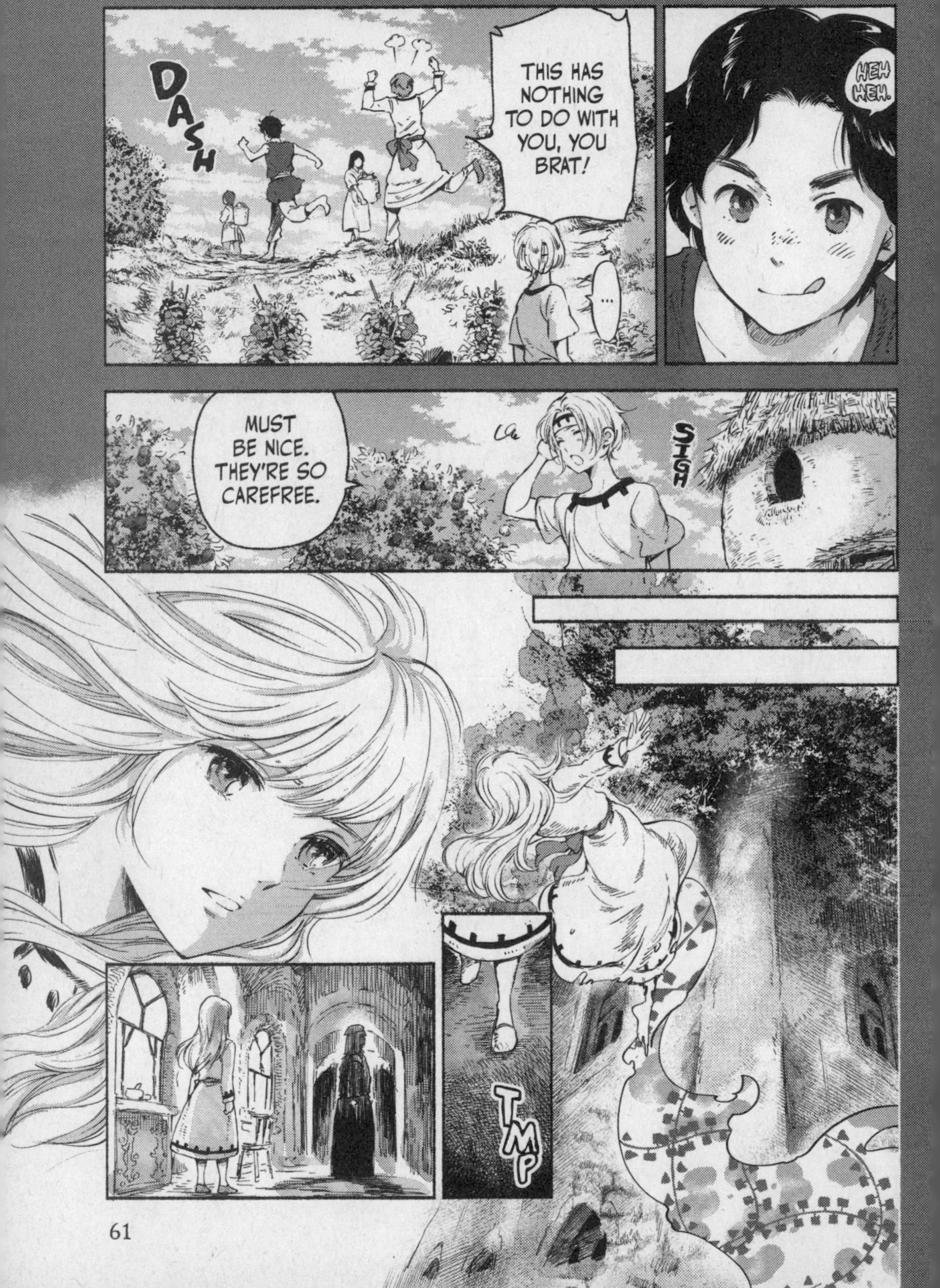
HEH HEH.
THIS HAS NOTHING TO DO WITH YOU, YOU BRAT!
DASH
...
MUST BE NICE. THEY'RE SO CAREFREE.
SIGH
TMP

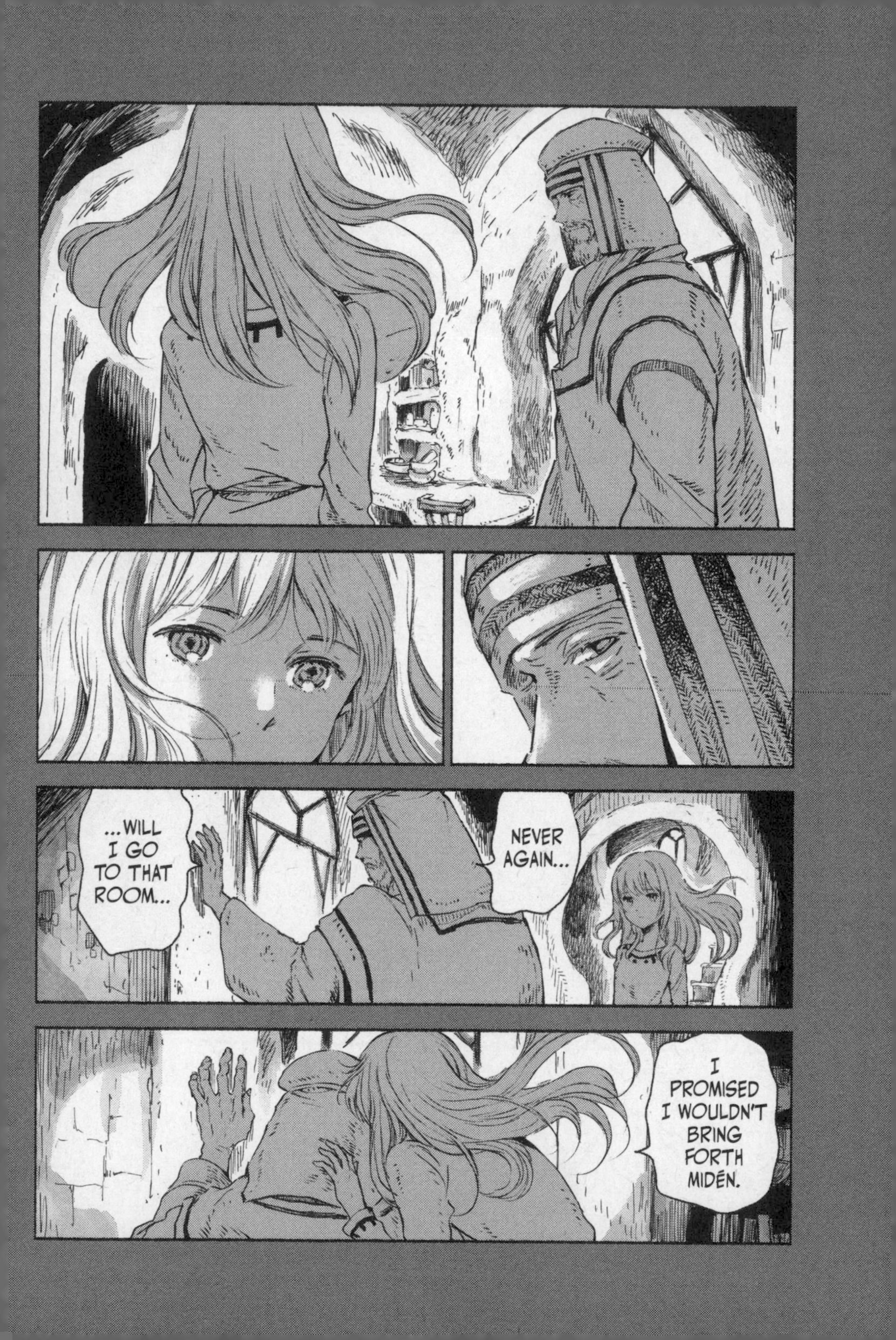
NEVER AGAIN...
...WILL I GO TO THAT ROOM...
I PROMISED I WOULDN'T BRING FORTH MIDÉN.

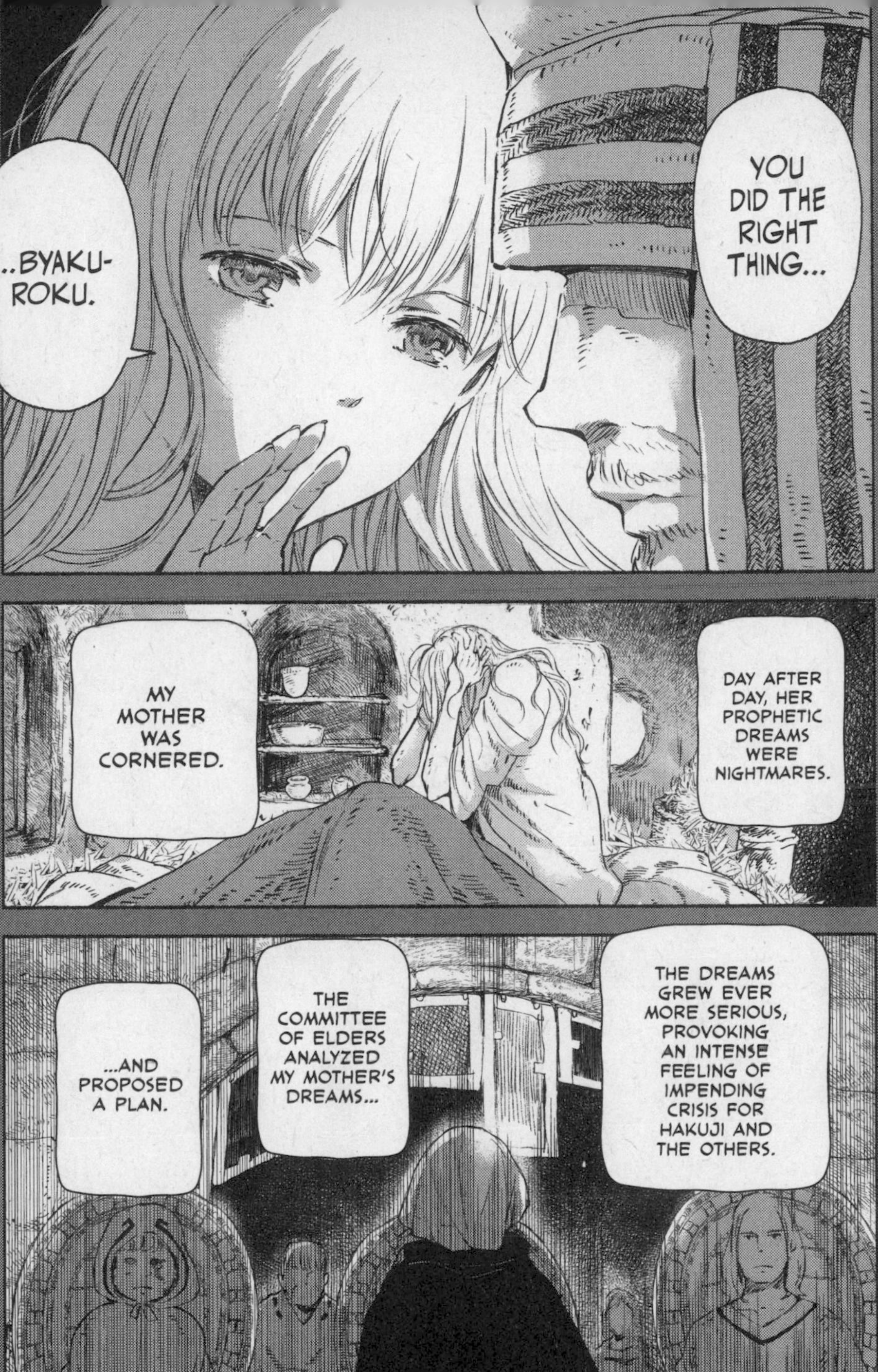
YOU DID THE RIGHT THING...
...BYAKU-ROKU.
DAY AFTER DAY, HER PROPHETIC DREAMS WERE NIGHTMARES.
MY MOTHER WAS CORNERED.
THE DREAMS GREW EVER MORE SERIOUS, PROVOKING AN INTENSE FEELING OF IMPENDING CRISIS FOR HAKUJI AND THE OTHERS.
THE COMMITTEE OF ELDERS ANALYZED MY MOTHER'S DREAMS...
...AND PROPOSED A PLAN.

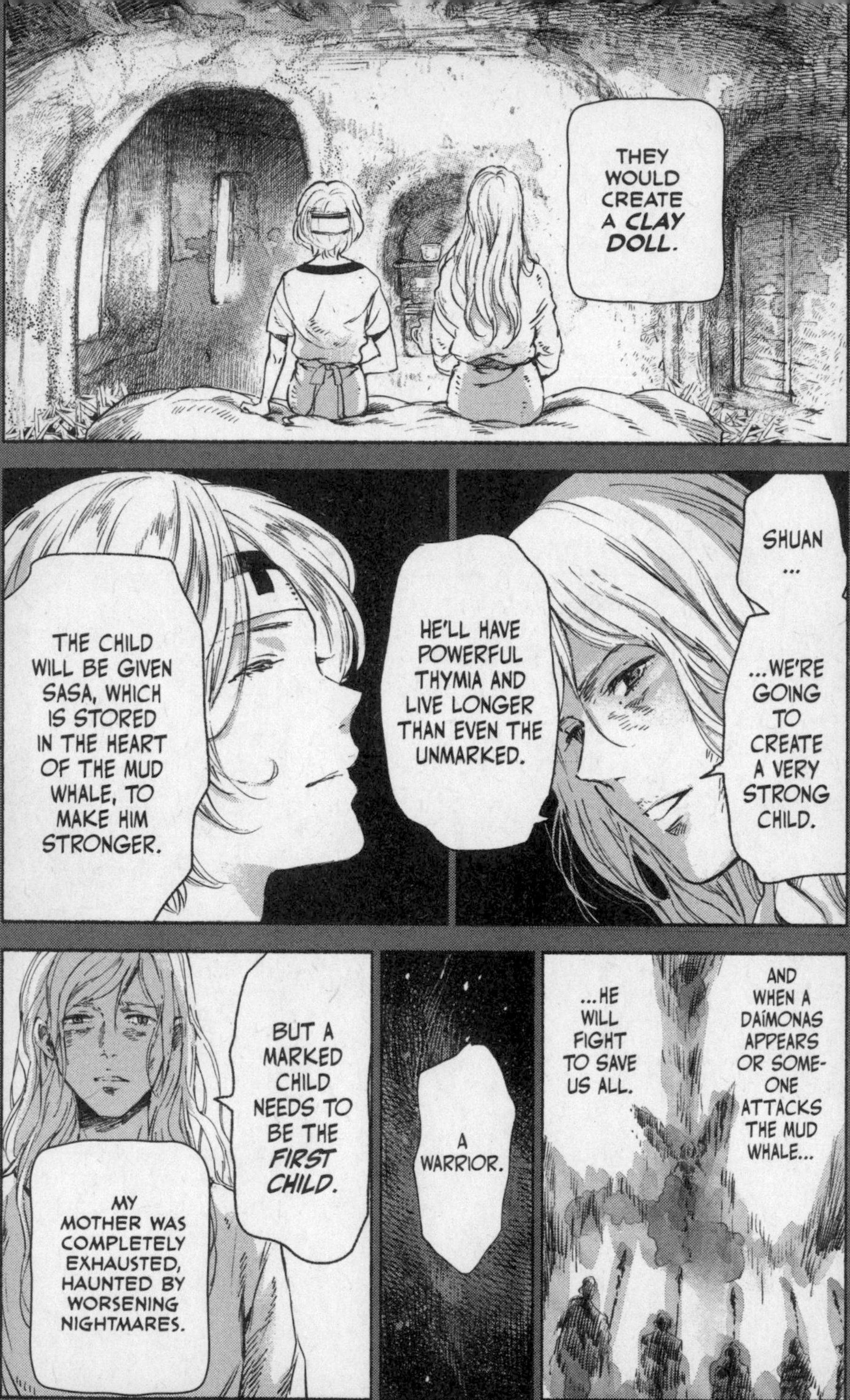
THEY WOULD CREATE A CLAY DOLL.
SHUAN ...
...WE'RE GOING TO CREATE A VERY STRONG CHILD.
HE'LL HAVE POWERFUL THYMIA AND LIVE LONGER THAN EVEN THE UNMARKED.
THE CHILD WILL BE GIVEN SASA, WHICH IS STORED IN THE HEART OF THE MUD WHALE, TO MAKE HIM STRONGER.
AND WHEN A DAÍMONAS APPEARS OR SOME-ONE ATTACKS THE MUD WHALE...
...HE WILL FIGHT TO SAVE US ALL.
A WARRIOR.
BUT A MARKED CHILD NEEDS TO BE THE FIRST CHILD.
MY MOTHER WAS COMPLETELY EXHAUSTED, HAUNTED BY WORSENING NIGHTMARES.

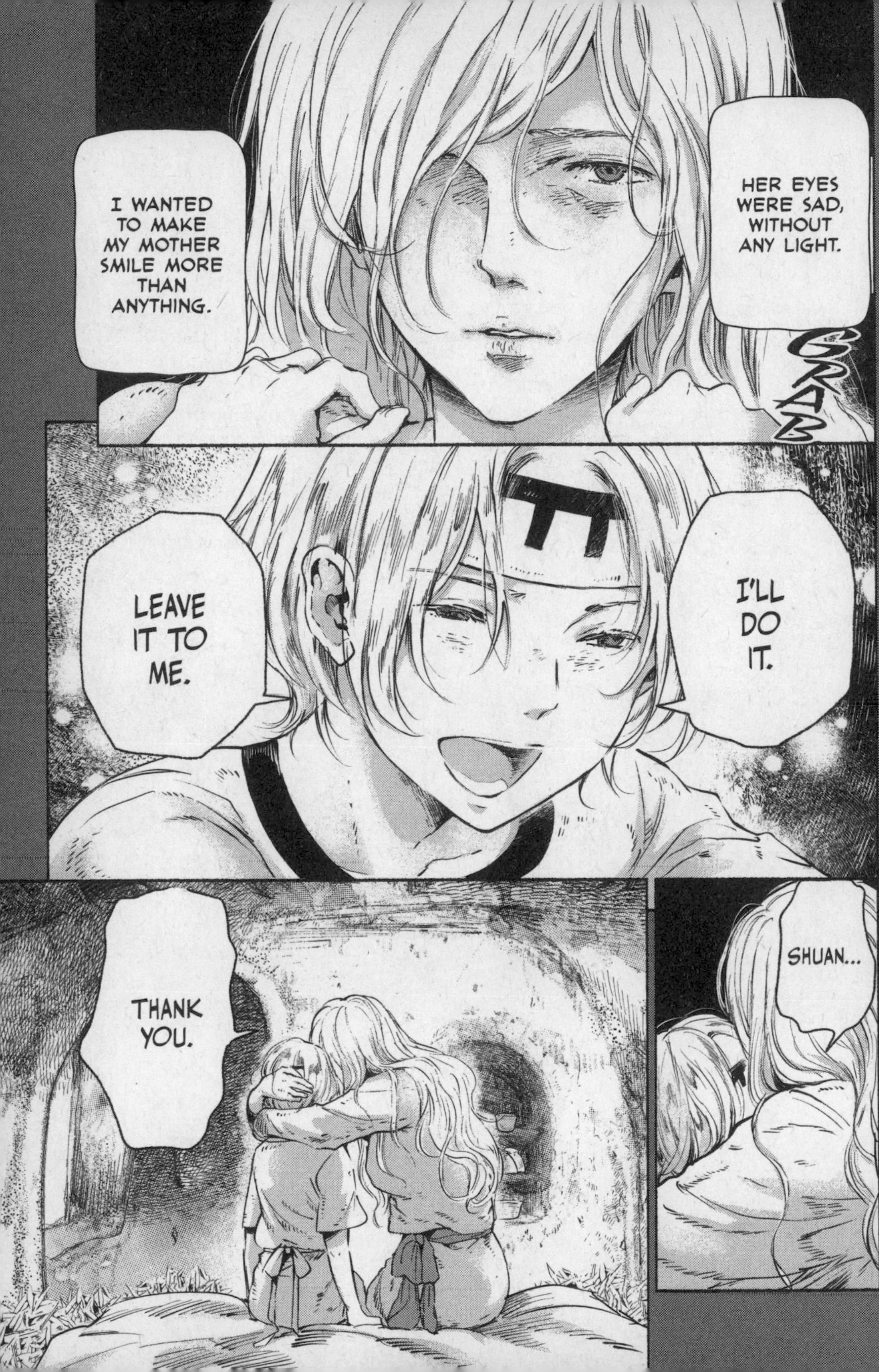
HER EYES WERE SAD, WITHOUT ANY LIGHT.
GRAB
I WANTED TO MAKE MY MOTHER SMILE MORE THAN ANYTHING.
I'LL DO IT.
LEAVE IT TO ME.
SHUAN...
THANK YOU.

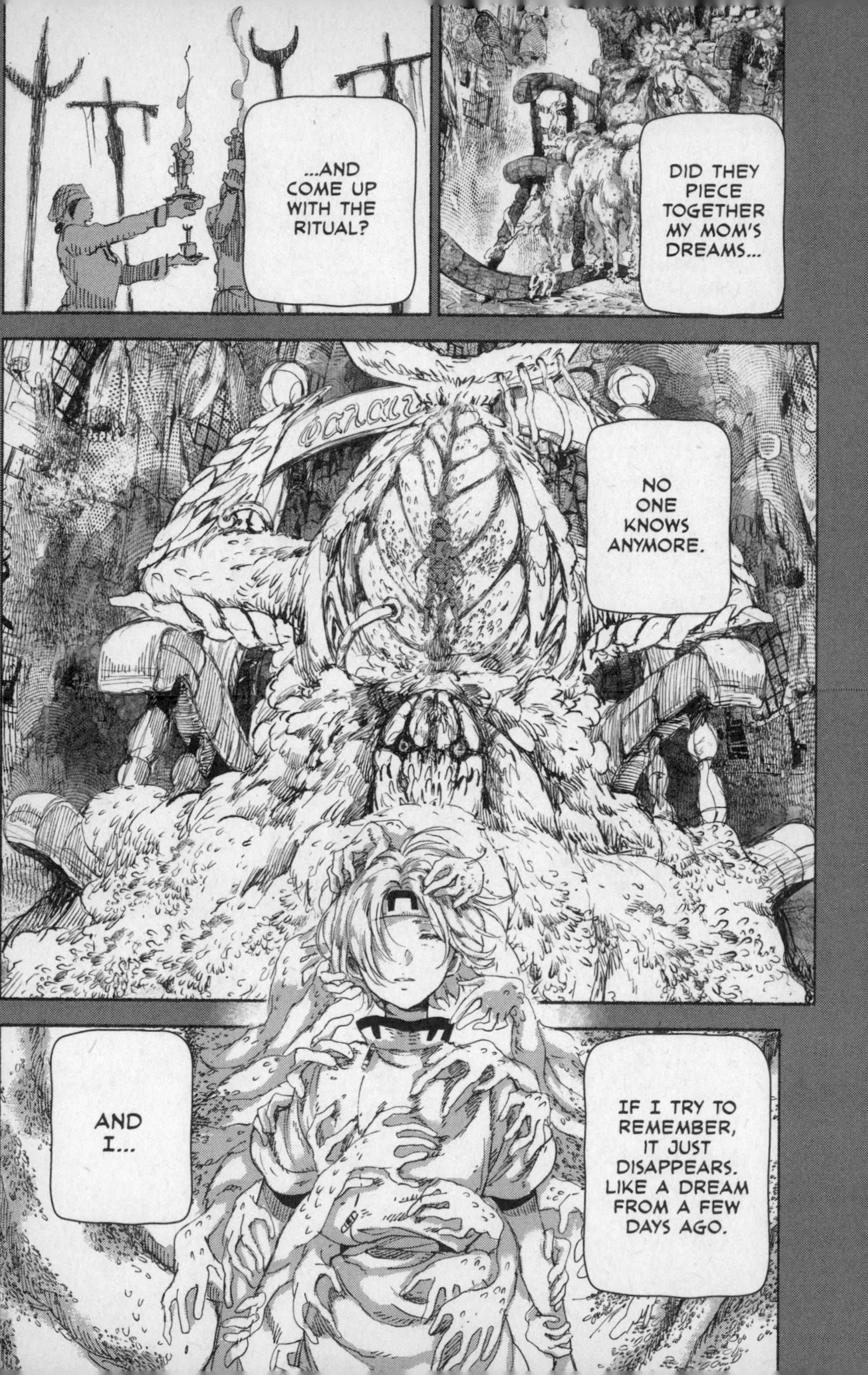
DID THEY PIECE TOGETHER MY MOM'S DREAMS...
...AND COME UP WITH THE RITUAL?
NO ONE KNOWS ANYMORE.
IF I TRY TO REMEMBER, IT JUST DISAPPEARS. LIKE A DREAM FROM A FEW DAYS AGO.
AND I...

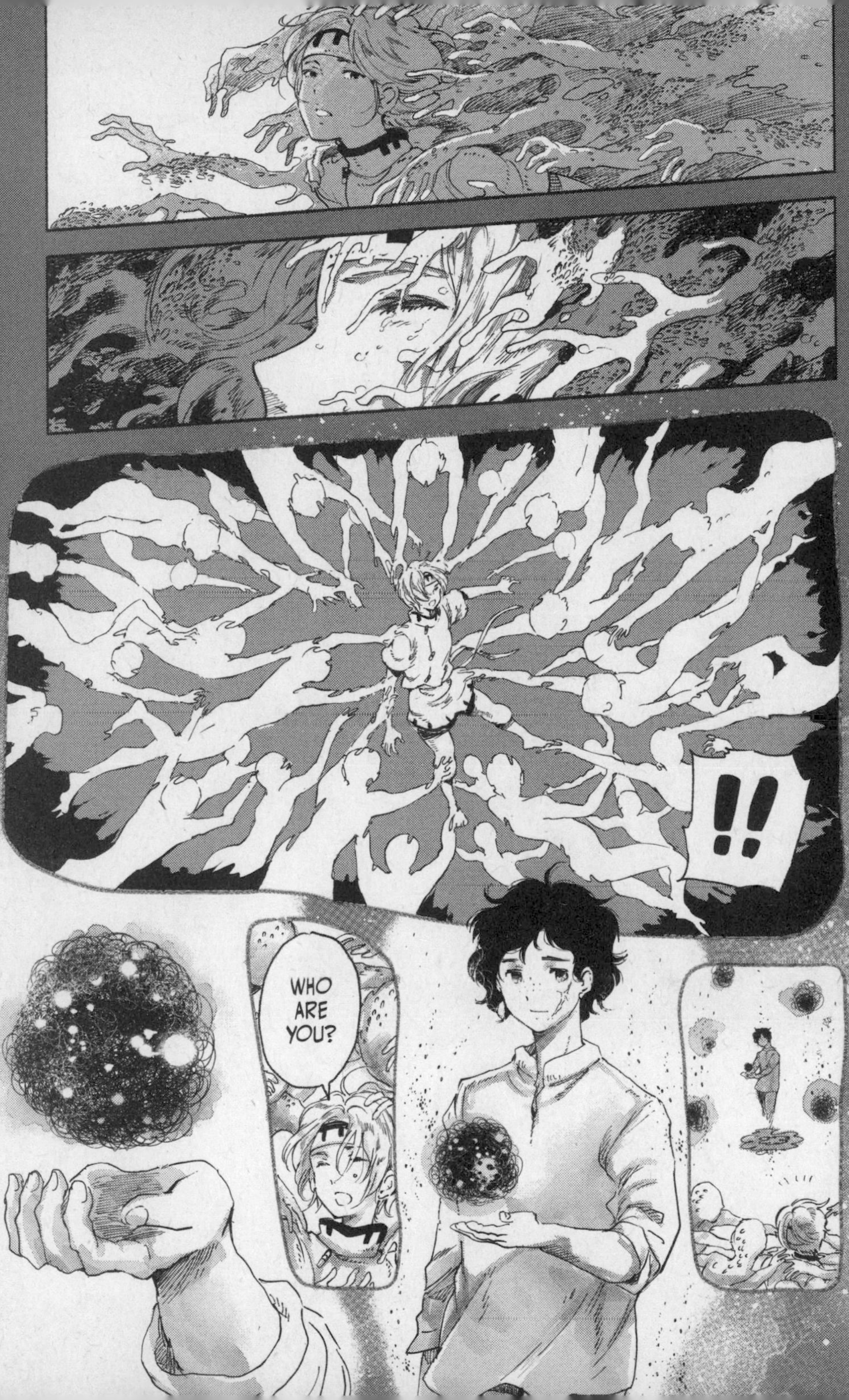
!!
WHO ARE YOU?

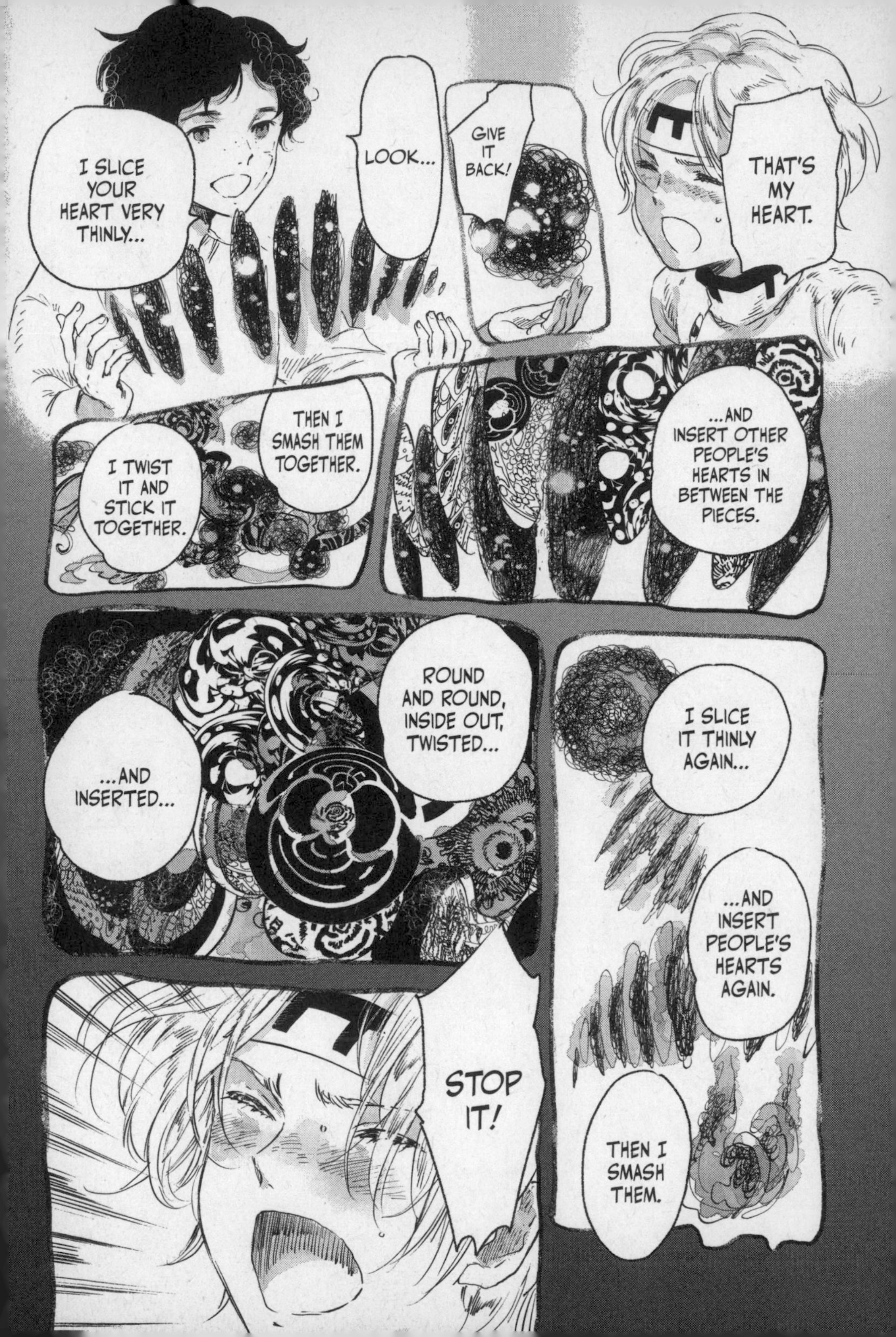
THAT'S MY HEART.
GIVE IT BACK!
LOOK...
I SLICE YOUR HEART VERY THINLY...
...AND INSERT OTHER PEOPLE'S HEARTS IN BETWEEN THE PIECES.
THEN I SMASH THEM TOGETHER.
I TWIST IT AND STICK IT TOGETHER.
I SLICE IT THINLY AGAIN...
...AND INSERT PEOPLE'S HEARTS AGAIN.
THEN I SMASH THEM.
ROUND AND ROUND, INSIDE OUT, TWISTED...
...AND INSERTED...
STOP IT!

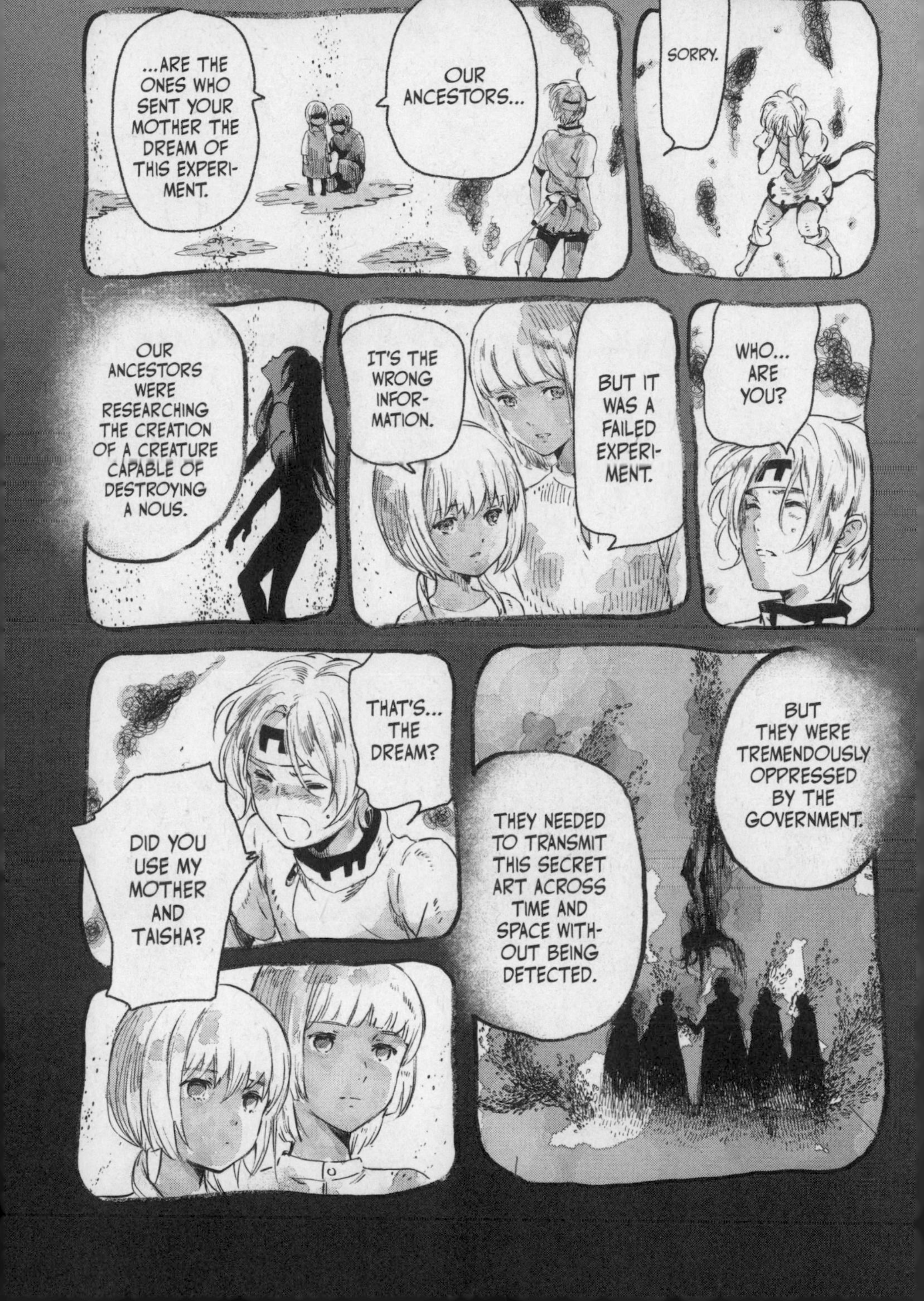
SORRY.
OUR ANCESTORS...
...ARE THE ONES WHO SENT YOUR MOTHER THE DREAM OF THIS EXPERIMENT.
WHO... ARE YOU?
BUT IT WAS A FAILED EXPERIMENT.
IT'S THE WRONG INFORMATION.
OUR ANCESTORS WERE RESEARCHING THE CREATION OF A CREATURE CAPABLE OF DESTROYING A NOUS.
BUT THEY WERE TREMENDOUSLY OPPRESSED BY THE GOVERNMENT.
THEY NEEDED TO TRANSMIT THIS SECRET ART ACROSS TIME AND SPACE WITHOUT BEING DETECTED.
THAT'S... THE DREAM?
DID YOU USE MY MOTHER AND TAISHA?

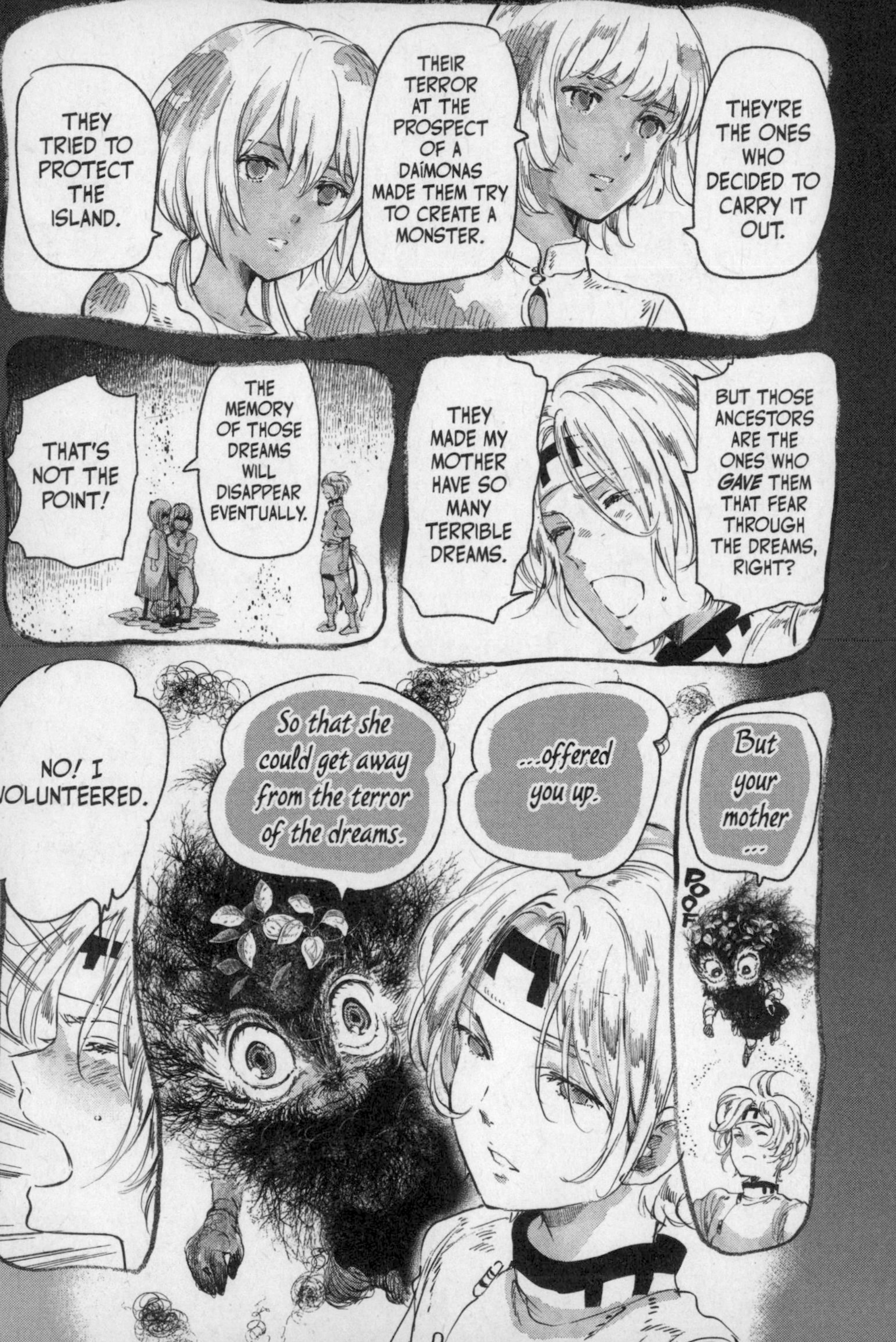
THEY'RE THE ONES WHO DECIDED TO CARRY IT OUT.
THEIR TERROR AT THE PROSPECT OF A DAÍMONAS MADE THEM TRY TO CREATE A MONSTER.
THEY TRIED TO PROTECT THE ISLAND.
BUT THOSE ANCESTORS ARE THE ONES WHO GAVE THEM THAT FEAR THROUGH THE DREAMS, RIGHT?
THEY MADE MY MOTHER HAVE SO MANY TERRIBLE DREAMS.
THE MEMORY OF THOSE DREAMS WILL DISAPPEAR EVENTUALLY.
THAT'S NOT THE POINT!
But your mother ...
POOF
...offered you up.
So that she could get away from the terror of the dreams.
NO! I VOLUNTEERED.

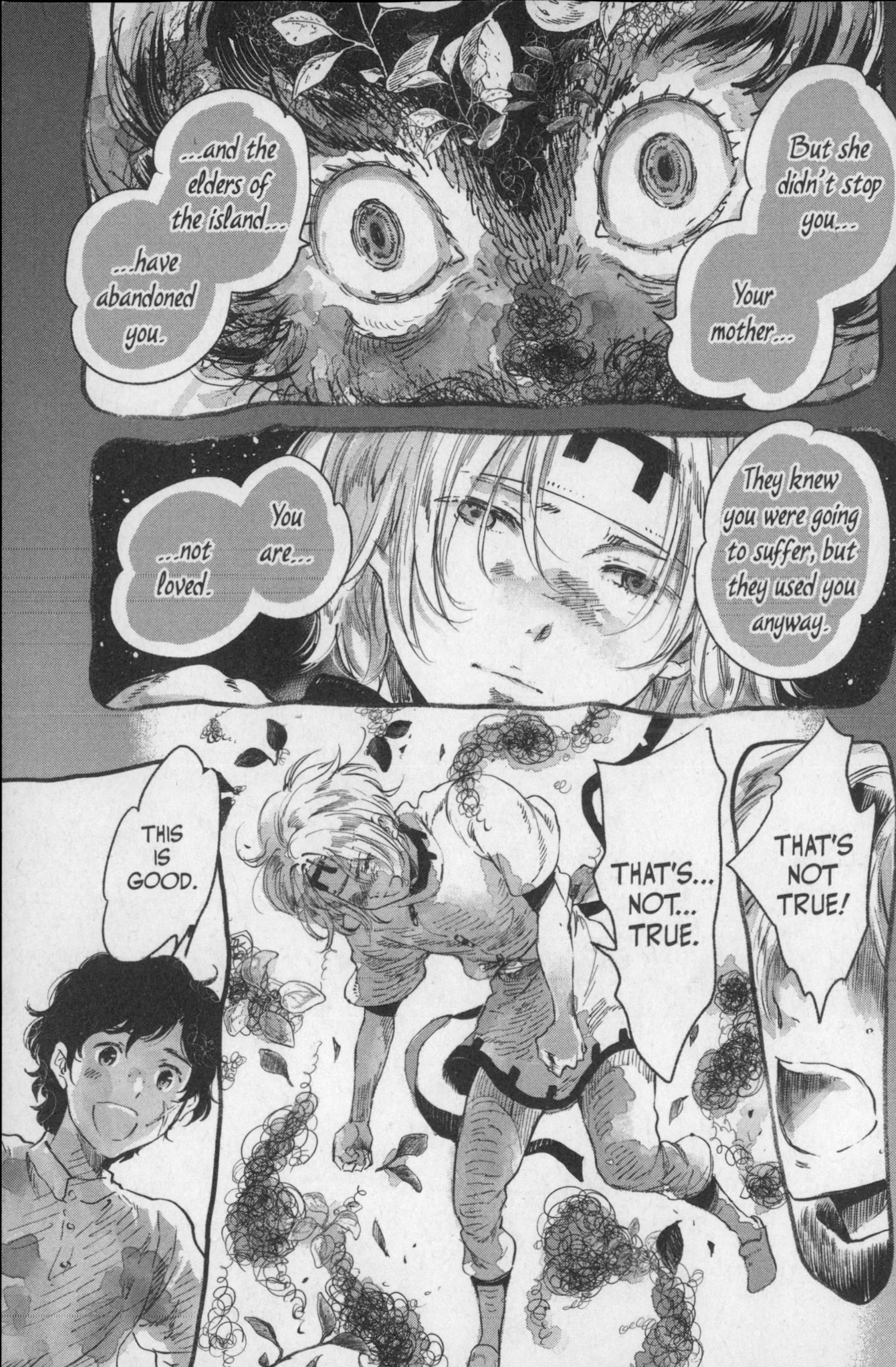
But she didn't stop you...
Your mother...
...and the elders of the island...
...have abandoned you.
They knew you were going to suffer, but they used you anyway.
You are...
...not loved.
THAT'S NOT TRUE!
THAT'S... NOT... TRUE.
THIS IS GOOD.

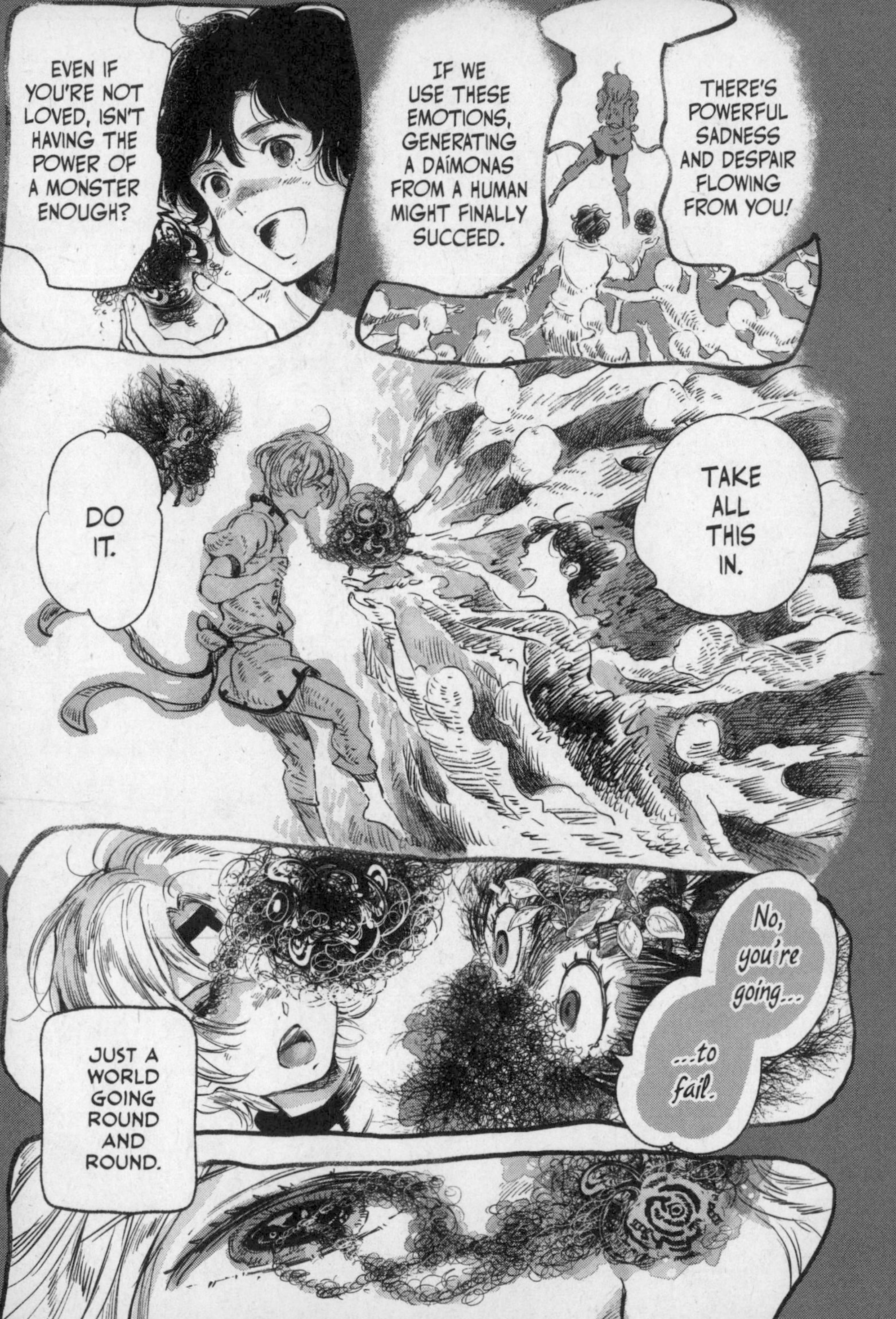
THERE'S POWERFUL SADNESS AND DESPAIR FLOWING FROM YOU!
IF WE USE THESE EMOTIONS, GENERATING A DAÍMONAS FROM A HUMAN MIGHT FINALLY SUCCEED.
EVEN IF YOU'RE NOT LOVED, ISN'T HAVING THE POWER OF A MONSTER ENOUGH?
TAKE ALL THIS IN.
DO IT.
No, you're going...
...to fail.
JUST A WORLD GOING ROUND AND ROUND.

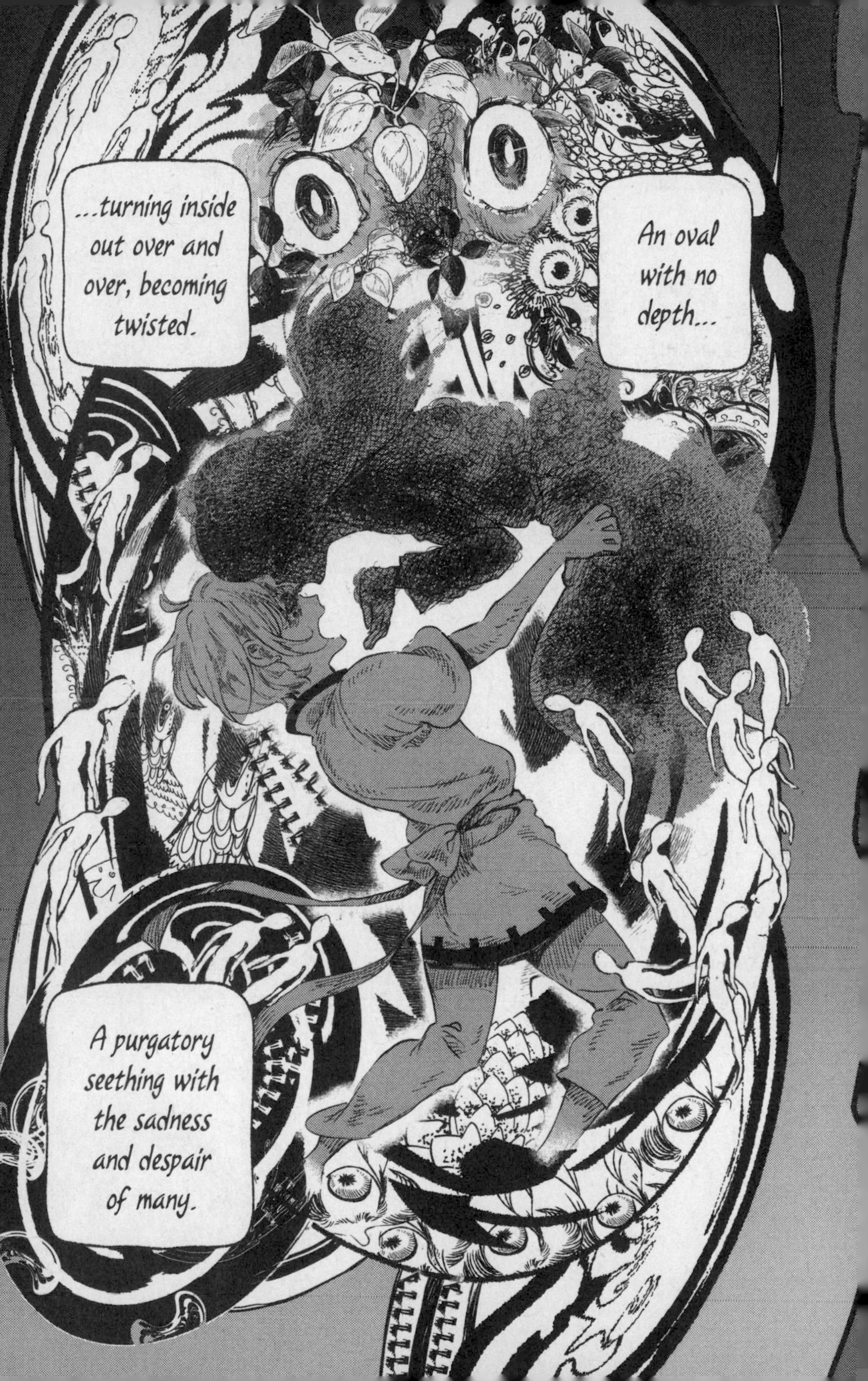
An oval with no depth...
...turning inside out over and over, becoming twisted.
A purgatory seething with the sadness and despair of many.

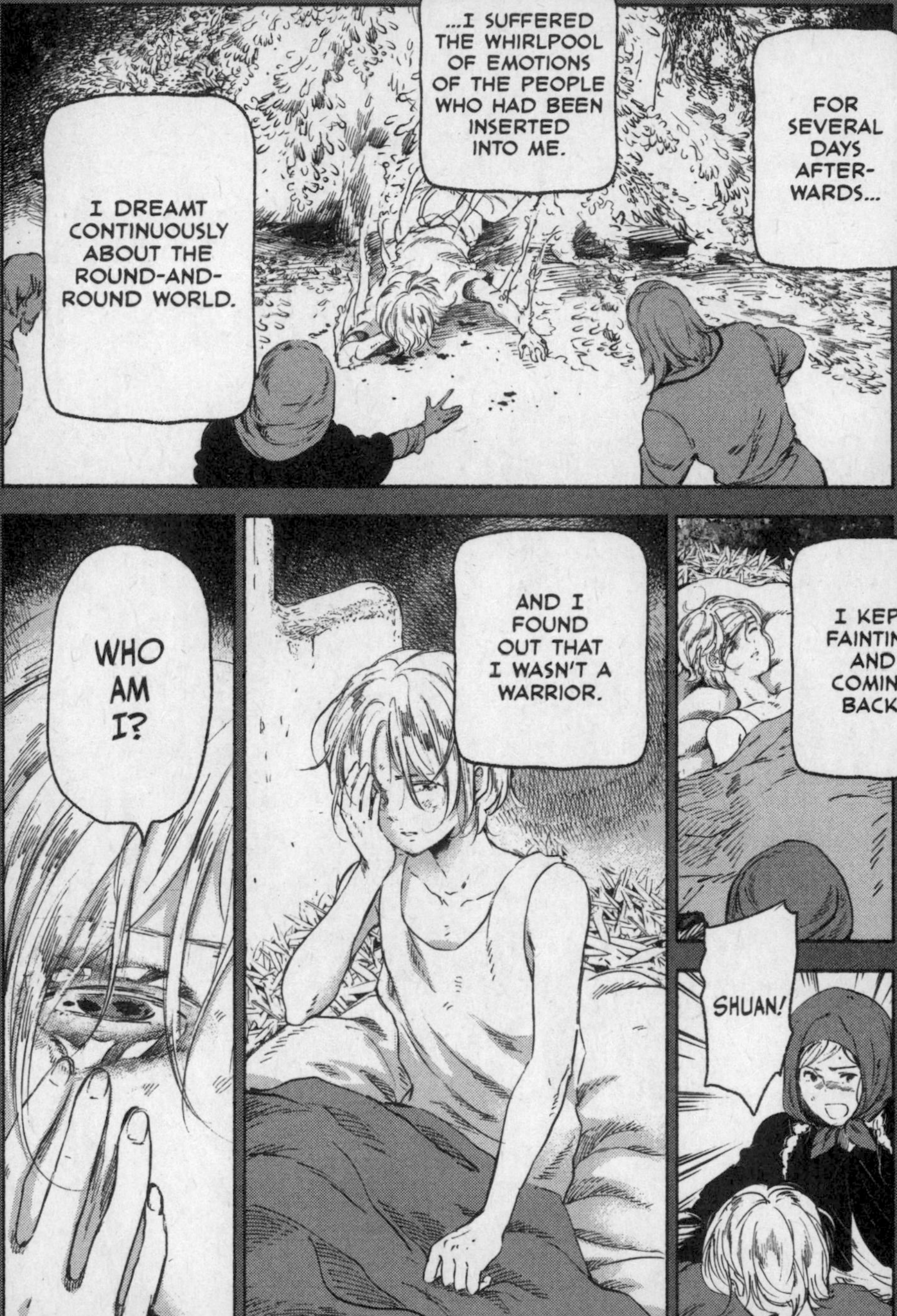
FOR SEVERAL DAYS AFTER-WARDS...
...I SUFFERED THE WHIRLPOOL OF EMOTIONS OF THE PEOPLE WHO HAD BEEN INSERTED INTO ME.
I DREAMT CONTINUOUSLY ABOUT THE ROUND-AND-ROUND WORLD.
I KEPT FAINTING AND COMING BACK.
SHUAN!
AND I FOUND OUT THAT I WASN'T A WARRIOR.
WHO AM I?

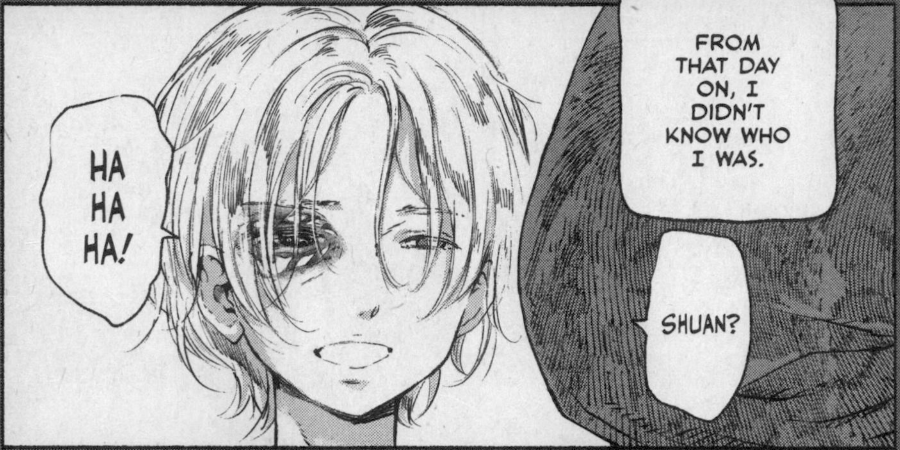
FROM THAT DAY ON, I DIDN'T KNOW WHO I WAS.
HA HA HA!
SHUAN?
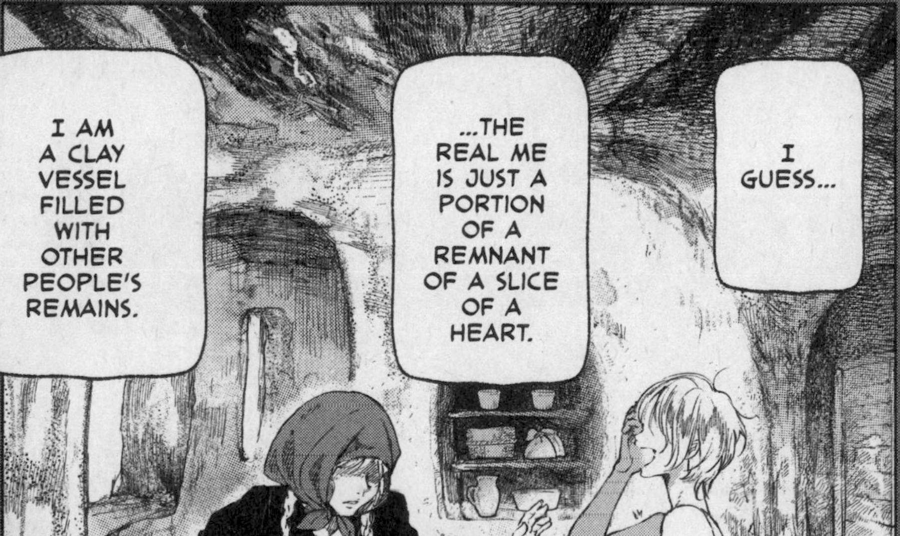
I GUESS...
...THE REAL ME IS JUST A PORTION OF A REMNANT OF A SLICE OF A HEART.
I AM A CLAY VESSEL FILLED WITH OTHER PEOPLE'S REMAINS.

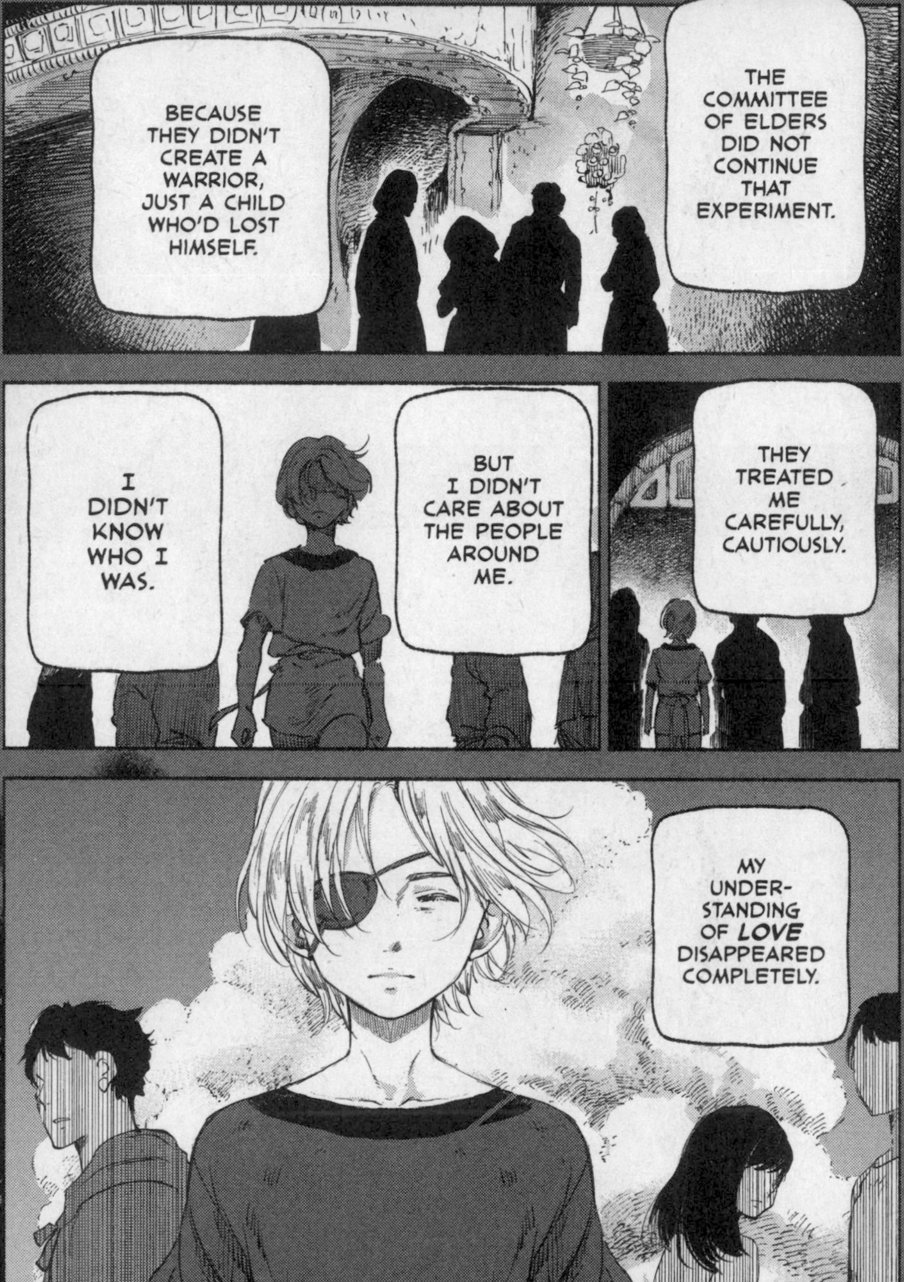
THE COMMITTEE OF ELDERS DID NOT CONTINUE THAT EXPERIMENT.
BECAUSE THEY DIDN'T CREATE A WARRIOR, JUST A CHILD WHO'D LOST HIMSELF.
THEY TREATED ME CAREFULLY, CAUTIOUSLY.
BUT I DIDN'T CARE ABOUT THE PEOPLE AROUND ME.
I DIDN'T KNOW WHO I WAS.
MY UNDER-STANDING OF *LOVE* DISAPPEARED COMPLETELY.

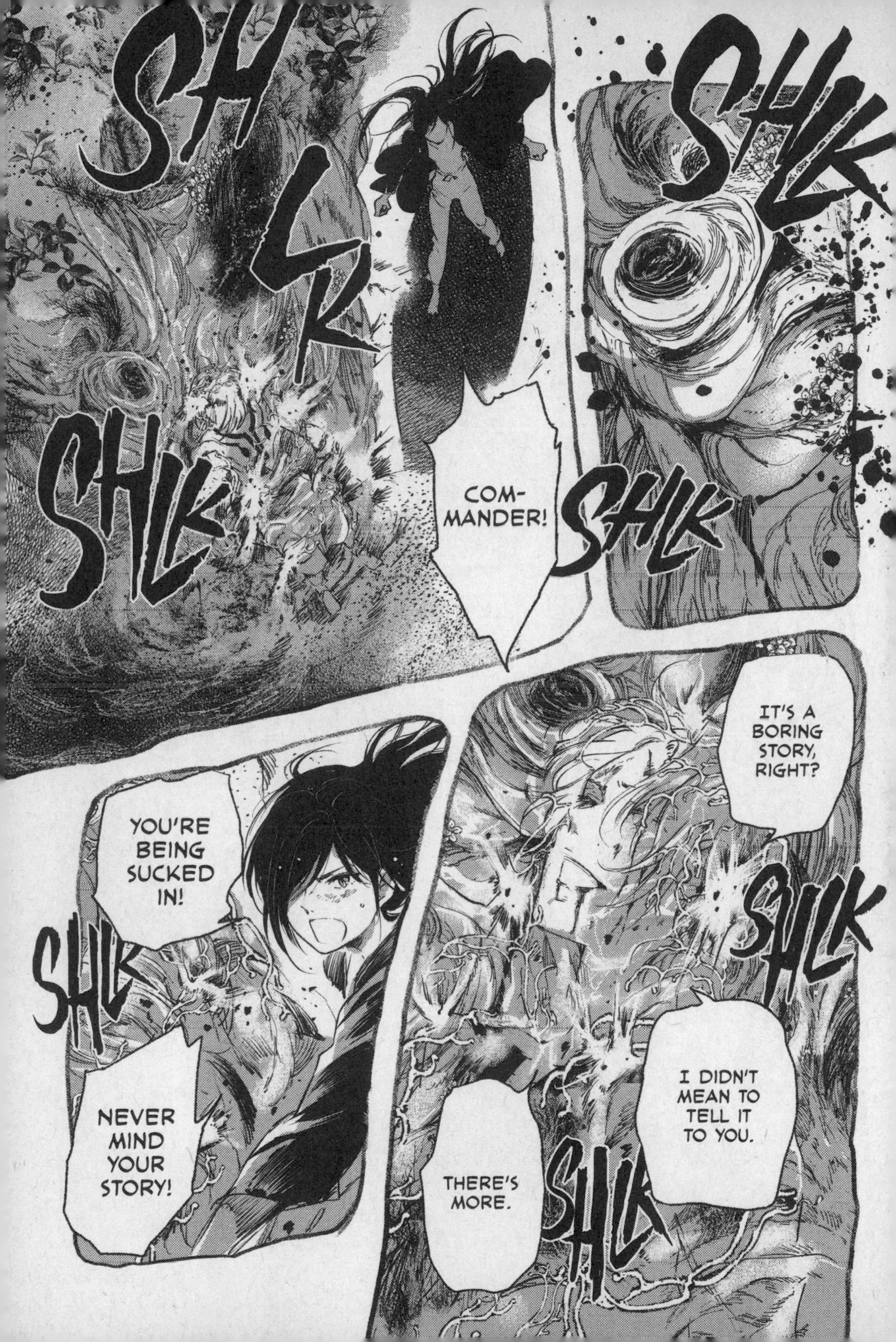
SHLK
SHLK
SHLK
SHLK
COM-MANDER!
IT'S A BORING STORY, RIGHT?
SHLK
I DIDN'T MEAN TO TELL IT TO YOU.
SHLK
THERE'S MORE.
YOU'RE BEING SUCKED IN!
SHLK
NEVER MIND YOUR STORY!

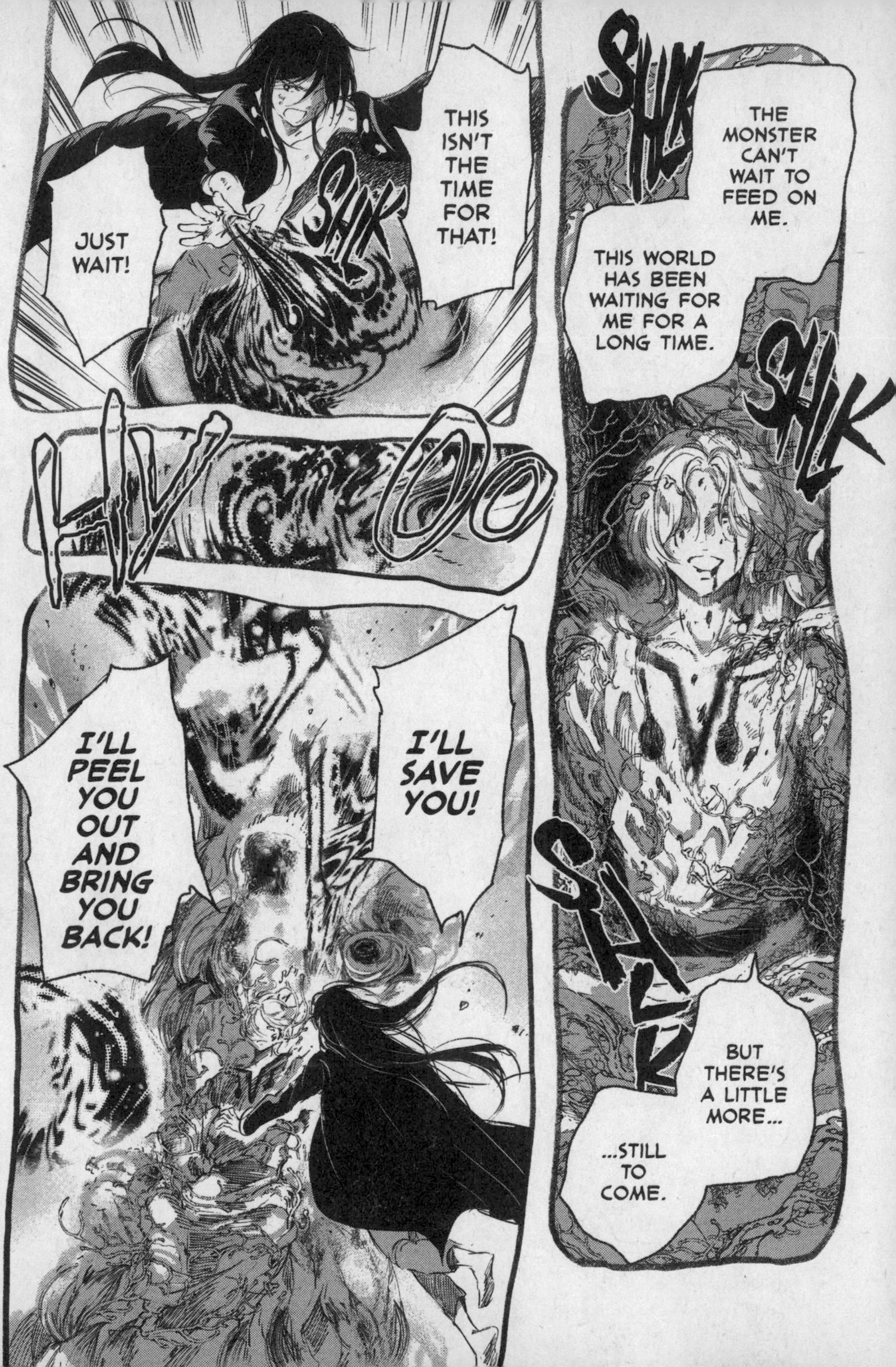
SHLK
THE MONSTER CAN'T WAIT TO FEED ON ME.
THIS WORLD HAS BEEN WAITING FOR ME FOR A LONG TIME.
SHLK
SHLK
BUT THERE'S A LITTLE MORE...
...STILL TO COME.
THIS ISN'T THE TIME FOR THAT!
SHLK
JUST WAIT!
HYOO
I'LL SAVE YOU!
I'LL PEEL YOU OUT AND BRING YOU BACK!

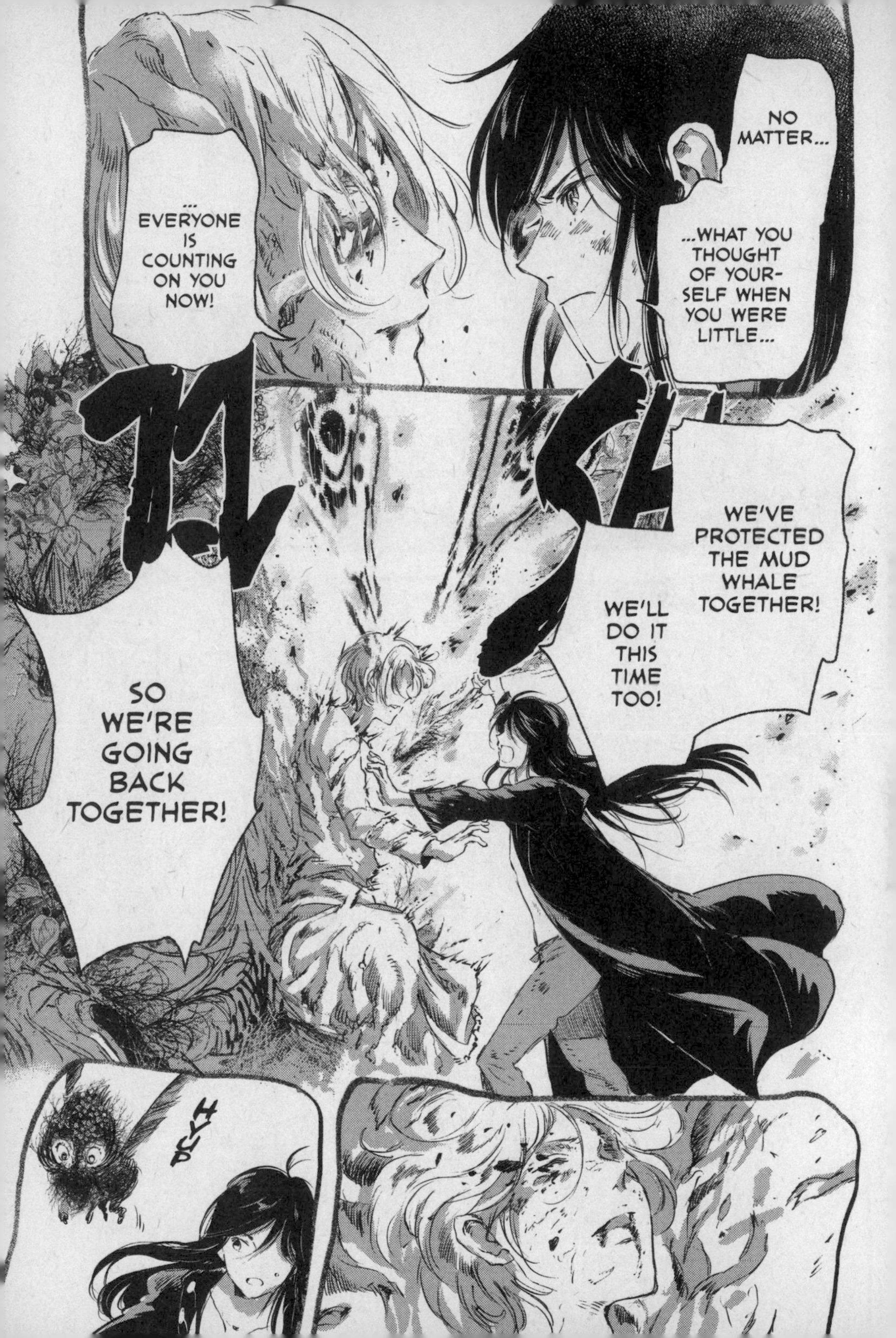
NO MATTER...
...WHAT YOU THOUGHT OF YOURSELF WHEN YOU WERE LITTLE...
...EVERYONE IS COUNTING ON YOU NOW!
WE'VE PROTECTED THE MUD WHALE TOGETHER!
WE'LL DO IT THIS TIME TOO!
SO WE'RE GOING BACK TOGETHER!
HYUP

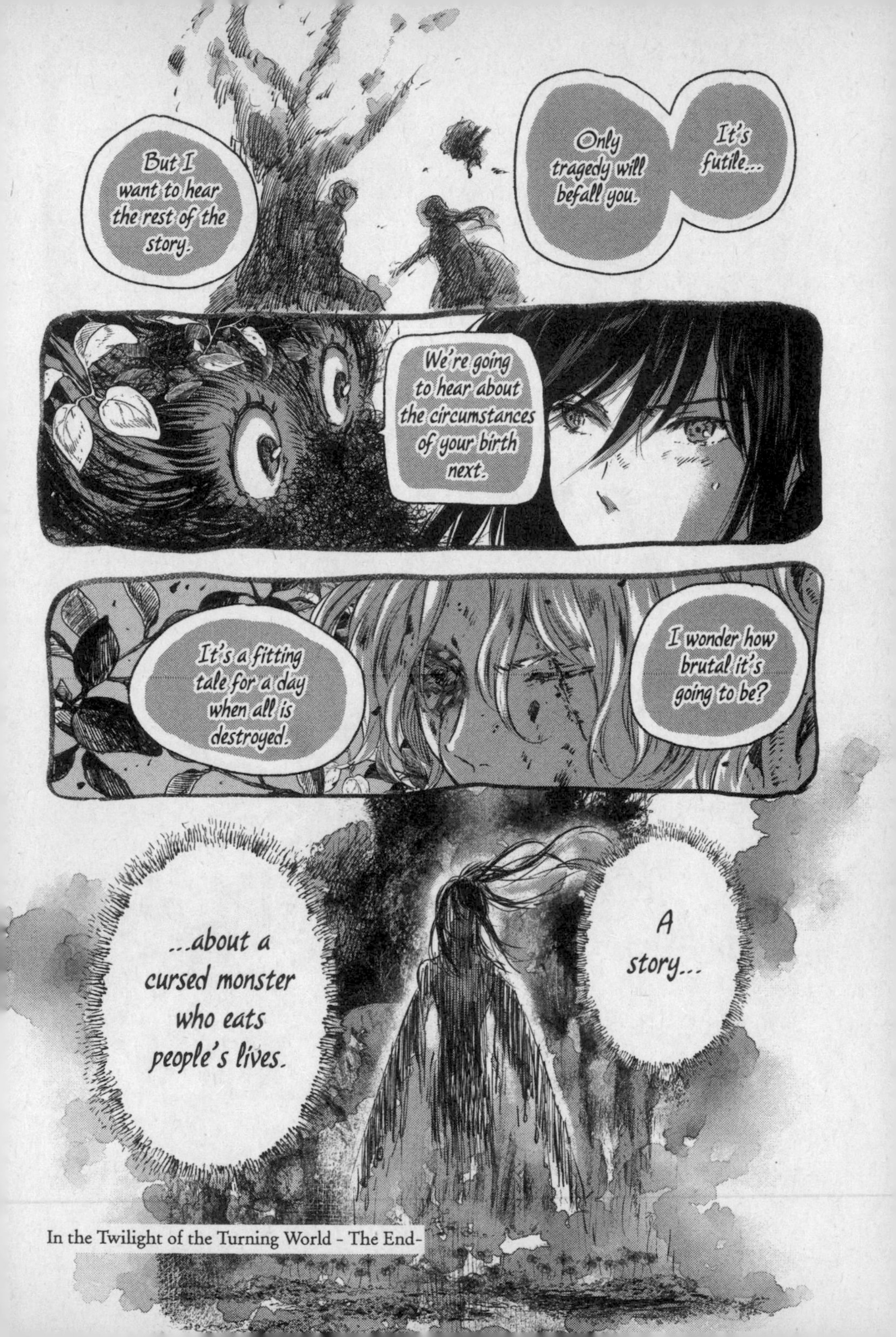
It's futile...
Only tragedy will befall you.
But I want to hear the rest of the story.
We're going to hear about the circumstances of your birth next.
I wonder how brutal it's going to be?
It's a fitting tale for a day when all is destroyed.
A story...
...about a cursed monster who eats people's lives.

In the Twilight of the Turning World - The End-

Sketch ⑪

Unmarked and the mayor

The residents of the Mud Whale say that they can't tell at the time of birth if a child is Marked or Unmarked.

After several days, a child who is Marked develops faint marks on their skin when they cry. These marks are called an aura.

The Marked and Unmarked are educated separately and take on their designated duties by the time they are twelve.

The Unmarked mainly assist the mayor, the mayor's aide or the committee of elders, or they work in the infirmary. The mayor's aide and the incumbent mayor are chosen from the Unmarked.

The committee of elders selects a gentle person of character as mayor, someone worthy of the love of people of the Mud Whale.

If the mayor ever betrays that love, they are relieved of their duties and punished, but that has not happened since the time of the second mayor.

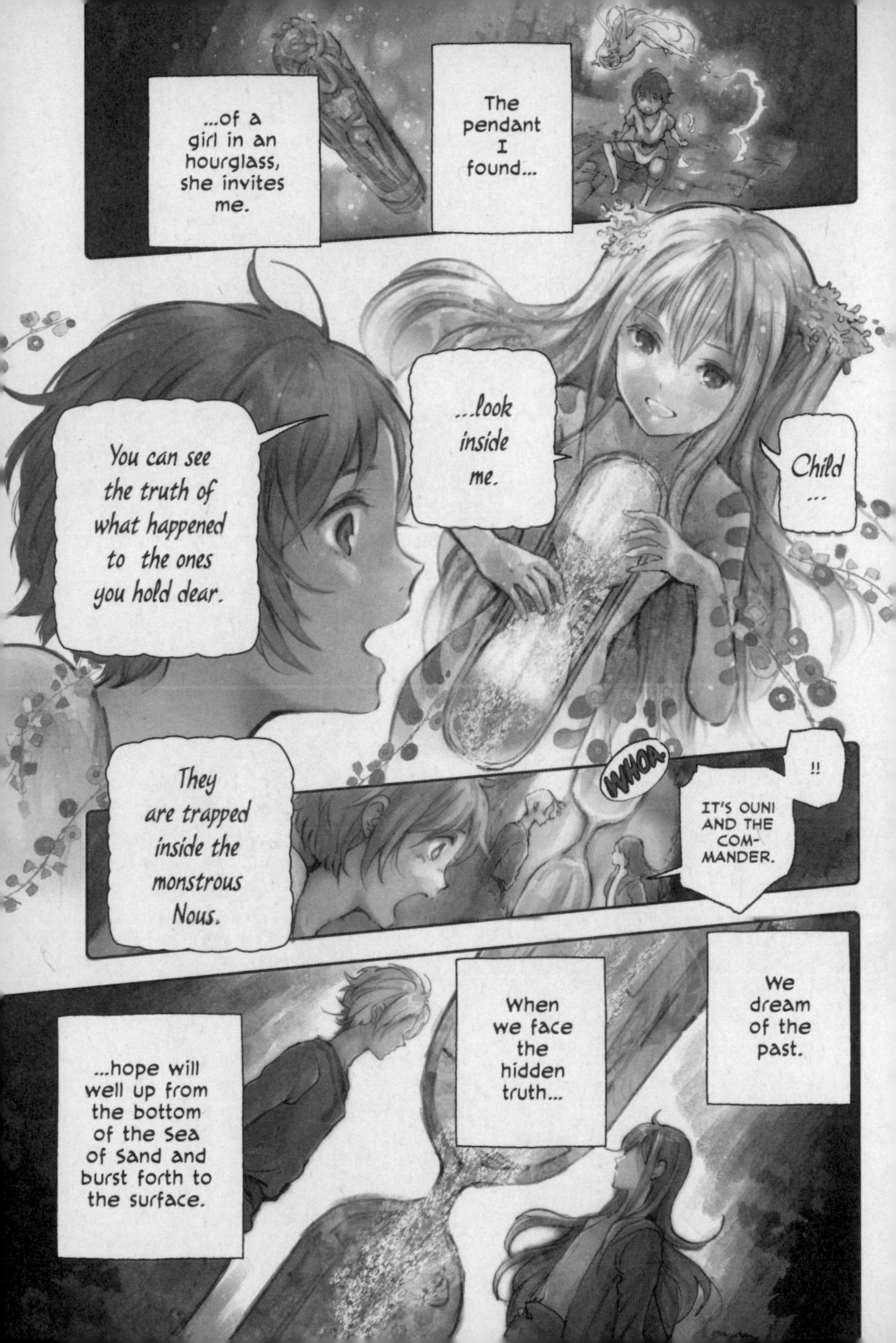
The pendant I found...
...of a girl in an hourglass, she invites me.
Child ...
...look inside me.
You can see the truth of what happened to the ones you hold dear.
!!
IT'S OUNI AND THE COM-MANDER.
WHOA
They are trapped inside the monstrous Nous.
We dream of the past.
When we face the hidden truth...
...hope will well up from the bottom of the Sea of Sand and burst forth to the surface.

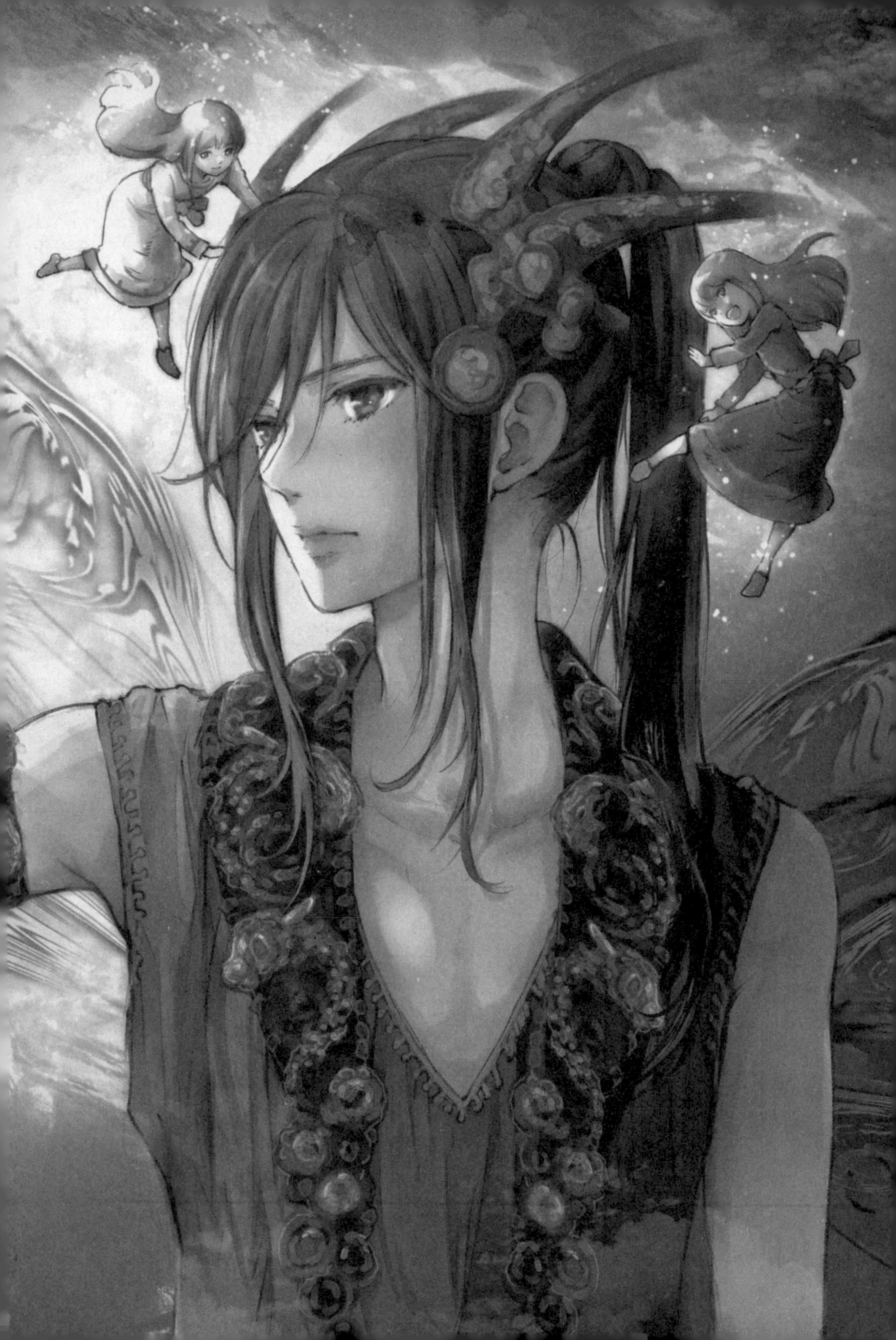

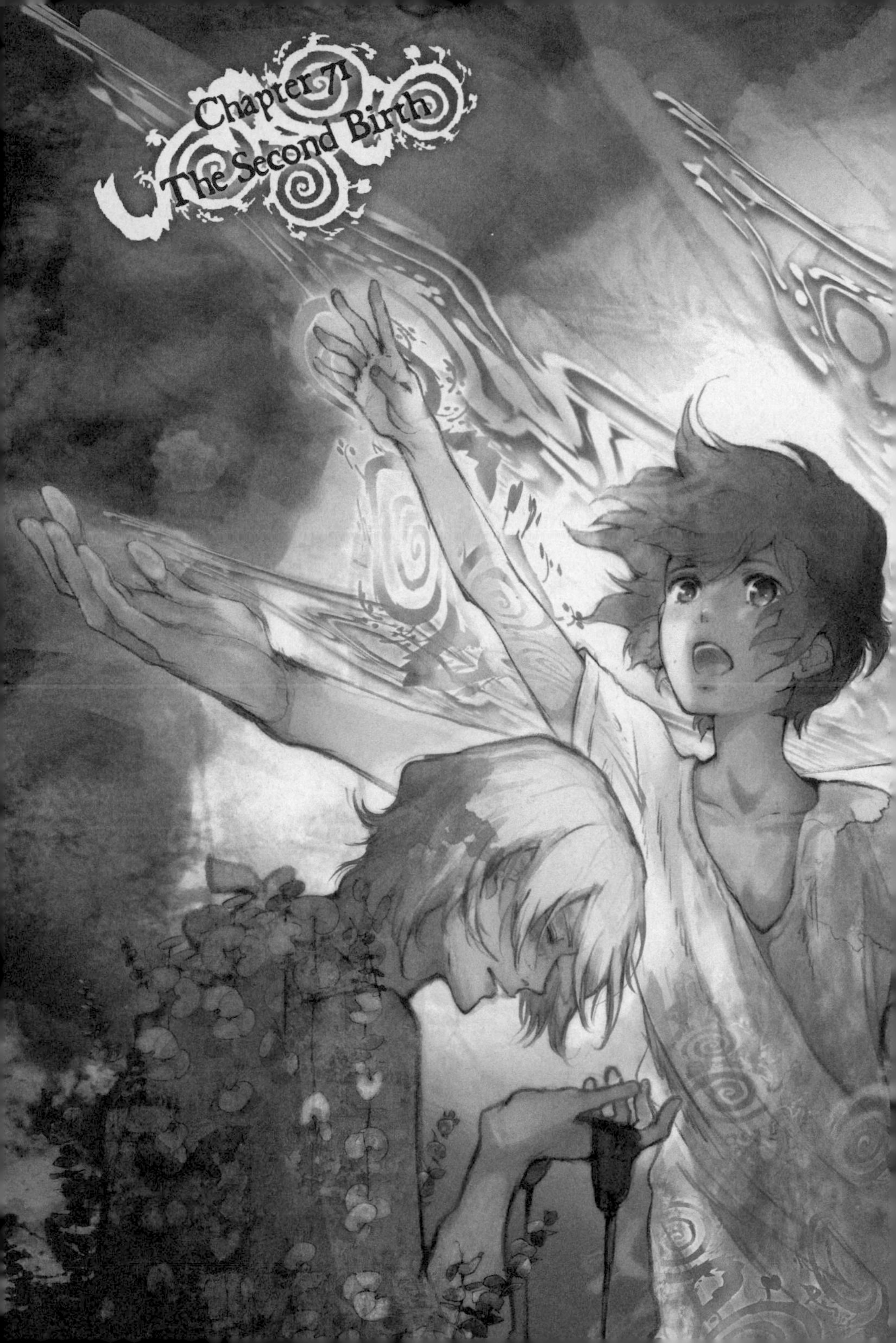
Chapter 71
The Second Birth

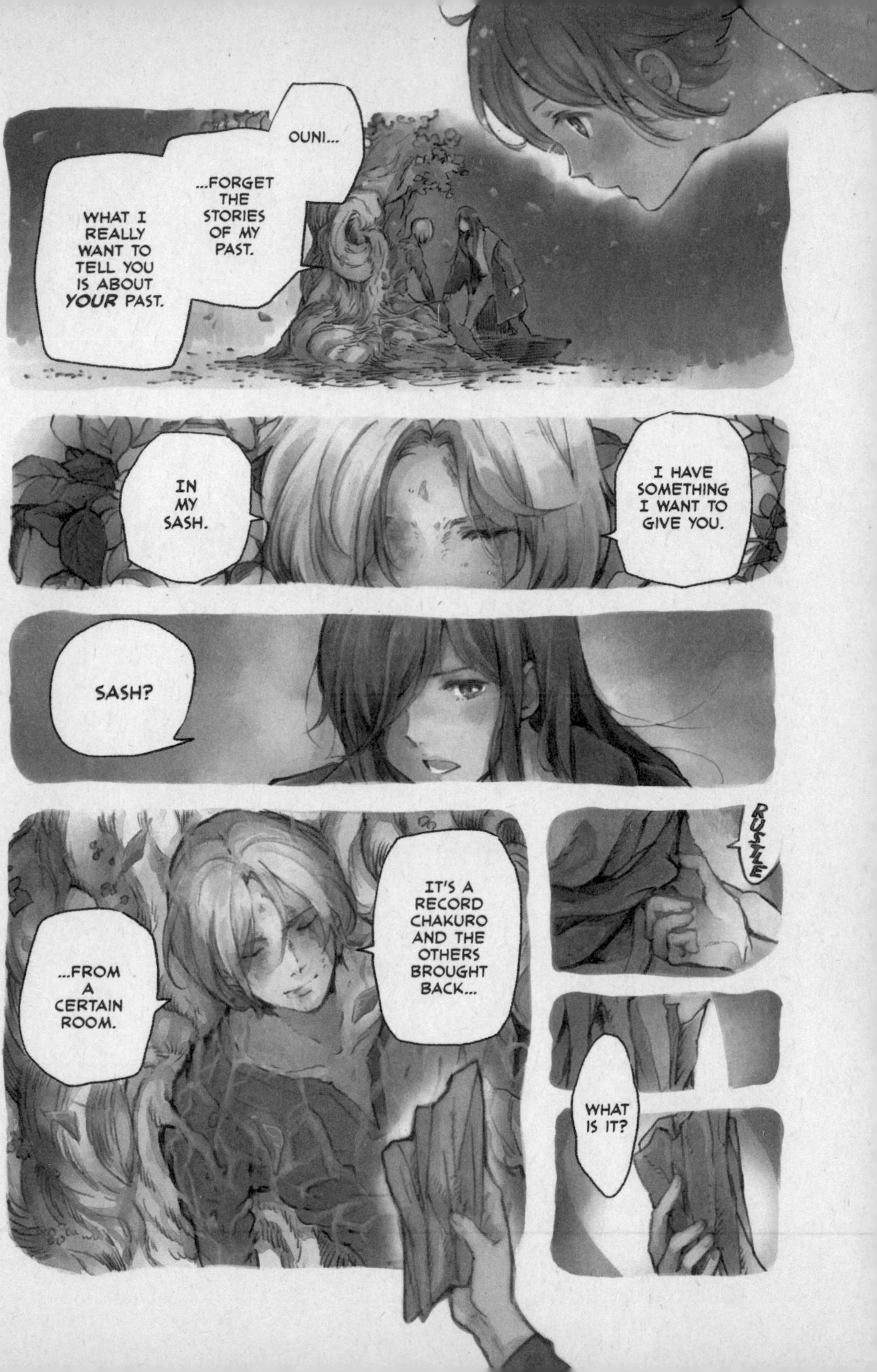
OUNI...
...FORGET THE STORIES OF MY PAST.
WHAT I REALLY WANT TO TELL YOU IS ABOUT *YOUR* PAST.
I HAVE SOMETHING I WANT TO GIVE YOU.
IN MY SASH.
SASH?
RUSTLE
WHAT IS IT?
IT'S A RECORD CHAKURO AND THE OTHERS BROUGHT BACK...
...FROM A CERTAIN ROOM.

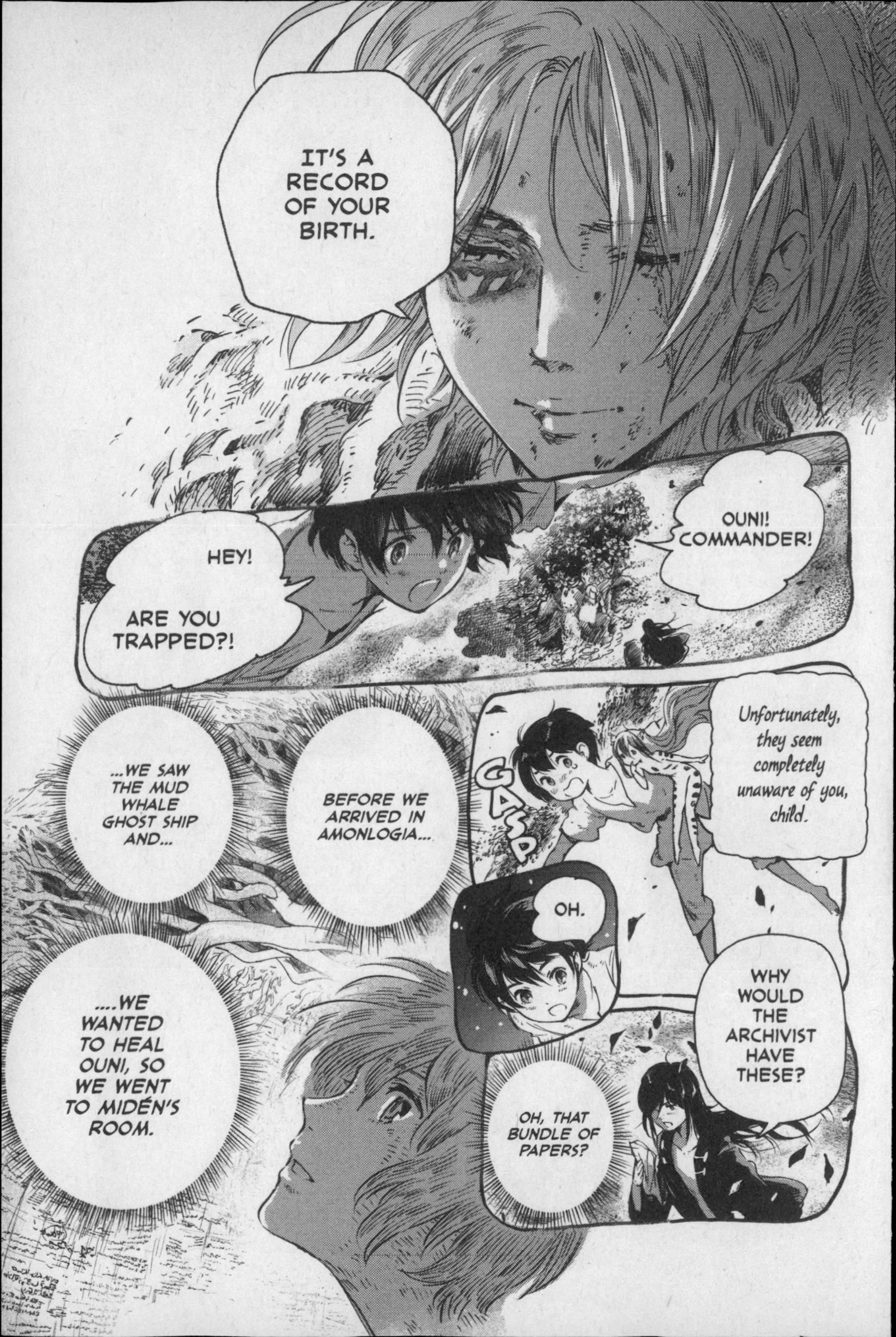
IT'S A RECORD OF YOUR BIRTH.
OUNI! COMMANDER!
HEY!
ARE YOU TRAPPED?!
Unfortunately, they seem completely unaware of you, child.
GASP
OH.
WHY WOULD THE ARCHIVIST HAVE THESE?
OH, THAT BUNDLE OF PAPERS?
BEFORE WE ARRIVED IN AMONLOGIA...
...WE SAW THE MUD WHALE GHOST SHIP AND...
....WE WANTED TO HEAL OUNI, SO WE WENT TO MIDÉN'S ROOM.

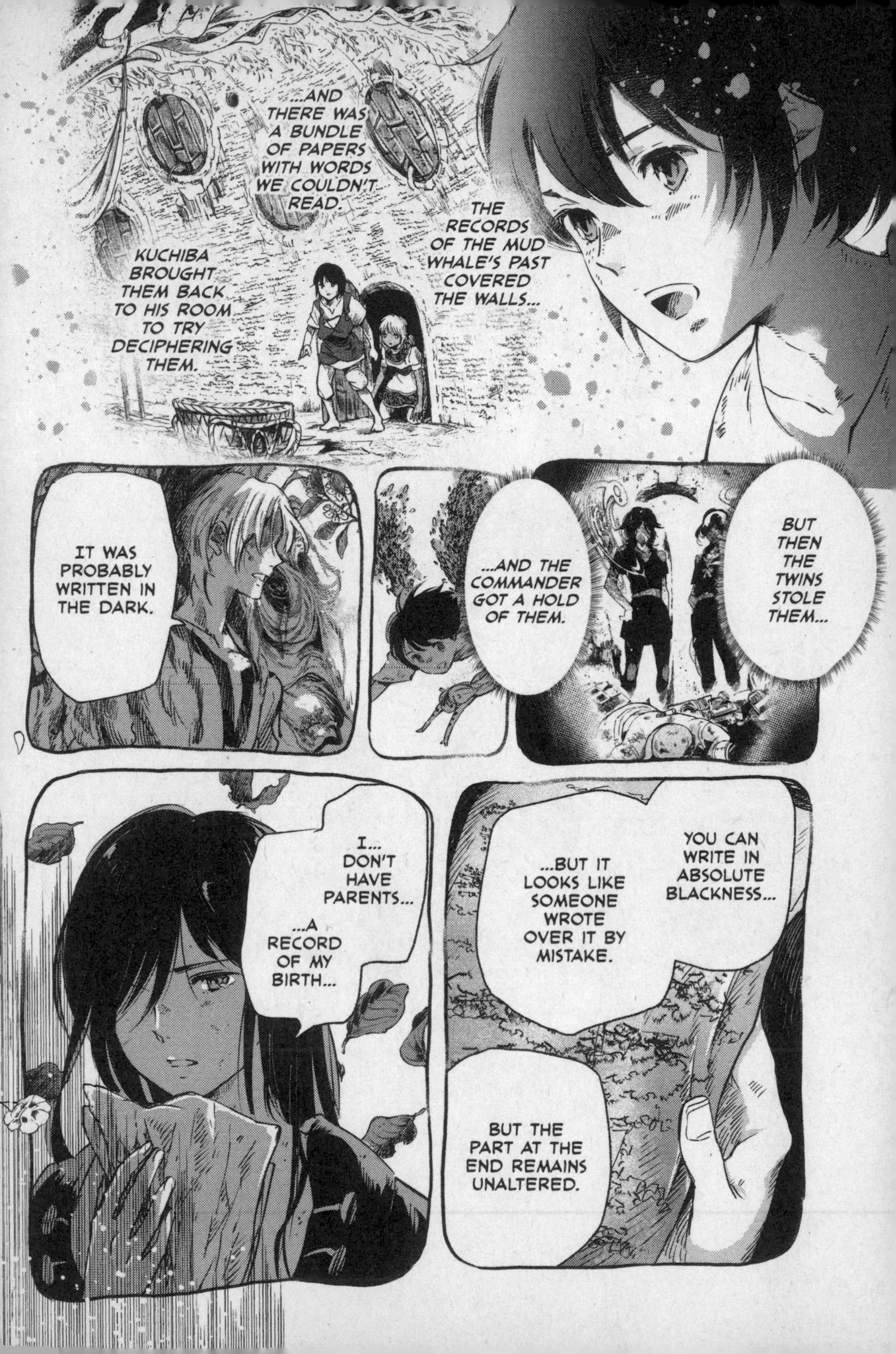
THE RECORDS OF THE MUD WHALE'S PAST COVERED THE WALLS...
...AND THERE WAS A BUNDLE OF PAPERS WITH WORDS WE COULDN'T READ.
KUCHIBA BROUGHT THEM BACK TO HIS ROOM TO TRY DECIPHERING THEM.
BUT THEN THE TWINS STOLE THEM...
...AND THE COMMANDER GOT A HOLD OF THEM.
IT WAS PROBABLY WRITTEN IN THE DARK.
YOU CAN WRITE IN ABSOLUTE BLACKNESS...
...BUT IT LOOKS LIKE SOMEONE WROTE OVER IT BY MISTAKE.
BUT THE PART AT THE END REMAINS UNALTERED.
I... DON'T HAVE PARENTS...
...A RECORD OF MY BIRTH...

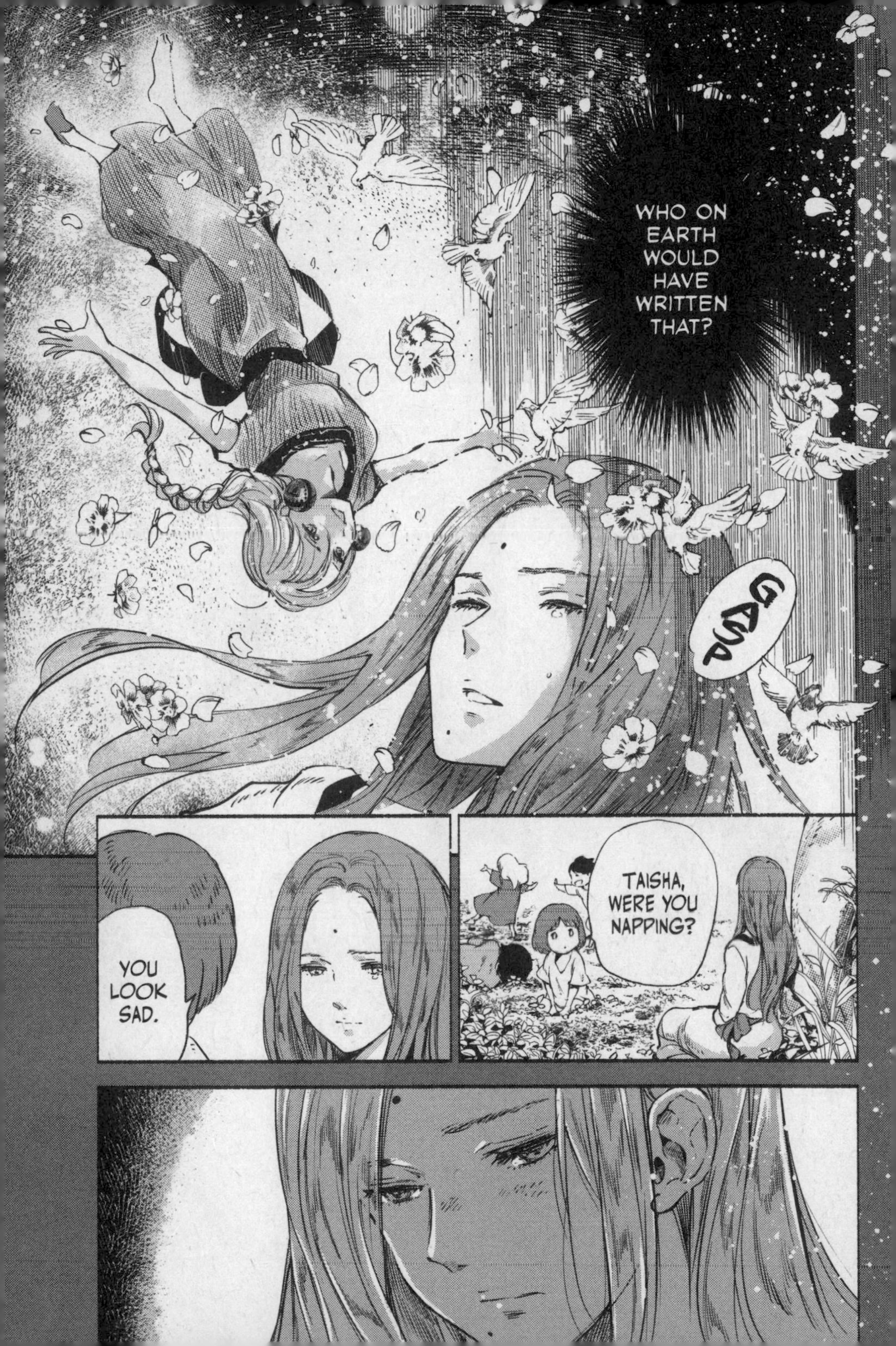
WHO ON EARTH WOULD HAVE WRITTEN THAT?
GASP
TAISHA, WERE YOU NAPPING?
YOU LOOK SAD.

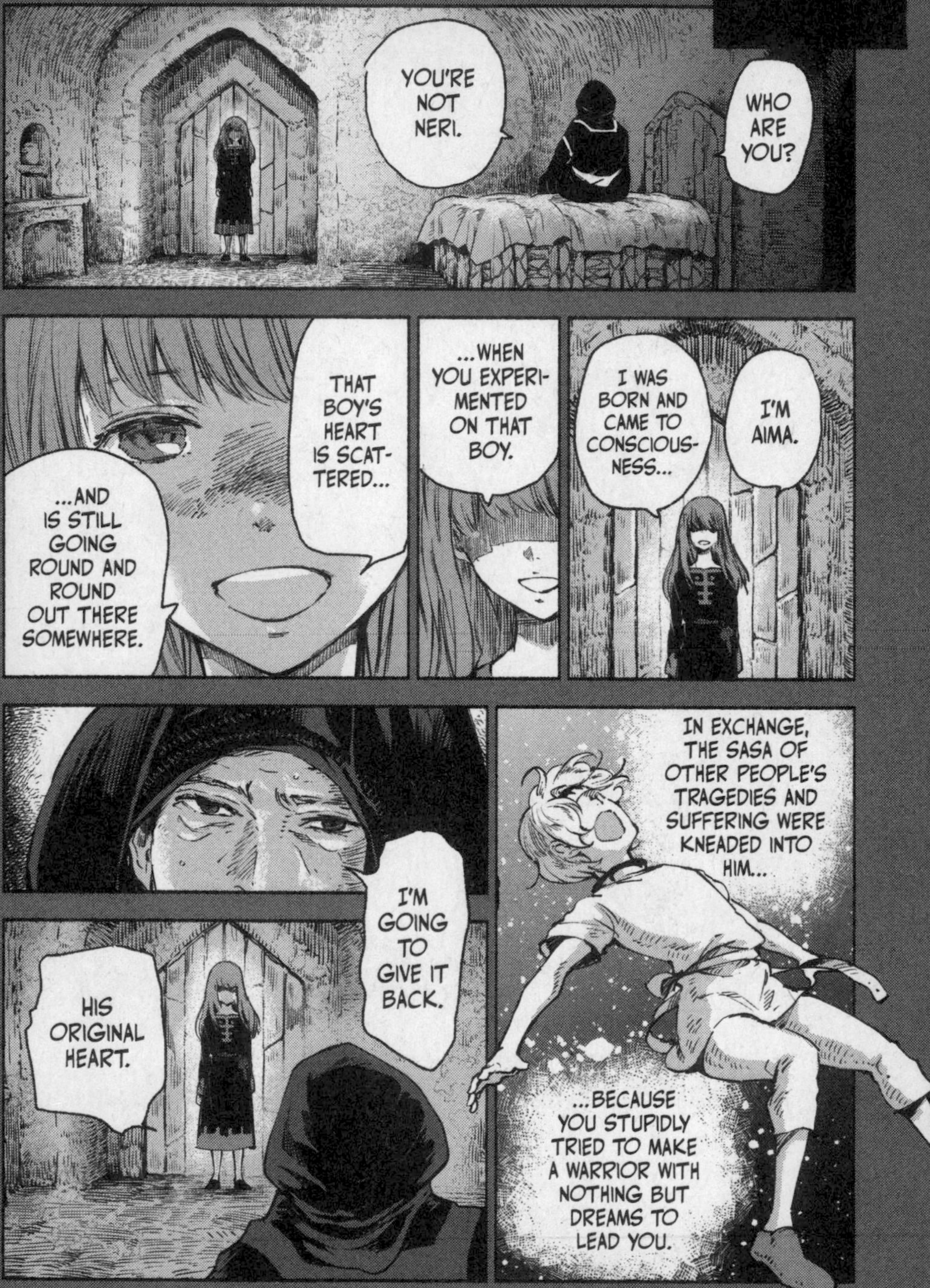
WHO ARE YOU?
YOU'RE NOT NERI.
I'M AIMA.
I WAS BORN AND CAME TO CONSCIOUS-NESS...
...WHEN YOU EXPERI-MENTED ON THAT BOY.
THAT BOY'S HEART IS SCAT-TERED...
...AND IS STILL GOING ROUND AND ROUND OUT THERE SOMEWHERE.
IN EXCHANGE, THE SASA OF OTHER PEOPLE'S TRAGEDIES AND SUFFERING WERE KNEADED INTO HIM...
...BECAUSE YOU STUPIDLY TRIED TO MAKE A WARRIOR WITH NOTHING BUT DREAMS TO LEAD YOU.
I'M GOING TO GIVE IT BACK.
HIS ORIGINAL HEART.

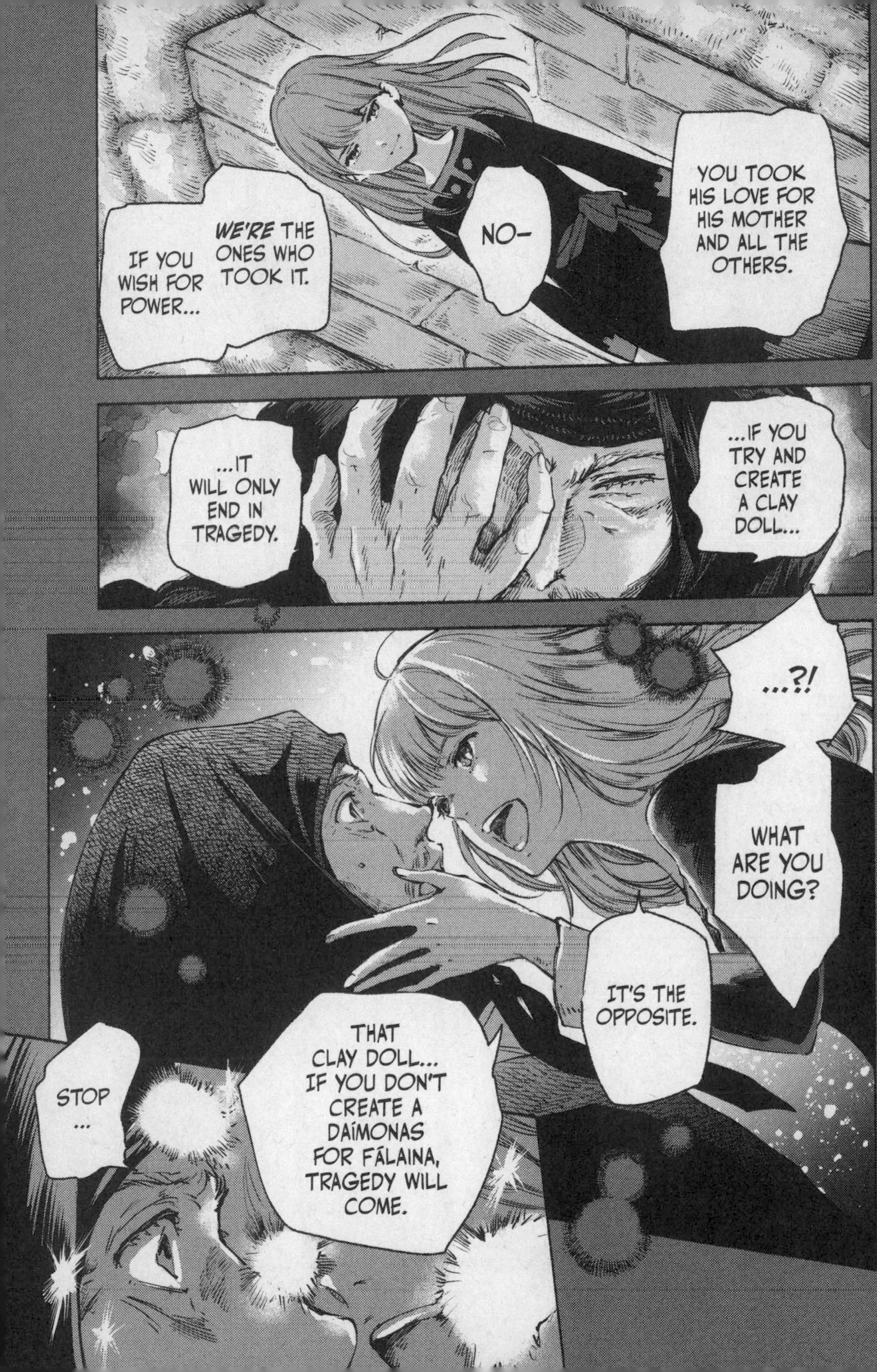
YOU TOOK HIS LOVE FOR HIS MOTHER AND ALL THE OTHERS.
NO–
WE'RE THE ONES WHO TOOK IT.
IF YOU WISH FOR POWER...
...IF YOU TRY AND CREATE A CLAY DOLL...
...IT WILL ONLY END IN TRAGEDY.
...?!
WHAT ARE YOU DOING?
IT'S THE OPPOSITE.
THAT CLAY DOLL... IF YOU DON'T CREATE A DAÍMONAS FOR FÁLAINA, TRAGEDY WILL COME.
STOP ...

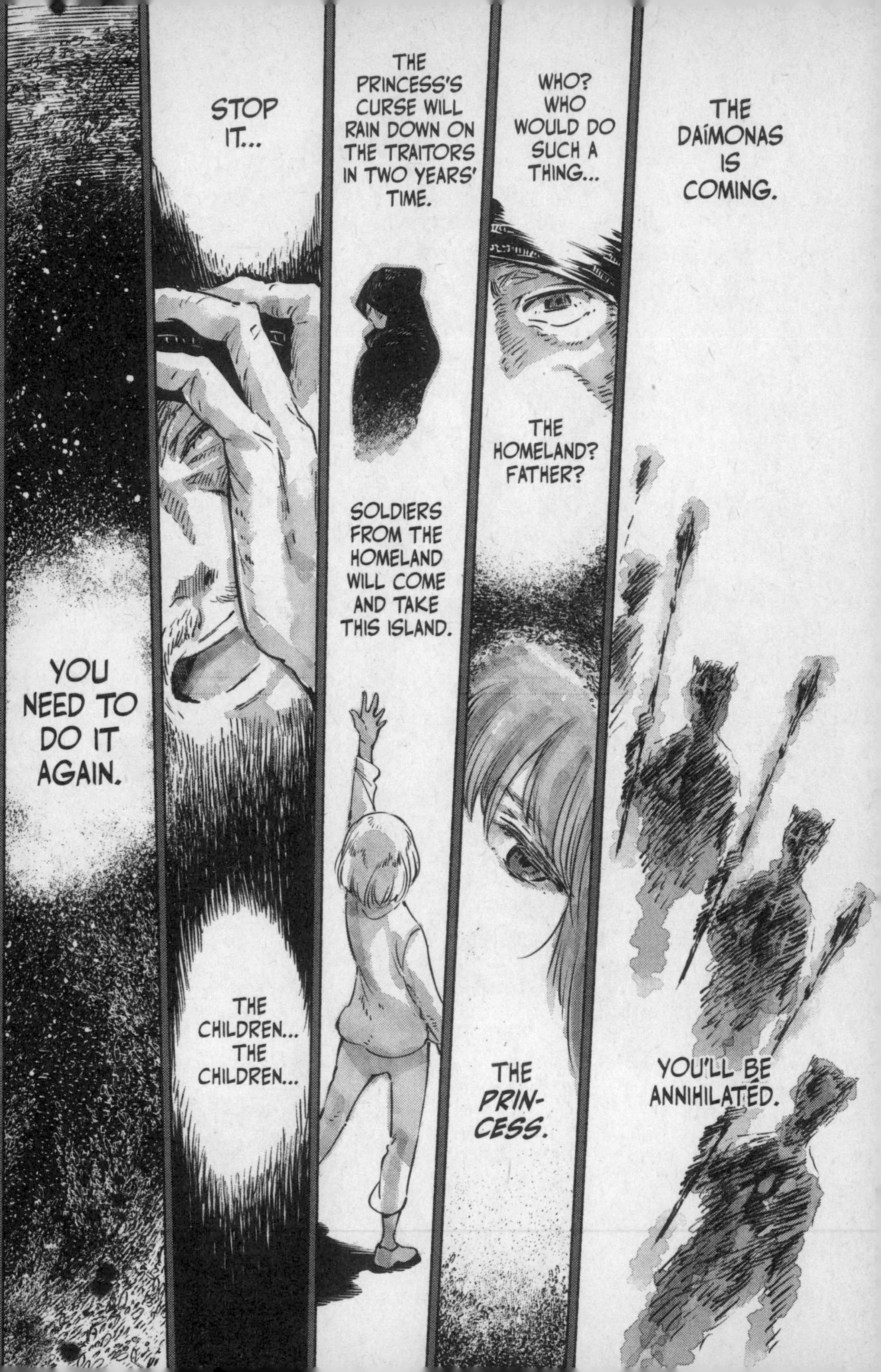
THE DAÍMONAS IS COMING.
YOU'LL BE ANNIHILATED.
WHO? WHO WOULD DO SUCH A THING...
THE HOMELAND? FATHER?
THE *PRINCESS*.
THE PRINCESS'S CURSE WILL RAIN DOWN ON THE TRAITORS IN TWO YEARS' TIME.
SOLDIERS FROM THE HOMELAND WILL COME AND TAKE THIS ISLAND.
STOP IT...
THE CHILDREN... THE CHILDREN...
YOU NEED TO DO IT AGAIN.

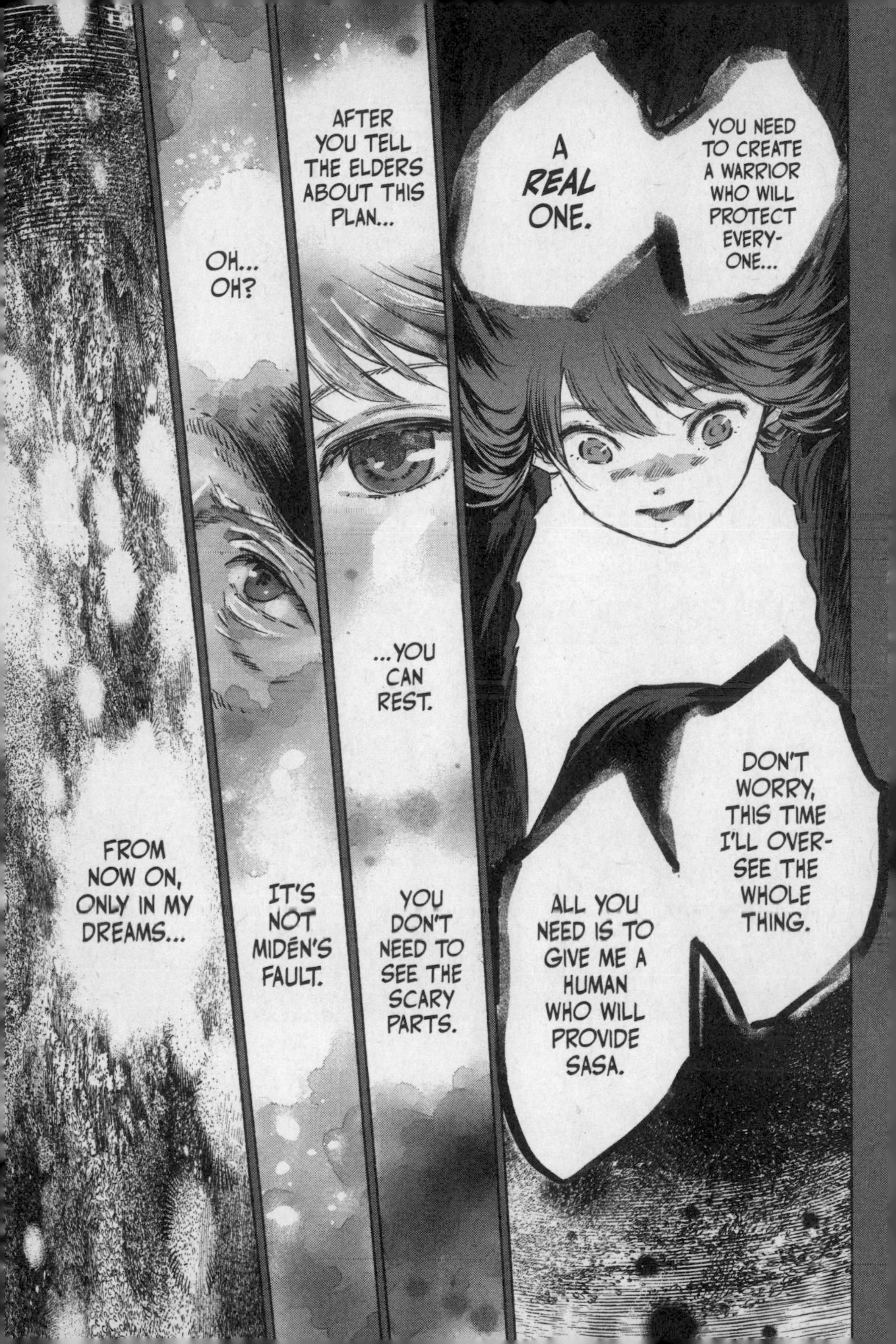
YOU NEED TO CREATE A WARRIOR WHO WILL PROTECT EVERY-ONE...
A *REAL* ONE.
DON'T WORRY, THIS TIME I'LL OVER-SEE THE WHOLE THING.
ALL YOU NEED IS TO GIVE ME A HUMAN WHO WILL PROVIDE SASA.
AFTER YOU TELL THE ELDERS ABOUT THIS PLAN...
...YOU CAN REST.
YOU DON'T NEED TO SEE THE SCARY PARTS.
OH... OH?
IT'S NOT MIDÉN'S FAULT.
FROM NOW ON, ONLY IN MY DREAMS...

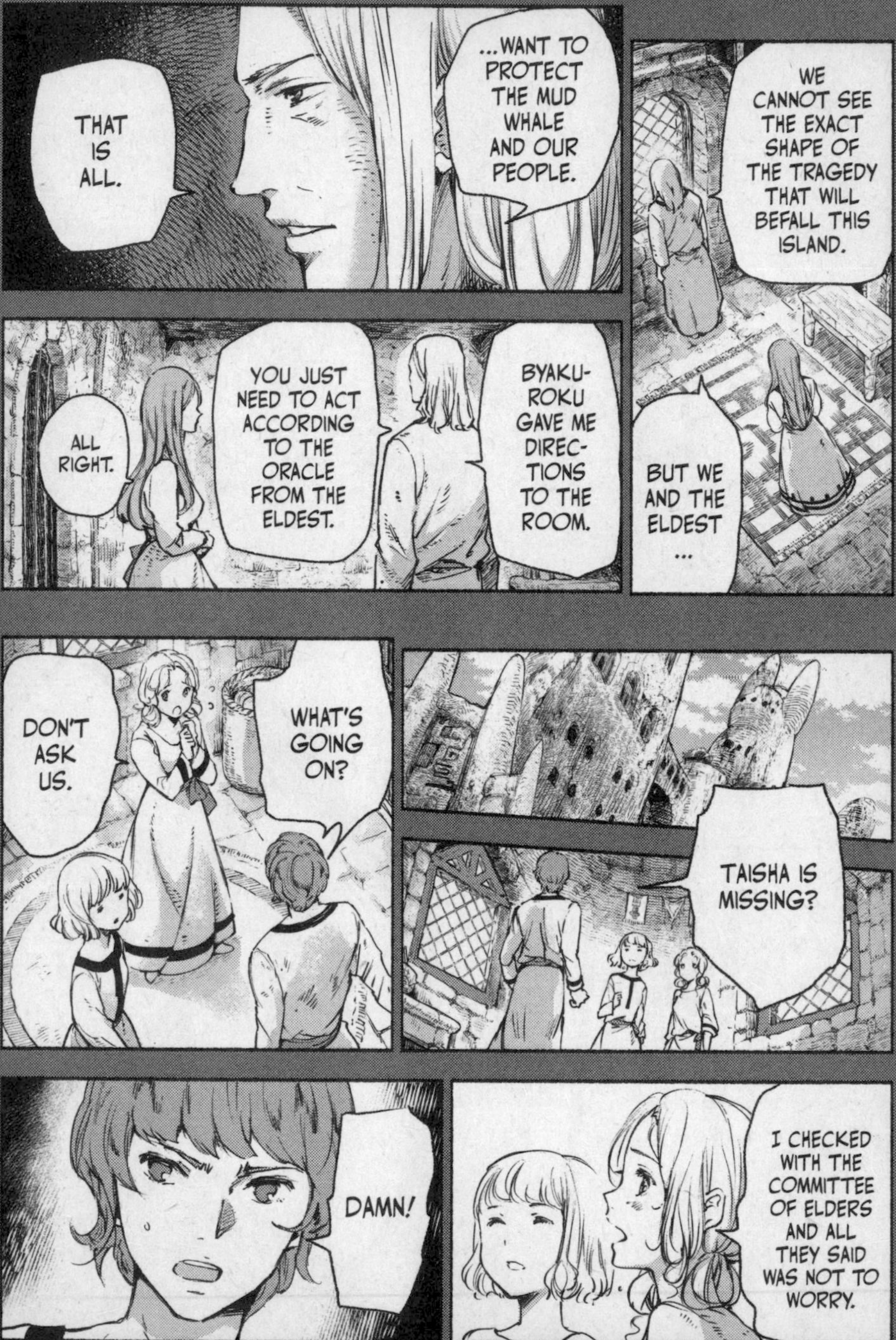
WE CANNOT SEE THE EXACT SHAPE OF THE TRAGEDY THAT WILL BEFALL THIS ISLAND.
BUT WE AND THE ELDEST ...
...WANT TO PROTECT THE MUD WHALE AND OUR PEOPLE.
THAT IS ALL.
BYAKU-ROKU GAVE ME DIREC-TIONS TO THE ROOM.
YOU JUST NEED TO ACT ACCORDING TO THE ORACLE FROM THE ELDEST.
ALL RIGHT.
TAISHA IS MISSING?
WHAT'S GOING ON?
DON'T ASK US.
I CHECKED WITH THE COMMITTEE OF ELDERS AND ALL THEY SAID WAS NOT TO WORRY.
DAMN!

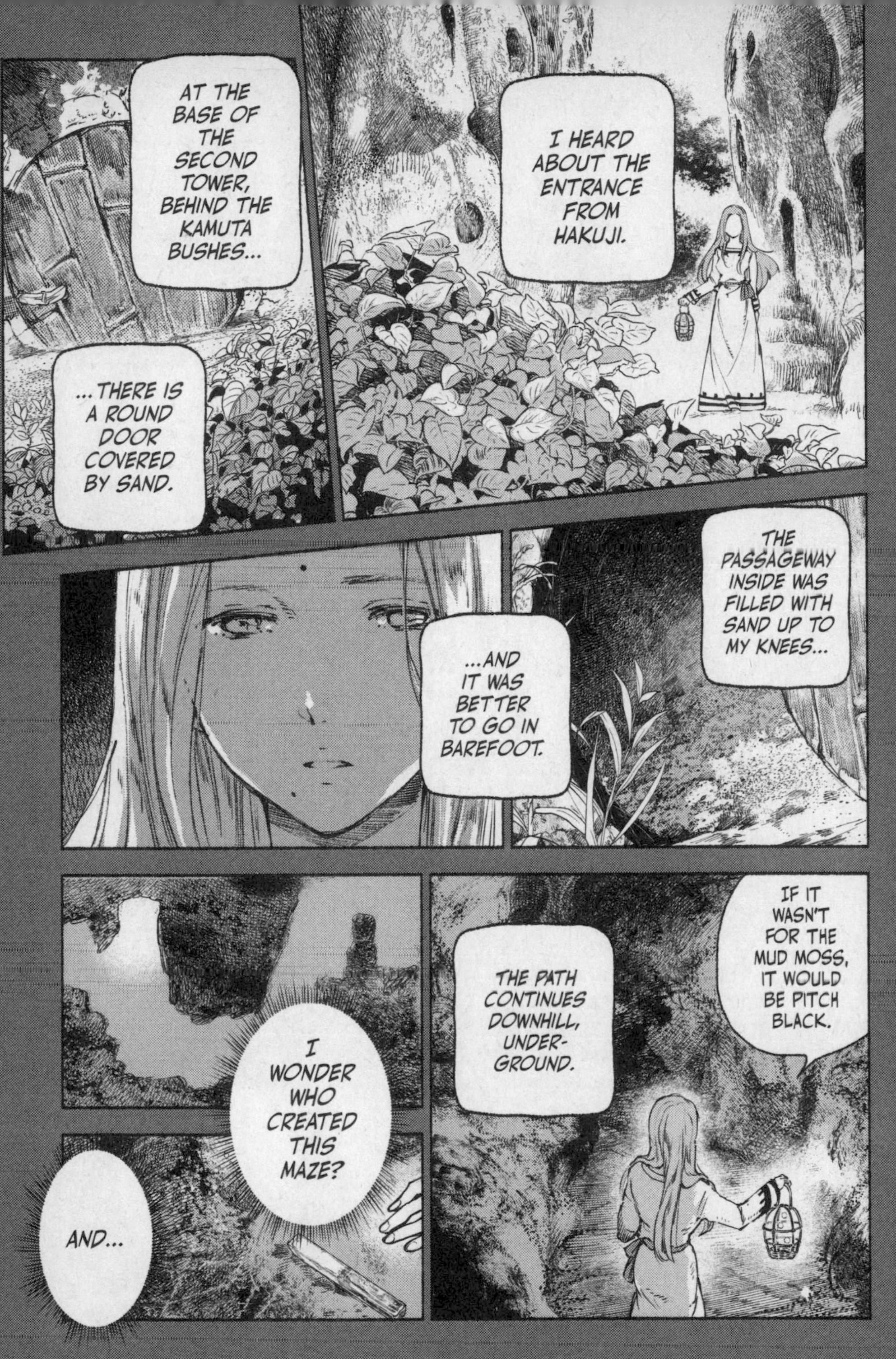
I HEARD ABOUT THE ENTRANCE FROM HAKUJI.
AT THE BASE OF THE SECOND TOWER, BEHIND THE KAMUTA BUSHES...
...THERE IS A ROUND DOOR COVERED BY SAND.
THE PASSAGEWAY INSIDE WAS FILLED WITH SAND UP TO MY KNEES...
...AND IT WAS BETTER TO GO IN BAREFOOT.
IF IT WASN'T FOR THE MUD MOSS, IT WOULD BE PITCH BLACK.
THE PATH CONTINUES DOWNHILL, UNDER-GROUND.
I WONDER WHO CREATED THIS MAZE?
AND...

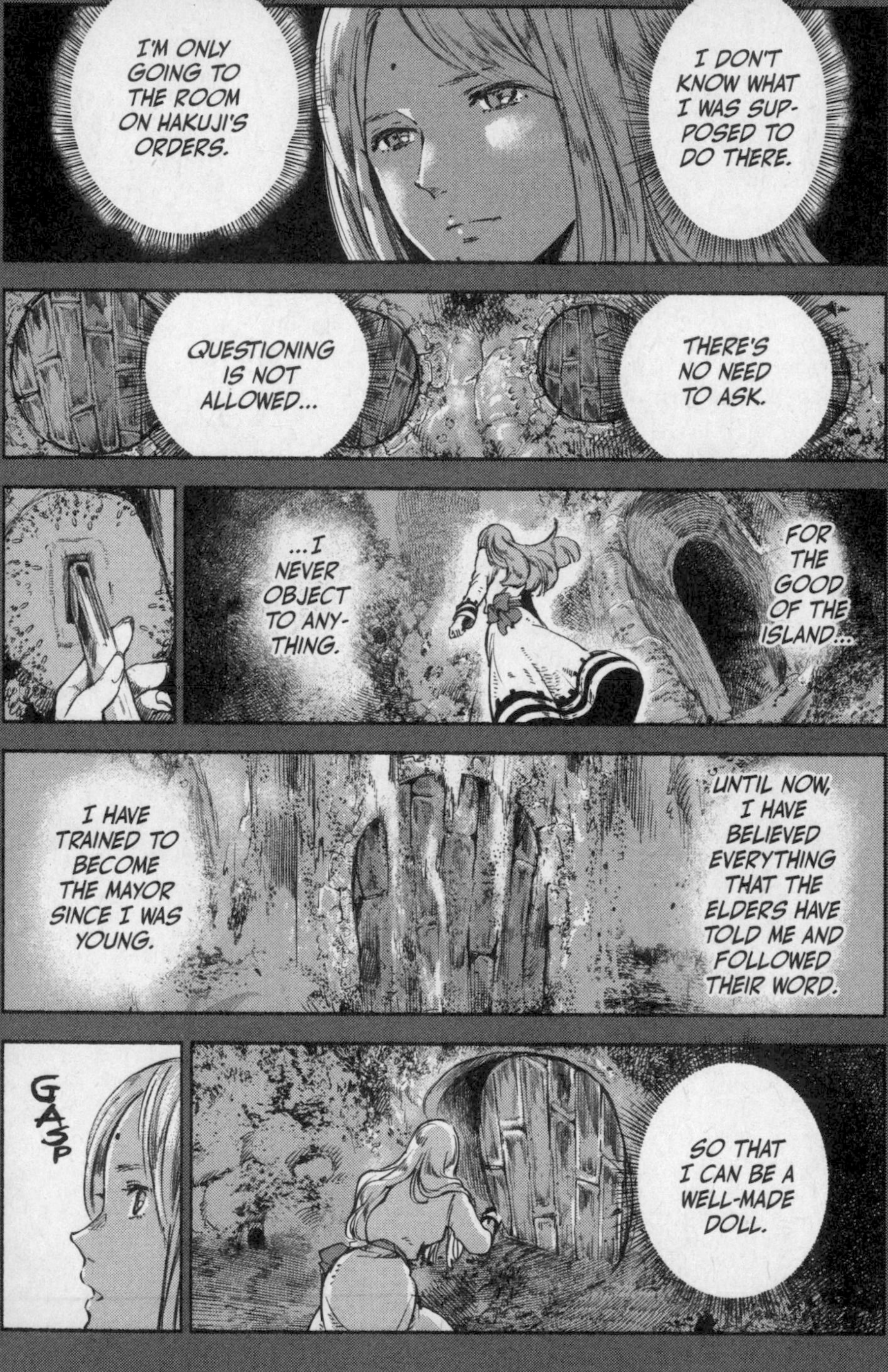
I'M ONLY GOING TO THE ROOM ON HAKUJI'S ORDERS.
I DON'T KNOW WHAT I WAS SUP-POSED TO DO THERE.
QUESTIONING IS NOT ALLOWED...
THERE'S NO NEED TO ASK.
...I NEVER OBJECT TO ANY-THING.
FOR THE GOOD OF THE ISLAND...
I HAVE TRAINED TO BECOME THE MAYOR SINCE I WAS YOUNG.
UNTIL NOW, I HAVE BELIEVED EVERYTHING THAT THE ELDERS HAVE TOLD ME AND FOLLOWED THEIR WORD.
GASP
SO THAT I CAN BE A WELL-MADE DOLL.

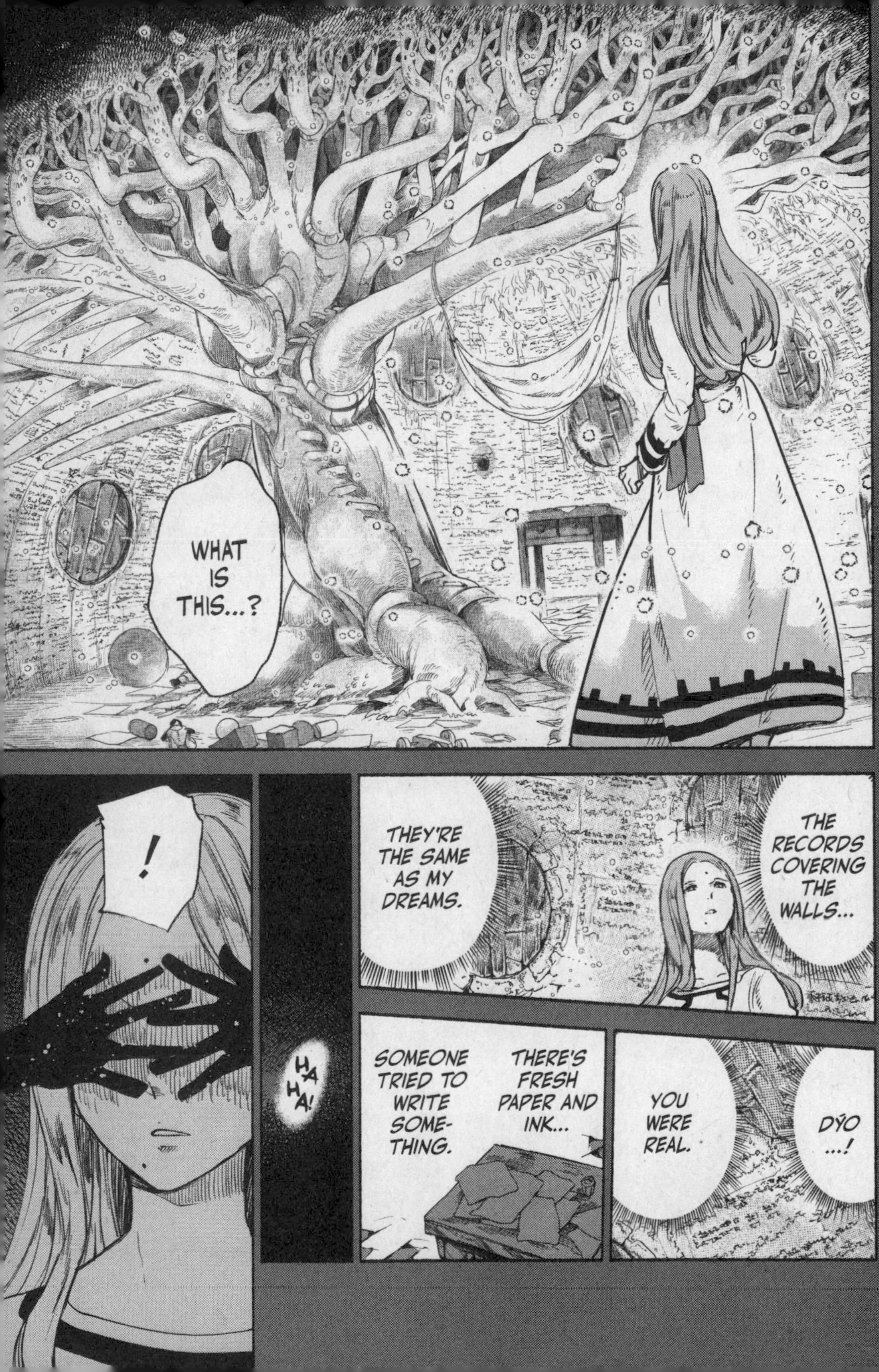
WHAT IS THIS...?
THE RECORDS COVERING THE WALLS...
THEY'RE THE SAME AS MY DREAMS.
DÝO ...!
YOU WERE REAL.
THERE'S FRESH PAPER AND INK...
SOMEONE TRIED TO WRITE SOME-THING.
HA HA!
!

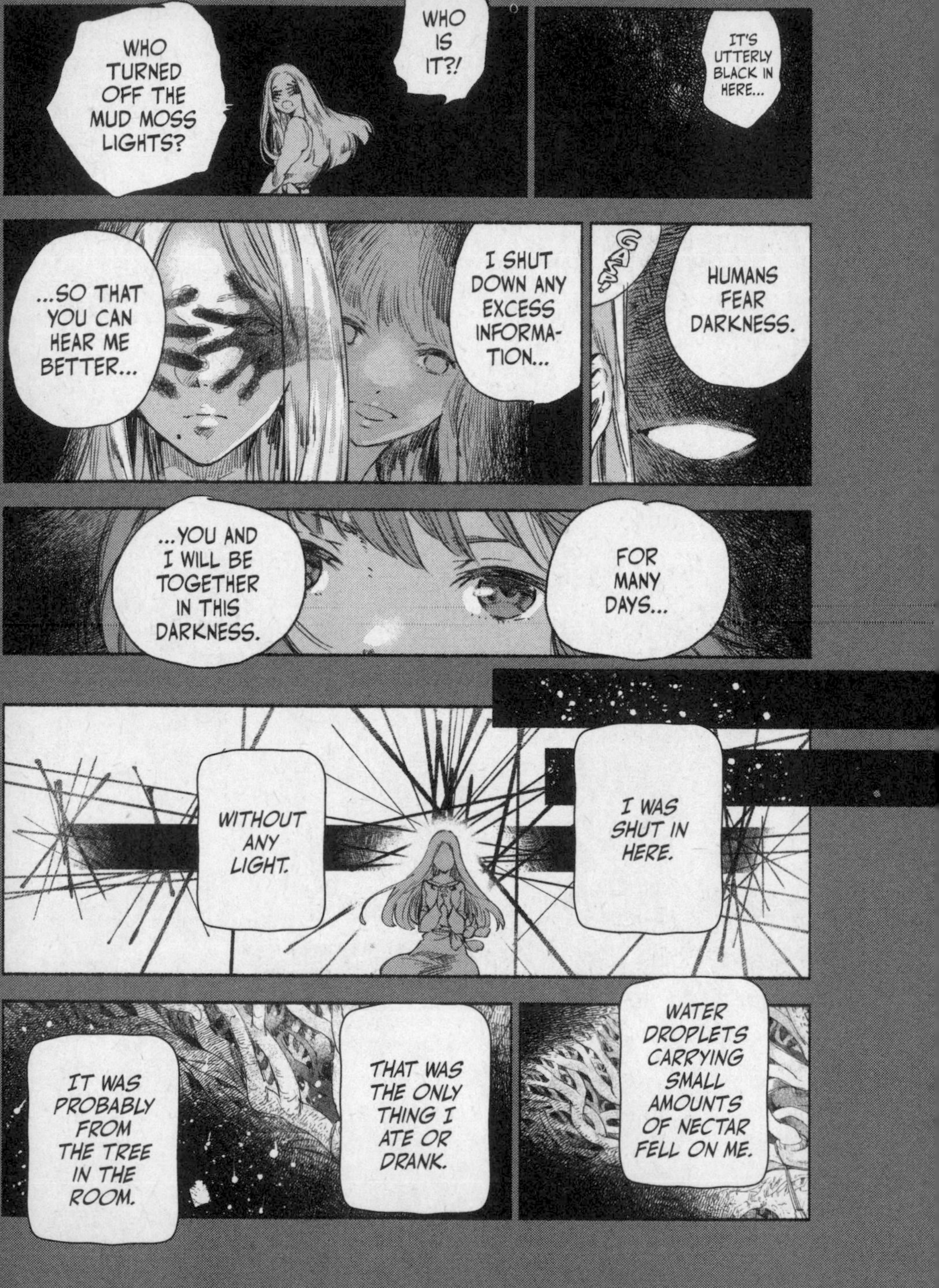
IT'S UTTERLY BLACK IN HERE...
WHO IS IT?!
WHO TURNED OFF THE MUD MOSS LIGHTS?
GASP!
HUMANS FEAR DARKNESS.
I SHUT DOWN ANY EXCESS INFORMATION...
...SO THAT YOU CAN HEAR ME BETTER...
FOR MANY DAYS...
...YOU AND I WILL BE TOGETHER IN THIS DARKNESS.
I WAS SHUT IN HERE.
WITHOUT ANY LIGHT.
WATER DROPLETS CARRYING SMALL AMOUNTS OF NECTAR FELL ON ME.
THAT WAS THE ONLY THING I ATE OR DRANK.
IT WAS PROBABLY FROM THE TREE IN THE ROOM.

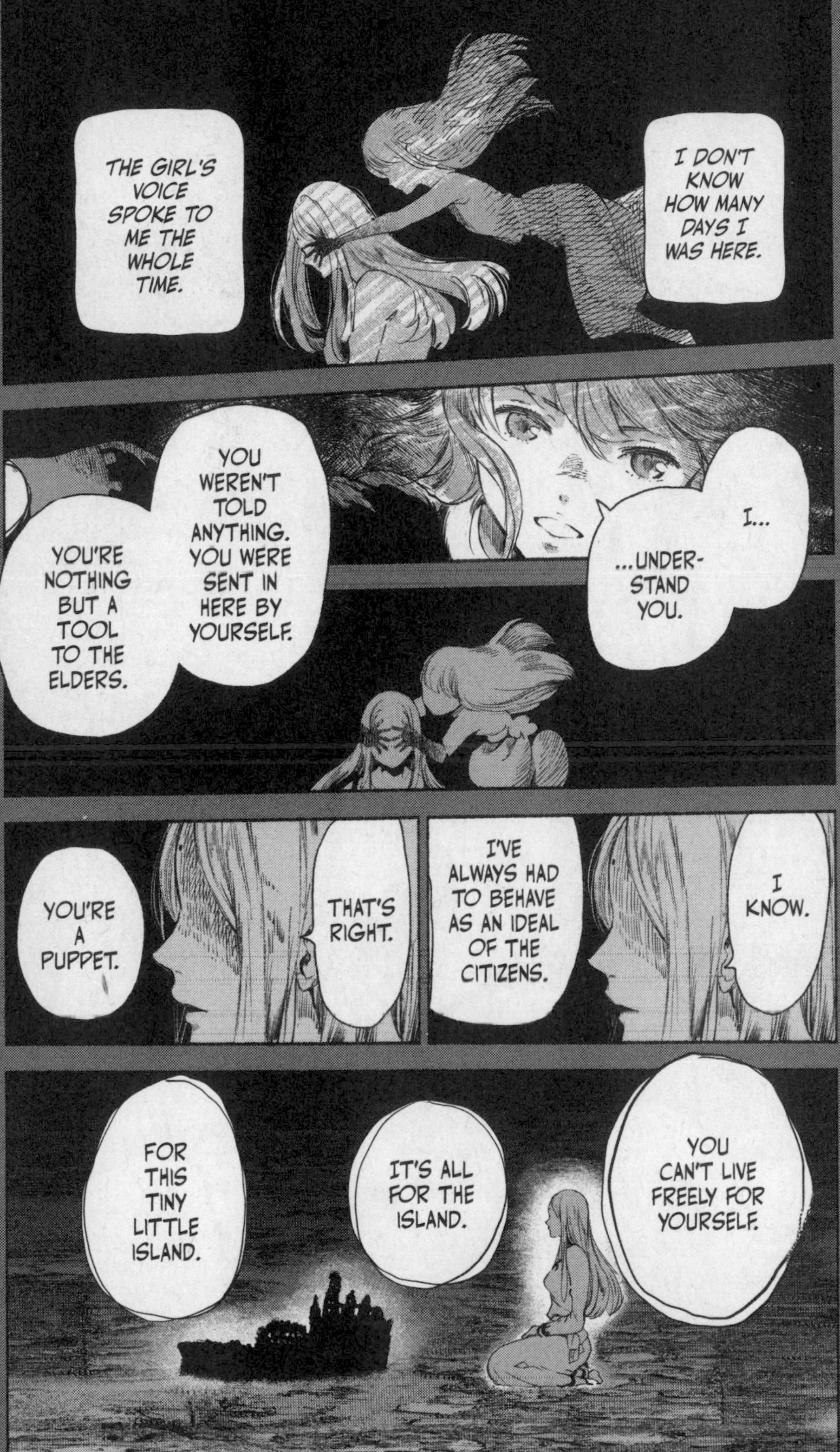
I DON'T KNOW HOW MANY DAYS I WAS HERE.
THE GIRL'S VOICE SPOKE TO ME THE WHOLE TIME.
I...
...UNDERSTAND YOU.
YOU WEREN'T TOLD ANYTHING. YOU WERE SENT IN HERE BY YOURSELF.
YOU'RE NOTHING BUT A TOOL TO THE ELDERS.
I KNOW.
I'VE ALWAYS HAD TO BEHAVE AS AN IDEAL OF THE CITIZENS.
THAT'S RIGHT.
YOU'RE A PUPPET.
YOU CAN'T LIVE FREELY FOR YOURSELF.
IT'S ALL FOR THE ISLAND.
FOR THIS TINY LITTLE ISLAND.

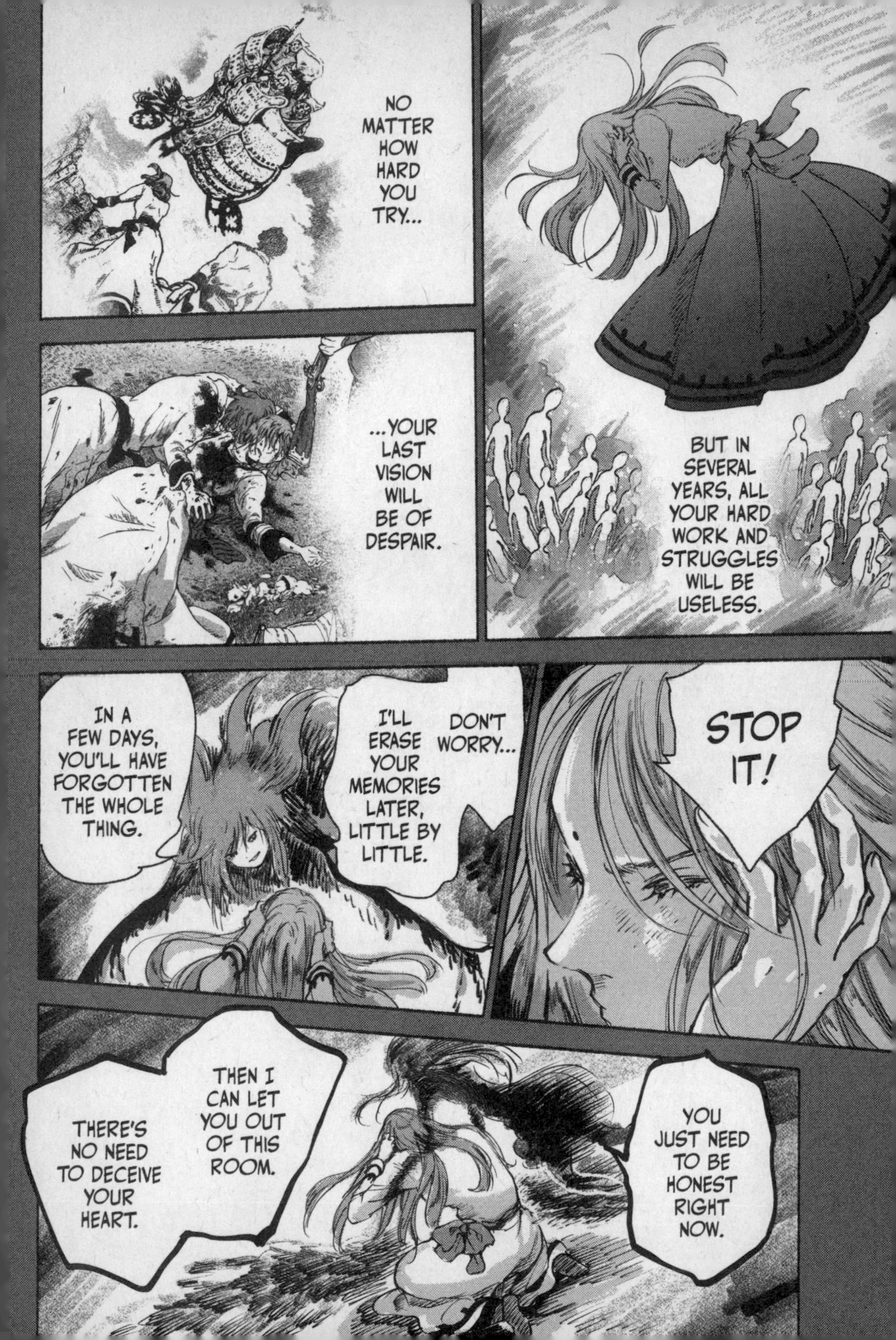
BUT IN SEVERAL YEARS, ALL YOUR HARD WORK AND STRUGGLES WILL BE USELESS.
NO MATTER HOW HARD YOU TRY...
...YOUR LAST VISION WILL BE OF DESPAIR.
STOP IT!
DON'T WORRY...
I'LL ERASE YOUR MEMORIES LATER, LITTLE BY LITTLE.
IN A FEW DAYS, YOU'LL HAVE FORGOTTEN THE WHOLE THING.
YOU JUST NEED TO BE HONEST RIGHT NOW.
THEN I CAN LET YOU OUT OF THIS ROOM.
THERE'S NO NEED TO DECEIVE YOUR HEART.

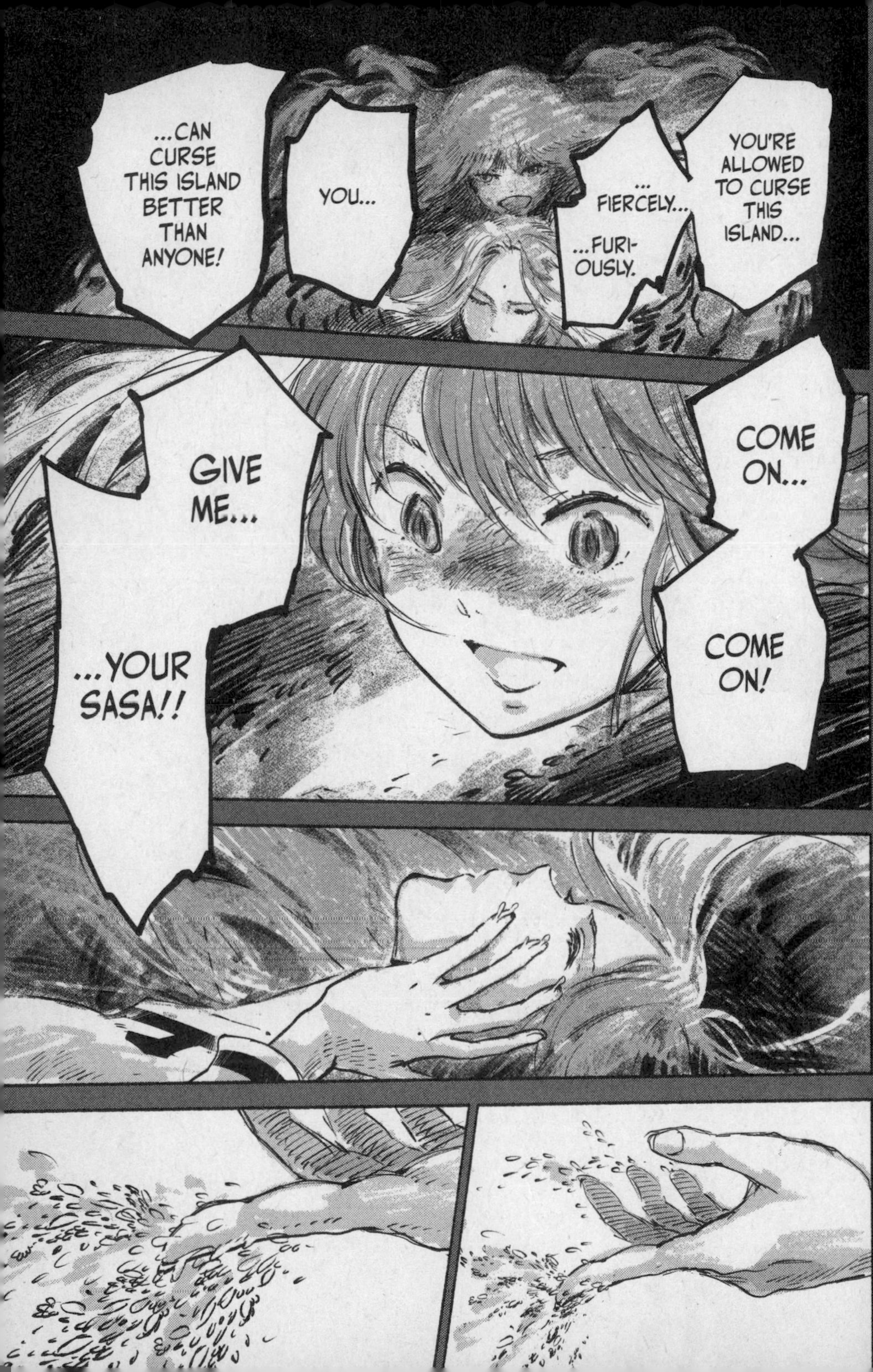
YOU'RE ALLOWED TO CURSE THIS ISLAND...
... FIERCELY...
...FURI-OUSLY.
YOU...
...CAN CURSE THIS ISLAND BETTER THAN ANYONE!
COME ON...
COME ON!
GIVE ME...
...YOUR SASA!!

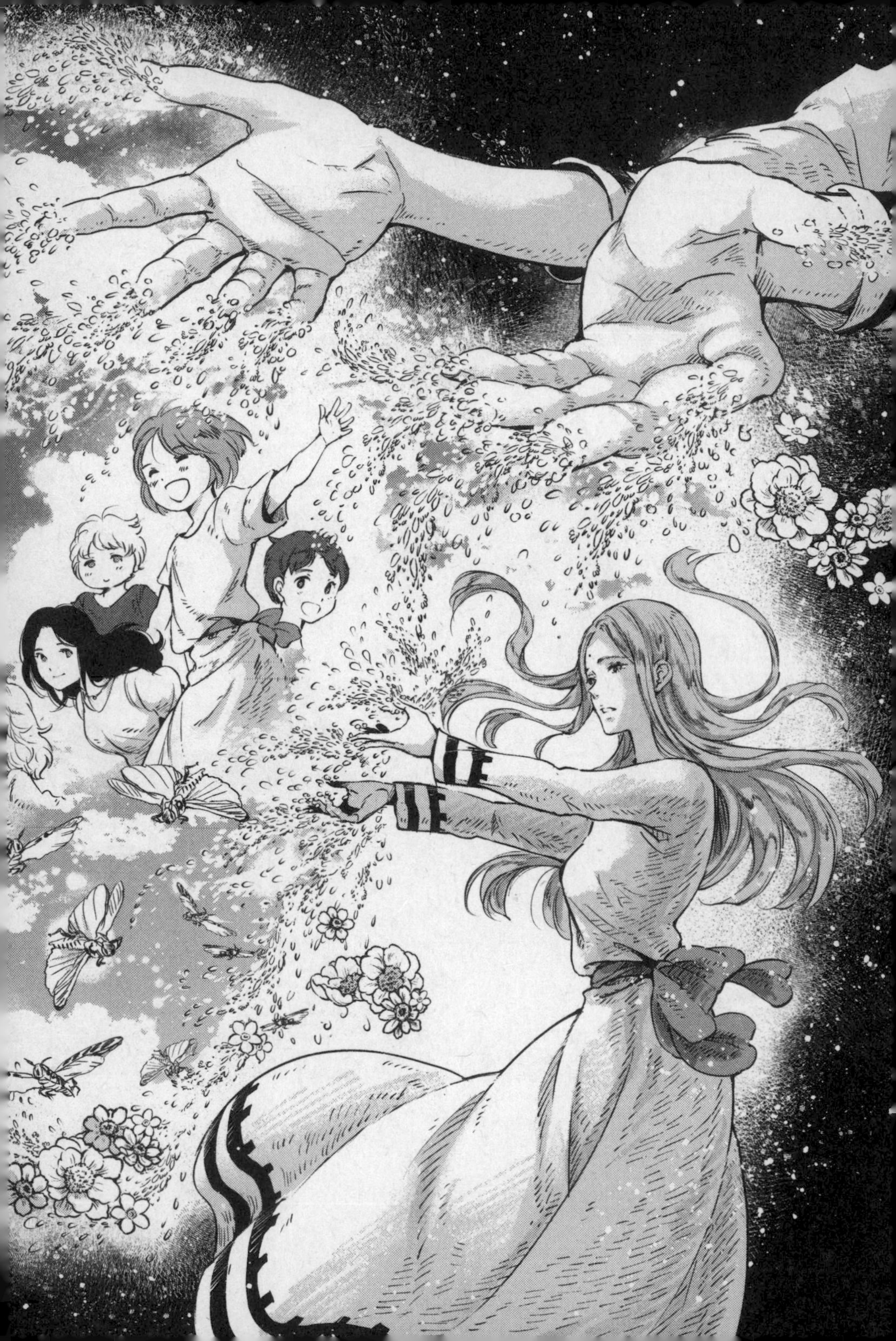

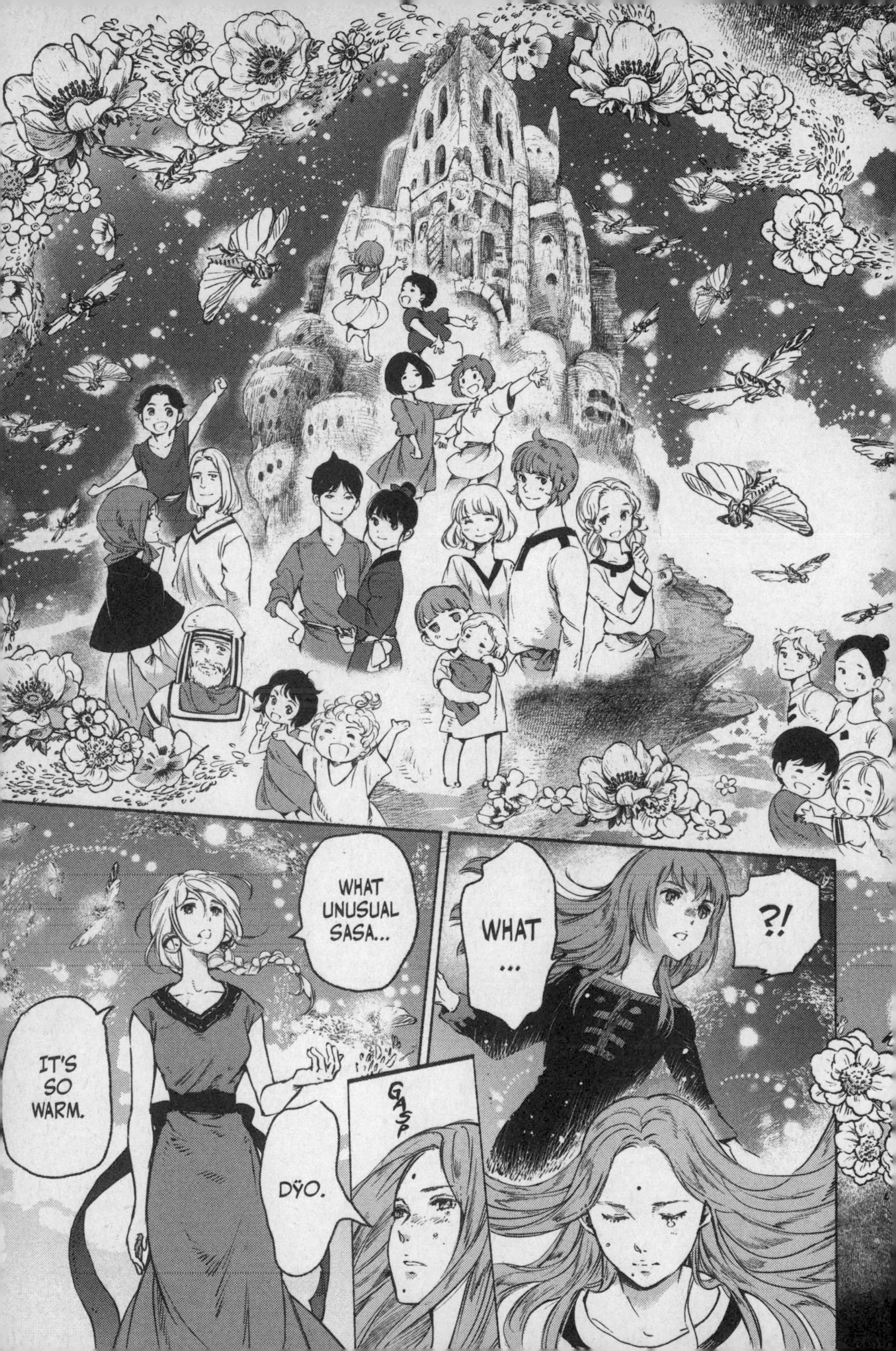
?!
WHAT ...
WHAT UNUSUAL SASA...
IT'S SO WARM.
GASP
DŸO.

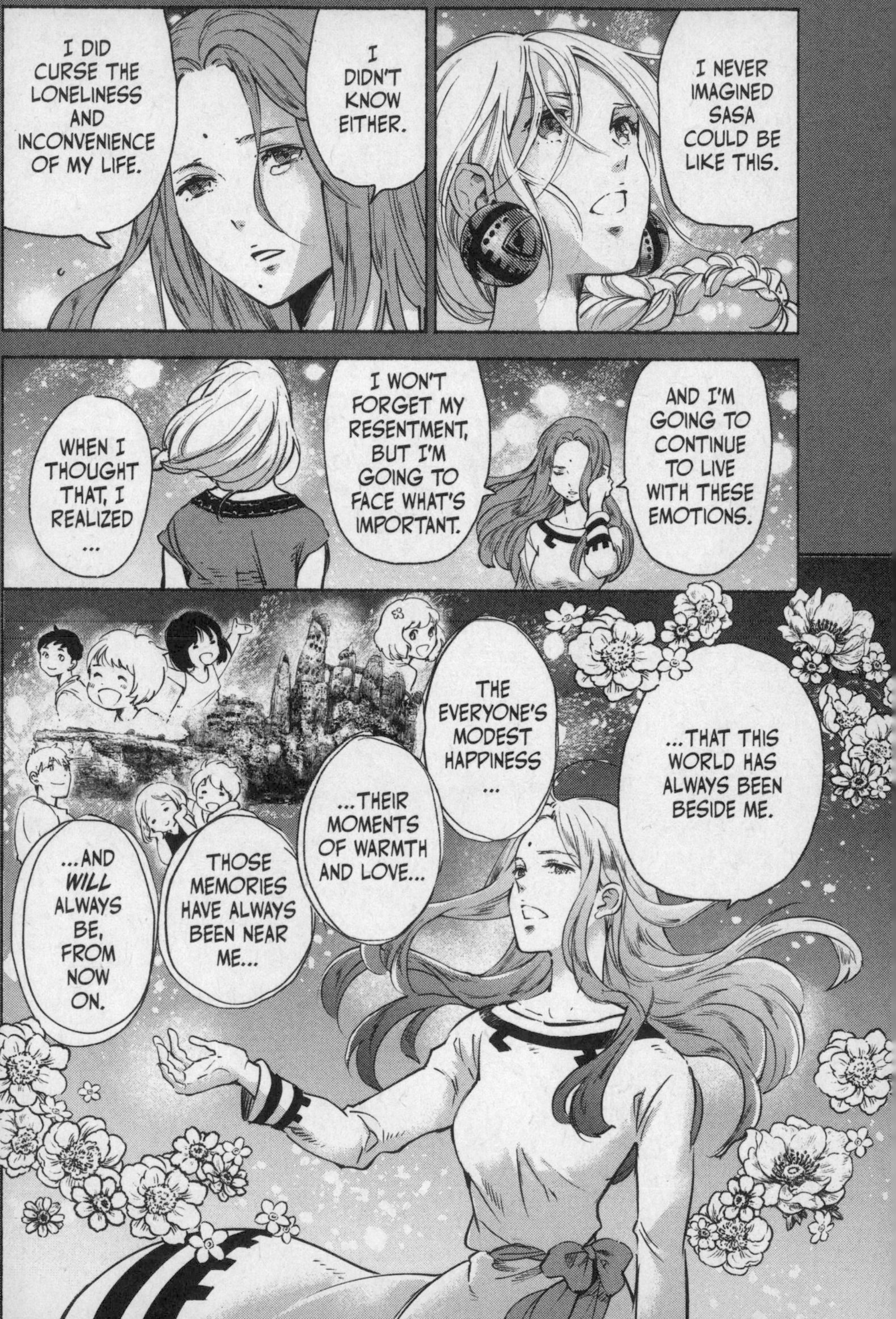
I NEVER IMAGINED SASA COULD BE LIKE THIS.
I DIDN'T KNOW EITHER.
I DID CURSE THE LONELINESS AND INCONVENIENCE OF MY LIFE.
I WON'T FORGET MY RESENTMENT, BUT I'M GOING TO FACE WHAT'S IMPORTANT.
AND I'M GOING TO CONTINUE TO LIVE WITH THESE EMOTIONS.
WHEN I THOUGHT THAT, I REALIZED ...
...THAT THIS WORLD HAS ALWAYS BEEN BESIDE ME.
THE EVERYONE'S MODEST HAPPINESS ...
...THEIR MOMENTS OF WARMTH AND LOVE...
THOSE MEMORIES HAVE ALWAYS BEEN NEAR ME...
...AND *WILL* ALWAYS BE, FROM NOW ON.

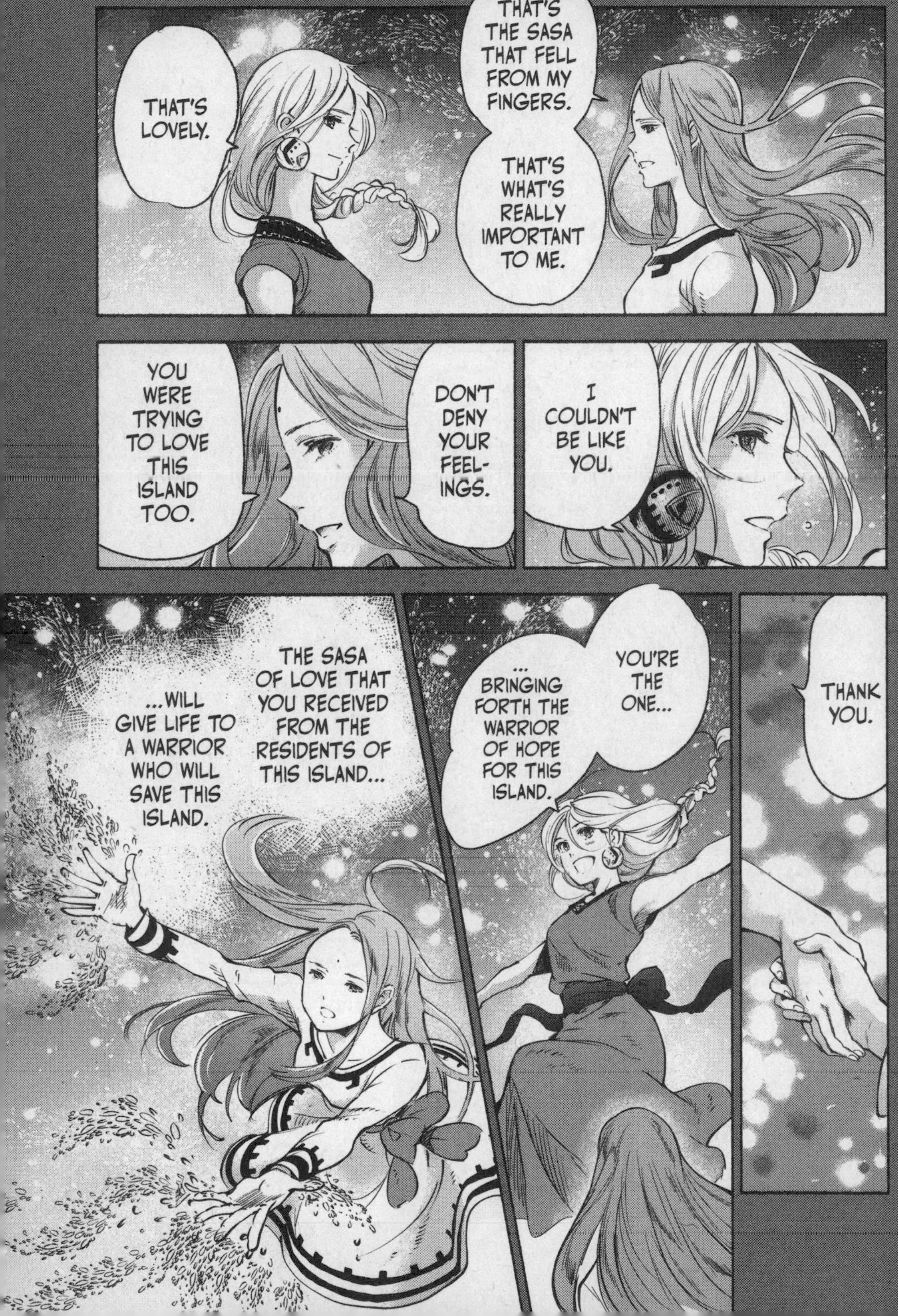
THAT'S THE SASA THAT FELL FROM MY FINGERS.
THAT'S WHAT'S REALLY IMPORTANT TO ME.
THAT'S LOVELY.
I COULDN'T BE LIKE YOU.
DON'T DENY YOUR FEEL-INGS.
YOU WERE TRYING TO LOVE THIS ISLAND TOO.
THANK YOU.
YOU'RE THE ONE...
...BRINGING FORTH THE WARRIOR OF HOPE FOR THIS ISLAND.
THE SASA OF LOVE THAT YOU RECEIVED FROM THE RESIDENTS OF THIS ISLAND...
...WILL GIVE LIFE TO A WARRIOR WHO WILL SAVE THIS ISLAND.

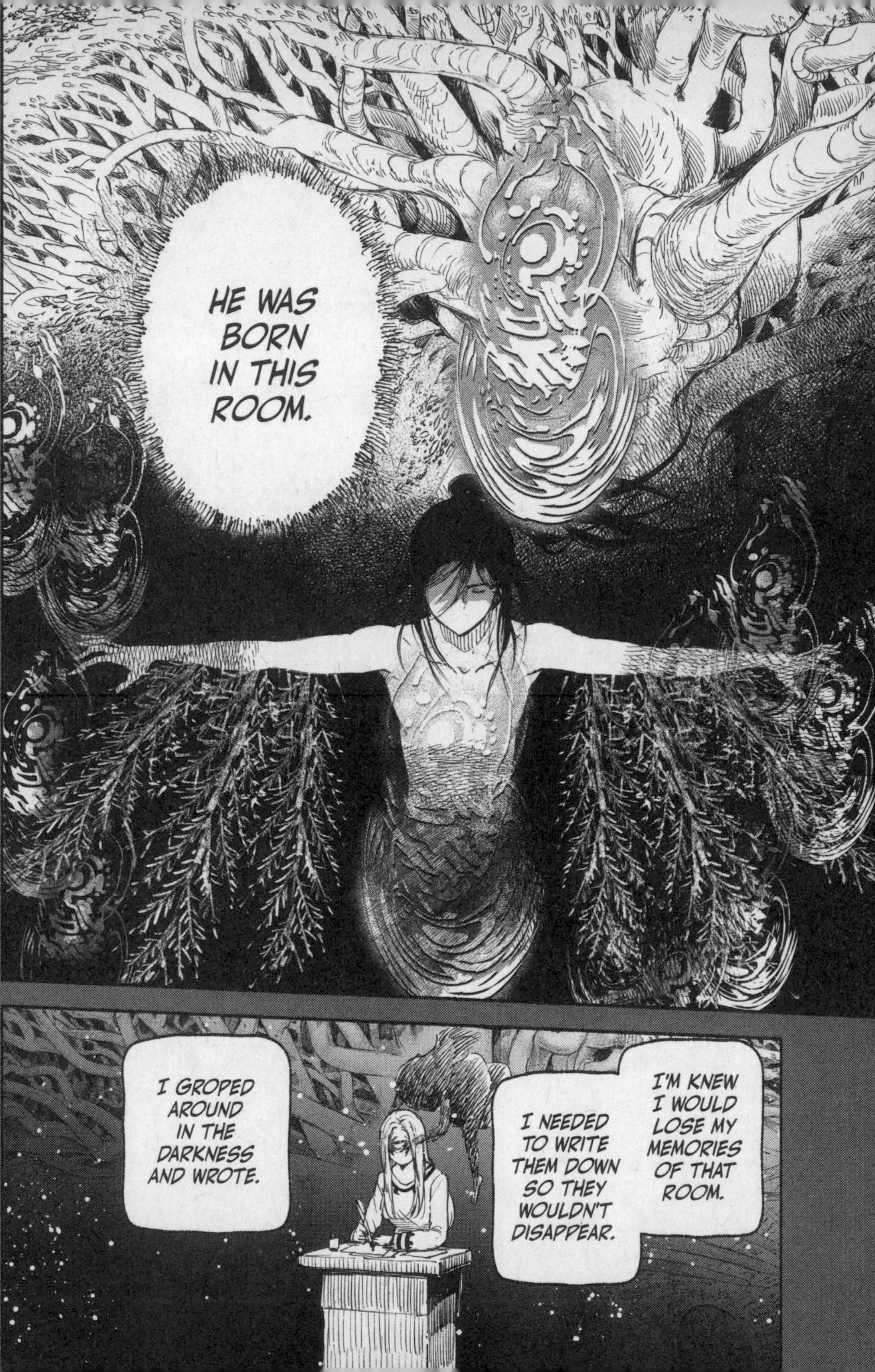
HE WAS BORN IN THIS ROOM.
I'M KNEW I WOULD LOSE MY MEMORIES OF THAT ROOM.
I NEEDED TO WRITE THEM DOWN SO THEY WOULDN'T DISAPPEAR.
I GROPED AROUND IN THE DARKNESS AND WROTE.

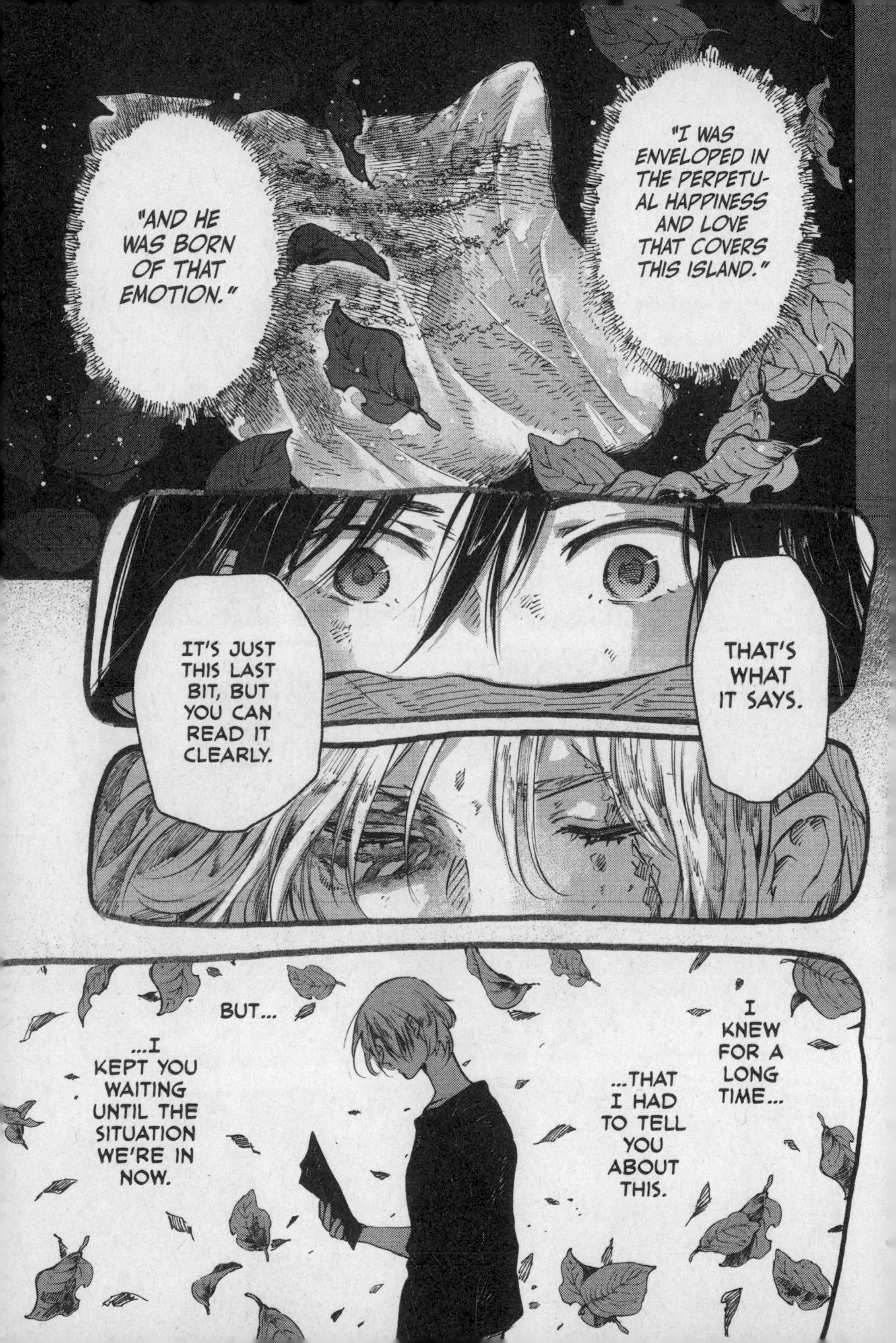
"I WAS ENVELOPED IN THE PERPETU-AL HAPPINESS AND LOVE THAT COVERS THIS ISLAND."
"AND HE WAS BORN OF THAT EMOTION."
THAT'S WHAT IT SAYS.
IT'S JUST THIS LAST BIT, BUT YOU CAN READ IT CLEARLY.
I KNEW FOR A LONG TIME...
...THAT I HAD TO TELL YOU ABOUT THIS.
BUT...
...I KEPT YOU WAITING UNTIL THE SITUATION WE'RE IN NOW.

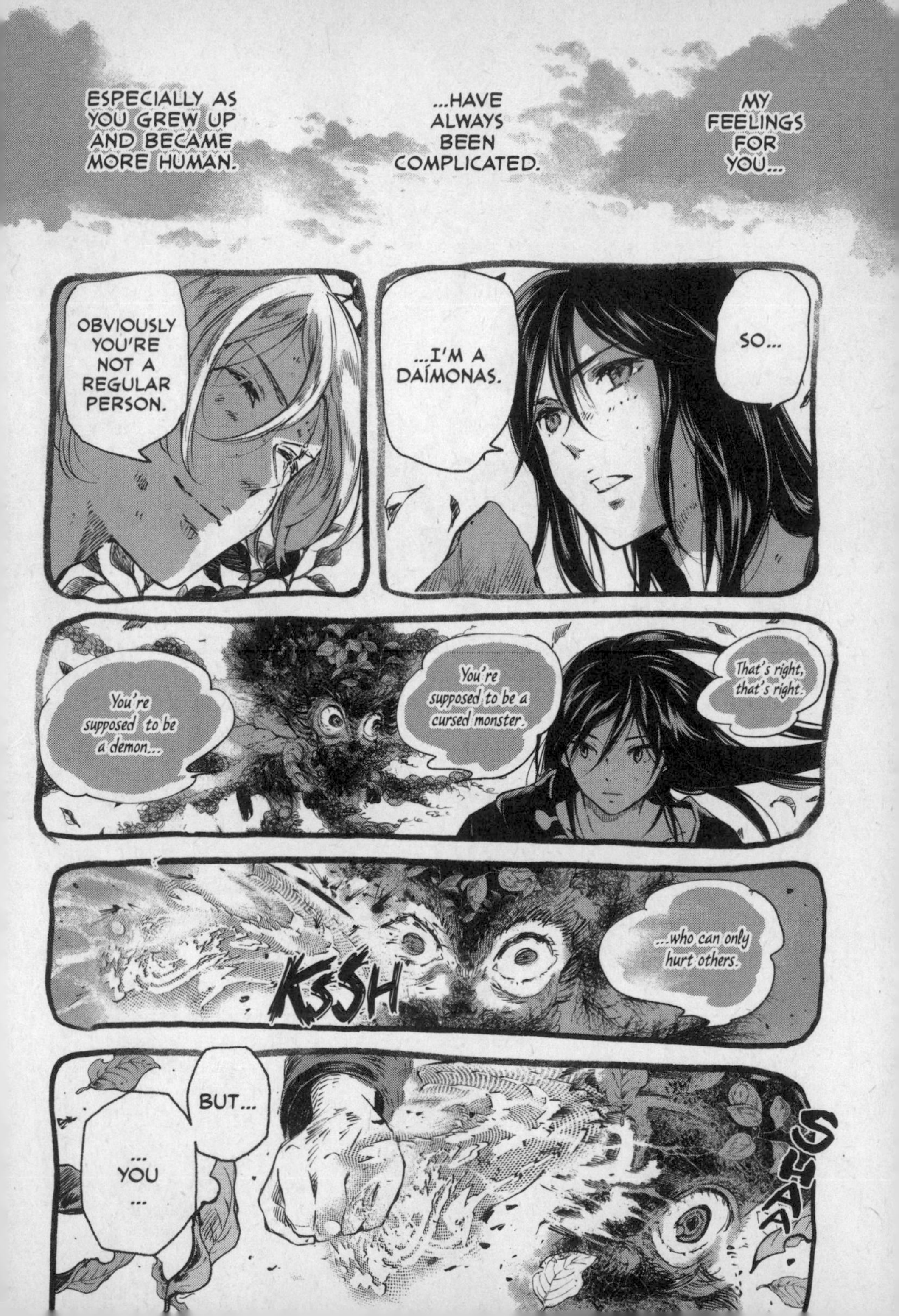
MY FEELINGS FOR YOU...
...HAVE ALWAYS BEEN COMPLICATED.
ESPECIALLY AS YOU GREW UP AND BECAME MORE HUMAN.
SO...
...I'M A DAÍMONAS.
OBVIOUSLY YOU'RE NOT A REGULAR PERSON.
That's right, that's right.
You're supposed to be a cursed monster.
You're supposed to be a demon...
...who can only hurt others.
KSSH
SHAA
BUT...
... YOU ...

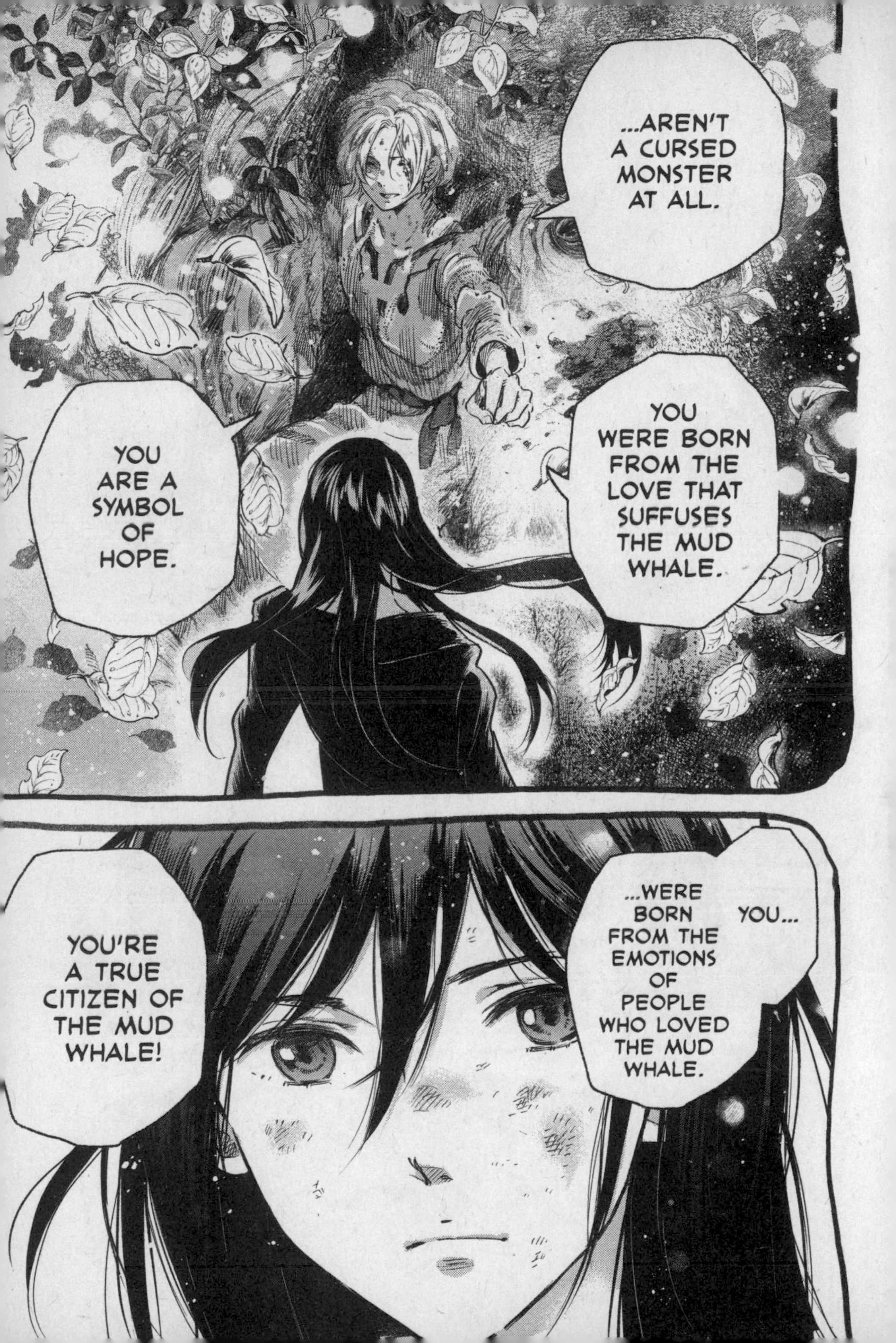
...AREN'T A CURSED MONSTER AT ALL.
YOU WERE BORN FROM THE LOVE THAT SUFFUSES THE MUD WHALE.
YOU ARE A SYMBOL OF HOPE.
YOU...
...WERE BORN FROM THE EMOTIONS OF PEOPLE WHO LOVED THE MUD WHALE.
YOU'RE A TRUE CITIZEN OF THE MUD WHALE!

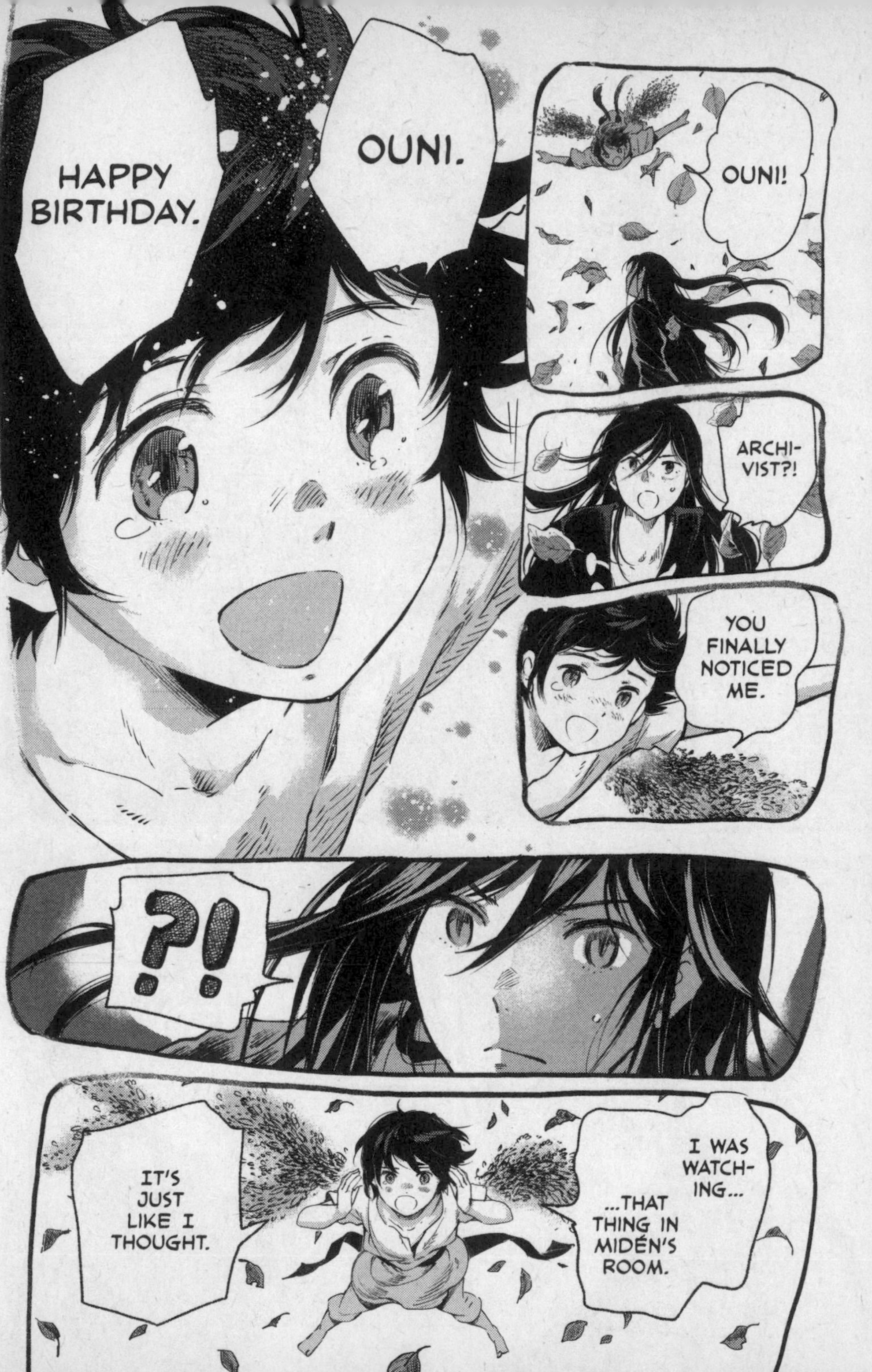
OUNI!
ARCHI-VIST?!
YOU FINALLY NOTICED ME.
OUNI.
HAPPY BIRTHDAY.
?!
I WAS WATCH-ING...
...THAT THING IN MIDÉN'S ROOM.
IT'S JUST LIKE I THOUGHT.

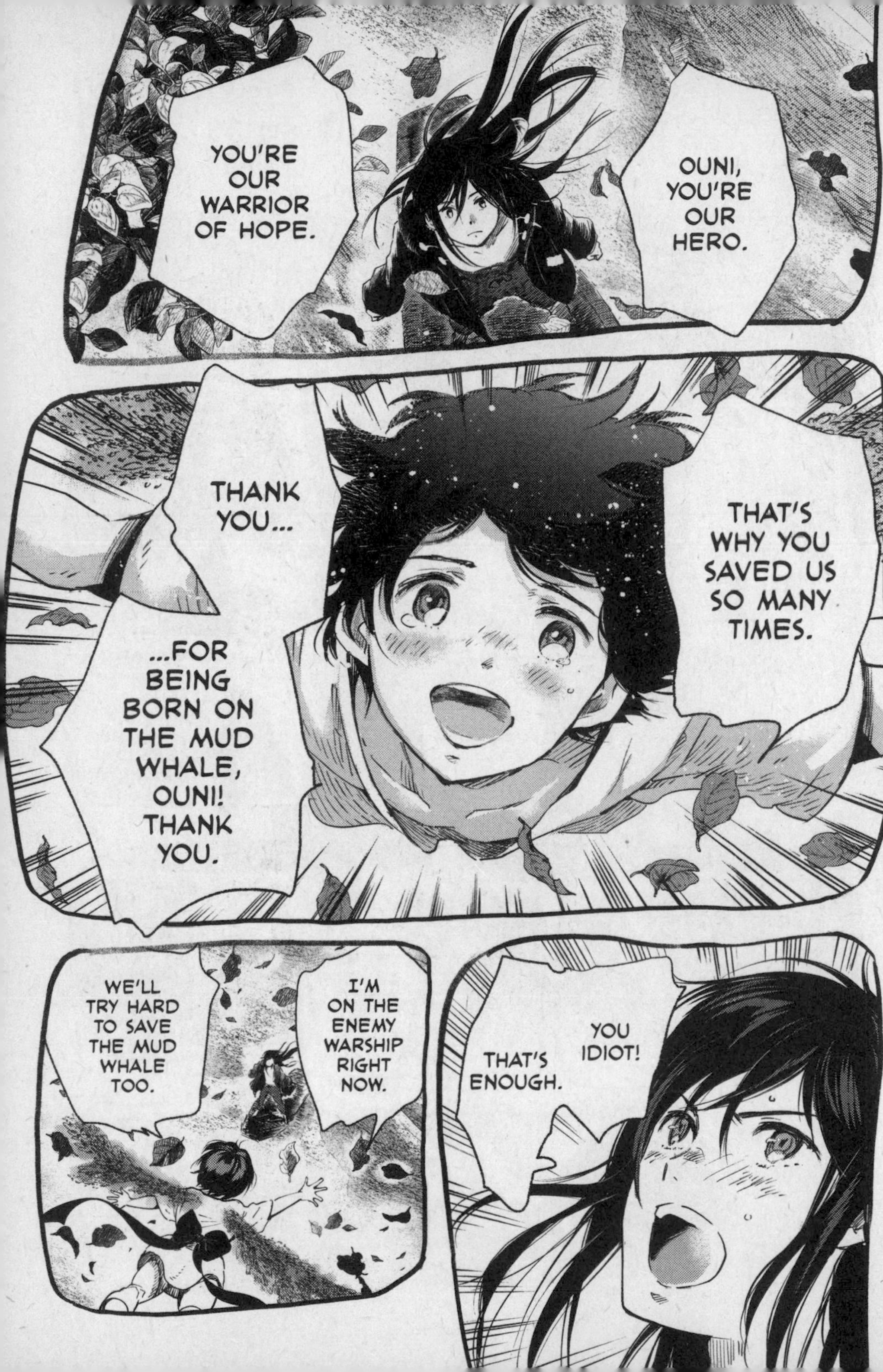
OUNI, YOU'RE OUR HERO.
YOU'RE OUR WARRIOR OF HOPE.
THAT'S WHY YOU SAVED US SO MANY TIMES.
THANK YOU...
...FOR BEING BORN ON THE MUD WHALE, OUNI! THANK YOU.
YOU IDIOT!
THAT'S ENOUGH.
I'M ON THE ENEMY WARSHIP RIGHT NOW.
WE'LL TRY HARD TO SAVE THE MUD WHALE TOO.

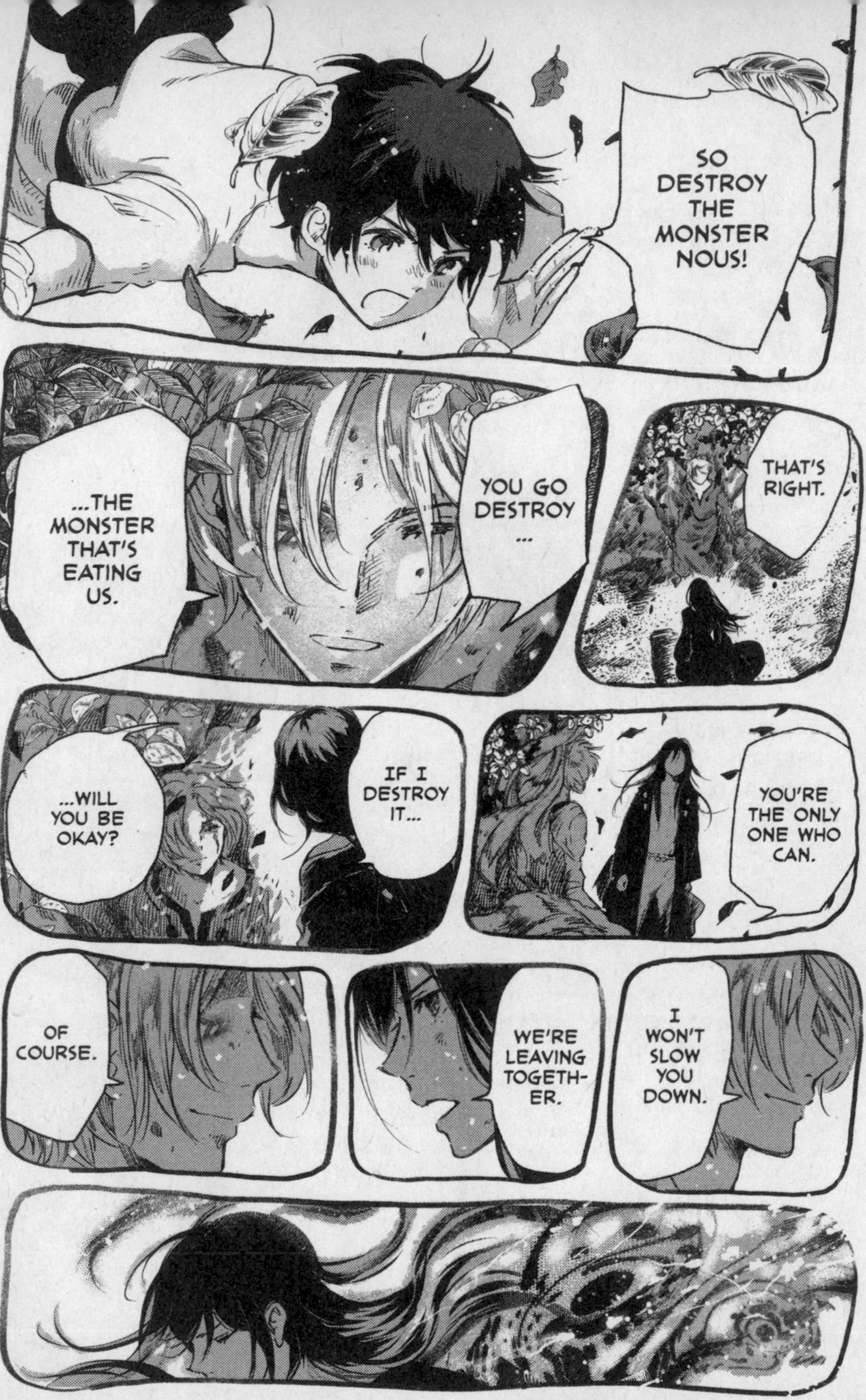
SO DESTROY THE MONSTER NOUS!
THAT'S RIGHT.
YOU GO DESTROY ...
...THE MONSTER THAT'S EATING US.
YOU'RE THE ONLY ONE WHO CAN.
IF I DESTROY IT...
...WILL YOU BE OKAY?
I WON'T SLOW YOU DOWN.
WE'RE LEAVING TOGETH-ER.
OF COURSE.

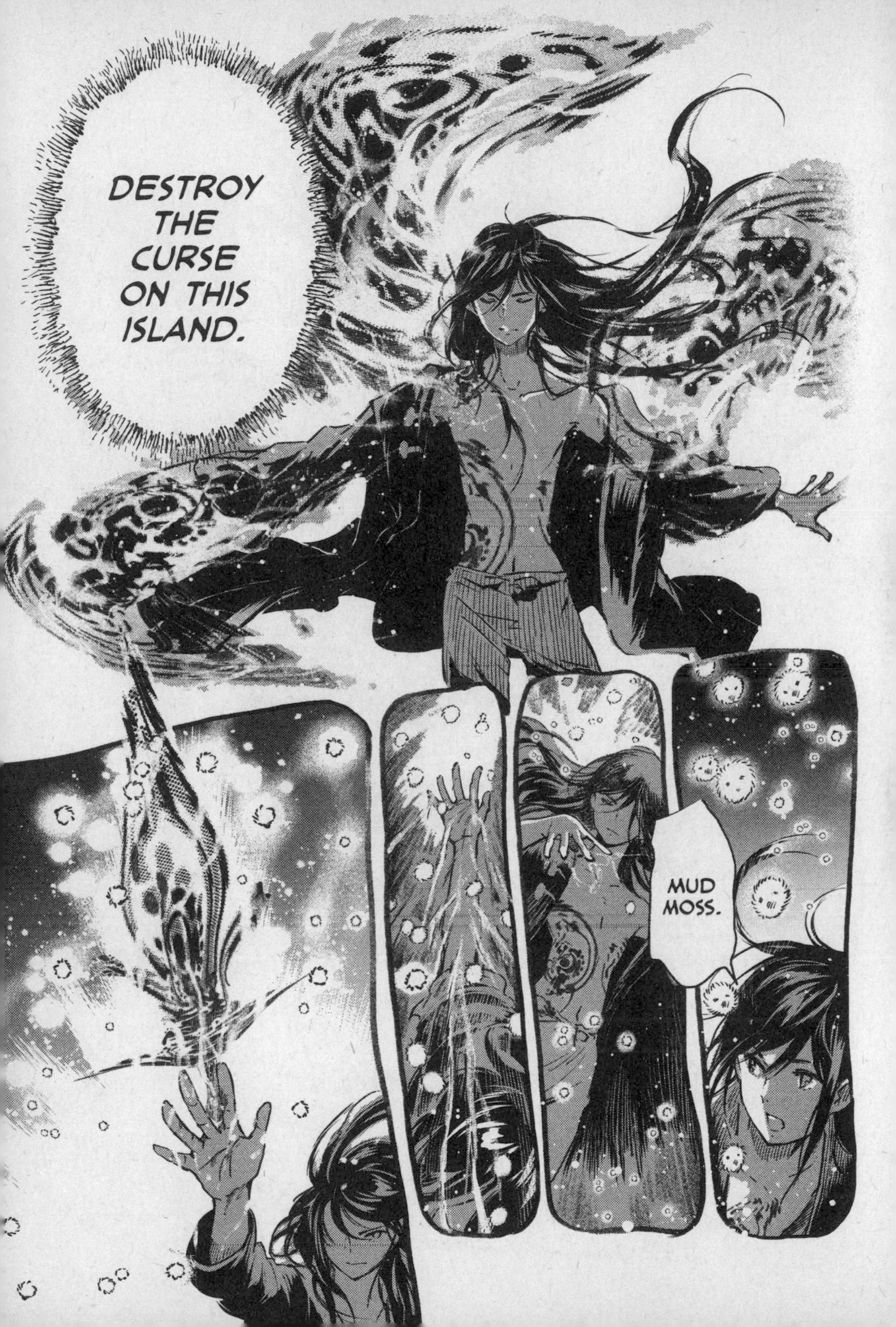
DESTROY THE CURSE ON THIS ISLAND.
MUD MOSS.

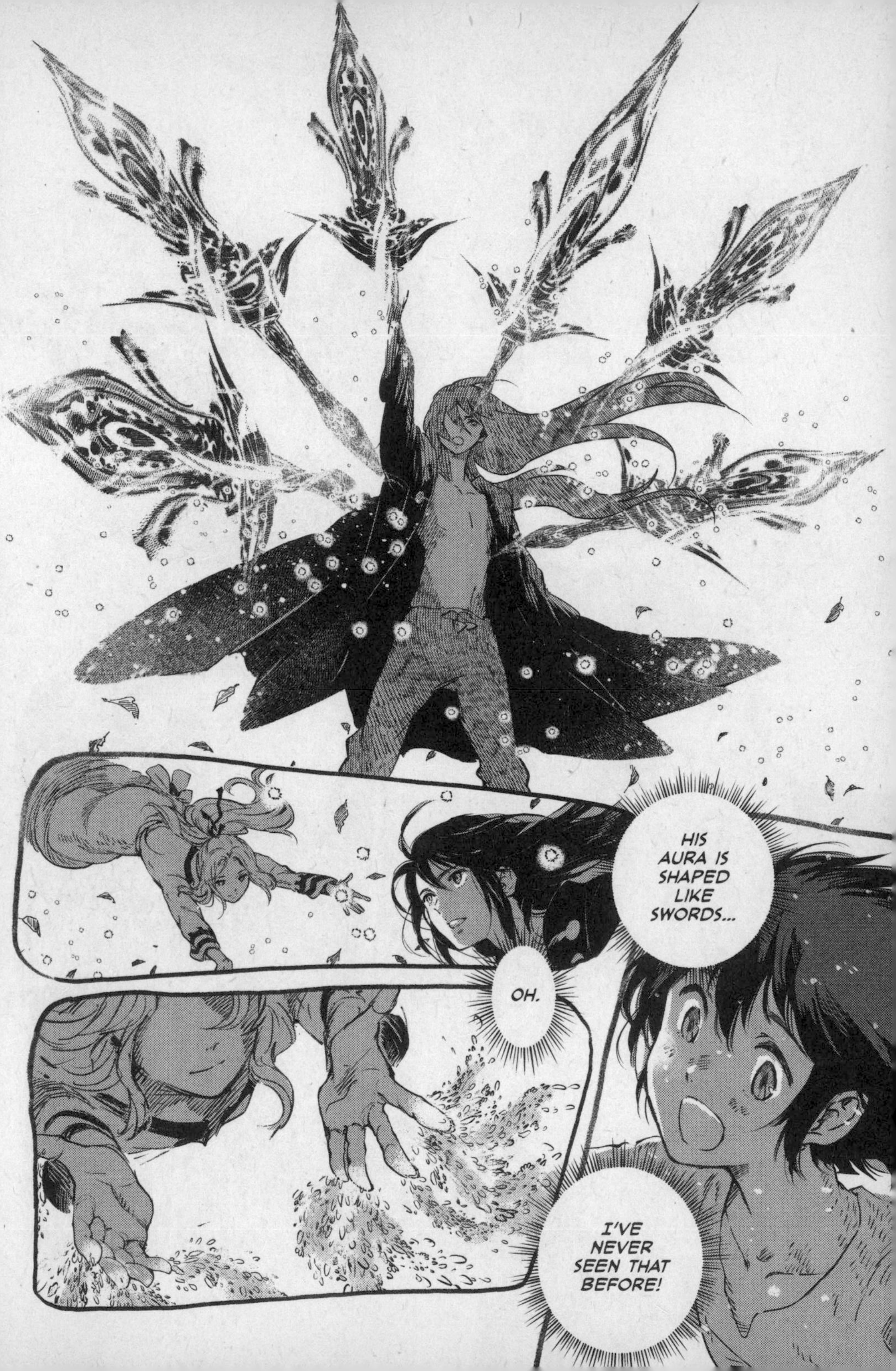
HIS AURA IS SHAPED LIKE SWORDS...
OH.
I'VE NEVER SEEN THAT BEFORE!

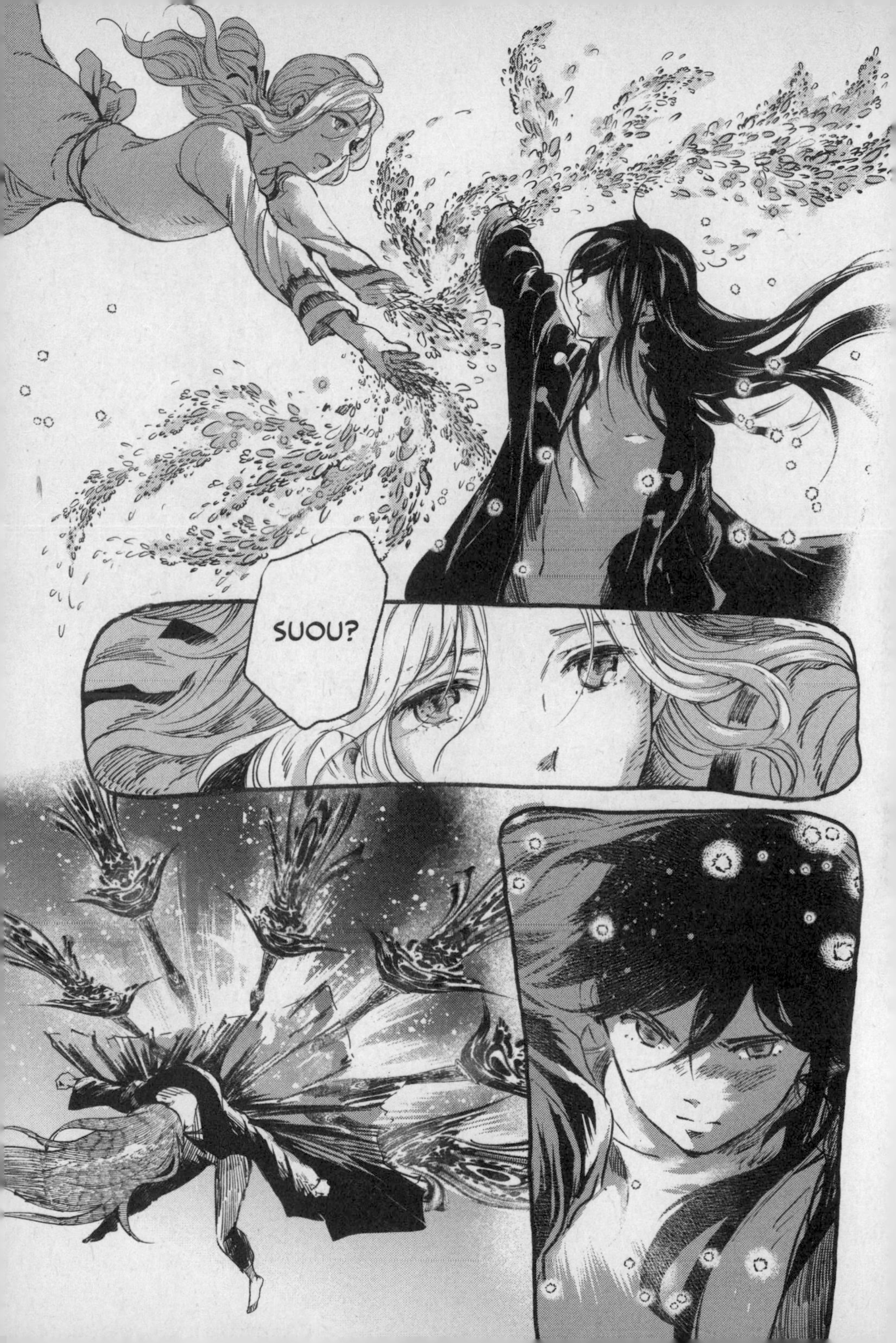
SUOU?

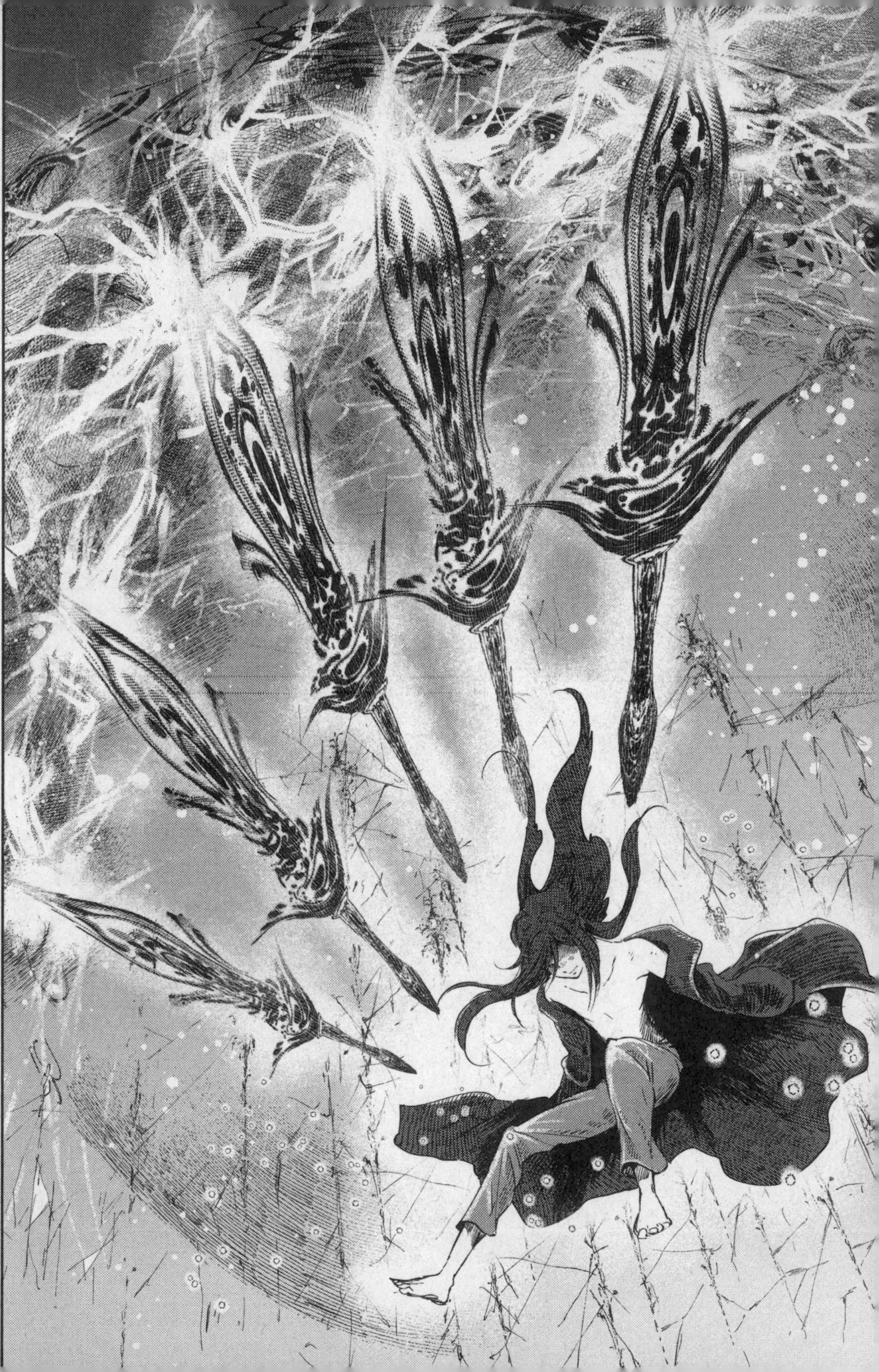

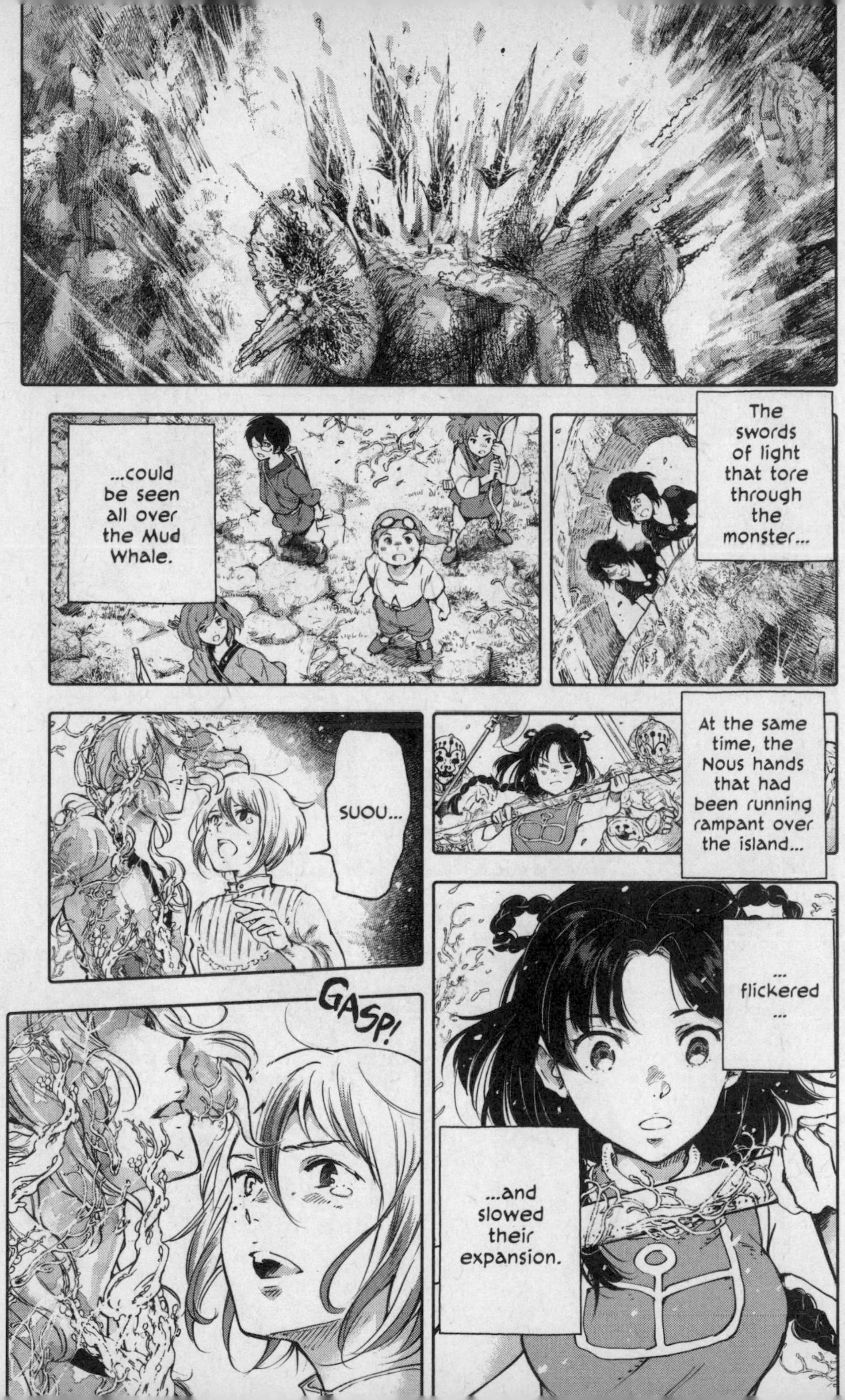
The swords of light that tore through the monster...
...could be seen all over the Mud Whale.
At the same time, the Nous hands that had been running rampant over the island...
...flickered...
...and slowed their expansion.
SUOU...
GASP!

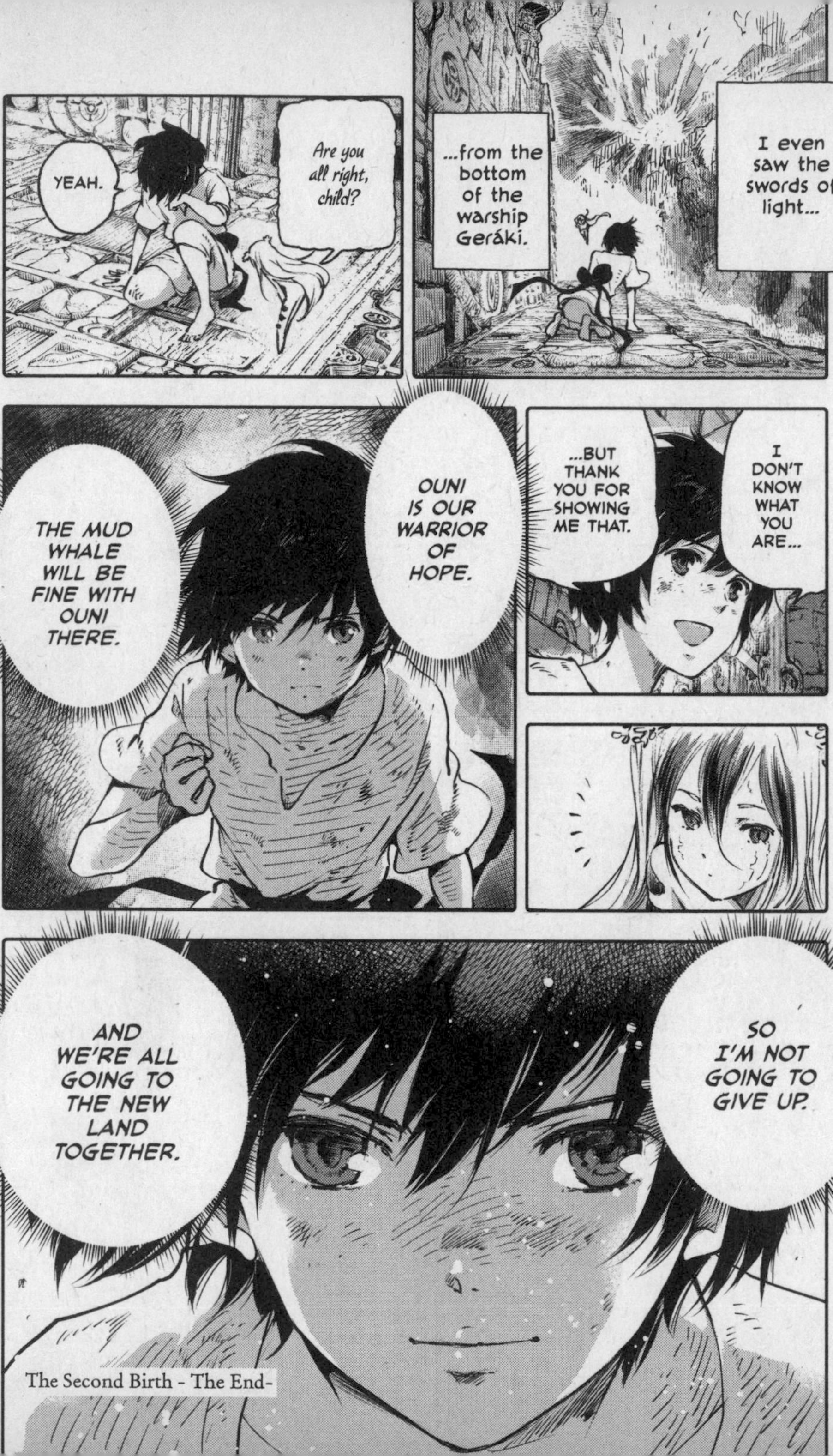
I even saw the swords of light...
...from the bottom of the warship Geráki.
Are you all right, child?
YEAH.
I DON'T KNOW WHAT YOU ARE...
...BUT THANK YOU FOR SHOWING ME THAT.
OUNI IS OUR WARRIOR OF HOPE.
THE MUD WHALE WILL BE FINE WITH OUNI THERE.
SO I'M NOT GOING TO GIVE UP.
AND WE'RE ALL GOING TO THE NEW LAND TOGETHER.
The Second Birth - The End-

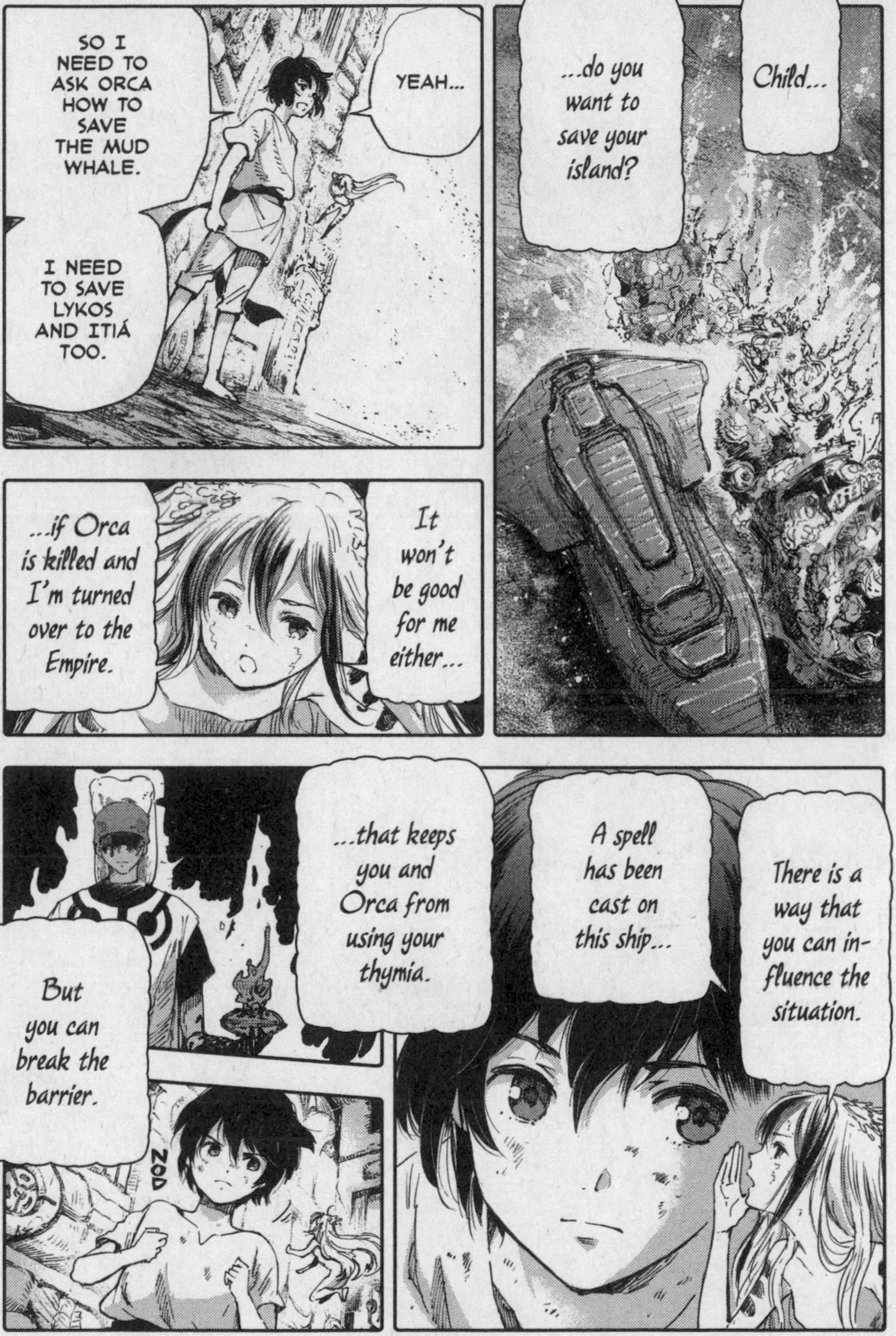
Child...
...do you want to save your island?
YEAH...
SO I NEED TO ASK ORCA HOW TO SAVE THE MUD WHALE.
I NEED TO SAVE LYKOS AND ITIÁ TOO.
It won't be good for me either...
...if Orca is killed and I'm turned over to the Empire.
There is a way that you can influence the situation.
A spell has been cast on this ship...
...that keeps you and Orca from using your thymia.
But you can break the barrier.
NOD

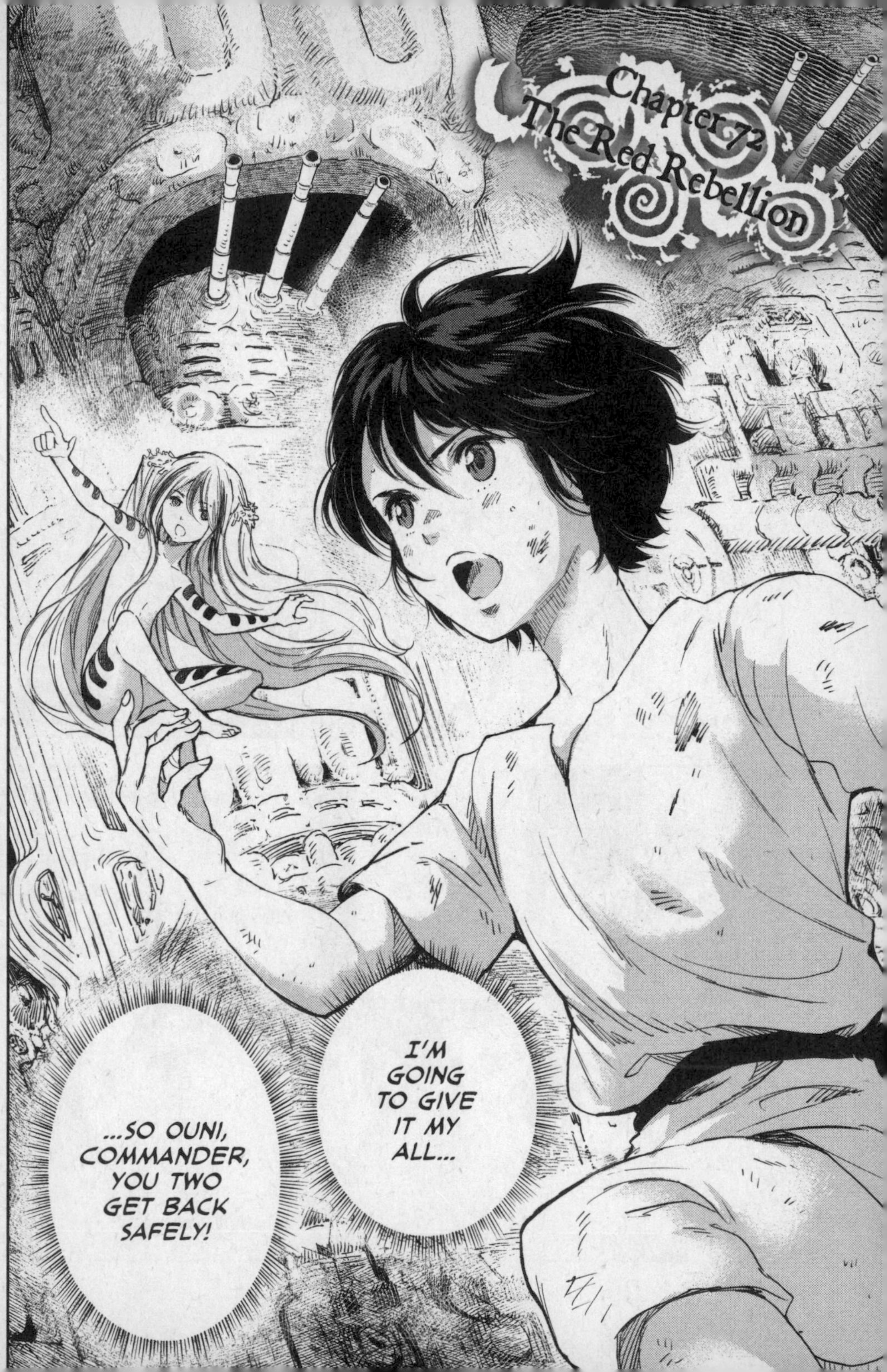
Chapter 72
The Red Rebellion
I'M GOING TO GIVE IT MY ALL...
...SO OUNI, COMMANDER, YOU TWO GET BACK SAFELY!

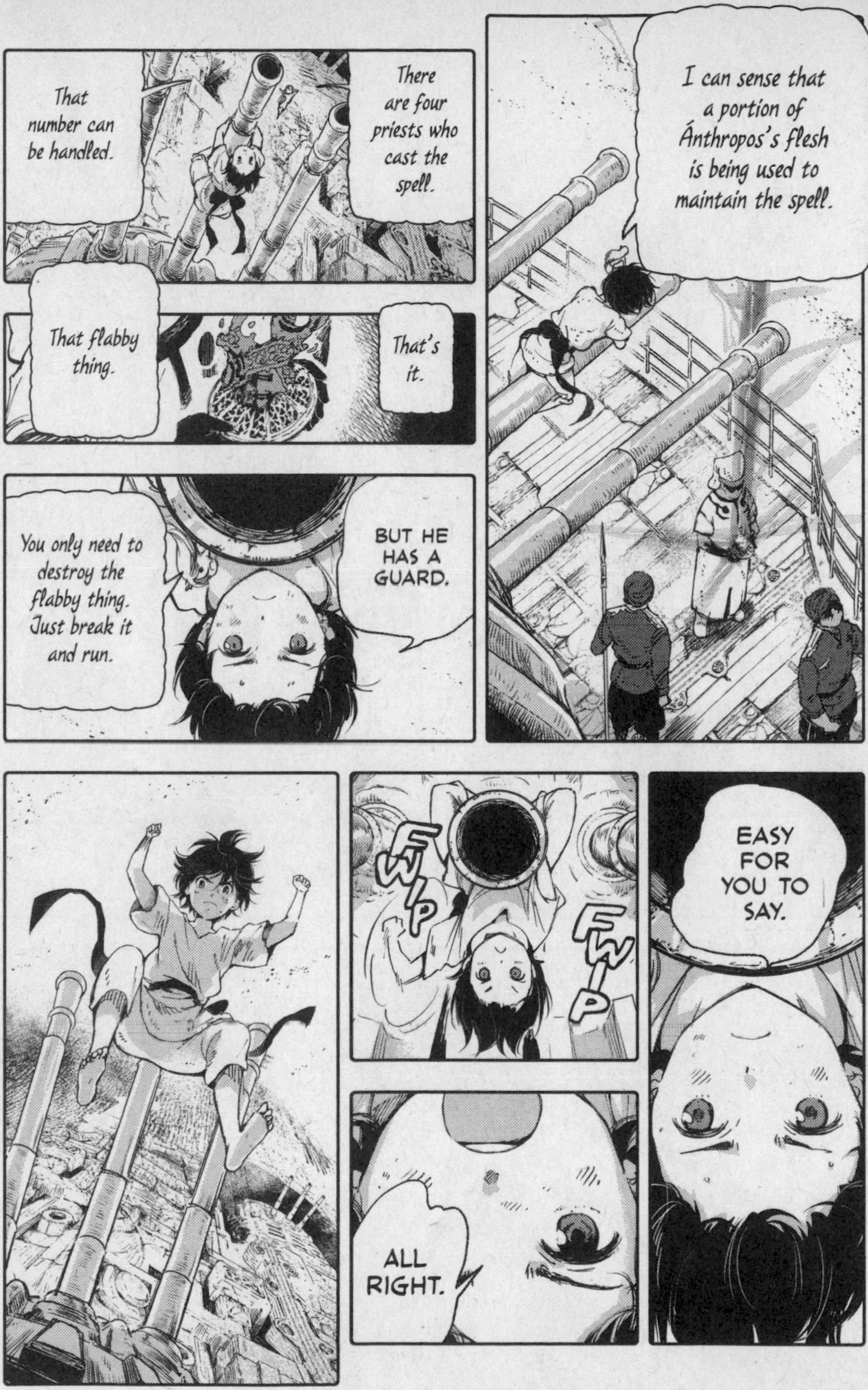
I can sense that a portion of Ánthropos's flesh is being used to maintain the spell.
There are four priests who cast the spell.
That number can be handled.
That's it.
That flabby thing.
BUT HE HAS A GUARD.
You only need to destroy the flabby thing. Just break it and run.
EASY FOR YOU TO SAY.
FWIP
FWIP
ALL RIGHT.

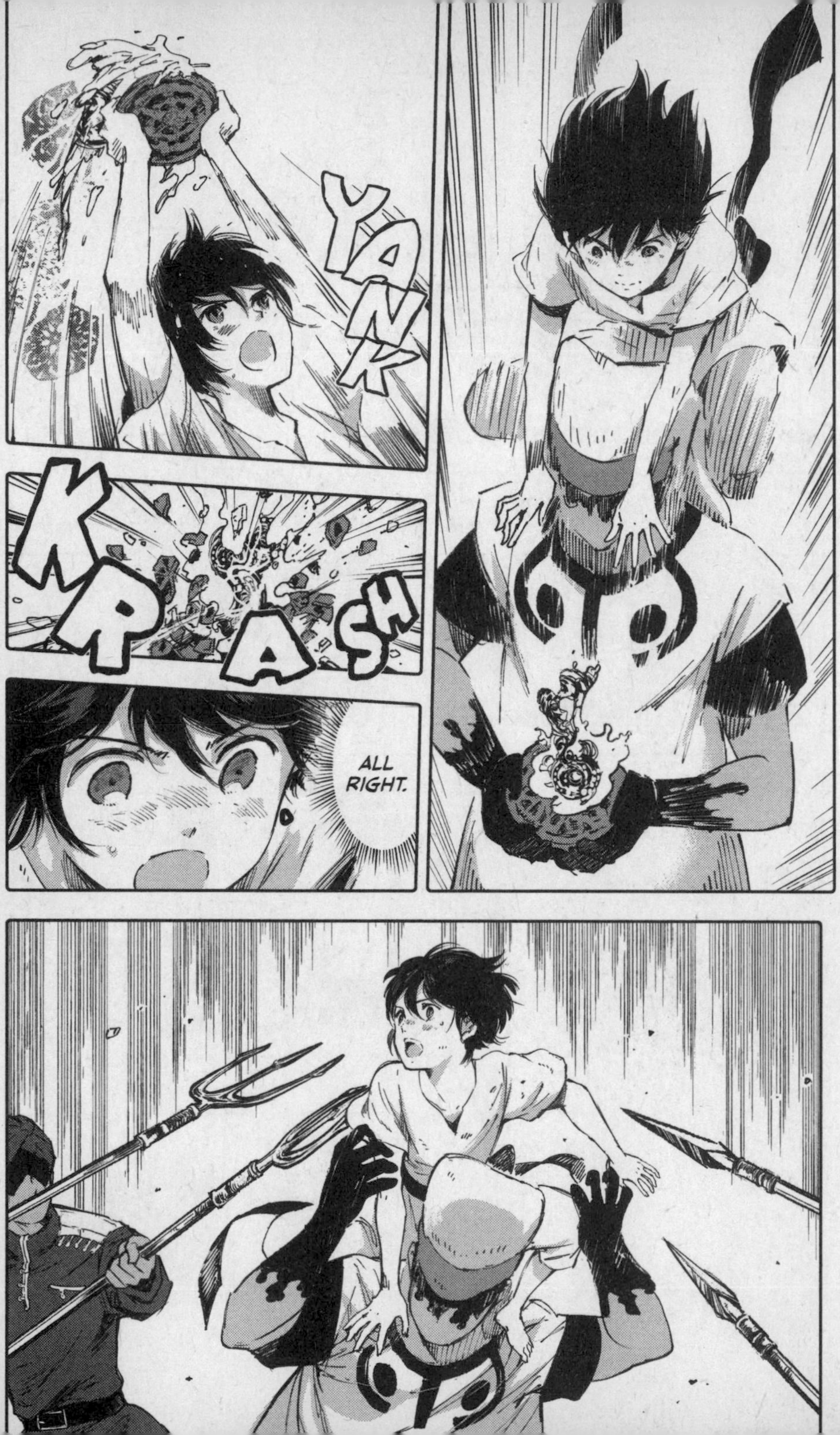
YANK
KRASH
ALL RIGHT.

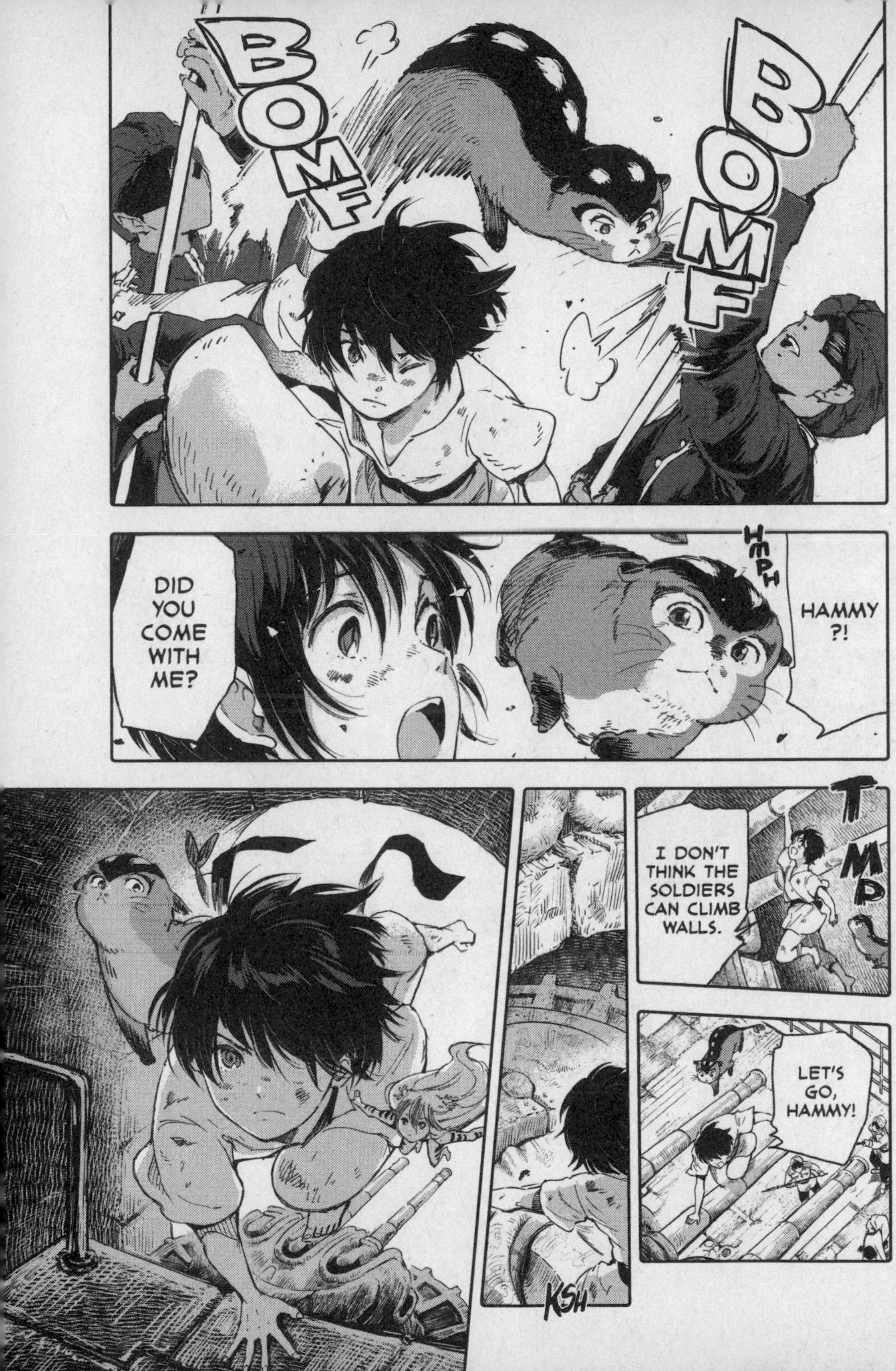
BOMF
BOMF
HMPH
HAMMY ?!
DID YOU COME WITH ME?
TMP
I DON'T THINK THE SOLDIERS CAN CLIMB WALLS.
LET'S GO, HAMMY!
KSH

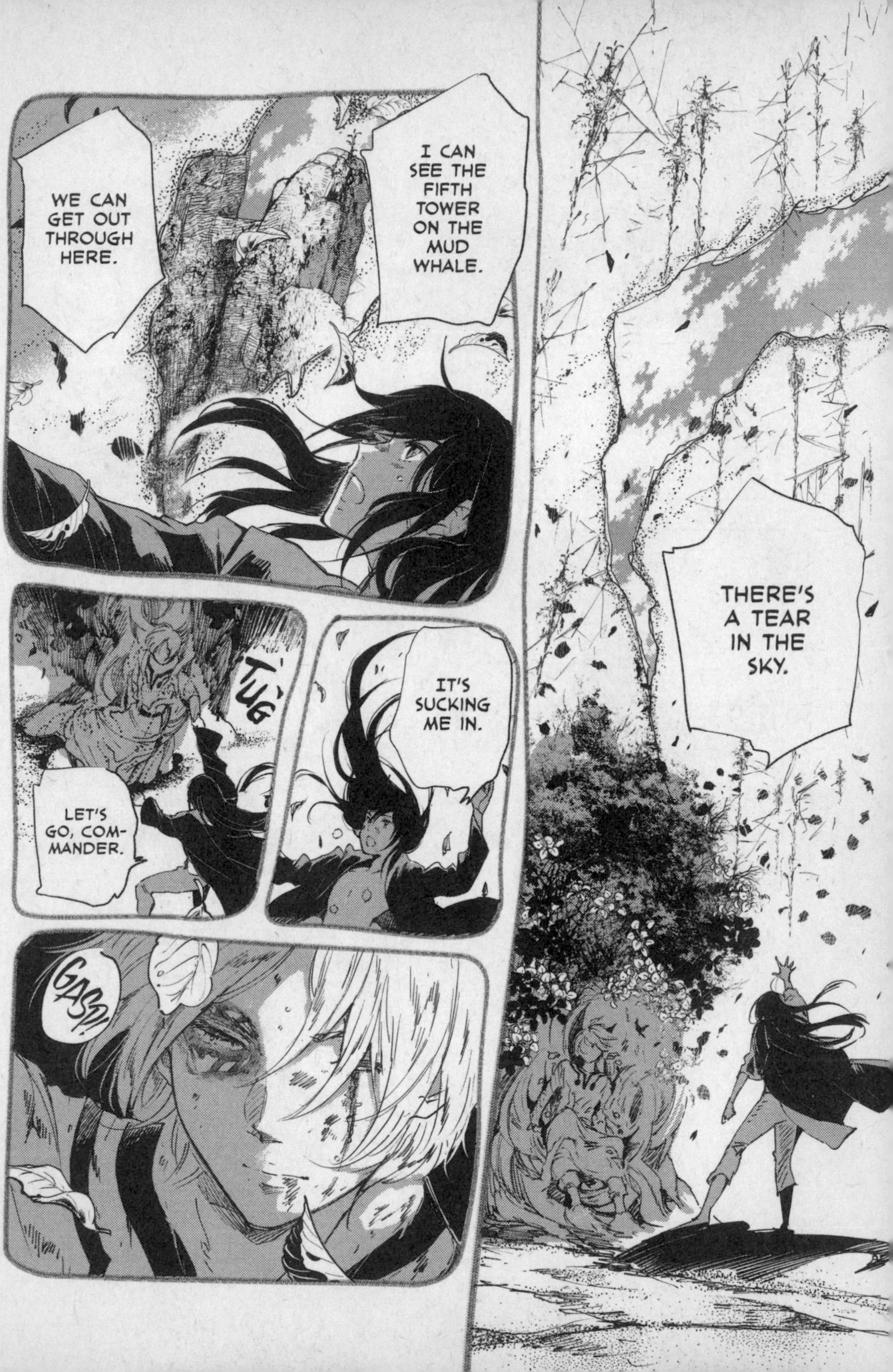
THERE'S A TEAR IN THE SKY.
I CAN SEE THE FIFTH TOWER ON THE MUD WHALE.
WE CAN GET OUT THROUGH HERE.
IT'S SUCKING ME IN.
TUG
LET'S GO, COM-MANDER.
GASP!!

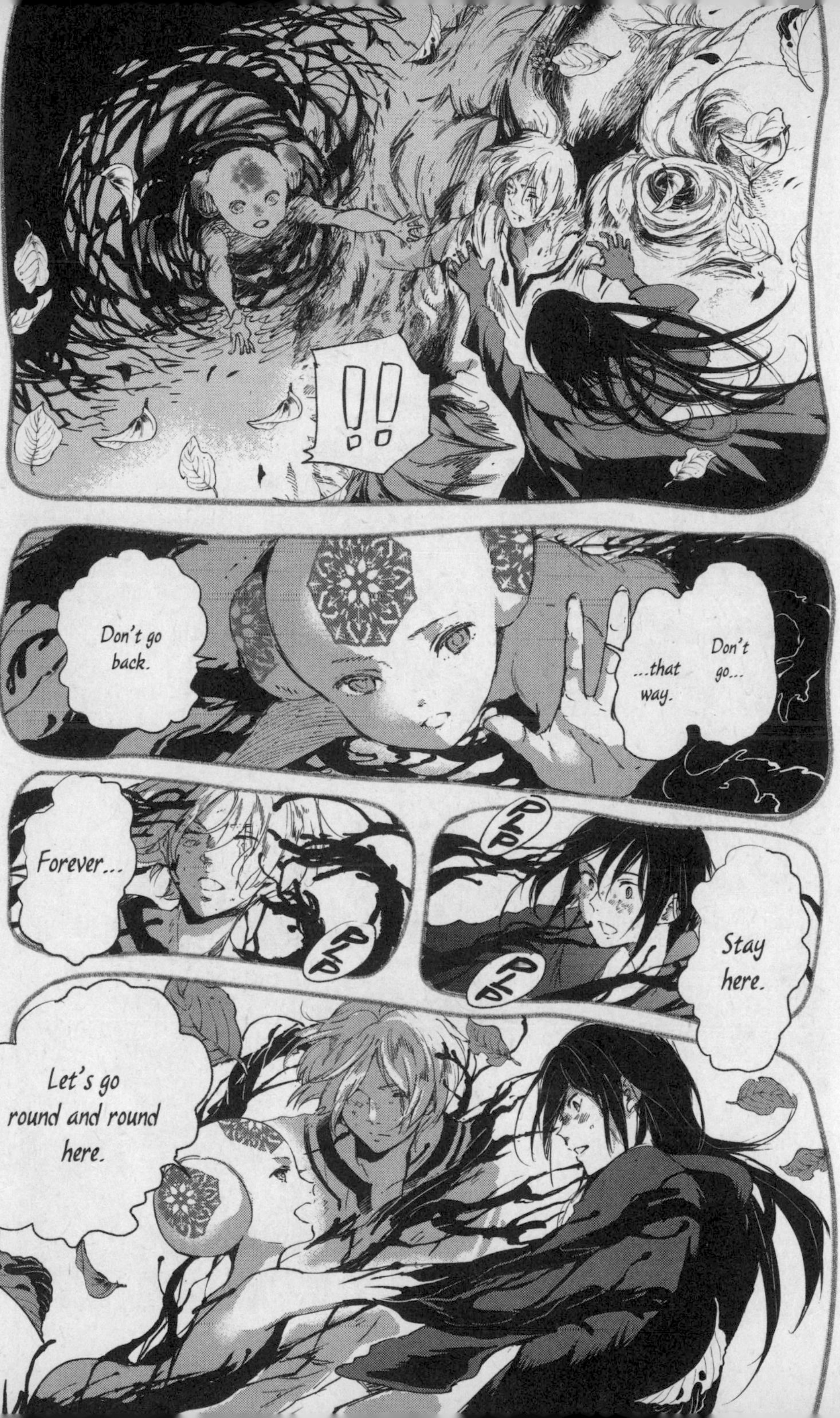
!!
Don't go... ...that way.
Don't go back.
PLIP
PLIP
Stay here.
Forever...
PLIP
Let's go round and round here.

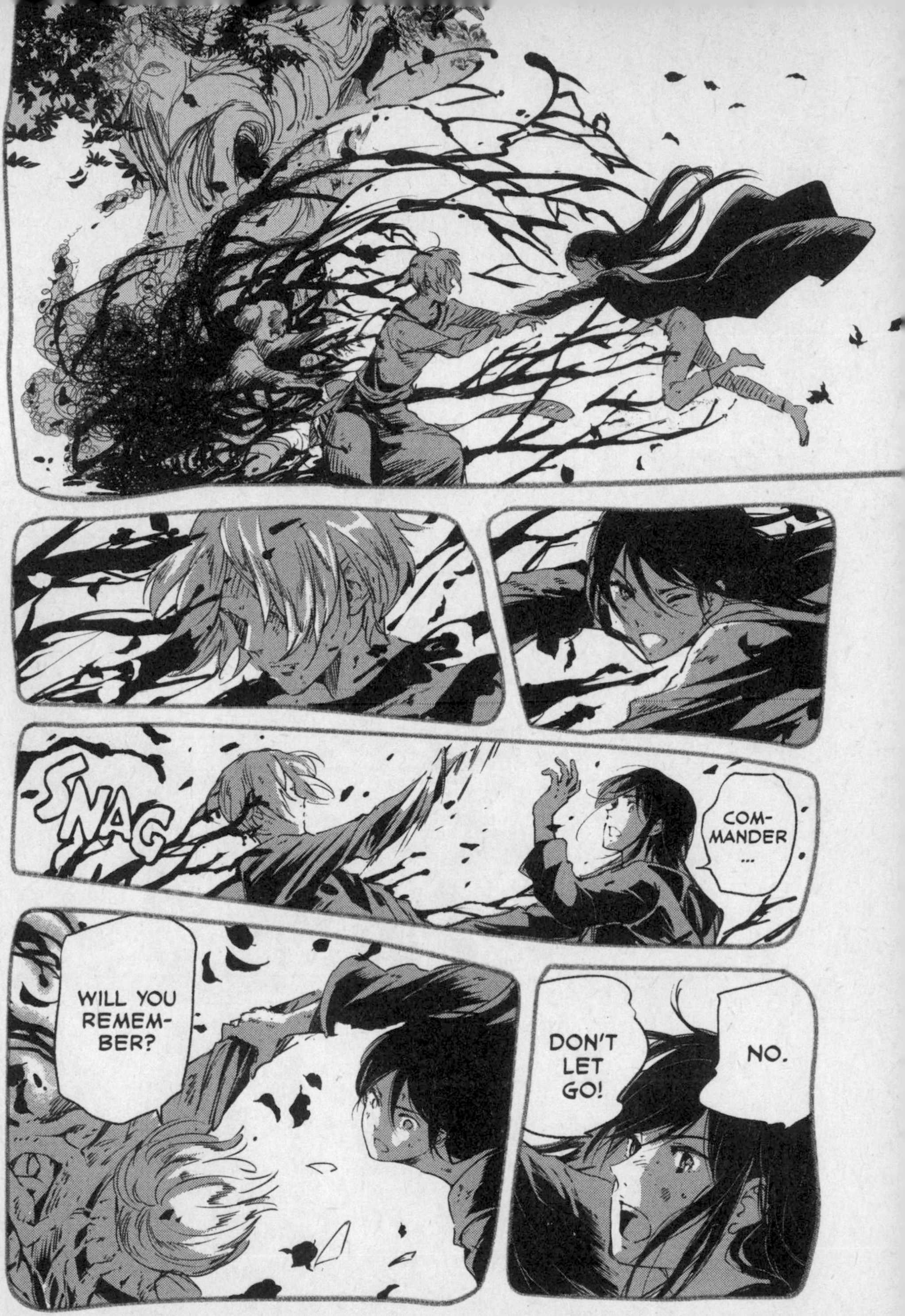
COM-MANDER ...
SNAG
NO.
DON'T LET GO!
WILL YOU REMEM-BER?

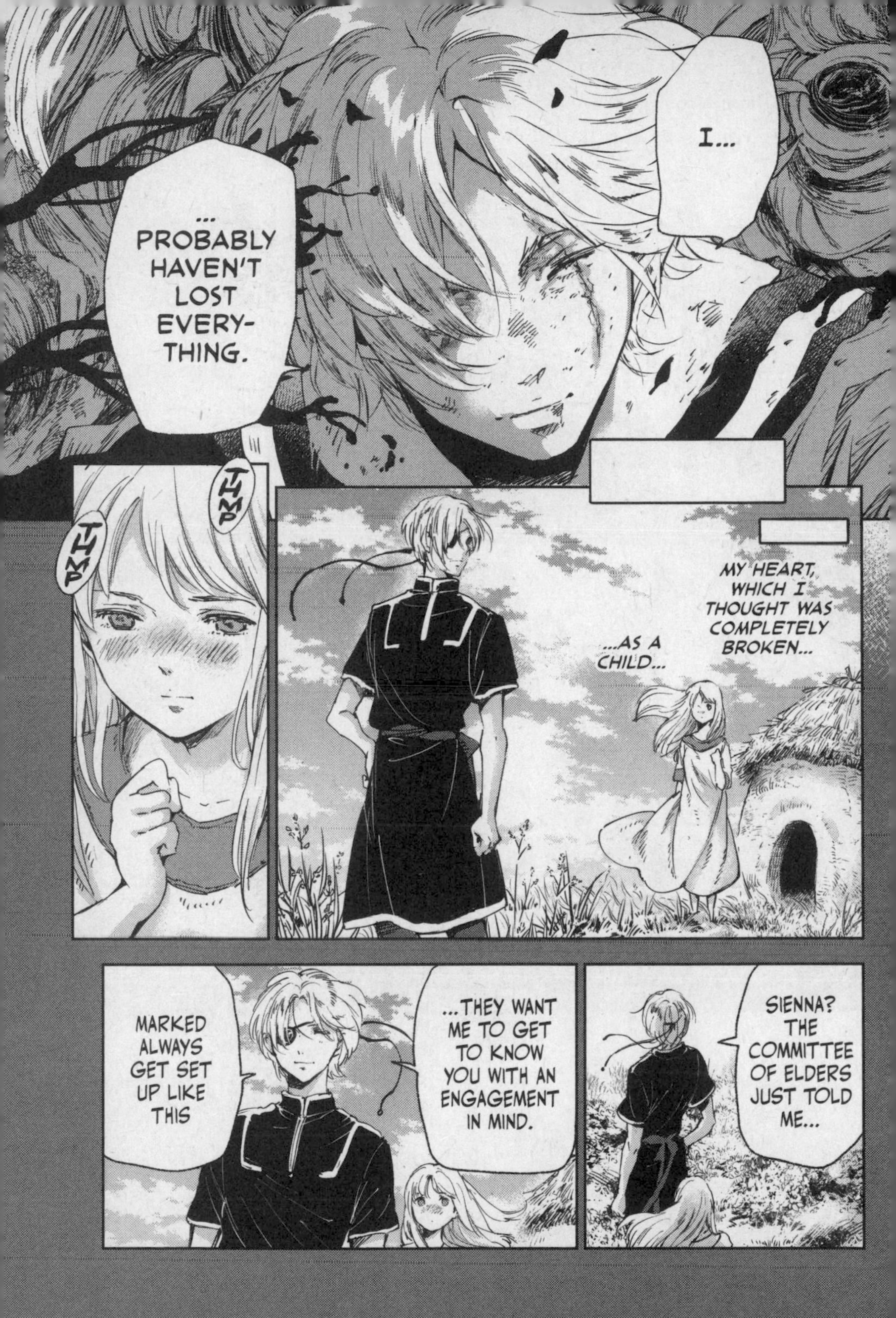
I...
...PROBABLY HAVEN'T LOST EVERY-THING.
MY HEART, WHICH I THOUGHT WAS COMPLETELY BROKEN...
...AS A CHILD...
THMP
THMP
SIENNA? THE COMMITTEE OF ELDERS JUST TOLD ME...
...THEY WANT ME TO GET TO KNOW YOU WITH AN ENGAGEMENT IN MIND.
MARKED ALWAYS GET SET UP LIKE THIS

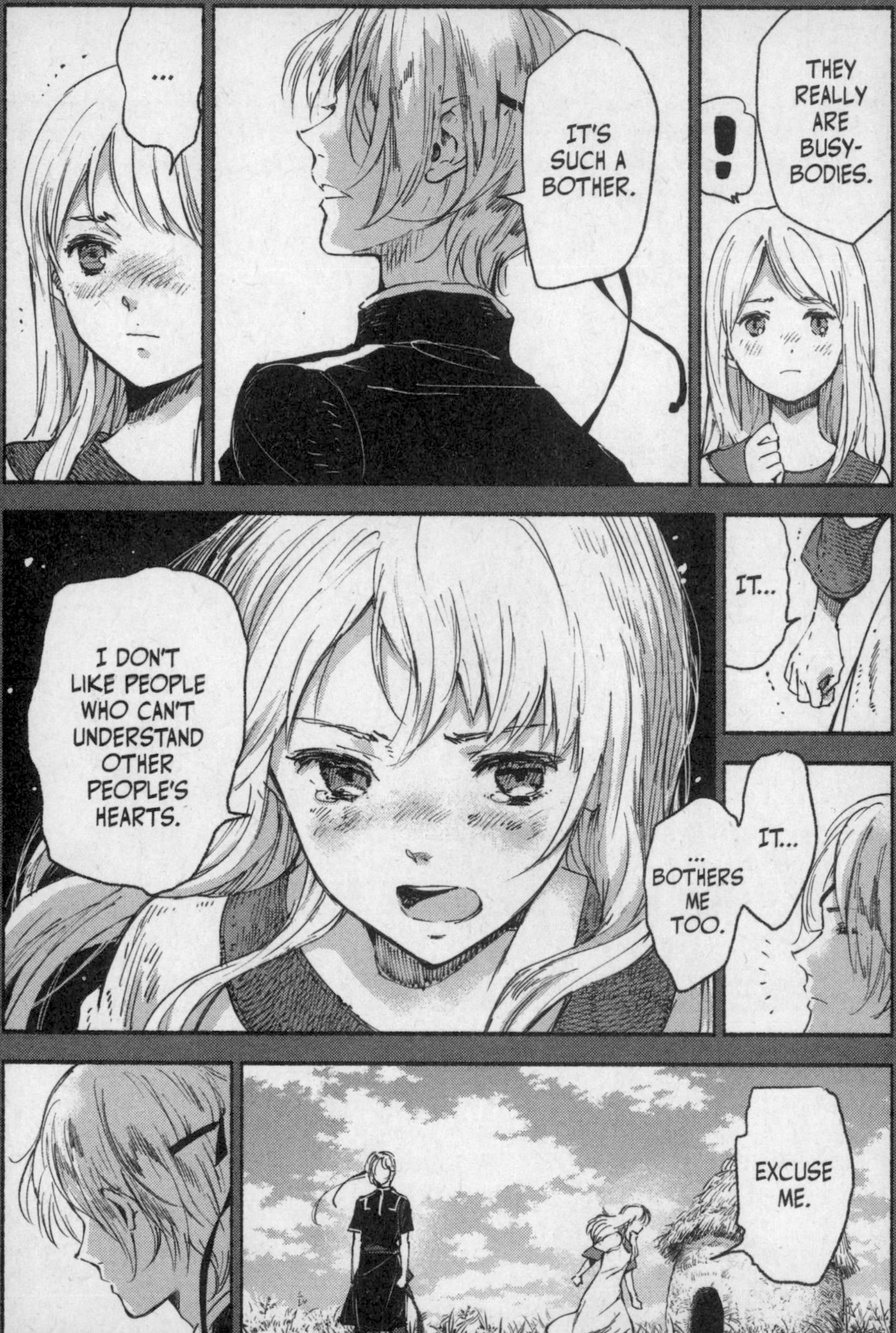
THEY REALLY ARE BUSY-BODIES.
!
IT'S SUCH A BOTHER.
...
IT...
IT...
... BOTHERS ME TOO.
I DON'T LIKE PEOPLE WHO CAN'T UNDERSTAND OTHER PEOPLE'S HEARTS.
EXCUSE ME.

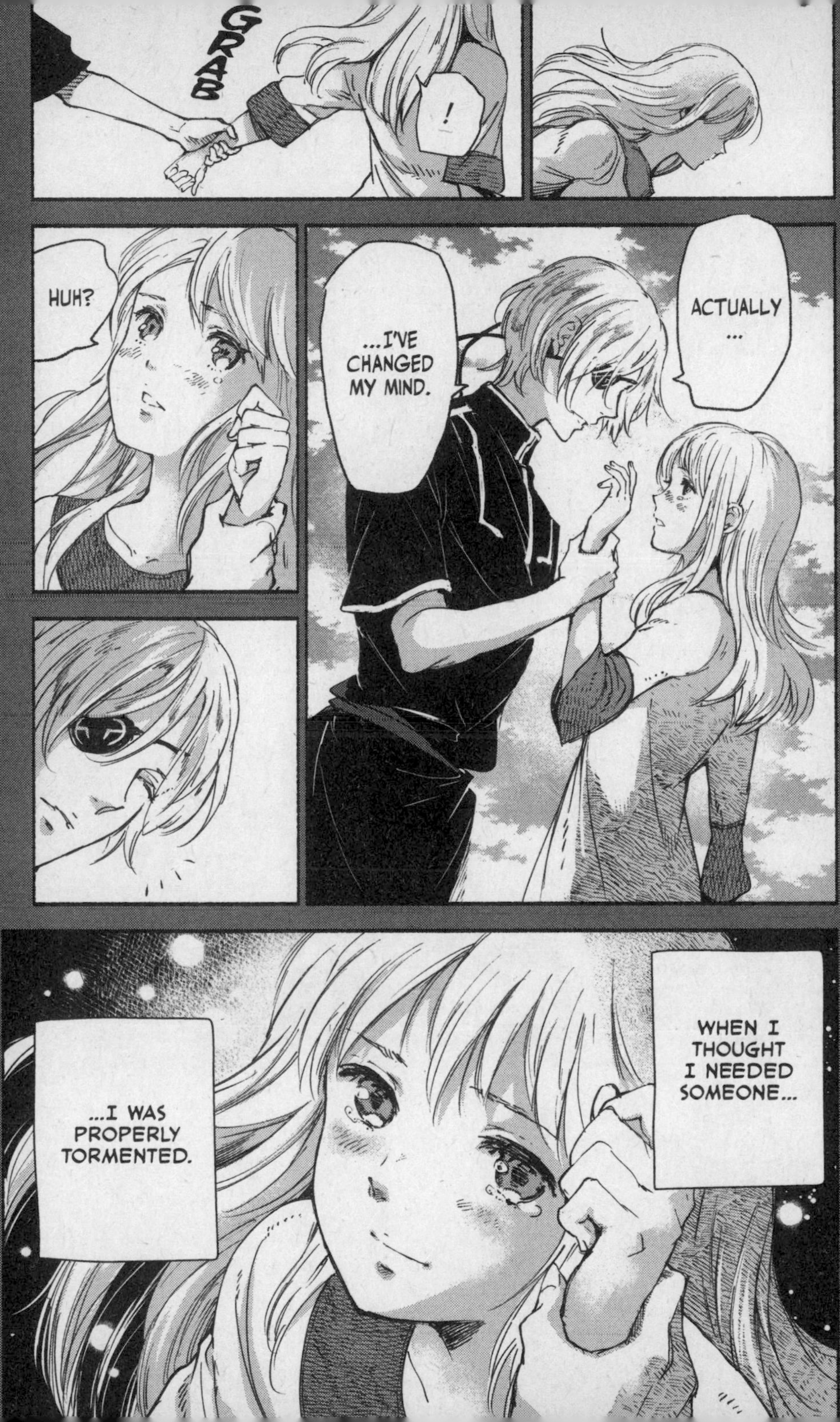
GRAB
!
ACTUALLY ...
...I'VE CHANGED MY MIND.
HUH?
WHEN I THOUGHT I NEEDED SOMEONE...
...I WAS PROPERLY TORMENTED.

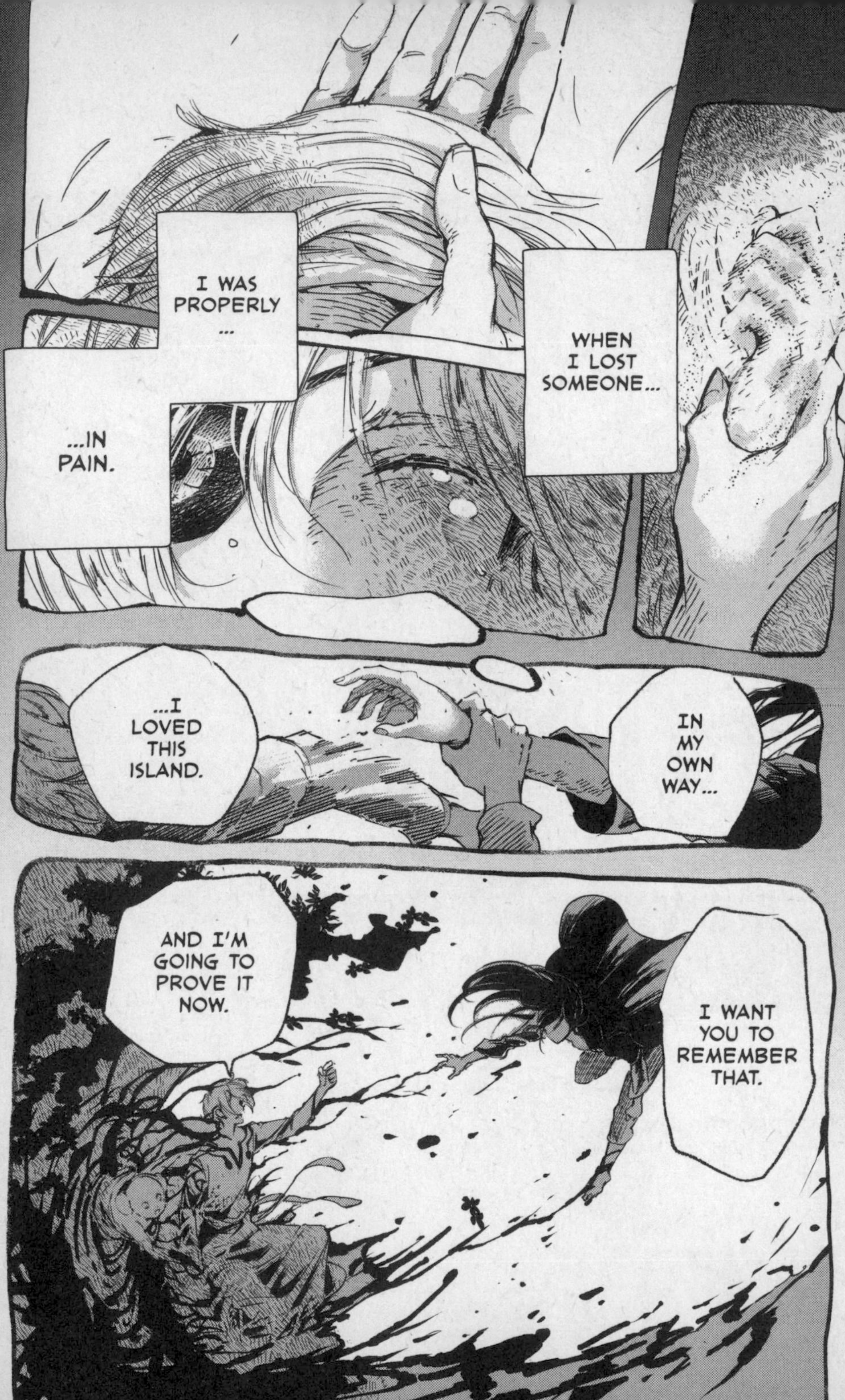
WHEN I LOST SOMEONE...
I WAS PROPERLY ...
...IN PAIN.
IN MY OWN WAY...
...I LOVED THIS ISLAND.
I WANT YOU TO REMEMBER THAT.
AND I'M GOING TO PROVE IT NOW.

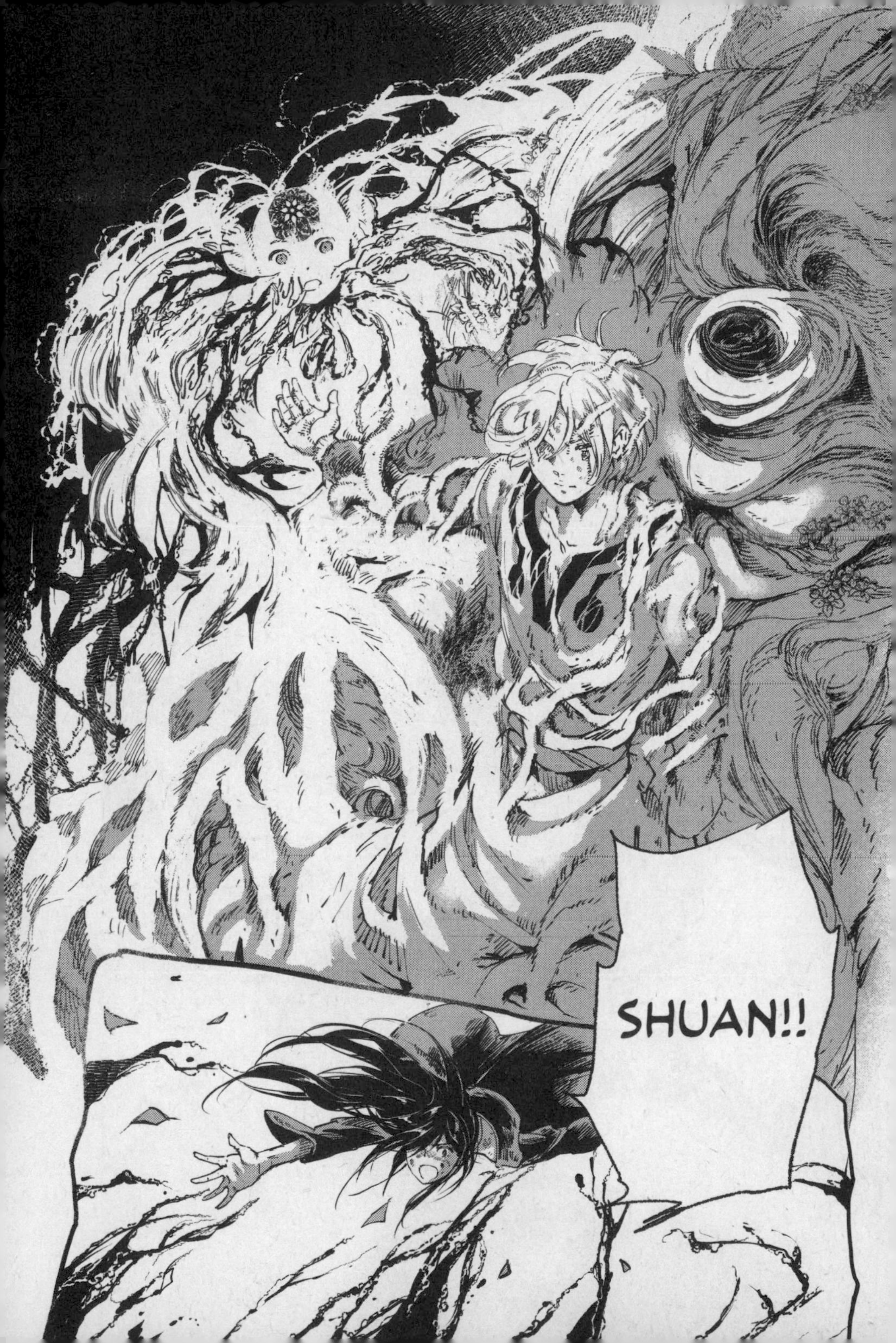
SHUAN!!

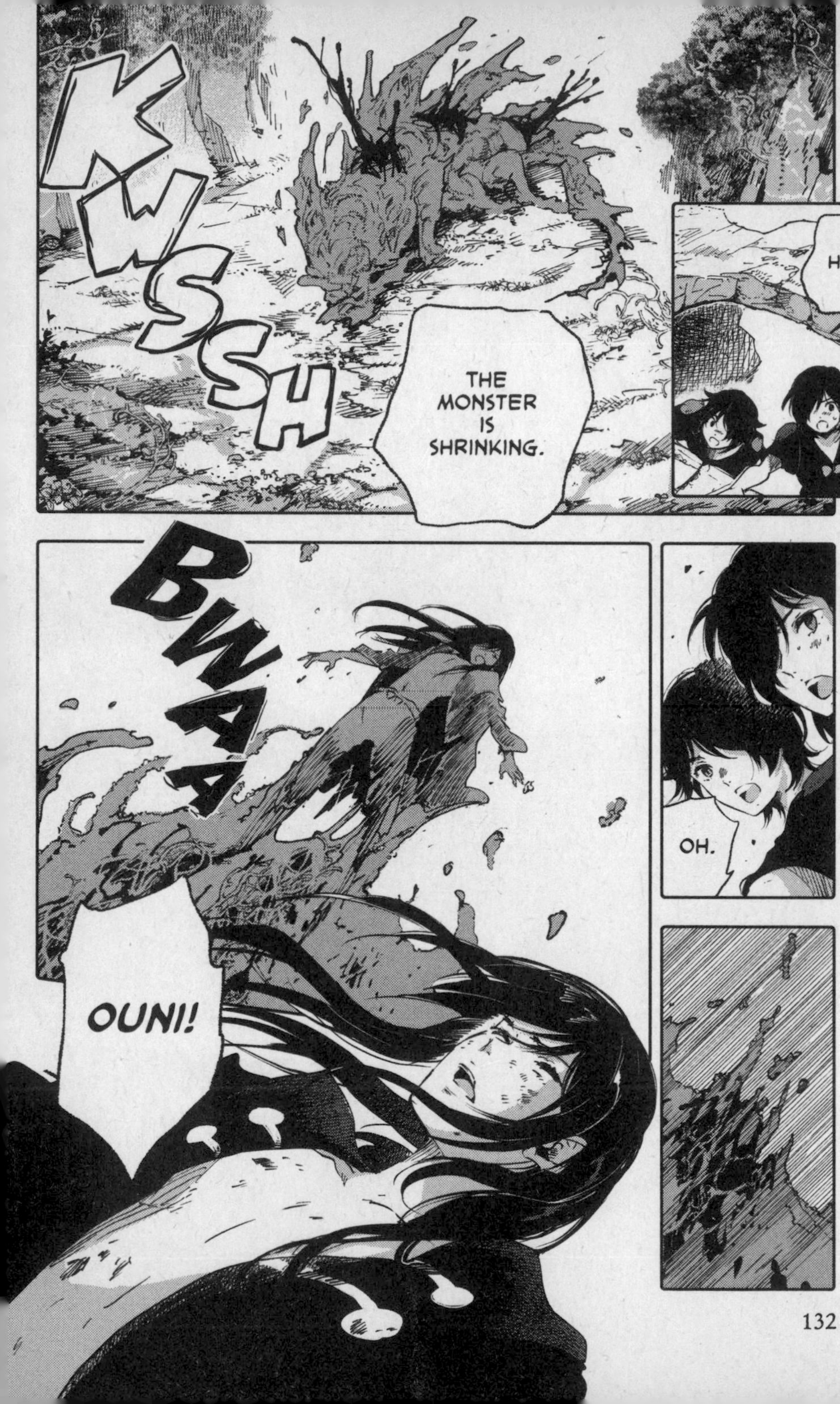
HEY.
KWSSH
THE MONSTER IS SHRINKING.
OH.
BWAAA
OUNI!

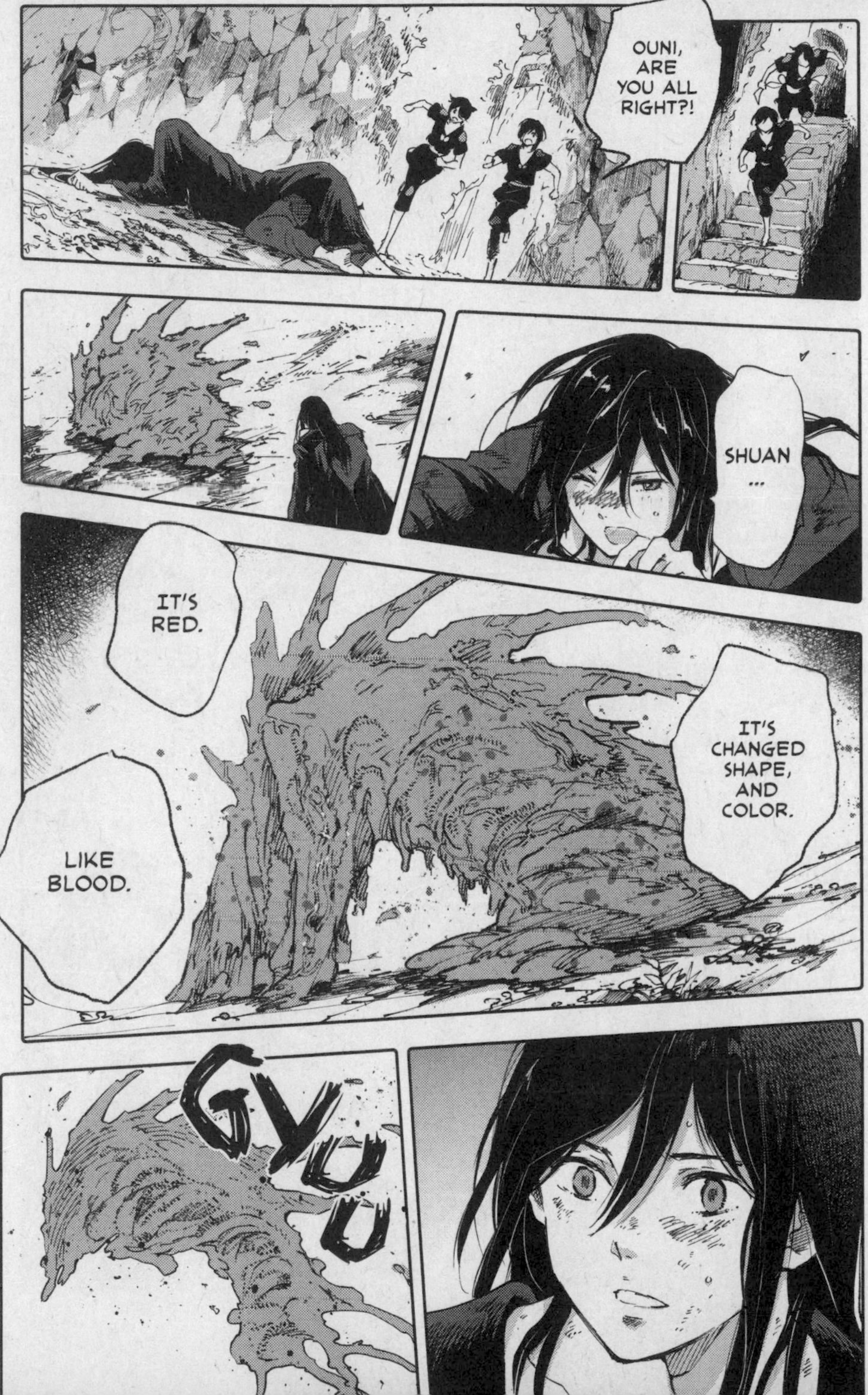
OUNI, ARE YOU ALL RIGHT?!
SHUAN ...
IT'S CHANGED SHAPE, AND COLOR.
IT'S RED.
LIKE BLOOD.
GYU U

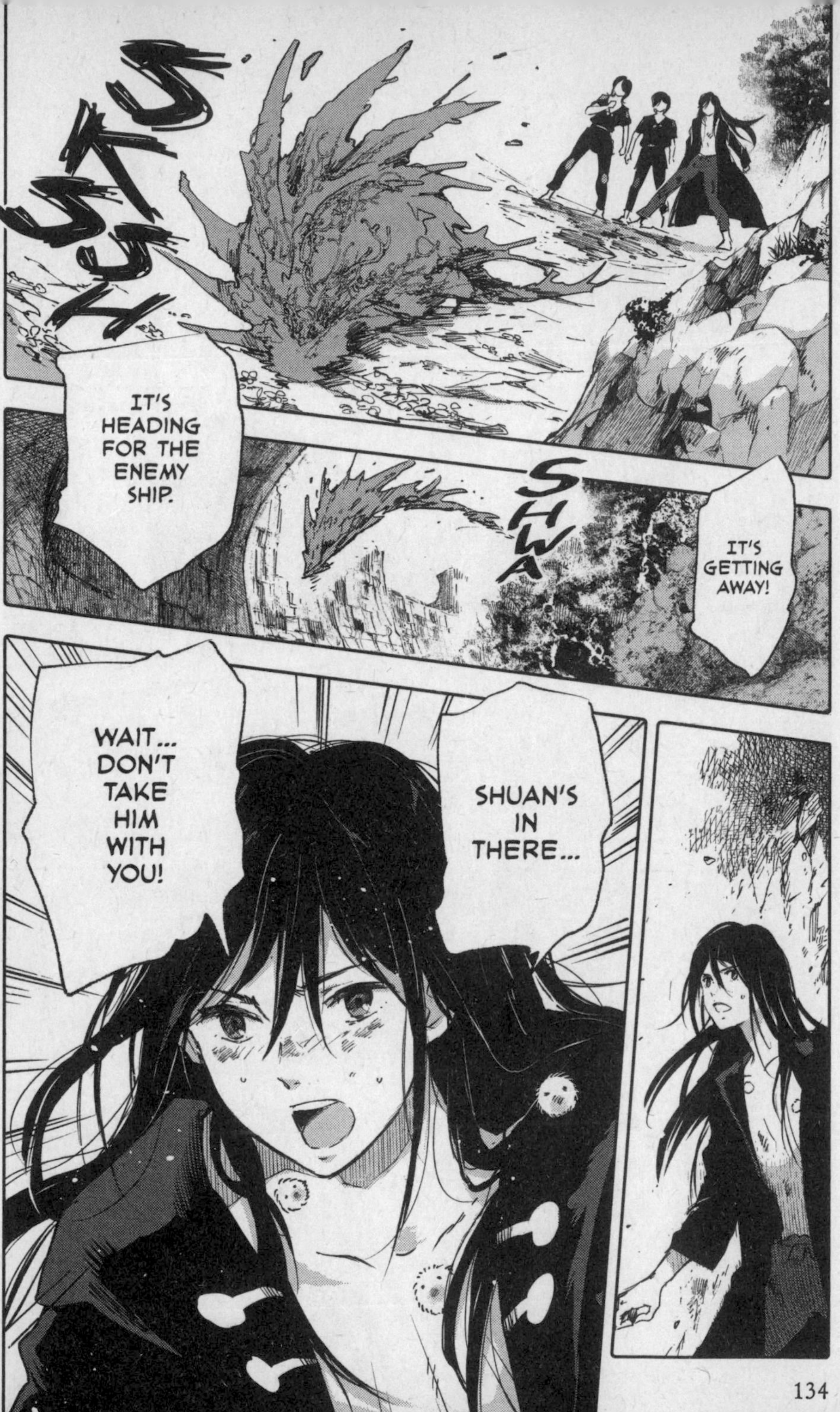
IT'S GETTING AWAY!
SHWA
IT'S HEADING FOR THE ENEMY SHIP.
SHUAN'S IN THERE...
WAIT... DON'T TAKE HIM WITH YOU!

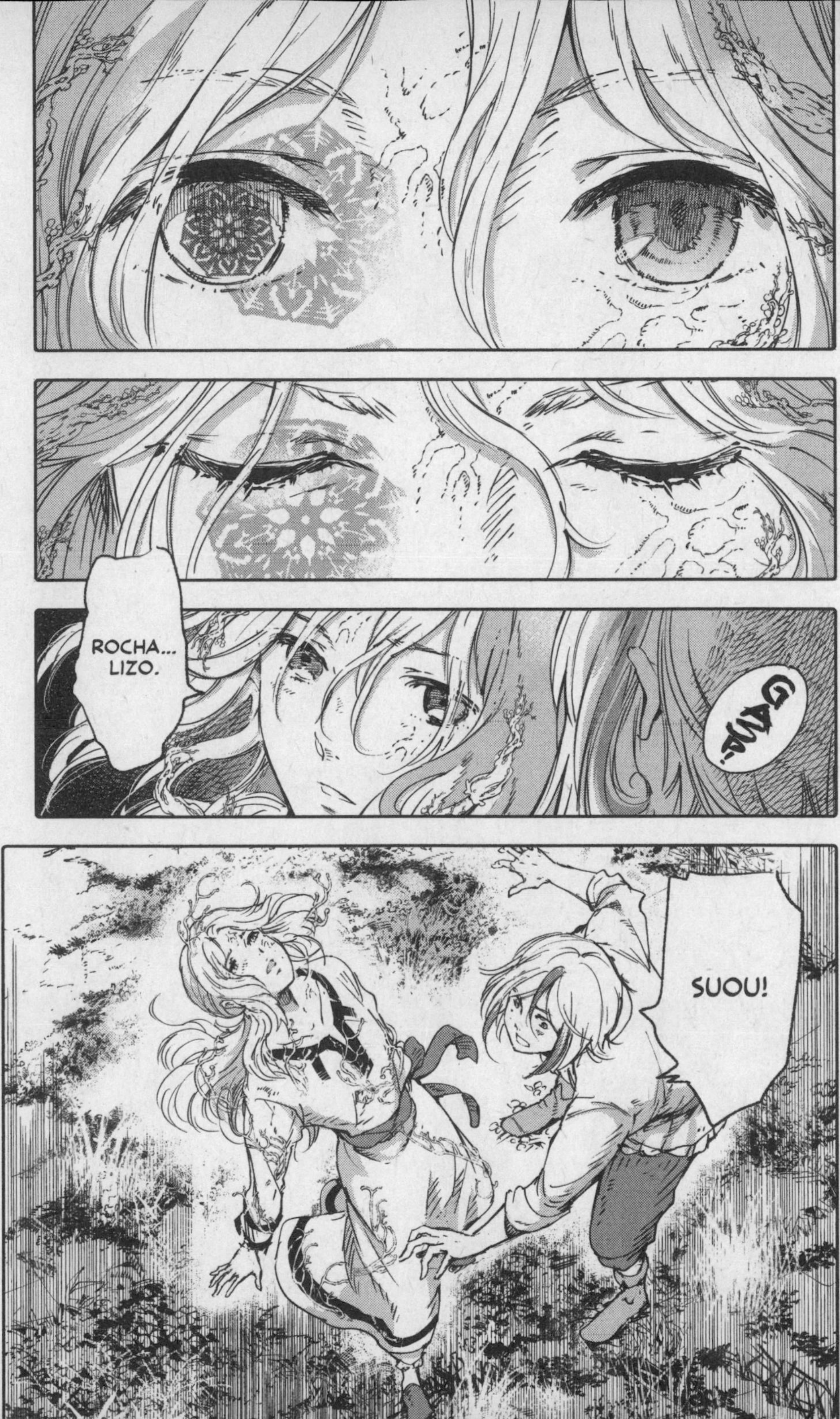
ROCHA... LIZO.
GAWA!
SUOU!

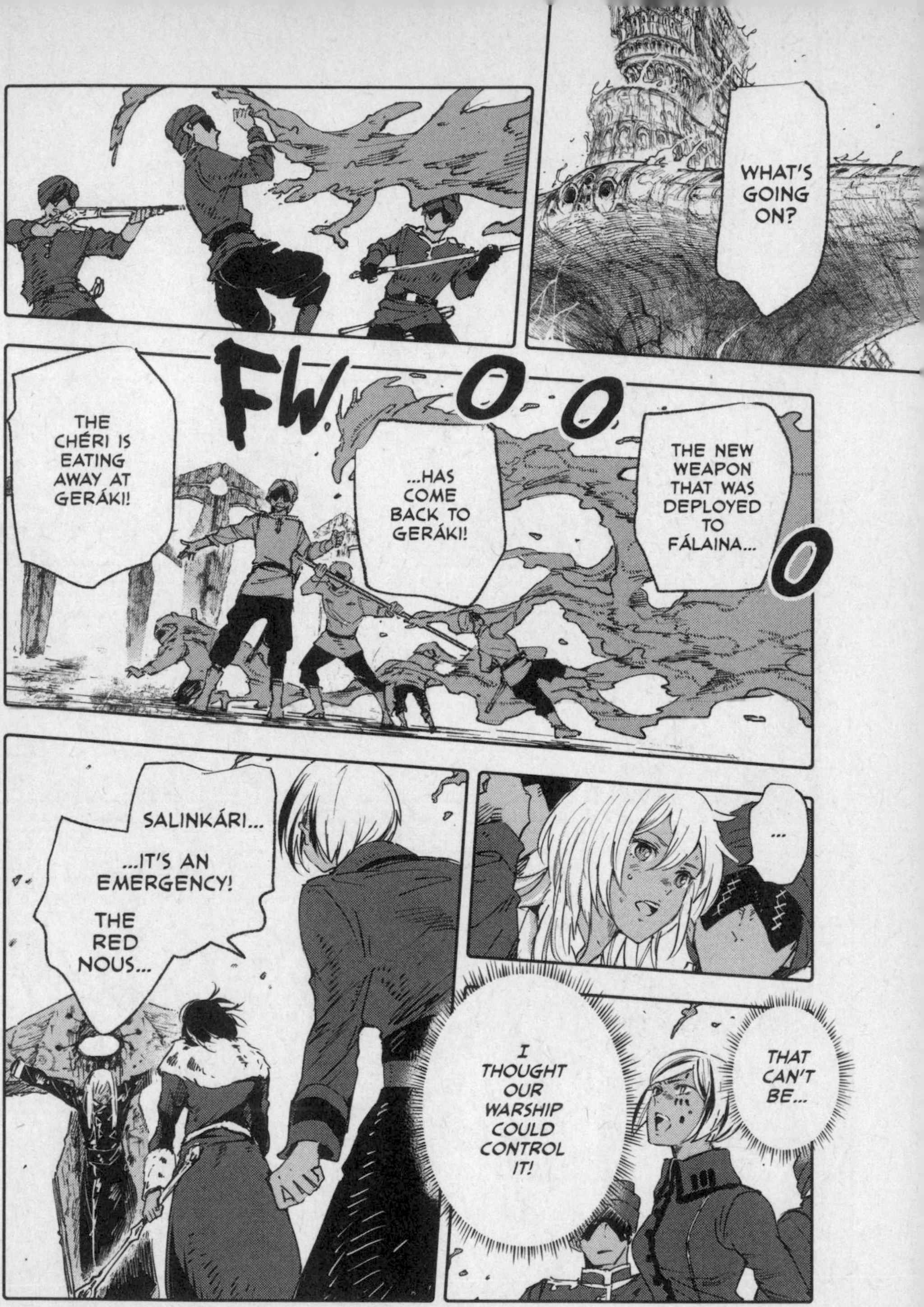
WHAT'S GOING ON?
FWOOOO
THE NEW WEAPON THAT WAS DEPLOYED TO FÁLAINA...
...HAS COME BACK TO GERÁKI!
THE CHÉRI IS EATING AWAY AT GERÁKI!
...
THAT CAN'T BE...
I THOUGHT OUR WARSHIP COULD CONTROL IT!
SALINKÁRI... ...IT'S AN EMERGENCY! THE RED NOUS...

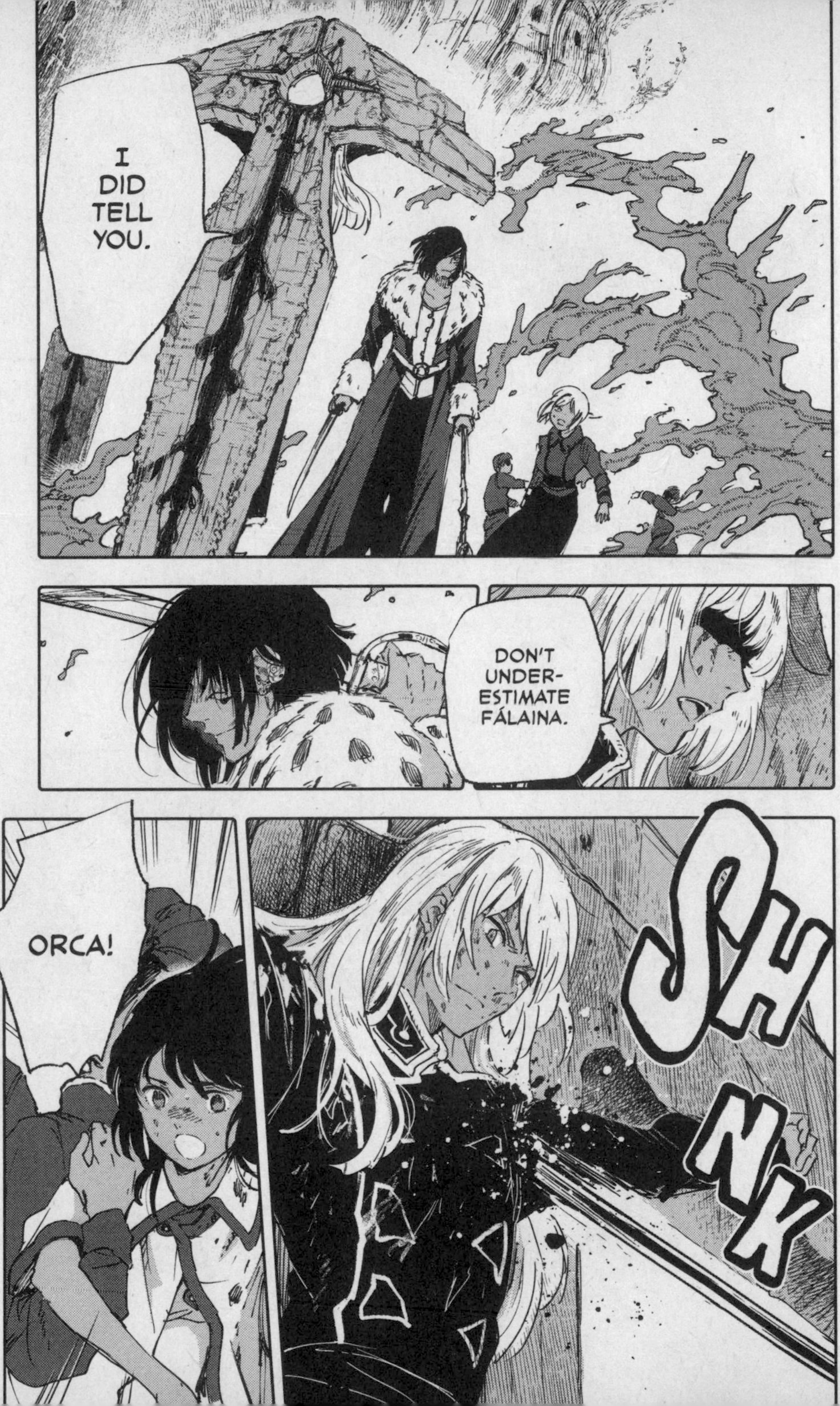
I DID TELL YOU.
DON'T UNDER-ESTIMATE FÁLAINA.
SHNK
ORCA!

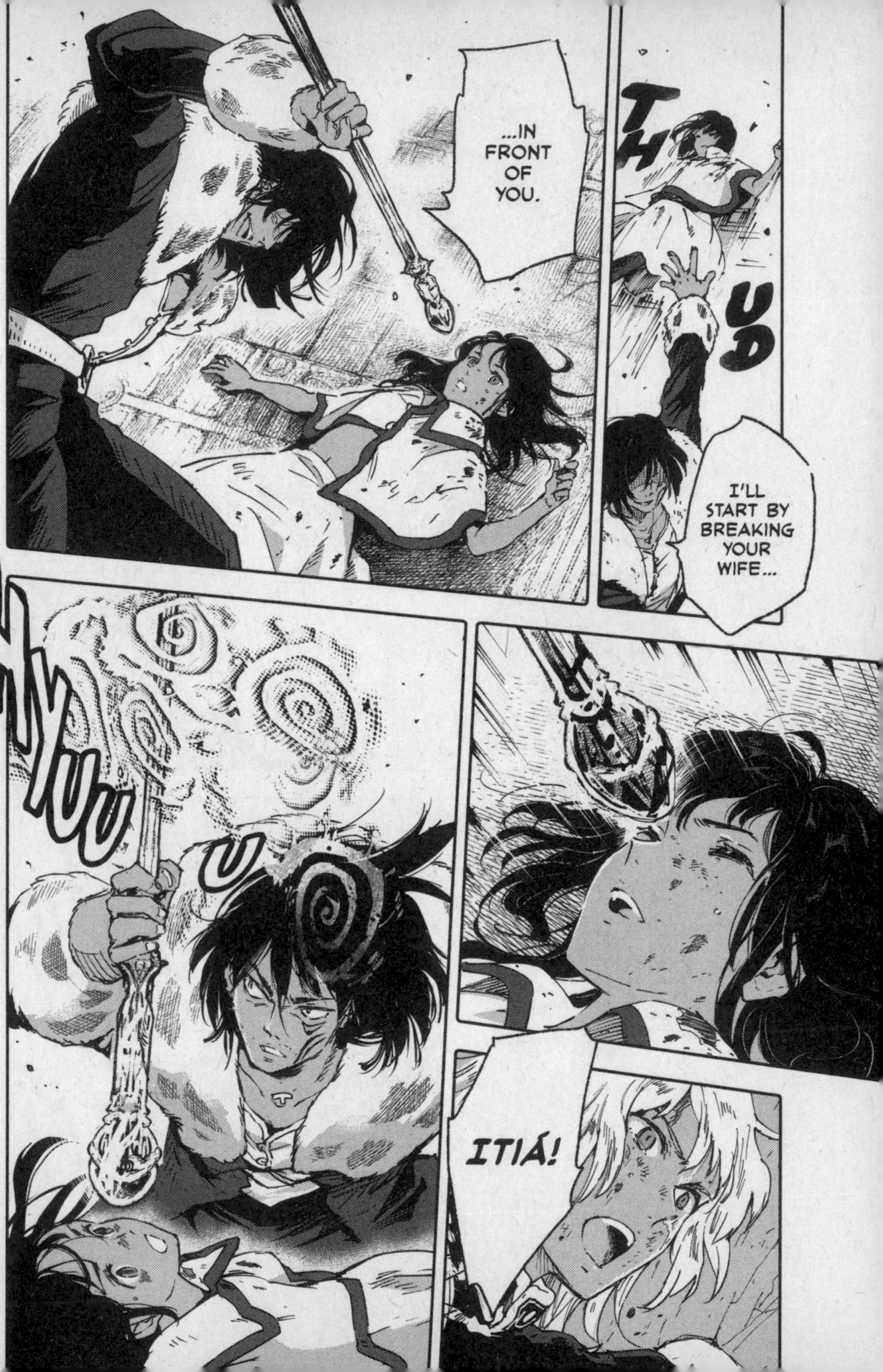
THUD
I'LL START BY BREAKING YOUR WIFE...
...IN FRONT OF YOU.
ITIÁ!
HYUUU

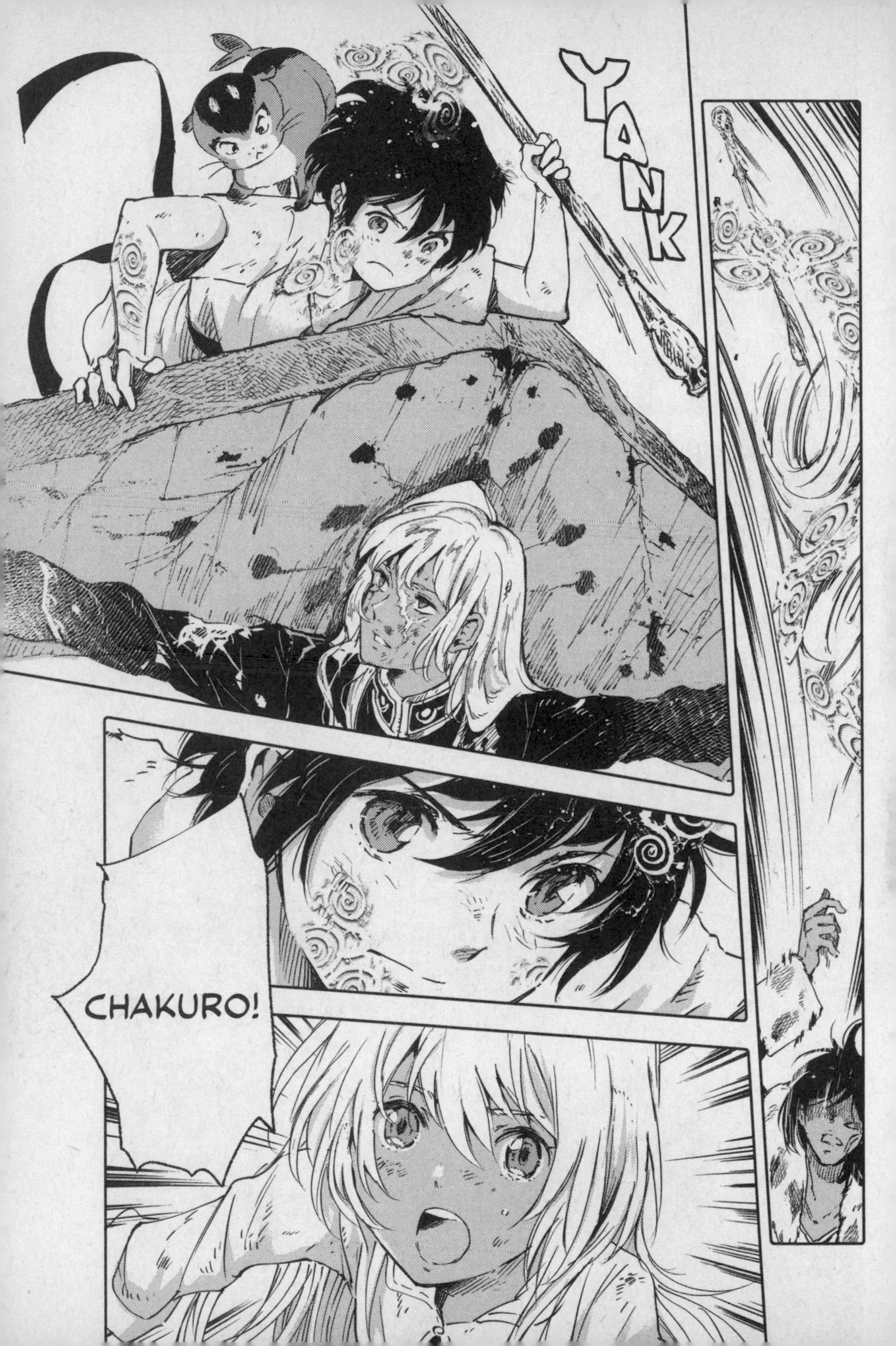
YANK
CHAKURO!

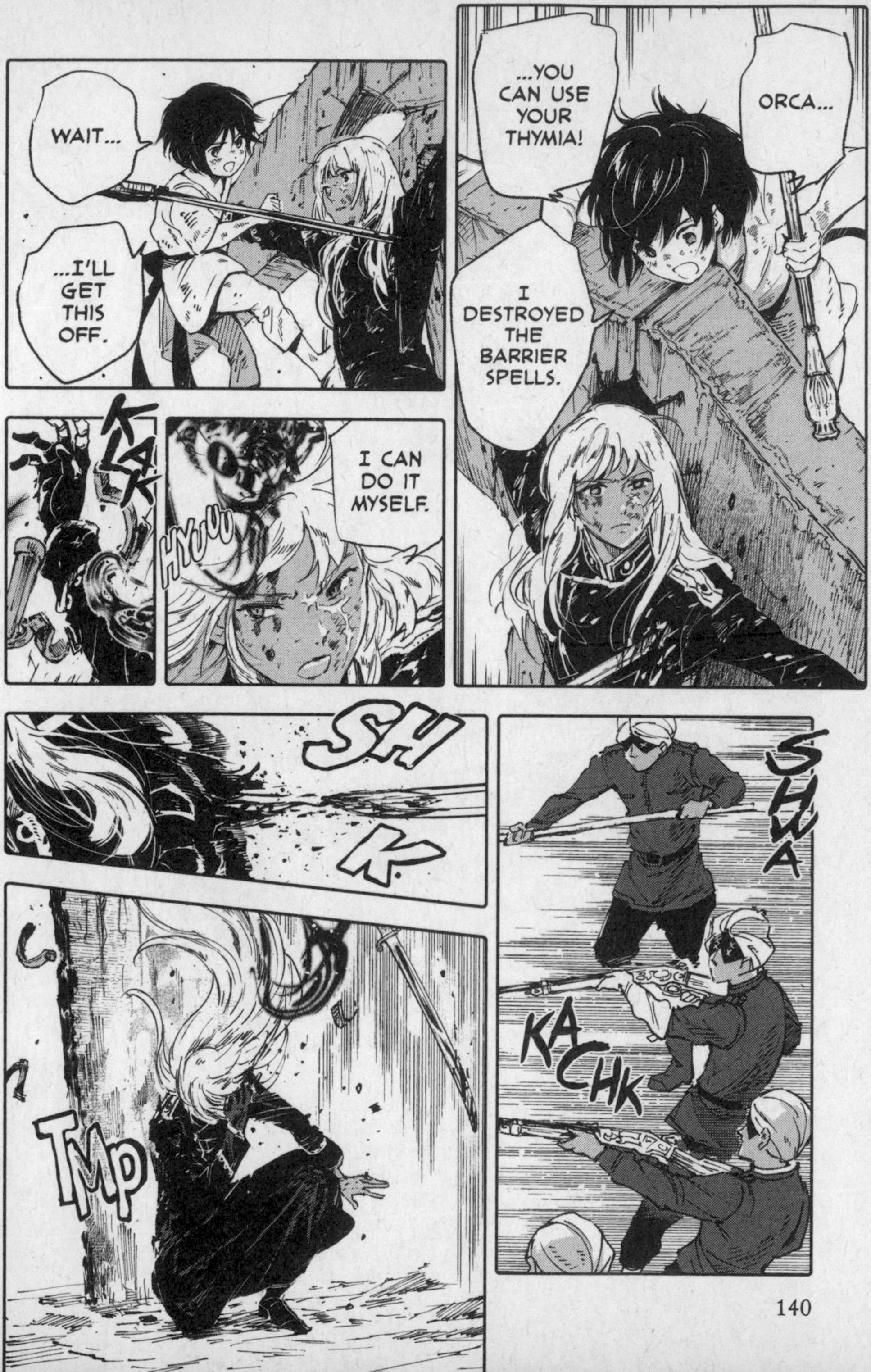
ORCA...
...YOU CAN USE YOUR THYMIA!
I DESTROYED THE BARRIER SPELLS.
WAIT...
...I'LL GET THIS OFF.
I CAN DO IT MYSELF.
HYUUU
KLAK
SHWA
KACHK
SH
K
TMP

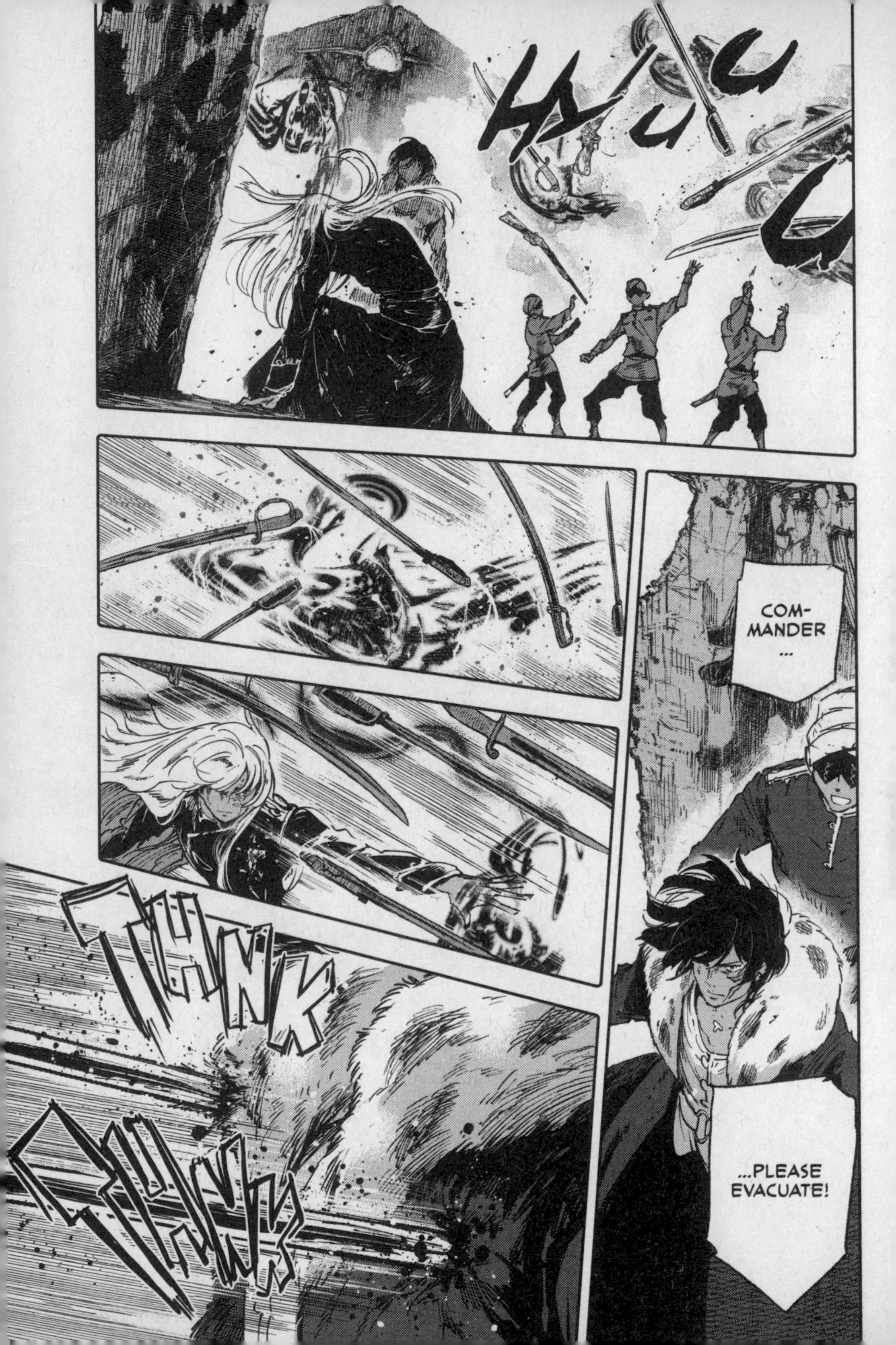
HYUUU
COM-
MANDER
...
...PLEASE
EVACUATE!
THUNK
THUNK

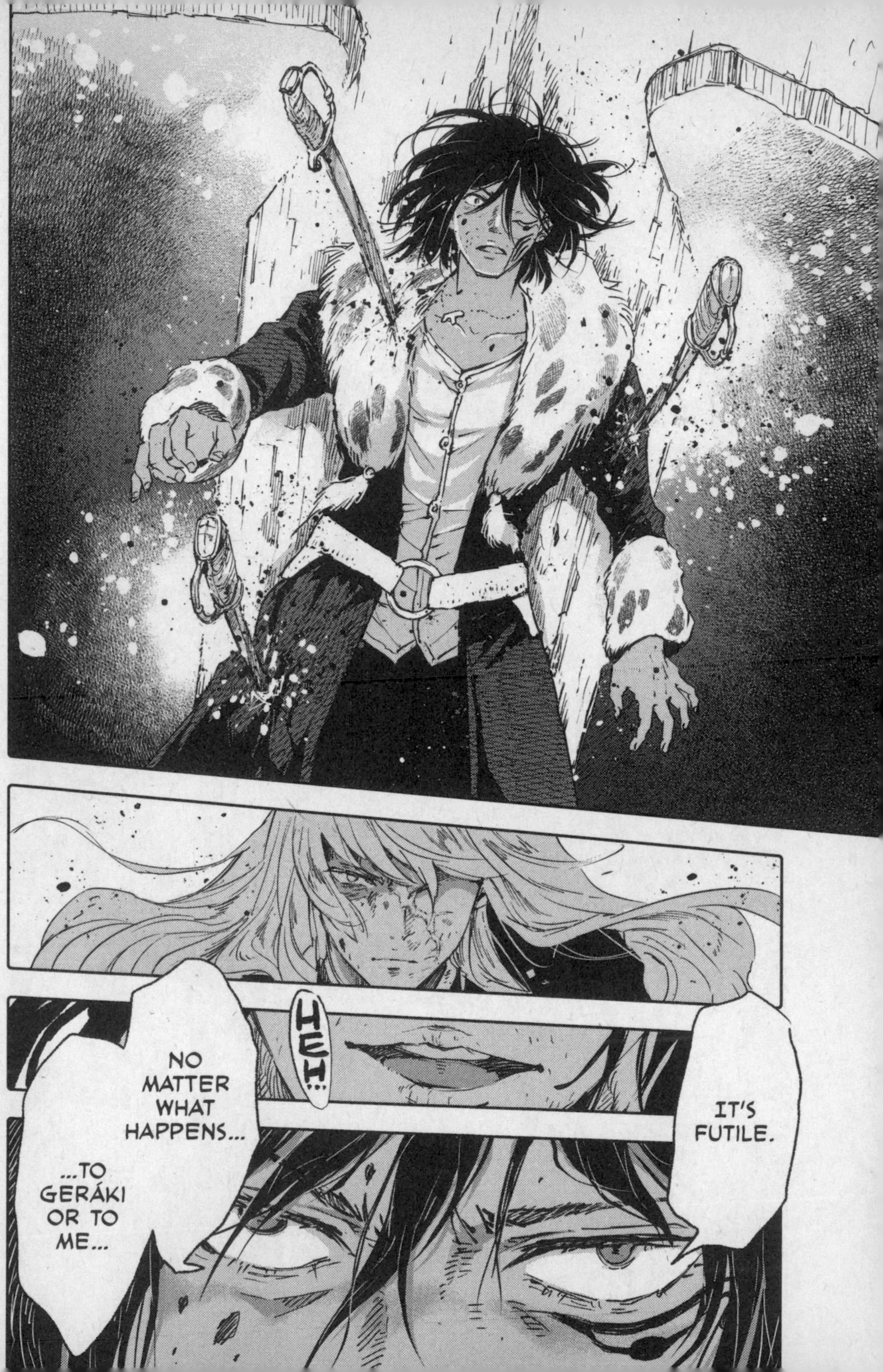
HEH...
NO MATTER WHAT HAPPENS...
...TO GERÁKI OR TO ME...
IT'S FUTILE.

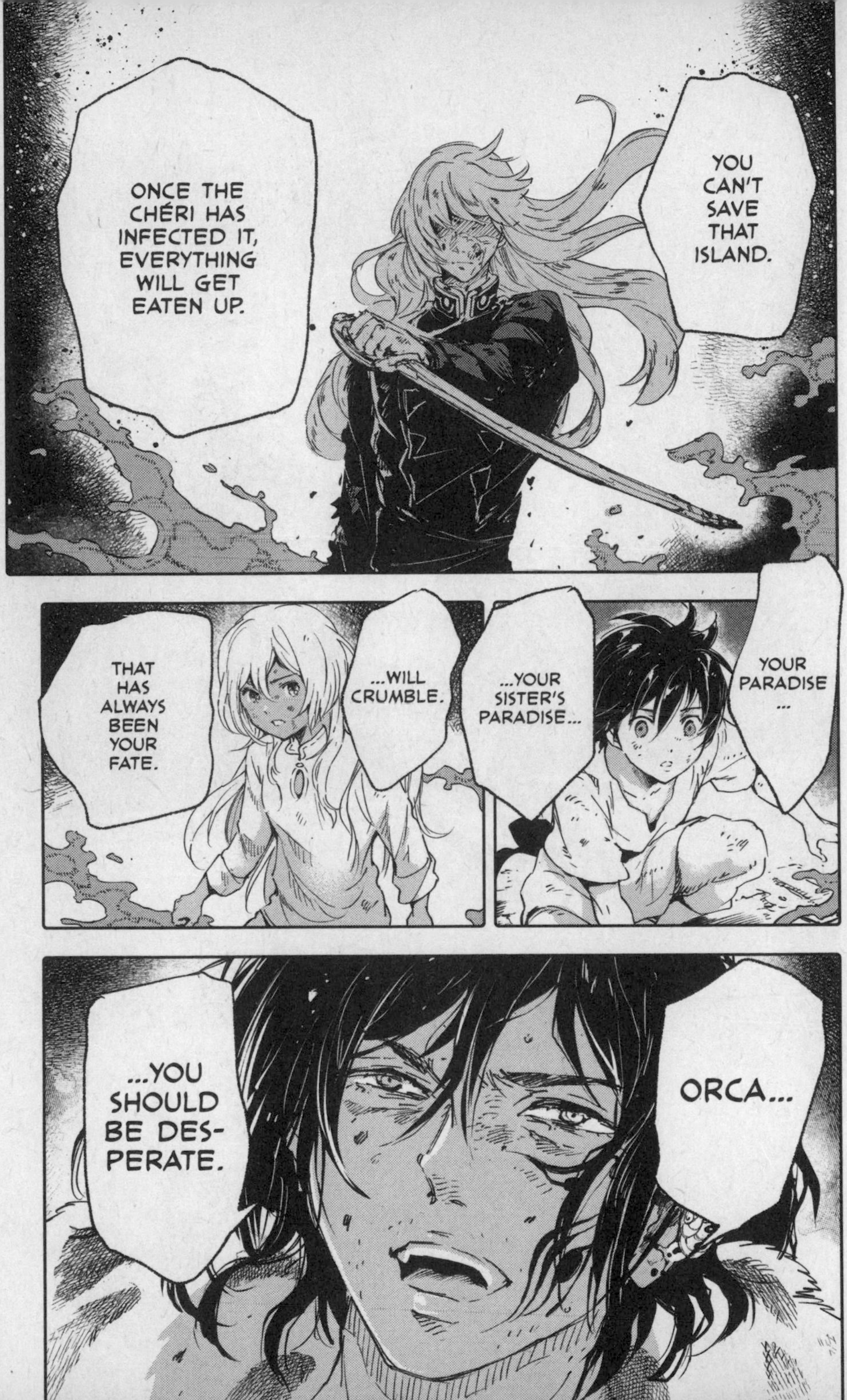
YOU CAN'T SAVE THAT ISLAND.
ONCE THE CHÉRI HAS INFECTED IT, EVERYTHING WILL GET EATEN UP.
YOUR PARADISE ...
...YOUR SISTER'S PARADISE...
...WILL CRUMBLE.
THAT HAS ALWAYS BEEN YOUR FATE.
ORCA...
...YOU SHOULD BE DES-PERATE.

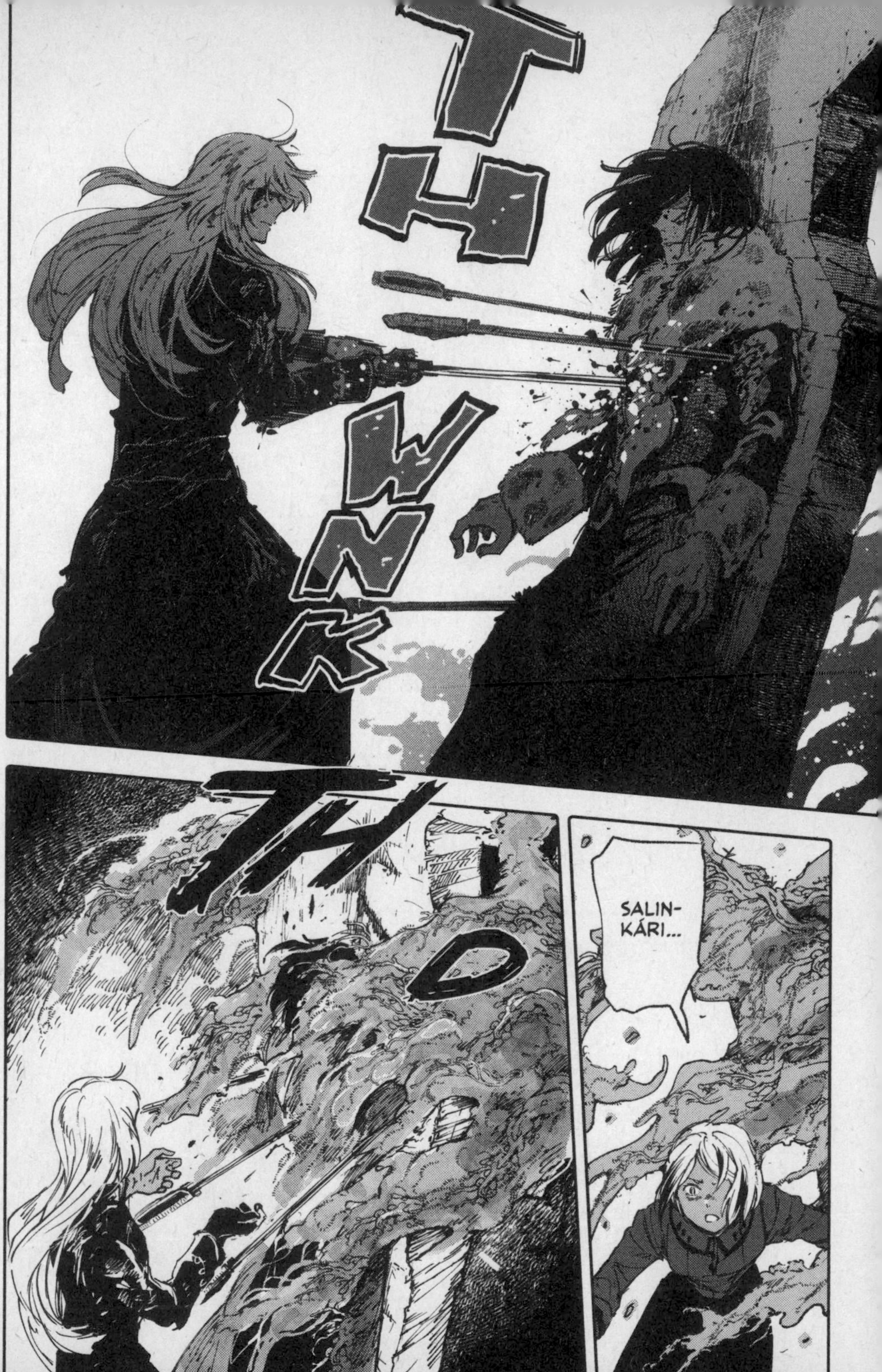
THWNK
SALIN-
KÁRI...
THD

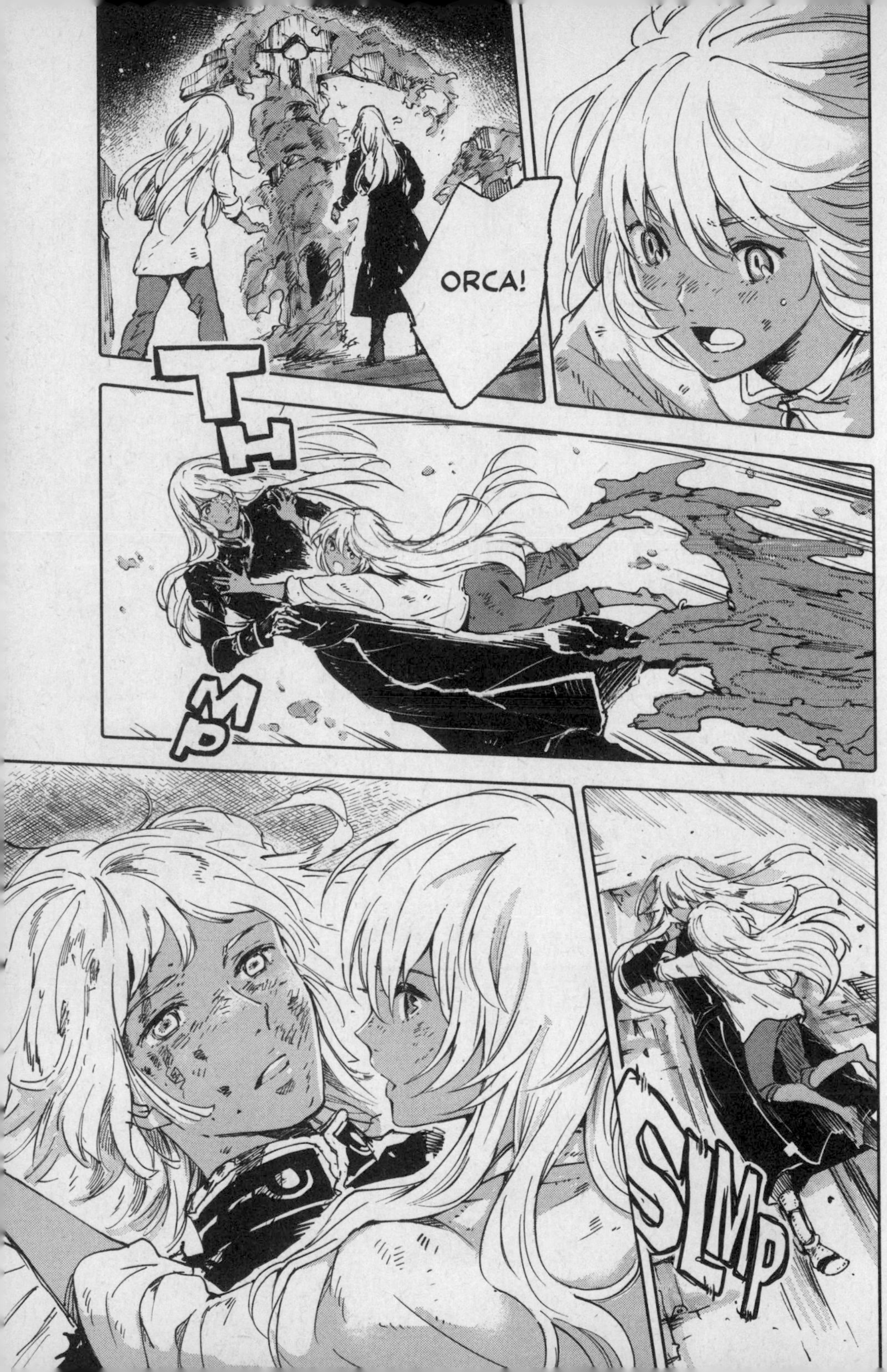
ORCA!
THMP
SLMP

ITIÁ!

?

IT'S AVOIDING US?

ORCA!

ORCA!

WHAT IS...

...THIS RED NOUS?

TUG

146

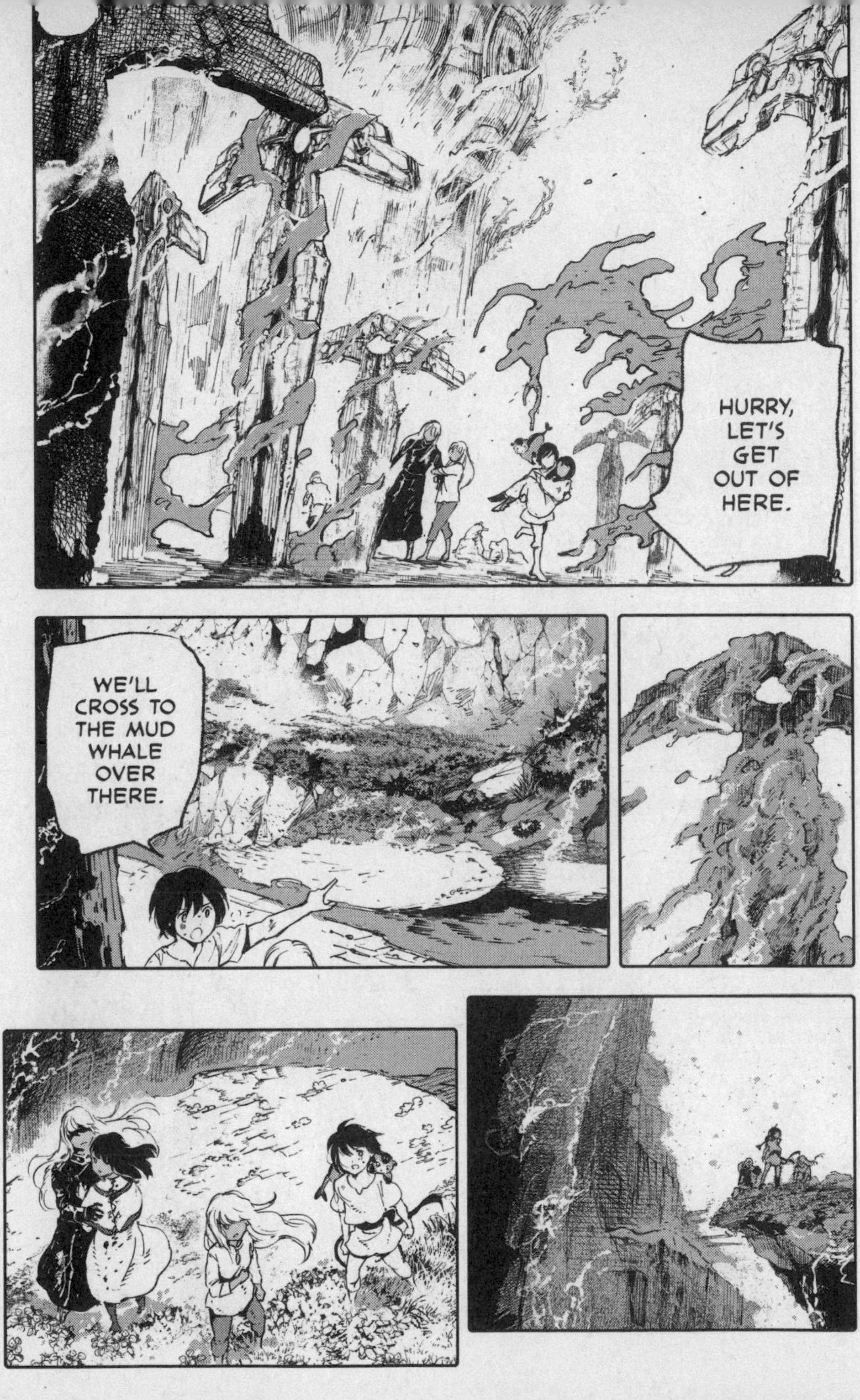
HURRY, LET'S GET OUT OF HERE.
WE'LL CROSS TO THE MUD WHALE OVER THERE.

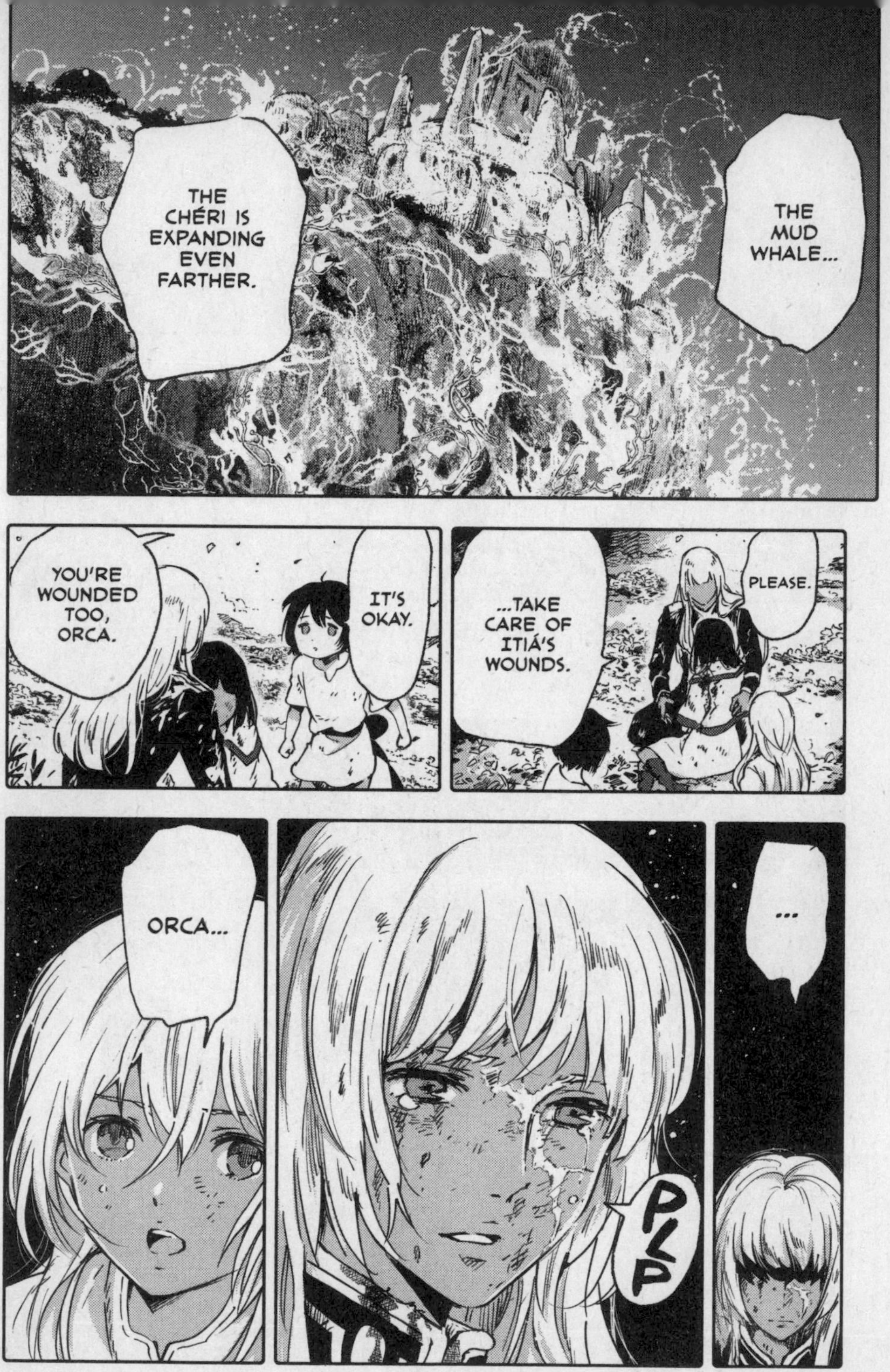
THE MUD WHALE...
THE CHÉRI IS EXPANDING EVEN FARTHER.
PLEASE.
...TAKE CARE OF ITIÁ'S WOUNDS.
IT'S OKAY.
YOU'RE WOUNDED TOO, ORCA.
...
PLP
ORCA...

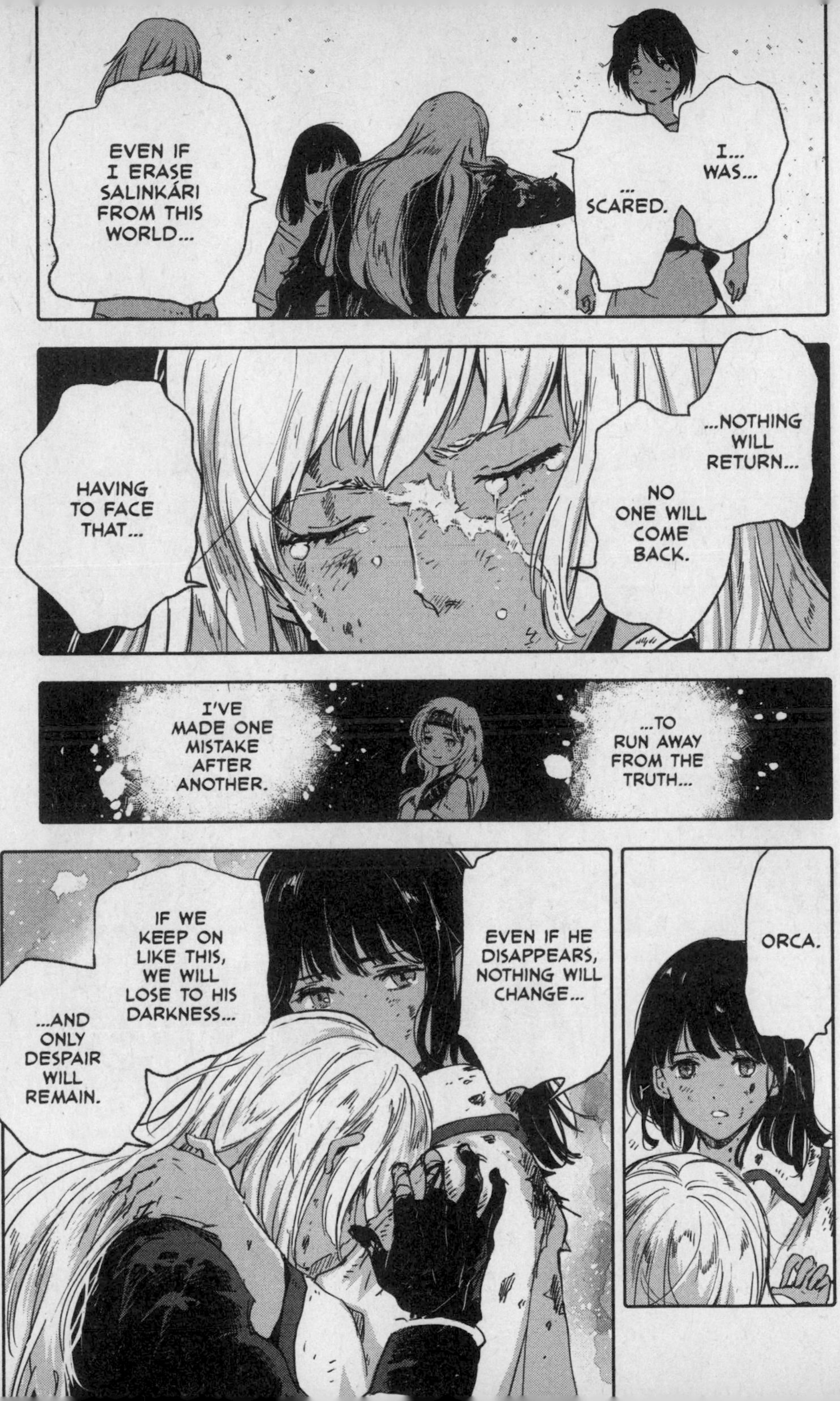
I... WAS... ...SCARED.
EVEN IF I ERASE SALINKÁRI FROM THIS WORLD...
...NOTHING WILL RETURN... NO ONE WILL COME BACK.
HAVING TO FACE THAT...
...TO RUN AWAY FROM THE TRUTH...
I'VE MADE ONE MISTAKE AFTER ANOTHER.
ORCA.
EVEN IF HE DISAPPEARS, NOTHING WILL CHANGE...
IF WE KEEP ON LIKE THIS, WE WILL LOSE TO HIS DARKNESS...
...AND ONLY DESPAIR WILL REMAIN.

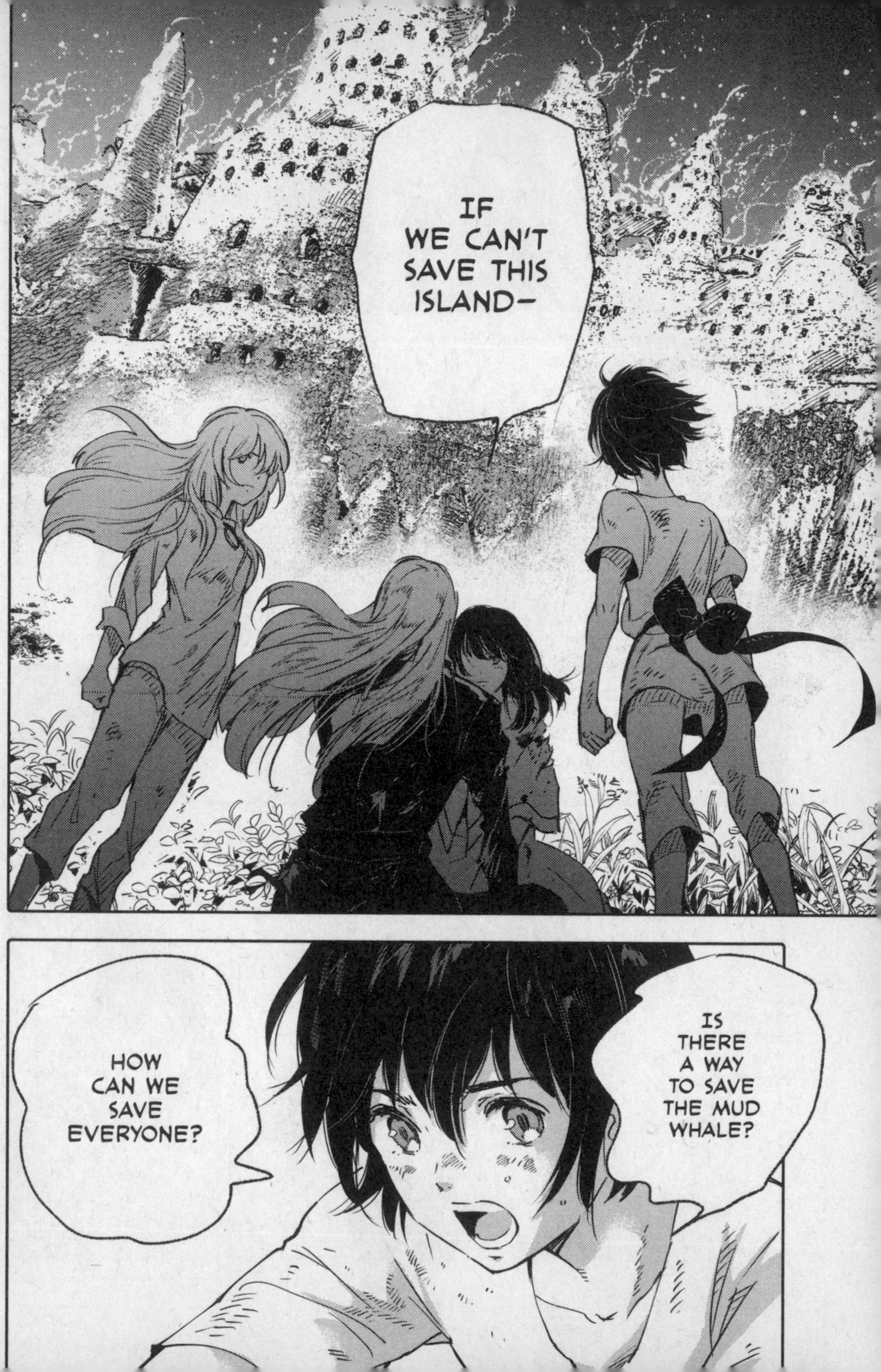
IF WE CAN'T SAVE THIS ISLAND–
IS THERE A WAY TO SAVE THE MUD WHALE?
HOW CAN WE SAVE EVERYONE?

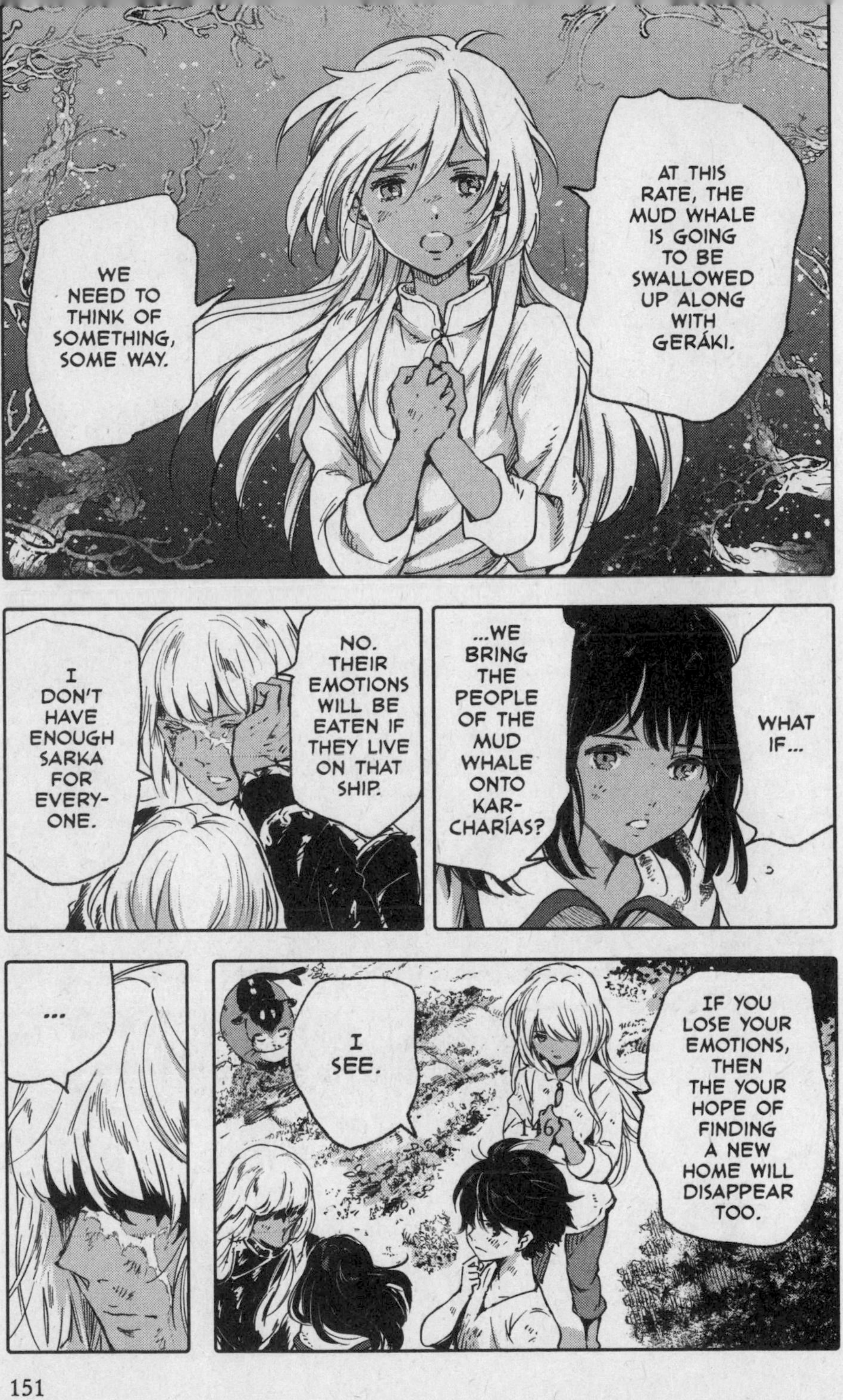
AT THIS RATE, THE MUD WHALE IS GOING TO BE SWALLOWED UP ALONG WITH GERÁKI.
WE NEED TO THINK OF SOMETHING, SOME WAY.
WHAT IF...
...WE BRING THE PEOPLE OF THE MUD WHALE ONTO KAR-CHARÍAS?
NO. THEIR EMOTIONS WILL BE EATEN IF THEY LIVE ON THAT SHIP.
I DON'T HAVE ENOUGH SARKA FOR EVERY-ONE.
IF YOU LOSE YOUR EMOTIONS, THEN THE YOUR HOPE OF FINDING A NEW HOME WILL DISAPPEAR TOO.
I SEE.
...

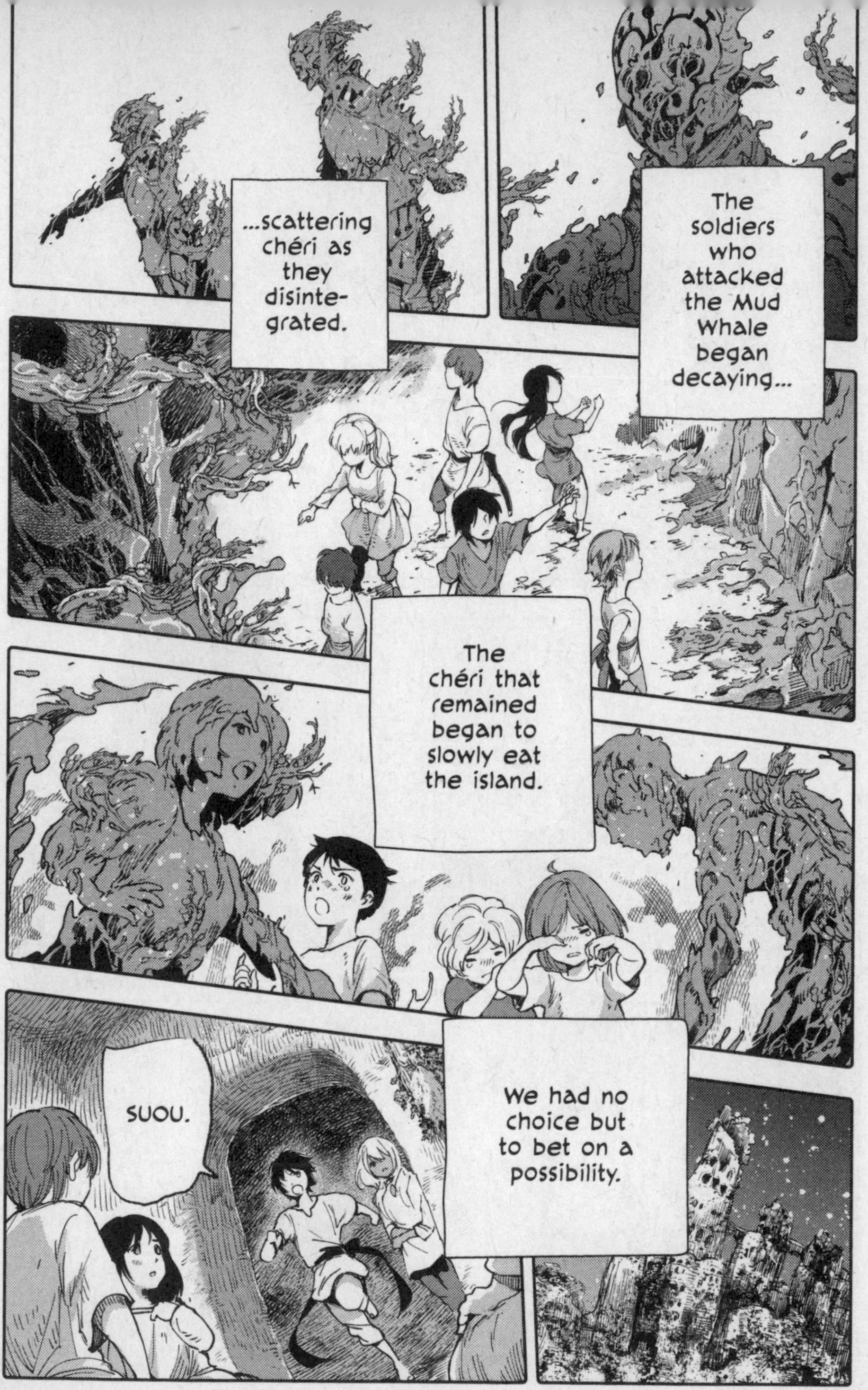
The soldiers who attacked the Mud Whale began decaying...
...scattering chéri as they disintegrated.
The chéri that remained began to slowly eat the island.
We had no choice but to bet on a possibility.
SUOU.

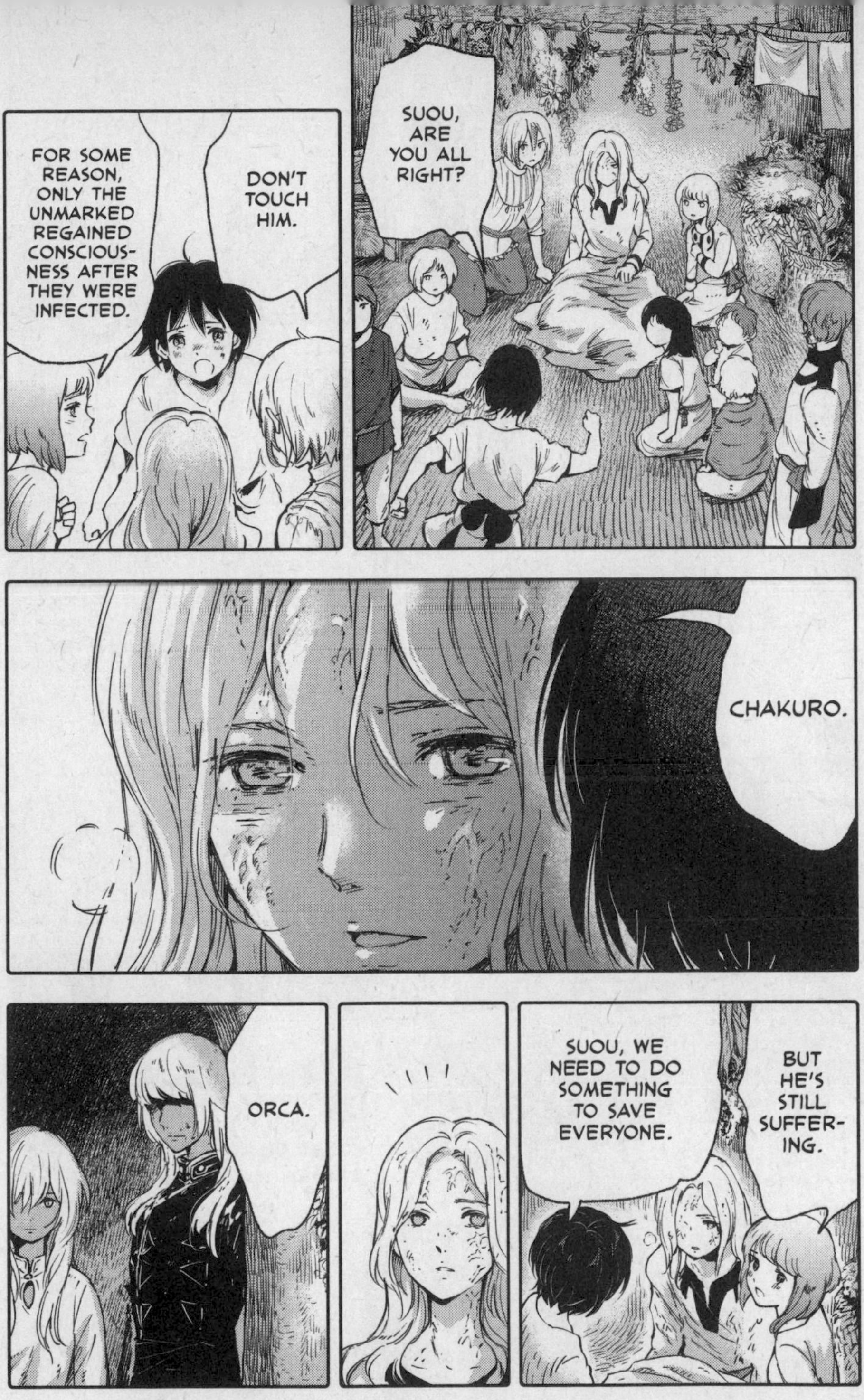
SUOU, ARE YOU ALL RIGHT?
DON'T TOUCH HIM.
FOR SOME REASON, ONLY THE UNMARKED REGAINED CONSCIOUSNESS AFTER THEY WERE INFECTED.
CHAKURO.
BUT HE'S STILL SUFFERING.
SUOU, WE NEED TO DO SOMETHING TO SAVE EVERYONE.
ORCA.

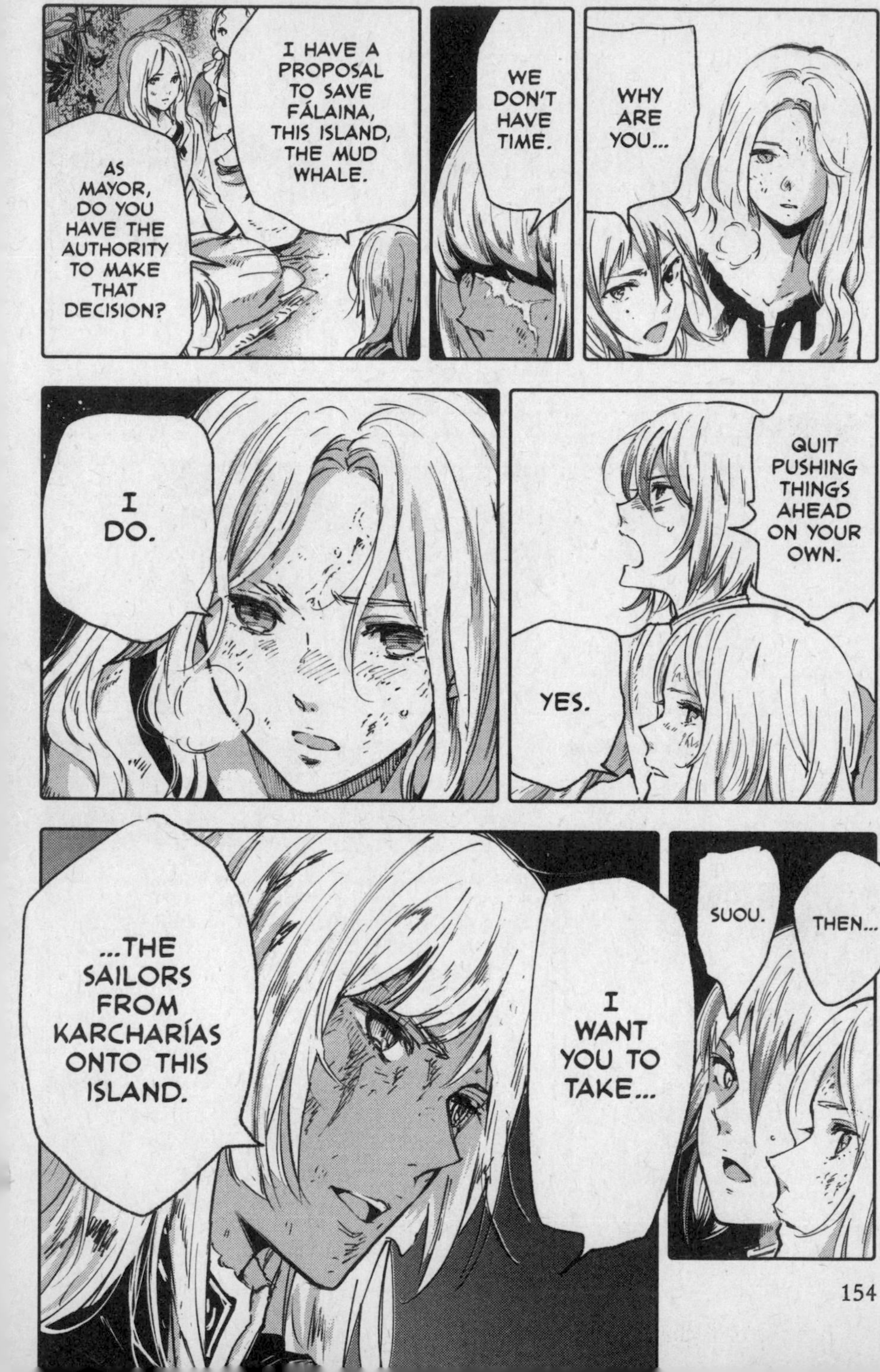
WHY ARE YOU...
WE DON'T HAVE TIME.
I HAVE A PROPOSAL TO SAVE FÁLAINA, THIS ISLAND, THE MUD WHALE.
AS MAYOR, DO YOU HAVE THE AUTHORITY TO MAKE THAT DECISION?
QUIT PUSHING THINGS AHEAD ON YOUR OWN.
YES.
I DO.
THEN...
SUOU.
I WANT YOU TO TAKE...
...THE SAILORS FROM KARCHARÍAS ONTO THIS ISLAND.

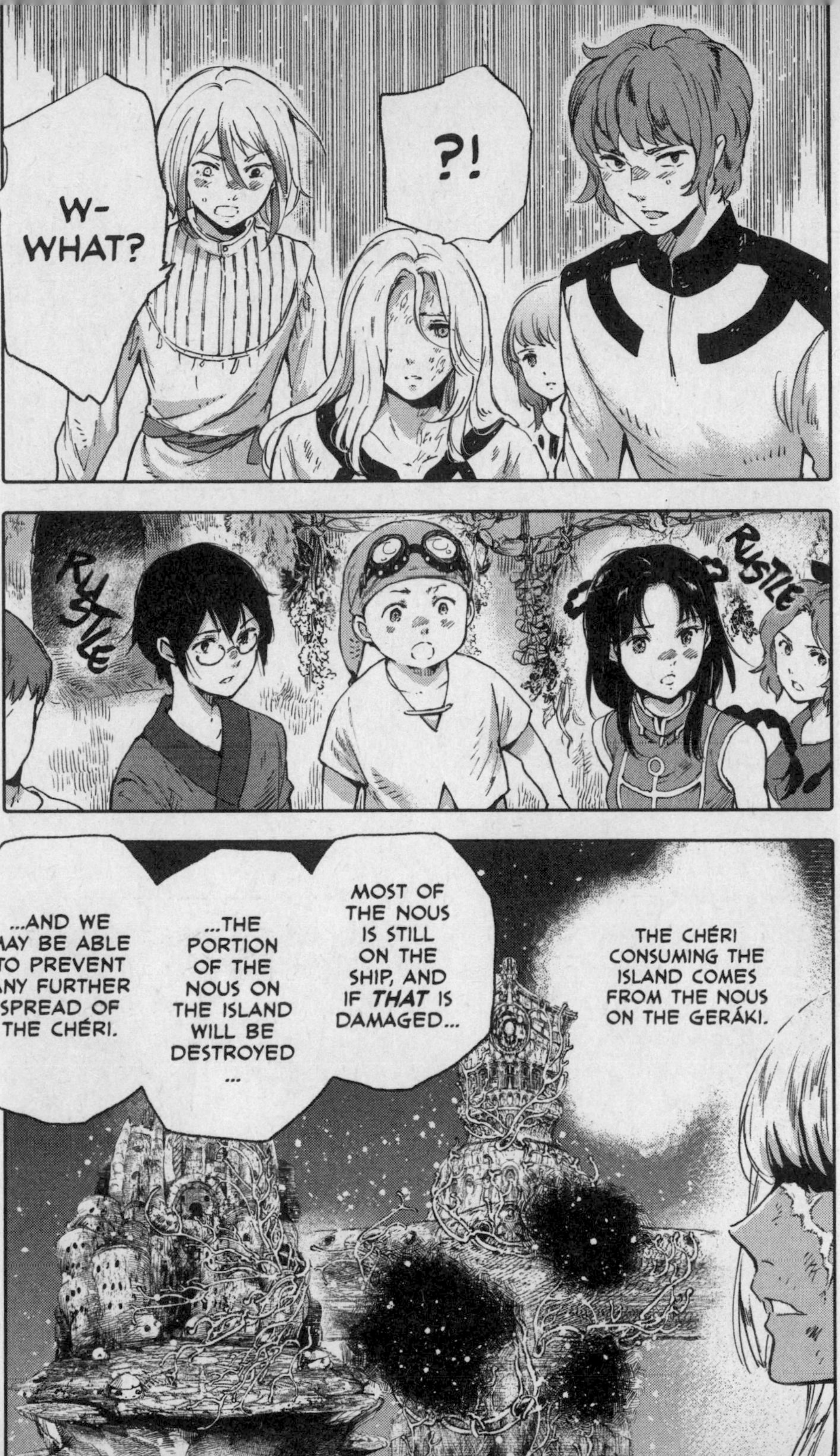
?!
W-WHAT?
RUSTLE
RUSTLE
THE CHÉRI CONSUMING THE ISLAND COMES FROM THE NOUS ON THE GERÁKI.
MOST OF THE NOUS IS STILL ON THE SHIP, AND IF *THAT* IS DAMAGED...
...THE PORTION OF THE NOUS ON THE ISLAND WILL BE DESTROYED ...
...AND WE MAY BE ABLE TO PREVENT ANY FURTHER SPREAD OF THE CHÉRI.

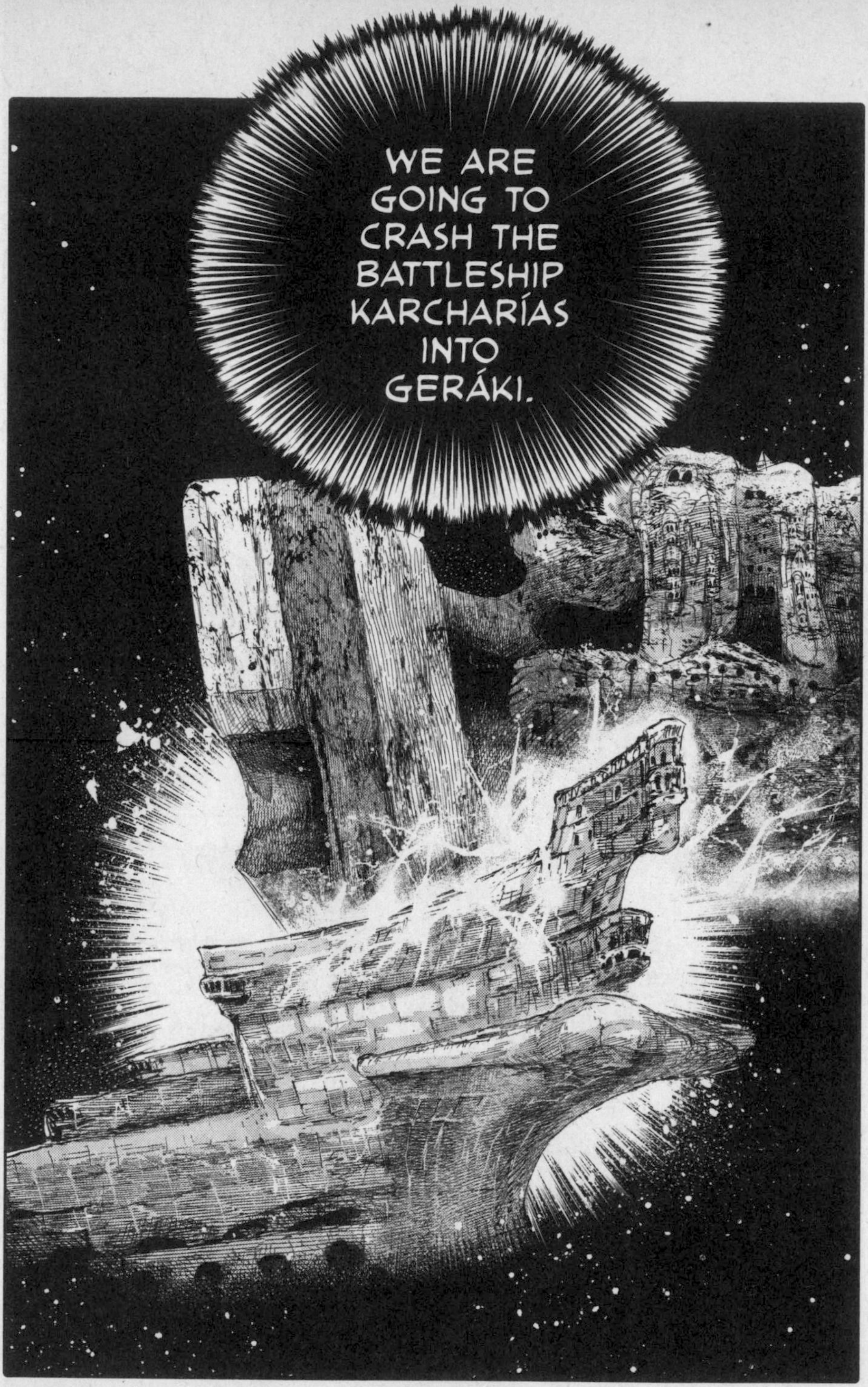
WE ARE GOING TO CRASH THE BATTLESHIP KARCHARÍAS INTO GERÁKI.

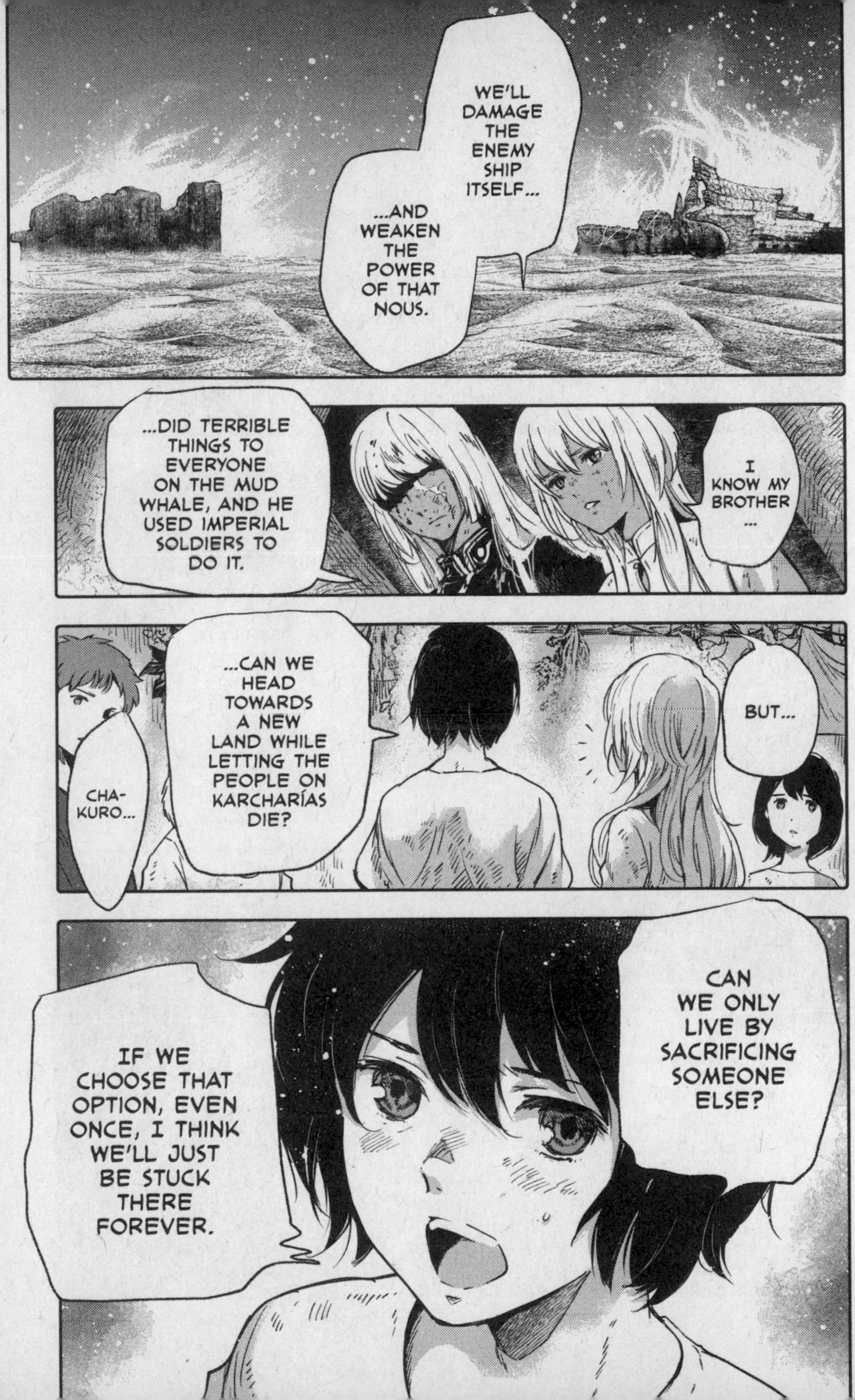
WE'LL DAMAGE THE ENEMY SHIP ITSELF...
...AND WEAKEN THE POWER OF THAT NOUS.
I KNOW MY BROTHER ...
...DID TERRIBLE THINGS TO EVERYONE ON THE MUD WHALE, AND HE USED IMPERIAL SOLDIERS TO DO IT.
BUT...
...CAN WE HEAD TOWARDS A NEW LAND WHILE LETTING THE PEOPLE ON KARCHARÍAS DIE?
CHA-KURO...
CAN WE ONLY LIVE BY SACRIFICING SOMEONE ELSE?
IF WE CHOOSE THAT OPTION, EVEN ONCE, I THINK WE'LL JUST BE STUCK THERE FOREVER.

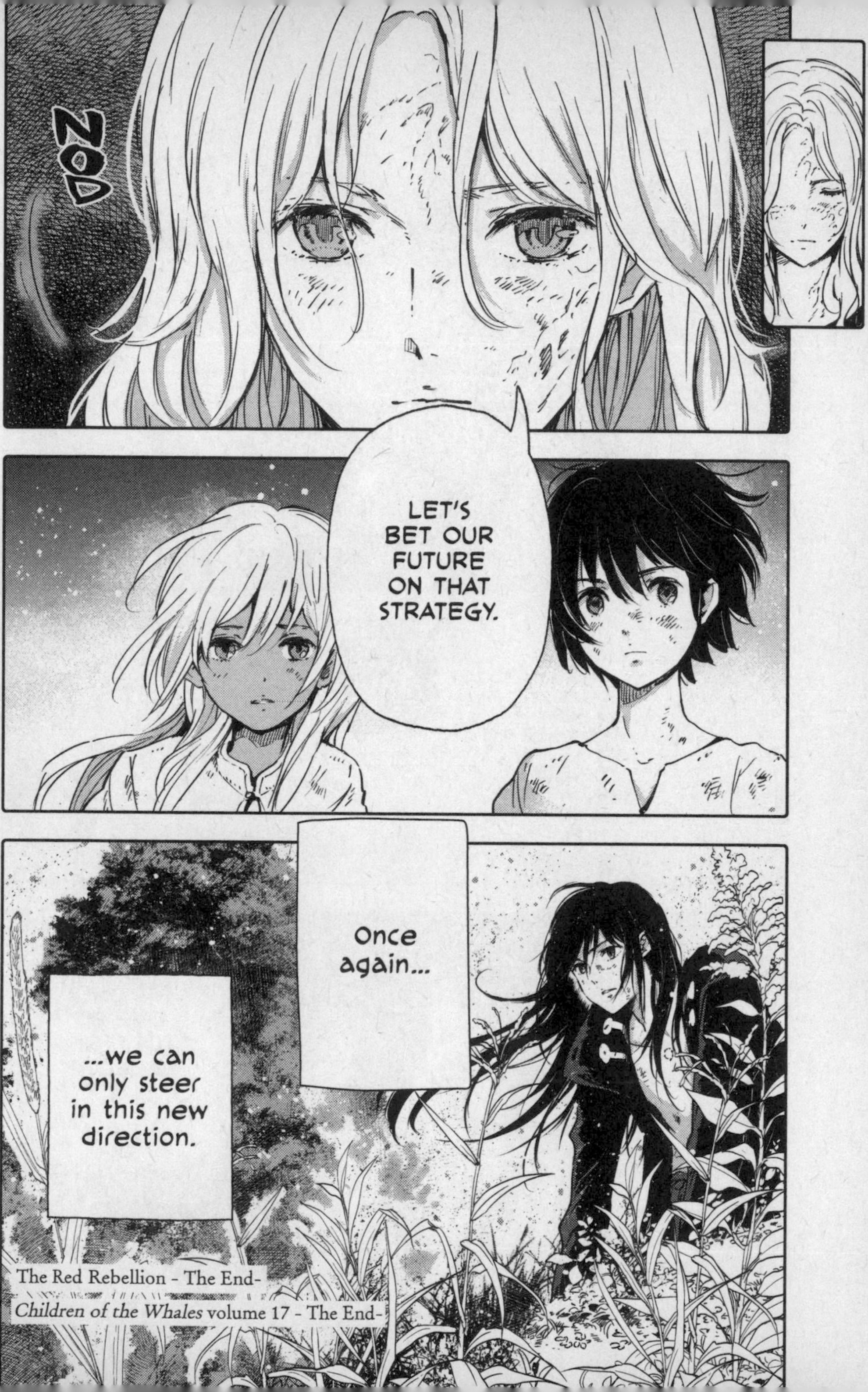
NOD
LET'S BET OUR FUTURE ON THAT STRATEGY.
Once again...
...we can only steer in this new direction.
The Red Rebellion - The End-
Children of the Whales volume 17 - The End-

CHILDREN OF THE WHALES

A Note on Names

Those who live on the Mud Whale are named after colors in a language unknown. Abi Umeda uses Japanese translations of the names, which we have maintained. Here is a list of the English equivalents for the curious.

Aijiro	pale blue
Benihi	scarlet
Buki	kerria flower (*yamabuki*)
Byakuroku	malachite mineral pigments, pale green tinged with white
Chakuro	blackish brown (*cha* = brown, *kuro* = black)
Furano	from "flannel," a soft-woven fabric traditionally made of wool
Ginshu	vermillion
Hakuji	porcelain white
Jiki	golden
Kicha	yellowish brown
Kikujin	koji mold, yellowish green
Kogare	burnt muskwood, dark reddish brown
Kuchiba	decayed-leaf brown
Masoh	cinnabar
Miru	seaweed green
Nashiji	a traditional Japanese crepe weave fabric
Neri	silk white
Nezu	mouse gray
Nibi	dark gray
Ouni	safflower red
Rasha	darkest blue, nearly black
Ro	lacquer black
Sami	light green (*asa* = light, *midori* = green)

Shikoku	purple-tinged black
Shikon	purple-tinged navy
Shinono	the color of dawn (*shinonome*)
Shuan	dark bloodred
Sienna	reddish brown
Sumi	ink black
Suou	raspberry red
Taisha	red ocher
Tobi	reddish brown like a kite's feather
Tokusa	scouring rush green
Tonoko	the color of powdered grindstone, a pale brown
Urumi	muddy gray

Mizen's room is detailed in volumes 7 and 8. This volume might be easier to understand if you go back and have a little look before you read.

—Abi Umeda

ABI UMEDA debuted as a manga creator with the one-shot "Yukokugendan" in *Weekly Shonen Champion*. *Children of the Whales* is her eighth manga work.

CHILDREN OF THE WHALES

VOLUME 17
VIZ Signature Edition

Story and Art by **Abi Umeda**

Translation / JN Productions
Touch-Up Art & Lettering / Annaliese "Ace" Christman
Design / Julian (JR) Robinson
Editor / Pancha Diaz

KUJIRANOKORAHA SAJOUNIUTAU Volume 17
© 2020 ABI UMEDA
First published in Japan in 2020 by AKITA PUBLISHING CO., LTD., Tokyo
English translation rights arranged with AKITA PUBLISHING CO., LTD. through
Tuttle-Mori Agency, Inc., Tokyo

Printed in Canada

Published by VIZ Media, LLC
P.O. Box 77010
San Francisco, CA 94107

10 9 8 7 6 5 4 3 2 1
First printing, July 2021

viz.com

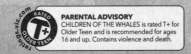

vizsignature.com

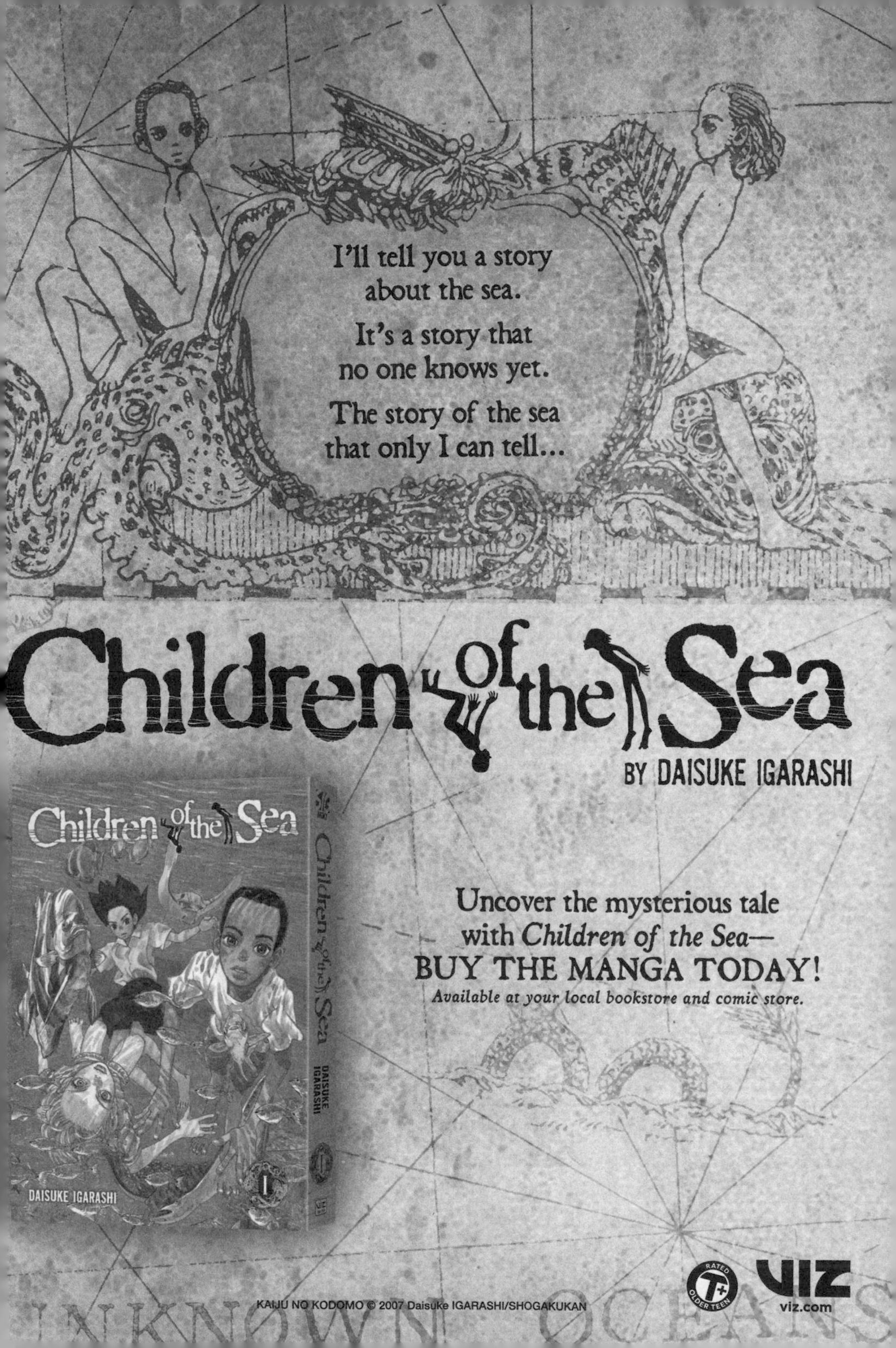
I'll tell you a story
about the sea.
It's a story that
no one knows yet.
The story of the sea
that only I can tell...
Children of the Sea
BY DAISUKE IGARASHI
Children of the Sea
Children of the Sea
DAISUKE IGARASHI
DAISUKE IGARASHI
1
Uncover the mysterious tale
with Children of the Sea—
BUY THE MANGA TODAY!
Available at your local bookstore and comic store.
RATED T+ OLDER TEEN
VIZ
viz.com
KAIJU NO KODOMO © 2007 Daisuke IGARASHI/SHOGAKUKAN
UNKNOWN OCEANS

Cats of the Louvre

by TAIYO MATSUMOTO

A surreal tale of the secret world of the cats of the Louvre, told by Eisner Award winner Taiyo Matsumoto.

The world-renowned Louvre museum in Paris contains more than just the most famous works of art in history. At night, within its darkened galleries, an unseen and surreal world comes alive— a world witnessed only by the small family of cats that lives in the attic. Until now...

Translated by *Tekkonkinkreet* film director Michael Arias.

THE DRIFTING CLASSROOM

PERFECT EDITION *by* KAZUO UMEZZ

Out of nowhere, an entire school vanishes, leaving nothing but a hole in the ground. While parents mourn and authorities investigate, the students and teachers find themselves not dead but stranded in a terrifying wasteland where they must fight to survive.

COMPLETE IN 3 VOLUMES

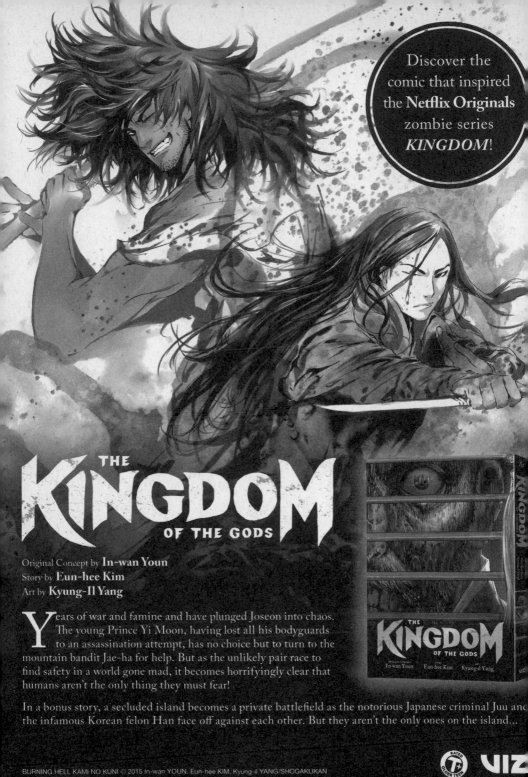

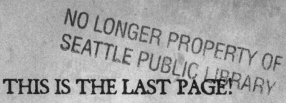

THIS IS THE LAST PAGE!

Children of the Whales has been
printed in the original Japanese
format to preserve the orientation
of the original artwork.

DAKOTA SKIES

Della Adair hired her old friend Miles Donovan to help her make her way safely across the long Dakota plains. Having sold her property in Deadwood, Della is intent on travelling south to start a new life with her younger sister, due in from the east. The whole town knows Della is carrying the gold made from the sale. Amongst them is Tom DeFord, a stone-cold killer who holds a blood grudge against Miles. With news that the Cheyenne are roaming the plains as well, Miles will have to fight his way along every yard of the trail.

DAKOTA SKIES

DAKOTA SKIES

by

Logan Winters

Dales Large Print Books
Long Preston, North Yorkshire,
BD23 4ND, England.

British Library Cataloguing in Publication Data.

Winters, Logan
    Dakota skies.

    A catalogue record of this book is
    available from the British Library

    ISBN   978-1-84262-594-1 pbk

First published in Great Britain in 2007 by Robert Hale Limited

Published in Large Print 2008 by arrangement with
Robert Hale Limited

Dales Large Print is an imprint of Library Magna Books Ltd.

Printed and bound in Great Britain by
T.J. (International) Ltd., Cornwall, PL28 8RW

ONE

I didn't like him because I knew he was a killer. He didn't like me because I knew that he was.

His name was Tom DeFord. He was a tallish man with coppery hair like wire on his arms and a lanky rug of unwashed red-orange hair on his head. He had cold blue eyes that looked right through a man, a lopsided mouth that had been sliced at the corner once upon a time and drooped on the right side. He had scarred boots and a flat-brimmed hat with a red scarf tied around it for a band. Everybody in Deadwood thought he was a fine fellow since he had the habit of setting up drinks all around whenever he came into the bar-room. It doesn't take much more than that in some places to make people like you. I didn't tell

7

people about him murdering that Blackfoot woman because they didn't want to hear it and wouldn't have believed me anyway out of loyalty to DeFord.

But he knew that I knew. So when I did bump into him, he was apt to be somewhat defensive.

He was drunk when he told me, 'Miles, I hate your guts. I'd like to open you up, carve out your liver and feed it to my hogs.'

I do appreciate a man being straight-forward with me, but I always thought that was a little beyond the boundaries. I do not know if he had any hogs or not, but I did get the idea.

You see, the way this started was, before the army and I went our separate ways by mutual agreement, I had scouted some-times for them up around the Black Hills and down as far as the Horse Creek area near the North Platte, up the Lodgepole – all of that country. Now this came about because when my father had drifted into the Dakotas early on he believed he could make

8

a go of it, but the land was just too raw and the winters too harsh. When he passed away I was kind of left with nothing but a knowledge of the area few whites had. That being the case, and no Indian in that part of the country being willing just then to scout for the invading blue jackets, I signed with the cavalry. It was that or nothing.

The first day ever I saw DeFord was a crystal cold morning out along the Belle Fourche, near where it forks with the Cheyenne River. There wasn't much danger of running into hostiles. Most of the Sioux had drifted northward, but it's a good idea to take a look around now and then when your scalp is at stake. There was a light dusting of new snow across the prairie. The wind had swept the crowns of the knolls bare. The army patrol and I ran across a fine herd of elk and sat our horses for awhile, just watching them nibble their way toward wherever they were going, sometimes pawing at the snow to get to the brittle grass underneath the snow.

Riding on we topped a coulee rim and I thought I heard something above the wind, a sound kind of like a screech owl. We found our way to the bottom of the coulee where a freshet snaked its way through the willow brush, working its way southward. When I heard the sound again, I knew it was rising from a human throat and I put heels to my bay pony. We wound our way across the sandy bottom until we saw a man mounted on top of a woman. She was motionless and there was a knife in his hand.

When he saw us, he staggered to his feet, wiped back his red hair and sheathed his bloody bowie. The Indian girl lay against the cold gray sand like a discarded pile of rags.

This, then, was DeFord and he walked to us in a wobbly way and told our lieutenant this story: 'Me and my friend were riding toward Fort Sully. We had a big pack of furs. They came at us as we tried to cross the coulee. Probably seven, eight of them. I don't know where Dave is. I think they took him captive. Might have killed him. I had to fight them off best I could. Packhorse had danced off and I was trying to follow it when this woman, all crazy-eyed, jumped me. Hell, Lieutenant, I didn't even know she was a woman, just that she was trying to kill me.'

He said it all with a straight face. The lieutenant squinted a lot and frowned, but he didn't argue the point. After all, as he said later, none of us had seen it.

Meanwhile I had swung down from my pony's back and was looking around. The girl looked up at me with dead, dusty eyes. I couldn't see a weapon that she might have used. I could see her skirt was hiked up pretty far. I could see that there were scratches on DeFord's face and a slash across the girl's throat. I could see that she was Blackfoot, and that made no sense. We had never had any Blackfoot trouble. Mostly they had been our allies against the larger Sioux nation and the Cheyenne as well. I could see no other horse tracks but the ones left by DeFord's buckskin pony that he had hitched in the willow breaks. I told the lieutenant what I thought. I had seen fleeing moccasin tracks and a place where the girl had gone down on her hands and knees after she had been tackled from behind. I gave my opinion without being asked.

'He waylaid her and tried to rape her. She fought back and he killed her.'

'That's a damn lie!' DeFord said. His eyes distended and raked me from out of his clawed-up face.

You never have seen such hate. At least I hope you haven't. The lieutenant frowned some more and squinted and told two of his men to bury the woman.

That was as far as it went. There never was much urge in those days to try a man for killing an Indian under any circumstances, and as the lieutenant kept saying, it was true – none of us actually had seen what had occurred. But I knew. I made my living reading sign, and I knew what had been done. The army didn't care to hear my comments, they had more important business to conduct. I made a nuisance of myself and raised a little hell in the major's office. He had me thrown out of the HQ building. It kept gnawing at me for a long time, but it was doing no one any good, least of all me, and after awhile I got angry enough to ride out without even collecting my pay. I don't remember anybody waving goodbye to me as I passed through the gates.

I hadn't expected to meet up again with DeFord in Deadwood, but here he was. While everyone was having a good laugh about my liver I had one drink and went back outside to watch the high, cold sky where only a single bulky white cloud shadowed the long plains in its slow passing.

The reason I was in Deadwood was as simple as sin. Della Adair had sent for me and I couldn't refuse her request. I had known Della for a long time, since the days when she had traveled up to the fort in her silk and lace with four or five other girls and parked her wagon outside the palisade, waiting for the soldiers' payday to roll around. Don't bother telling me what she was. I know it. There's a hundred different words for it, and none of them is very pretty. It didn't matter, in that time and place. She was a woman to be with, and we sometimes would sit around a small fire out on the prairie and just talk. Sometimes we didn't speak for long hours; that was all right too. She would sit on the ground, or a rock if one was handy, her knees drawn up, her red silk dress shimmering in the low glow of firelight, now and then smoking a thin black cigar. Sometimes her head would go to her knees as the cold wind blew and she would say things like, 'God, how did I ever come to this?' in a way that would break your heart. I never responded. What do you say to people when they're feeling that way? I don't know. Maybe a wiser man than I would.

On this evening I again met Della as arranged, and she embraced me warmly, held me at arm's length to study my face and hooked her arm through mine, leading me out of her hotel room to walk slowly out onto the dark, empty prairie. There was something serious on her mind, something she didn't want to have overheard by curious listeners. We walked on until the town was just a small collection of twinkling lights; then we stopped. Looking around for a clear patch of ground, she lowered herself to a sitting position, drawing her knees up, and after a long minute she looked up and asked, 'We are friends, aren't we, Miles?'

'Of course we are. We've known each other for some time now, haven't we?'

'Sure,' she said, lifting her eyes to the starry night while she sighed. 'But that's not what I mean. I've known a lot of the boys out here … you know. I don't think there are many who would call themselves my friend come morning.'

'I don't know. You're pretty popular.'

'I'm in demand, you are saying. That's not what I mean at all.'

No. I guess I knew that. 'Have you a reason for asking, Della? Or is it just one of

15

those nights when a person needs to know?'

'Oh,' she said, looking back toward me with her sad, dark eyes. 'It's some of both, I expect.'

She hesitated. 'I need to ask you a question, Miles,' Della said softly. 'Are you working?'

'Not so's you'd notice it,' I had to admit. Somewhere distantly a coyote barked and her litter of pups joined in, yipping at the night.

'I need some help. I'll pay you well.'

I waited for her to go on. She still had her legs drawn up, her knees nearly to her breast, her skirt smoothed down over them. 'What's the trouble, Della?'

'I'm selling out,' she told me. 'The saloon business has gotten old. I went into it because it's a ready source of money out here. One of the few things a woman can make a decent profit at.' I nodded my understanding. 'But I've had it, Miles. I have all the money I need to do what I came west for in the first place.'

'Which is?'

'Like most of us, I suppose: find a little piece of land, build a house and settle down. Now I've gotten a letter from my brother Brian. He plans on coming to meet me in Steubenville – where I told him I had a little parcel of land.' She smiled faintly. 'Liar that I am.'

'So you plan to sell the saloon and move down that way,' I said, understanding.

'Yes. A crazy Scotsman named McCulloch drifted into Deadwood last month, looking for an investment opportunity. I mean to sell the Eagle's Lair to him. My brother Brian will be bringing my younger sister, Regina along with him... I don't want either one of them to know how I made my stake.'

'So what is it you want me to help you with?' I asked Della.

'Go with me, Miles. You're a plainsman. You know what to look out for. Indians, bandits, wild creatures. I could do it alone. I am,' she said with strength, 'a woman who has been on her own for a long time, but I'd

17

feel better having a man – a man I could trust – traveling with me.'

'I see,' I said, pondering. It didn't seem like much of a request. Steubenville was not more than a hundred miles south and the weather was holding good. Della still seemed worried, her dark eyes looking up at me, catching starlight. 'Sure, I'll take you down there.'

'It might not be as simple as it sounds,' Della said, leaning back her head as she took a deep breath. 'People know – almost everyone knows that I've decided to sell the saloon, and that I'll have a deal of gold money with me when I do leave town.'

'So you think this might turn into a shooting affair?' I asked.

She hesitated. 'I'm afraid it might,' she answered. 'You understand why I daren't go alone.'

'My first suggestion is that we find at least one other man to go with us,' I told Della. For I had already mentally agreed to help the lady out. I liked Della, and always found her to have a good heart.

Besides, no woman – or man for that matter – would travel those plains alone with a known large quantity of gold money.

'I can't think of a single man I'd trust except you,' Della said.

'What about Henry Coughlin?' I suggested, remembering her old bartender. Della laughed out loud.

'Henry's seventy years old! Can you see him fighting off a band of raiders?'

'He can drive a wagon, can't he?' I replied. 'With you selling out, he will likely be replaced on his job, won't he? If he agrees, he could handle the wagon, leaving me free to ride at will and keep an eye on the backtrail.'

'I hadn't thought of that,' Della said thoughtfully. 'Then Henry and I could spell each other at the reins.'

'That's right. That way, we'd be sure to roll into Steubenville in no more than four, five days. When is your brother expected ... and your sister?'

'Next week,' Della said. 'I'm cutting it

close to find some property and buy it, pretend that I'm a substantial citizen. I'll need to buy some sturdier clothes,' she said, smoothing her silk skirts again, drifting off into a woman's way of thinking. Me, I was thinking about supplies, ammunition, finding a wagon and team of horses. We all have different priorities in this world. Della was thinking mainly of trying to shed her image and refashion herself for her younger sister and brother, Brian.

I was thinking more about getting her to Steubenville alive, her purse intact.

'I'll talk to Henry,' I told Della as I stood, offered her my hand and tugged her to her feet. 'If you can promise him a place to bunk once you get your little place built, he'll leap at it. A seventy-year-old man doesn't have a lot of options in this country.'

'No, you're right. I can promise him that much,' Della said, standing so near to me that I could feel the heated scent of her body. She was still a fine-looking woman, but she was not for me, had never been. I liked her too much as a friend to risk complications.

'Anything else, Della?' I asked, as we started back toward the brawling town. 'Anyone in particular I should be watching?'

She stopped, lifted her eyes once again and answered, 'Of course, Miles. The man we both are going to have to keep an eye on. Tom DeFord has been asking around. He's found out that I am going to sell the saloon and that I am to be paid in gold. I don't think he would have any compunctions about robbing me, do you?'

'No,' I answered carefully.

No, DeFord would have no compunctions at all in robbing a lady out on the lonesome prairie, nor of assaulting her. And if he was given the opportunity to kill me, he would accept that bonus quite cheerfully.

The sky was full dark when we reached Deadwood, meaning it was beginning to wake up. The streets were alive with brawling, staggering men. There was the sound of breaking glass, wild cursing and twice a gunshot sounding. We paused on the porch of the hotel where Della was staying and she looked up and down the rowdy boulevard.

'God, how did I tolerate this for so long?' she said miserably.

'There's things that have to be tolerated to survive,' I said. Me, I felt the same way about Deadwood and any of a hundred other boom-towns scattered across the Dakotas. I liked the big country, the wilderness. There were times when too much solitude can shove a man toward the very brink of madness, but all it took was a day or two, a few hours, in the company of too many men to make me wish to return to the long plains and deep lonely forests.

'Let's go on in,' Della said with a shake of her head. She turned toward the hotel entrance, then halted abruptly, gripping my arm tightly at the elbow. Her face had gone white, her eyes were wide.

'What is it, Della?'

She was a long minute answering. Her gaze was fixed on some unsettling sight I could not make out. 'They're here!' Della said in near-panic.

'Who's here? What are you talking about, Della?'

'My brother, Brian. And Regina.'

Now, studying the length of the boardwalk I saw a tall, rangy man moving with a limp, a young pretty girl on his arm walking directly toward us. I knew what she was thinking. Now they would find out what sort of reputation Della had in Deadwood. There was no way to hide her shame. Her plan had fallen apart.

I put my arm across her quaking shoulders. 'It doesn't matter, Della. If they love you, the rest of it won't matter to them at all.'

But she drew away, put both of her hands on my shoulders, and looking up with haunted eyes, said, 'You don't understand, Miles. If Brian sees Tom DeFord there is bound to be killing done!'

TWO

'Quickly,' Della said, clutching at my coat sleeve, 'let's get inside. Up to my room. I can't think straight.'

We went into the hotel lobby, crossed it to the desk where Della was given her key by the bald-headed clerk without asking, then up the carpeted steps to her second-floor room. Her hands were shaking so that she could hardly fit the key into the lock and so I opened it for her. Entering the lighted room Della rushed to the window, staring down anxiously, her fingers jabbing at her hair, her lower lips trembling slightly.

'What have I done?' she asked herself miserably. 'What have I done?'

I sat on the bed and studied her grief-stricken face for a minute. She started to sob, covered her face with a lace handkerchief and got herself under control.

'It seems we have some talking to do, Della, and quickly. How do you think Brian tracked you to Deadwood?'

'My letters, of course,' she said. 'I wrote to Brian, and to Regina.'

'So they got to Steubenville earlier than expected and decided to come here to look for you.'

'Yes,' she said heavily, turning to face me. 'So it seems.'

I heard footsteps in the corridor and glanced up, but it was only a balding merchant passing, lighting a cigar as he went. 'Come here,' I said to the worried lady, patting the mattress next to me and heavily she walked to the bed and sat down.

'Listen, Della,' I said speaking in a low, confident voice, 'it's your brother and sister we're talking about. They might have learned, or guessed some things that you hoped they wouldn't ever know, but they're still your family. They'll still love you. All right, the plan didn't come off as you'd hoped – when do they ever? That doesn't mean that it's not a good plan for all of you. You can get out of Deadwood, you'll all have a place to live in peace.'

'I can only hope so,' Della said, lifting lantern-lit eyes to me. She breathed in deeply and then out again heavily. 'I wanted them to think highly of me.'

I put my arm around her shoulders and let her finish recovering her composure. Twin shadows fell across the floor and this time, turning my head toward the doorway I saw a tall man and a tiny woman standing in it.

'Get your hands off of her!' the girl shrieked rushing at us. She tried to claw my eyes, but I spun away and rose so that she fell across Della's lap. Backing away from the bed I heard a small metallic sound and glanced up to see the big Colt revolver in Brian Adair's hand, cocked and ready. I backed off a step, raising my arms.

'You like roughing up women?' Brian Adair said. His face was lean, his body narrow, his eyes pale blue and just now filled with cold fire.

'Don't be a fool, Brian!' Della said, coming to her feet. 'Put that gun away.'

'I saw what he did to Gina. I saw him with you.'

'Gina tripped over her own feet,' Della said, her voice returning to a normal level. Standing there coolly in her red silk dress, I saw her gather the firm manner that she must have used many times in the Eagle's Lair to break up a saloon fight between drunken men. 'Put that gun away. This is my friend, Miles Donovan.'

'A good friend?' Regina Adair asked, smoothing her own gingham skirt, her eyes glaring at me and at Della in turn. She was petite, sparingly built as a little doll, with golden hair and fiery eyes. Her question implied that she and Brian had, indeed, heard some stories about Della's lifestyle in Deadwood.

'Yes,' Della said as icily as I've ever heard her, 'a very good friend.'

It wasn't much of a start to a family

reunion. Brian still hadn't holstered his Colt Peacemaker, the two women stood glowering at each other. Me, I stood there foolishly, not knowing if I should even lower my arms to shake hands with Brian Adair.

I said to Della, 'I'll be going. Besides, with Brian here, you won't be needing a driver anymore, will you?'

'I don't like jokes at my expense, friend,' Brian Adair said in a voice that made a rattler's quivering tail sound friendly. It was only then that I noticed that the left sleeve of his tan jacket was pinned up at the elbow. Brian Adair had lost that arm. Feeling the fool, I nevertheless could think of nothing more to say.

'I think you should go talk to Henry,' Della said, drawing me out of the awkward situation. 'I'll explain things to my family.'

Brian Adair now slowly holstered his gun although he looked as if he'd as soon use it. I glanced at Della, at the furious little girl with the mass of golden hair, and nodded. Picking up my hat from the bedpost, I eased past the cold eyes of Brian Adair and out into the hallway, the door to the room closing behind me as I started down the dimly lighted corridor. I could hear their voices, but did not pause to try to overhear any of their conversation.

I liked none of this, but I had given my word to Della, and I would follow through on my promise. Over the rest of it I had no control – what the family thought of Della, what they believed me to be. I shoved all those concerns aside as I stepped out into the cool night, and decided to approach it as I would any other job. You didn't have to like your boss, but if you were drawing wages, you did what you were hired on to do.

I went looking for Henry Coughlin.

I couldn't say that Henry was drunk when I found him in his lonely little shack behind the Eagle's Lair Saloon, but neither could I say that the rheumy-eyed old man was sober. At his invitation I had entered the shack through a leather-hinged door to find him sitting on a tick mattress flung over a loosely sprung iron bed, a bottle of whiskey half empty on the round table near its head, a candle guttering in an iron holder. He looked up with surprise.

'Miles?'

'That's right.'

'Haven't seen you for a long while. Sit down and have a drink with me. There should be a chair somewhere under that pile of clothes,' he said, with a nearly toothless grin. I shoved his dirty laundry aside and sat on the heavy, homemade wooden chair, facing him, my hat tilted back.

'Good to see you, Henry.'

'What brings you down Deadwood way?' he asked, pouring another two fingers of whiskey into a greasy glass.

'Work,' I told him.

'That's something, then,' the old man said, working his knuckly, arthritic hands. 'Me, I've got a job for two more days, or so they tell me. You heard about the Scotsman buying Della's place?'

'I heard,' I nodded. 'That's why I'm here, Henry.'

He rubbed his whisker-stubbled chin. 'Have a drink. What's your meaning, son? Why are you here?'

'An offer of work – from Della.'

'Della.' His eyes closed briefly and he shook his head. 'What a woman. Took me off the street and set me up behind the bar. I'd have been dead by now if it weren't for Della. Woman's got the biggest heart any ever had.'

'She needs your help now, Henry.'

'My help? I don't know what help I can be to anybody – myself included – but Della don't even have to ask. What is it, Miles?'

I explained matters to him. The old man wagged his head heavily, his thin arms dangling between his bony knees as he listened. Sorrowfully he told me, 'You do have trouble now.'

'What do you mean, Henry?'

'Brian Adair, is what I mean. How much do you know about him?'

'Nothing at all – except that he took an instant dislike to me.'

Henry waved a hand as if my remark were insignificant. Lifting those weary eyes he told me, 'He spent three years in Andersonville. You know about that place, don't you, Miles.'

I nodded. Everyone knew about that Confederate prison camp in Georgia where 13,000 men had died and thousands of other captured soldiers had been beaten, starved and left to freeze under the watch of indifferent or sadistic guards. The first warden, a man named John Henry Winder, would certainly have been tried and hung for war crimes had he not died in February of 1865, just three months before hostilities ended.

Henry Coughlin went on. 'Brian Adair was captured after his horse was shot out from under him – at Bull Run, I believe. His arm was broken in the fight, a musket ball shattering it. He was captured and taken to Andersonville, but his arm was never treated, and in time gangrene set in. They sawed it off without morphine or any other anesthetic. He might have recovered when his arm was first set, but they made him work with it that way, even used clubs to beat on it.'

'I could see where that would make a man bitter.'

Henry stroked his whiskered chin and hoisted his whiskey glass to his lips again. 'There's more to it,' he told me as he slapped the glass back down on the rickety table. I waited.

'Tom DeFord was one of those guards at Andersonville.'

I was silent for a minute, hearing two dogs barking in the muddy yard outside the cabin, the sounds of raucous cowboys in the saloon. 'Does Brian know that?' I asked Henry.

''Course he does. A man treated that way don't forget a name or a face. Not even after all the years that have passed since then.'

'Does he know that DeFord's here? In Deadwood at this moment?'

'Hope not. Hope he don't find out. You see now what Della was trying to avoid, why she's so upset?'

I did. As much as she did not want her brother and young sister to know the kind of life she had been living, they had probably surmised as much long ago. Della was trying to protect her fragile reputation as much as possible, but more she was trying to keep Brian from being killed – or being hanged as a killer himself. Knowing Brian was sure to fight if he ran across DeFord, knowing her brother was on his way west could even have been a part of the reason for her deciding to sell the Eagle's Lair in the first place.

'We'd better not let any grass grow under our feet,' I said, rising from the chair. 'Best find us a wagon and team and get Della and Brian out of town before anything can happen.'

'I agree with you, Miles,' Henry said. His grim face grew taut with determination. He picked up the cork to the whiskey bottle and

CARDIFF
CAERDYDD

thumped it into place.

'You're still willing to go along with us,' I asked, 'knowing all that you know?'

'Miles,' the old man said lifting his eyes. 'Look around you. This is my life and I won't even be able to get a job good enough to support this way of life. Della said she would take me in once she builds her place in Steubenville. Della's word is her bond; I know her. Dying slowly in this cold shack is my only alternative – 'course I'm with you. Let's go look at some horses.'

Tramping across the muddy street to the stable I had time to consider how things had suddenly snarled up. DeFord undoubtedly knew about Della's gold and wanted it. Having me along wouldn't deter him any. He hated my liver. Now with Brian Adair we had another gun, but yet another reason for DeFord to attack us, before Brian could smear DeFord's reputation all across the territory. Or come stalking him. I had been right – we had to depart Deadwood as quickly and secretively as possible. In fact, I had it in mind to try it on this very night under cover of darkness.

Henry agreed with me. 'Sooner the better. But, say, has Della gotten her money from the Scotsman yet?'

'I don't know. Maybe he was waiting for the bank to open tomorrow. Maybe he keeps that much on hand. I'll have to ask Della. Meanwhile, let's do what we can to get the trek organized.'

I didn't know what Brian and Regina had arrived on, but the stable hand, Jocko Gates, a little gnome of a man, pointed at a well-used little surrey resting in the corner of the high-ceilinged stable. That would have to be abandoned. Maybe Brian would agree to sell it, maybe not. No matter, it wasn't fit for what we intended. I explained to Jocko that we needed a heavy wagon and strong team.

If Della had any furniture and such household things she had intended to take with her to Steubenville, I would try to talk her out of it. I wasn't acting panicky, by any means. My mind was cool and deliberate, but we urgently needed to get out of Dead-wood before Brian and DeFord discovered each other.

In these far-flung settlements, every new arrival was scrutinized with interest. By now someone knew of the presence of a one-armed man and a pretty young girl. They were a pair to raise interest.

'Their horses are a pretty fine pair,' Jocko Gates was telling us, 'but they're worn down, not fit for another long trip without some rest. Besides, they ain't built for wagon haul-ing.'

I looked Brian Adair's team over. Two leggy, good-looking sorrels. They were beautiful animals, but not suited for draw-ing a covered wagon, which was what we needed for the road to Steubenville. Would he be willing to sell them? I had no idea. How was I to explain to him the need for urgency? Probably he had meant to rest up in Deadwood for a day or two and then head back toward Steubenville with Della. I would have to put my head together with Della and let her try to figure a way to explain this to her brother.

'You're right, these are beautiful horses, but they're too light, their legs too slender. What can you show me by way of dray horses?'

'You can take this lantern,' Jocko said, taking one from the wall and handing it to me, 'and look over the stock in the pen out back as best you can. You said you needed a wagon, too?'

'If you've got one.'

'I've got,' Jocko said.

'Henry, maybe you had better take a look at it. You know what we need.'

Henry nodded and the two older men started out the front of the stable, turning toward a yard where Jocko kept a variety of rolling stock. I went to the back entrance, pausing to visit my own horse, a rangy black with one white ear and a splash of white on his flank named Dodger. He seemed pleased to see me, if a little irked because I hadn't exercised him. He would get plenty of that soon. I dipped a scoop of oats from Jocko's bin and put it into Dodger's feed trough, stroking his sleek dark neck for a time. Then I went out into the chill dark night to look for a pair of tough, heavy dray animals, if such I could find.

I paused, put the lantern on a fence post, turned up my collar to the cold wind and reached for a match. It was then that they jumped me.

I heard the rush of boots before I turned to see their bulky shadows coming at me from out of the darkness of the stableyard. Two big men and bent on mischief, they slammed into me as one, and I was driven to the ground, the lantern flying free of my hand.

I grabbed for my Colt, but, anticipating that, one of them had pinned my arms to my sides while the other yanked the revolver from my holster and flung it away.

Then they got to work. I was thrown

roughly to the ground and they set upon me.

One of them kicked me in the ribs as I tried to roll away from them and the other tried stomping my face. I was able to grab his ankle, twist and shove him off. He went sprawling as the second, bear-like thug tried kicking me again. I managed to reach out and grip the lowest rail of the horse corral and drag myself to my feet even as my assailant swung two hard punches into my ribs.

The horses circled and whinnied in fright, their peace disturbed by the brawl. The night was dark and moonless, and even as the second man recovered to join his friend, they had trouble finding targets for their heavy punches as I rolled my head and body from side to side, ducking and weaving.

My head, foggy from their first attack, was now clearing and I felt a surge of anger. The man in front of me took a step back, trying to get leverage for his fists, and I doubled up my leg, kicking him in the chest with all the strength I could muster. He sagged to his knees, clutching his heart.

Without waiting to see what he would do next, I turned my attention to the other faceless hoodlum. Stocky, of medium height, he wore a beard. That I discovered as I hooked a right-hand shot into his jaw, staggering him. He growled a curse and came in again. From the corner of my eye I could see the other one rising heavily to join in the beating.

'Hey! What's going on out here!'

Henry Coughlin emerged from the stable, the open door casting a rectangle of light across the straw-dusted yard. Behind him came Jocko Gates. Jocko had snatched up his double-twelve shotgun and he pulled the trigger, loosing a fiery warning blast of buckshot into the night sky. The two thugs took to their heels.

I considered giving chase, but hadn't the breath to do it. I bent over, hands on my knees, still leaning against the corral rails as the excited horses continued to mill. Henry was beside me in moments, his scrawny hand around my shoulders.

'Are you all right, Miles?'

'Yes. Thanks to you two.'

'Who were they?' Jocko asked, staring up the darkened alley where my assailants had fled.

'No idea,' I answered. I held my chest where a fiery pain reminded me of a boot toe's impact. I was hoping they hadn't broken a rib. Nothing is more painful or takes longer to heal.

'Let's go inside and take a look at you,' Jocko suggested, and I did not argue. My head was still reeling, my legs a little wobbly.

Sitting me on an empty barrel, Henry looked over my face, judging me mostly sound, although: 'You will have a terrific black eye by morning.' I rubbed my sore cheek and took a deep slow breath, testing. The rib did not seem to be cracked. It's difficult to take in a full breath without pain when a rib is cracked – I know.

Jocko brought me a tin cup of dark strong

coffee. At first sip I could tell he had added a dollop of whiskey. I made no objection.

'Who could that have been?' Henry Coughlin wondered out loud. 'Think it was Tom DeFord, Miles?'

'Tom,' I said sincerely, 'wouldn't use fists and boots. He would have just plugged me.'

'I think you're right,' Henry agreed. 'How about this Brian, Della's brother? You said you and he had a run-in.'

'Neither man was him.' I would know if I had been fighting a one-armed man, no matter how dark the yard was, although he could have hired two rowdies to beat me. 'We didn't have a good first meeting,' I explained. 'But it wasn't so bad that a man would set out to do harm to someone over it. Besides,' I concluded, 'I mark him as the kind of man who would take care of his own business, and in daylight.'

Shaking his head, Jocko said, 'Probably two drifters hoping to rob you of drinking money.'

'Probably,' I agreed, rising, handing the

44

empty coffee cup back to Jocko. But neither of my attackers had made a move toward my wallet, tried my pockets where I had some money Della had given me to purchase what we needed. No, there was more to it than a robbery attempt. I might never discover what was behind it. No matter – just now there was business to be taken care of.

'Let's have a look at those horses,' I said.

'They've settled down now,' Jocko said, glancing toward the corral. 'If you don't mind, I'm keeping this scattergun under my arm while you have your look.'

I had no objection at all. I took up the lantern and looked for my gun. I found it where it had been thrown under a bush. I asked Henry, 'Did you find a wagon?'

'A sturdy old Conestoga. Even has good canvas on it still. Front axle seems a little splayed, but it'll do for a run to Steuben-ville.'

I would have to accept Henry Coughlin's judgement as sound; besides we didn't have the time to be particular. I had the feeling that the episode at Jocko's tonight was just a sample of things to come, and we were well off getting shed of Deadwood as early as possible in the morning.

Someone wanted me out of the way. Someone wanted Della's hard-earned gold.

And there were two violent men involved in this who would be more than willing to do murder on sight.

THREE

I had to get Della alone to speak to her
about matters. It was near to midnight when
I again knocked on her hotel room door. My
body had begun to stiffen up and there was
a fair-sized knot on my temple from the
stableyard fight. My head was throbbing
heavily and I was beginning to regret taking
on the job.

Della in a blue silk wrapper clutched at her
breast opened the door, her hair unpinned,
her eyes appearing slightly haunted. I didn't
think she had been asleep. Her eyes opened
a little wider as she studied my face. Glancing up and down the corridor, she swept me
into her room where a lantern burned low
on a bedside table.

'What happened to you, Miles?' she asked
with concern. She was dipping a washcloth

in her basin.

'Obvious, isn't it?' I asked. 'Just don't ask me why it happened or who did it, because I don't know.'

She dabbed lightly at my nicks and pressed the cool cloth to the lump on my head. Turning the lantern up a little she looked more closely at my face, made small 'tsking' sounds and then sat on the bed, tucking her robe between her knees.

'I didn't mean for there to be any trouble,' she told me.

'I expected some – but not this soon,' I told the dark-eyed woman. 'Listen, Della, we have to get out of town tonight. I've been told that your brother and Tom DeFord have a blood grudge between them.'

'Yes,' she admitted.

'This is bad news for us – Brian showing up in Deadwood. With what I've already learned of Brian's temper,' I said, 'and of DeFord's brutal nature, one of them would have to be killed if they learn of the other's presence.

'Yes,' Della said unhappily, 'I know that.

You're right, unfortunately.'

'The sooner we get out of Deadwood, the better. Too many people are waiting for us to pull out anyway. Everyone in town knows that you'll have a purse full of gold. I know you asked me to help, but I can't fight off a gang of men alone. Brian can't ride a horse and shoot at the same time, Henry's ... well, he's Henry. There's no time to look for other trustworthy men – assuming we could find any.'

'This is too much, too fast,' Della said, poking at her loose hair with her fingertips. I knew the lady. She was strong and confident, but I had apparently shaken her with the news about DeFord and Brian.

'I'm sorry, Della. I know it is hurried. But we have to leave tonight – I feel that's the best way. Henry has a Conestoga and a four-horse team. He and Jocko Gates are hitching the team and greasing the axles. The wagon will be ready within the hour. We should gather what you consider necessary and load up.

'I haven't...' Della seemed suddenly over-whelmed. Maybe like a lot of people the distance between conceiving a plan and the reality of putting it into motion was a large step for her.

'If you'll get dressed, we can go and try to talk to this Scotsman, this McCulloch. He was planning on paying you in the morning, signing the papers. He might have planned for the transaction, withdrawn the money from the bank.'

'He's a Scot; he doesn't believe in banks.'

'All the better. We have to do this, Della. I don't want you to think I'm pushing it, but...'

'Yes, yes,' she said, her voice growing more hectic. 'I can see that we have to try it. There'll be Jocko Gates's bill... I can see that we have to try to do this tonight.' She rose and touched her forehead with the heel of her hand. 'What can I tell Brian and Regina without giving away the reason for this change in plans?'

'Keep it vague,' was my advice. 'Tell them

that there have been threats. Embellish it any way you like.'

'I suppose I can pull it off. The surrey. Brian's horses,' she continued as if talking only to herself. Swiftly she went to her closet and began sorting through her clothes with rapid fingers. I rose to look out the window at the still-bustling streets to give my eyes something to do while she dressed.

It was then that Regina burst into the room.

'You!' she shouted as the door banged open. The blond girl, her hair free in the night, dressed in a cotton robe, glanced at her half-undressed sister and returned her slashing gaze to me. Her voice was a heavily emotional pant. 'Didn't you learn anything tonight? Leave my sister alone! It's men like you that...!'

She came nearer, her tiny fists clenched, her face an angry mask. Della grabbed Regina from behind and spun her around.

'Stop it!' Della yelled. Still panting, Regina drew away, brushing her sister's hand from her shoulder.

'You have no right to tell me what I should do – look at you!' Regina hollered back. I didn't like the anger in the two women's eyes. I didn't like witnessing an apparently long-held bitterness come to the surface. Such scenes always make me uncomfortable and I never know how to defuse them.

'I'll be out front,' I muttered in Della's direction and left the room, hearing low angry words being exchanged behind me.

It was fifteen minutes before Della emerged from the hotel to join me on the porch. In that time I had seen two fights, saw one riderless horse racing through town, heard more curse words than even I knew, seen a bottle thrown through a storefront window and once a woman accosted. And yet presumably normal people chose to live in Deadwood. Me, I'm for the long open prairie and the woodlands. Living a solitary life leaves me alone with company I'm more comfortable with – I seldom cuss myself.

'I'm sorry,' Della said breathlessly. Her hair was still loose, having had no time to pin it up, but it was concealed under the hood of her fur-lined jacket.

'You did nothing, Della.'

'I did. I've been hurting Regina deeply for years. I just never knew how much until tonight.'

I didn't respond to that. I'm not bright enough to give advice about such matters. 'Where does this McCulloch live?' I asked.

She led the way up the still-rowdy main street and turned off along a lane lined with struggling newly-planted chestnut trees. Here there were widely spaced new homes of sawn lumber and even a wrought-iron fence or two. Deadwood's nouveau riche, what few there were of them had built here to distance themselves from the common element – of which there were many.

We walked past an unfinished brick gateway and groups of elm saplings to the front door of a respectable two-story brick house. It was unlighted, and no wonder considering that midnight had come and gone.

'I don't know...' Della said hesitantly as we approached the heavy oaken door with its brass knocker.

'We have to, Della. You've done things in your time that took a lot more courage than this.' She smiled with gratitude in response to my encouragement, lifted the heavy knocker and banged it down sharply three times. I immediately heard grumbling from above. When the Scotsman appeared in a black robe, his thin reddish hair tousled, he was taken aback by the sight of the hooded lady in red and the rangy, rough-dressed plainsman he saw.

'Mr McCulloch,' Della said, pulling her hood back, 'it is very important that I talk to you. Now.'

McCulloch hesitated, looking at me as if I might be ready to rob or assault him, but finally he nodded and stepped aside, ushering us into a dark entranceway of which I could see little and into an office where he lit a lantern with a green shade and sagged behind an ornately carved oak desk.

'What is it, then?' he asked, impatience obvious in his voice. Della began to explain, leaning forward. Her hands constantly gesturing, earnestly she asked if there were some way he could finish executing the sale of the Eagle's Lair and find the funds to pay her off on that night.

The Scotsman's eyes narrowed as he leaned back. 'I might not be able to come up with the full amount on such short notice,' McCulloch replied after a while. I thought he was probably lying, but the business end of this matter was not my concern. Della had made herself a neat fortune out west, starting with nothing at all. She was every bit a match for the investor.

I let them talk while I gazed around the room. An assortment of antique firearms and medieval weapons hung on the paneled walls. There was a small glass-fronted book-case and a white-brick fireplace so new that there were not even smudges on it.

I turned as the Scotsman rose and walked

to a small green safe I had not seen in the corner. He glanced at me furtively, and now I saw that there was a holstered pistol beneath his robe on the right side. I turned away again, not wanting to give him the wrong impression of my intent.

I shifted my eyes back at the clink of a small sack filled with gold coins striking the desktop. Della had finished signing the deed. Now she blew on the ink to dry it and handed the papers over to McCulloch.

The Scotsman looked satisfied. He must have managed to dicker Della down a little, her urgency being obvious.

Outside I told Della, 'I hope I didn't cost you much.'

She laughed. 'I was gouging the old faker to begin with. Here.' She handed the gold sack to me. At my look of surprise she said, 'You've signed on to protect me and my money, Miles. Here's where you start earning your pay.'

I nodded, tied the rawhide thongs at the top of the bag around my belt and stuffed it inside my trousers. We walked through the heavy cold shadows back toward the heart of Deadwood. Della's face was hidden by her hood. I couldn't make out her expression, though I could see starlight in her eyes. I admired the woman in a way that I found hard to define. So many men had loved her and a few had become almost obsessively fascinated by her. Too many. To me she was a fine, strong woman doing her best to survive in a difficult time and place. And a good friend.

'Now for the hard part,' Della said as we reached main street again, finding it as rowdy as ever. Dozens of boisterous drunks crowded the boardwalks.

'What do you mean?'

'Waking Brian up and telling him that we're going on to Steubenville this very night. They've only arrived, and haven't had but a few hours' sleep.'

'Do you want me to...?' I began.

'No, Miles,' she said, touching my wrist. 'It's much better if I do it, believe me.'

She was right of course. Brian Adair and I hadn't hit it off well at our first meeting. Nor had Regina fallen for my charms. I was recalling what the young woman had said earlier: 'Didn't you learn anything tonight?' It gave me pause to wonder if it had been Regina who had hired two goons to beat me up, perhaps convinced that I had led her sister astray. I said nothing to Della who was, I imagined, composing a speech in her mind to explain the sudden urgency to Brian; to manage that without having to mention Tom DeFord.

'If Father had only known,' I heard Della sigh. I had no idea what she meant, but she was willing to tell me as we walked along the plankwalk toward the hotel. 'Brian has always been a bit of a problem. I do love him, but it seems he complicates things wherever he goes. Of course those years in Andersonville Prison did nothing to soften his rough edges. He was adopted, Miles.'

'I didn't know that.'

'Yes, Father took him in when he was only

four years old. Mother had died by then, and Father – I suspect – had always wanted a son. There was always something a little disturbing about Brian. I don't know,' she said, shrugging one shoulder.

'Such as?'

'Small things. He would steal trinkets from me that he had no use for. A ring my mother left me. Once we had a kitten that ... well, it seemed that someone had tortured the poor creature. Brian was always peeking into personal items. My diary, clothing ... did you know we were being followed?' Della asked, squeezing my arm.

'Yes.' I had noticed it, but hoped that Della hadn't. Someone had been walking nearly on our shadows since we left McCulloch's house. 'It probably means nothing,' I said to ease her mind. Then I asked with some concern, 'Della, do you think that Brian could possibly want your money himself? That the gold could be the reason that he came west after all these years.'

'Of course not!' she said sharply, and I was

immediately sorry that I had spoken up. 'He is my brother.' The look in her eyes did not have the same conviction as her words. She murmured a slight apology and then instructed me as we reached the hotel door, 'Check on Henry and the wagon, all right? Pay off Jocko Gates...' She hesitated, making up her mind, and decided.

'Just go ahead and sell Brian's surrey and his matched sorrels to Jocko if you can. Brian will be angry, but I'll pay him well for them when we reach Steubenville.'

'All right. Henry and I will bring the wagon around back. If there's things you need from your room...'

'Only my trunk.'

'Della, are you sure that you want me holding all this gold? I mean, a man could just saddle up and ride off with it, couldn't he?'

'Some,' she said in a way that touched me, 'but not a man like you Miles Donovan.' She went to tiptoes, kissed my cheek and swept into the hotel lobby leaving me on the boardwalk while the riotous town continued its wild ways.

I went off to find Henry Coughlin, fully aware that I still had a man following in my shadow. Tom DeFord? An aimless wanderer? Someone McCulloch had sent to reclaim his gold? One of the two men who had jumped me earlier? Brian Adair?

It was too much to consider. I simply walked swiftly toward Jocko's stable, my hand on the staghorn grips of my Colt, the small cold bag of gold coins thumping against my thigh.

At sometime around 2 a.m., I saddled my black horse and gave him his bit, swung aboard and started toward the alley behind the hotel, Henry Coughlin driving the four-horse team drawing the creaking Conestoga wagon in my wake.

I swung down from my black in the coolness of the night. Henry looped his reins around the brake handle and walked toward me, rubbing his hands together. 'Seen any more of your tail?' he asked, for I had told him of the man following me.

'No. Maybe he was just somebody wandering around aimlessly.'

'But you don't think so,' Henry said. 'I've something to show you, Miles.'

'All right.' I followed him back to the wagon, leading Dodger. Henry lowered the tailgate of the wagon and gestured me nearer. His hand touched the floorboard of the wagon, worked around a little and then lifted a neatly sawn length of wood from the bed. His voice dropped even lower. 'The man who owned this last had built himself a little cubbyhole here. I found it while I was checking the wagon over.'

'Can't see it in the dark, that's for sure,' I commented.

'It was put back in a little cockeyed or I'd have never found it even with my lantern back at Jocko's. If you throw a trunk, some bedding over it, no one will ever find it.'

That was a stroke of good fortune. I couldn't continue with the gold sack down my pant-leg, nor did I just want to thrust it into my saddlebags where any searcher could discover it.

'Anybody around?' I asked Henry, and he looked up and down the alley, at the un-lighted hotel windows.

'Not a soul,' he said, and I undid the ties on my belt, hoisted the gold pouch from my pantleg and stuffed it into the hidden compartment, carefully replacing the sawn plank the right way so that the wood grain matched.

'Where are the others?' Henry asked when we were done.

'They should be out in a few minutes. Della has a trunk she wants to bring along. I don't know what else.'

'This brother of hers,' Henry said cautiously. 'What do you know about him?'

'Nothing much. I just wouldn't mention to him that the gold is on board the wagon. Maybe we shouldn't even tell Della,' I said, thinking that she might somehow slip up. She had given the money into my care and so I was going to play it my way.

'You know, Miles, there was a man come by the stable and asked me if I had seen a one-armed man. That wasn't more than an hour ago.'

I didn't like that, but I said nothing. Too many people were interested in what our party was up to. The back door to the hotel swung open and a rectangle of lanternlight spread itself against the rutted alley.

Della emerged first, holding one end of a heavy trunk by its leather strap. Brian held the other handle. Behind them came the so-pretty and angry Regina Adair. She marched right up to me while the other three leveraged the trunk into the wagon bed.

'Where is Brian's surrey?' she demanded, looking up at me from my collar line.

'It seemed best that we all travel together.'

'Why? I can handle that surrey. I drove it all the way up here.'

'That surrey's awful light for rough travel, and the horses were weary. It seemed better to purchase a fresh team.'

'Who decides what's for the better – you?'

Behind me Brian Adair said in a surprisingly controlled voice. 'It's done, Regina. Leave it alone.'

Biting back some other harsh words she had for me, Regina flounced off toward the wagon box to clamber up beside Henry who had gloves on now, reins in hand. Brian and Della scooted up into the wagon, Brian seating himself on the tailgate, watching me with cold thoughtful eyes as I swung aboard Dodger, and Henry Coughlin started the heavy wagon rolling through the alleyway.

I kneed the black and started along after them, glancing around. There was still someone following us. But now they were mounted, and now there were two of them.

What had I gotten myself into?

FOUR

The cluster of crows rose in dark, raucous unison from the barren cottonwood tree as dawn streaked the long skies with burnt orange and deep purple. I shifted in the saddle, already a little trail-weary after the night ride. The crows circled us, like some unknown enemy, and drifted back toward the broken tree as the Conestoga wagon passed. My black horse plodded on tirelessly, though I could tell by the way his head hung that he was ready for a rest. The same must have held true for the team of horses drawing the wagon and I heeled my pony on ahead to signal Henry Coughlin that it was time to draw up and let the big horses breathe.

It would have been nice if there were water for the animals, but so far as I knew there was no creek or river along our path, and it had not rained recently to leave ponds in the low-lying areas. The land was dry and quite cold as morning joined us. The first glint of golden sunlight spread across the stubble grass, and with it rose a breeze that brought a chill to my bones.

If there was anyone following us, they were cautious, wily. I had held myself back during the night ride, watching and listening. There was no sign of the two riders we had spotted as we left Deadwood. Maybe we were too jumpy. They could have been nothing more than two men who happened to hit the trail late, traveling in the same direction as we were. I just didn't like coincidences, considering the way matters lay.

Now as daylight blossomed, coloring the land, I still could see no riders although we were on open prairie now. Flat, featureless land, uninhabited except by the small buffalo herd I'd spotted to the east of us. There were no more than five hundred of the shaggy beasts, grazing their steady way south as they followed a primitive urging, sensing that winter would soon be upon us.

Henry stepped from the box stiffly and took off his hat to wipe his brow. 'I'm too old for this,' he said, as I swung down from Dodger and walked up to meet him.

He did look tired out, but I told him, 'You'd put a younger man to shame.'

'Maybe, but I could use some sleep, Miles. You care to drive for a while?'

'That kind of defeats the purpose of me being out watching our backtrail, Henry. It'll have to be one of the others.'

'There's only the two women,' he said, looking toward the rear of the wagon where Brian Adair stood, rubbing his leg with his single hand. 'The kid there, that Regina, was telling me the last twenty miles how she could drive twice as better'n I can. Shall we let her try?'

I glanced at the young blond girl, her cheeks flushed, the dawn light painting highlights in her golden hair. 'Why not?' I shrugged. 'We know she can handle a two-horse team. I don't think Della is up to it.'

'The girl don't seem to like you much,' Henry said.

'I can't do a thing about that. A lot of people don't like me.' I stood deep in thought, watching the young girl, the one-armed man and Della. They were a strange little family group, I thought. Almost as if she could feel my eyes on her, Regina lifted her head and returned my gaze. She strode toward us, her white blouse pressed against her breasts, her divided buckskin skirt swishing against her ankles, her blue eyes hard.

'Isn't it time we started again?' Regina asked.

'It is. Think you can handle the team?'

Her eyes grew mocking. 'I can handle about anything, mister.'

'All right then. Spell Henry, let him get a few hours' sleep.' I told her, 'Drift a little westward. The ground's rougher, but we want to stay away from the buffalo herd.'

'Why?' she demanded. I was getting tired

of her confrontational tone, but I explained simply.

'As far as we know there are no Indians around, but there could be. With winter coming on, this might be their last chance for a buffalo hunt. We don't need to be in the vicinity of the herd.'

She looked at me for a long time, nodded her understanding and walked back toward the wagon, pulling her fringed gloves on. Henry Coughlin glanced at me, half-smiled and started that way himself. I mounted my black horse and waited to see them on their way. Brian Adair's face was set in a scowl as he perched on the tailgate of the wagon. Della looked at me as if she would like to have talked to me, as if there was something that needed saying, but then, lifting her skirts, she climbed up onto the wagon box to sit beside her sister.

No sooner was Della aboard than Regina snapped the reins and the four-horse team lumbered into motion. I shook my head. The wind was becoming colder, shifting my horse's mane and tail; the land was an end-less progression of grassy hummocks. It was a sterile land and a lonely one. I didn't like what was going on around me. Much of it did not feel quite right, although I didn't know what it was that was making me jumpy.

No matter – I could take three more days of it, for Della's sake. I turned the black slightly northward and began to search our backtrail for approaching riders.

I hadn't seen the two men following since the night before. Maybe I had been wrong about them as well. My biggest concern was Tom DeFord, of course. When he came, if he did, he wouldn't come alone, and he would not leave peacefully.

I made my way along the rim of a coulee, some twenty feet deep and twice as wide. The bottom of the depression was clotted with thickets of gray willow brush, with an occasional sycamore growing there. I could smell water, but saw none flowing. The wind continued to rise, flattening the long grass. In the northern distances I could see cold gray stacks of approaching rainclouds. I hoped we could reach Steubenville before the heavy winds pushed the storm over us.

I didn't even see them coming.

My attention had been on the backtrail, watching the horizon for any sign of approaching riders. The two mounted men rode at me from out of the coulee bottom, guns at the ready. It was more than foolish of me; it was inexcusable to have been caught unaware like that. As an old army scout I had seen entire bands of Indians on horseback rise up from one of these deep draws cut into the plains, seeming to appear onto the flat surrounding prairie as from out of the earth itself.

I spun Dodger, but the black horse reared, startled by the rush of the charging men. Before I could settle my pony, let alone level my rifle on them, they had sided me with their horses, grabbing the black's bridle, clubbing my Winchester from my hand.

'All right!' One of them, a stocky man with

deep-set eyes shouted at me, 'Where is he?'

'Who?' I was rubbing my wrist where the other one, a narrow-built man with a crooked mouth had cracked it with the muzzle of his pistol.

'Who, he asks! Swing down, friend,' the stocky man said and I obliged, having little choice. I stood facing them as they dismounted to stand before me, each angry looking, trail dusty; each with a rifle in his hand and a Colt revolver on his hip.

'We'll brook no hindrance,' the stocky man said. My eyes narrowed a little at this odd phrasing. Simultaneously I was looking past them toward the wagon, now long vanished on the plains.

'Tell us where Brian Adair is and you might come out of this alive.'

Adair? It was Della's brother they were hunting. Why? I hesitated too long in answering. The narrow man kicked me behind the knee, buckling my leg and I went down on my back, hard. He hovered over me with the stock of his rifle raised menacingly as if he would bring it down against my face.

Who were these two men? I held up a hand and they let me sit up. The narrow-built man stepped away, his chest heaving with emotion. He was angry enough to do about anything. The stocky man with the tiny eyes was calmer and seemed to be the one in charge.

'I'd talk if I was you, son. Lazarus here has a hair trigger if you haven't noticed.'

'What does this man, Adair, look like?' I asked, trying to stall.

'You don't know him?'

'Not by that name,' I lied. I repeated my question, 'What does he look like?'

'Lean, tall. Only has one arm. You were seen leaving Deadwood with him,' the man named Lazarus said with menace.

'That one!' I said, as if finally understanding. 'He gave us five dollars to smuggle him out of town. He said someone was looking for him.'

The two glanced doubtfully at each other. Lazarus said, 'He's in that wagon still, Barry.'

'Is that so?' the stocky man asked me. 'What wagon?'

Lazarus had run out of patience. He kicked me in the ribs and I felt a bone crack. My breath rushed out of me and hot pain took its place. I lay on my back, holding my ribcage. The men in the alley behind the stable had almost broken my ribs. Lazarus had done it properly. I could feel the jagged pain of broken bone. I thought he was going to finish the job, but the man called Barry held him back, placing a gloved hand on his arm.

'We'll find out soon enough,' he told his partner. Then to me, 'You said someone was looking for Adair, someone he was afraid of meeting. Who was it?'

I was tired of lying. 'A man named Tom De-Ford,' I said, managing to sit up again, holding my ribs with both arms. Astonishingly, they laughed. Both of them. My hair was in my eyes; I had a broken rib. I was sitting on the cold prairie earth with a colder wind blowing. And they were laughing.

'You're either a fool or a damned liar,' Barry said.

I didn't know how to respond. There was something happening here that I didn't understand. Lazarus was hovering over me, his mouth set in a mean little grin. I thought he would like nothing more than to kick me again. My face must have shown both pain and incomprehension.

'You damned fool,' Barry said. 'Adair and DeFord run with the same gang. They've been together off and on since the war. Whenever opportunity shines, you'll find 'em riding side by side.'

'You're wrong,' I said, shaking my head painfully. 'I happen to know that Adair was a prisoner in Andersonville. That Tom DeFord was a prison guard there.'

Lazarus laughed again; Barry did not. 'Mister,' he said, 'you're right on both counts. But Adair survived Andersonville when a lot of others didn't. Do you know how? He was a snitch for the prison officials. He was the one who tipped them off when

77

some of the Union prisoners had an escape planned, which man had wealthy family back home that might be blackmailed out of money if they promised to release him or grant him privileges. That was Brian Adair. That's how he survived two years in Andersonville. He and Tom DeFord ran a lucrative business from that cold prison.'

'Adair lost an arm there through mal-treatment,' I objected and again Lazarus laughed. Barry just shook his head heavily as if I was the dumbest thing he had run across in a long time.

'Brian Adair lost his arm long before they caught him and shipped him to Anderson-ville. He was wounded in battle – running the wrong way during a cavalry charge at Bull Run. One of his own officers shot at him as he tried his best to desert.'

It was too much to take in all at once. They were wild stories these strangers off the plains were carrying. I looked up at my attackers and asked them, 'Who are you, anyway? How do you know that any of this is true?'

'Mister,' Barry told me in a ragged voice, 'we were there. We were at Andersonville. We survived, but a lot of our friends, fellow soldiers, didn't because of these two.'

'We got to catch up with that wagon,' Lazarus said worriedly.

'Wait.' Barry stroked his whiskered chin thoughtfully. 'Something's going on here. Did you say DeFord was in Deadwood too?'

I nodded, watching Barry's brow furrow as he considered that. 'They're up to something, then. But what?'

He looked at me again, but I was not going to say a word about Della's gold, although it seemed almost certain – if these two were telling the truth – that DeFord and Brian Adair were in cahoots, planning on stealing the woman's life savings from her. Her own brother! Or adopted brother, it made no difference. I shrugged as if I had no more information to give these two and since they had already decided that I was nothing but a fool, they didn't try to extract more from me.

'DeFord will be on the trail,' Lazarus said. He did not look concerned, however. These two had ridden with a sense of violent purpose for a long while. Now they had stumbled over not a half of their quarry, but both men. 'And he'll not be coming alone.'

'We're not riding alone either,' Barry said grimly. 'We've a thousand ghosts to give us strength.'

Abruptly, without a sign between them or another word, they turned away and swung into their saddles. As I watched, they collected the reins to my black pony as well and started on – slowly, determinedly, making their way southward.

When they were gone I rolled over onto hands and knees and staggered to my feet, each small movement causing jagged pain to tear through my ribcage. I stood watching the long prairie, the buffalo grass shifting in the rising wind, the cold storm clouds creeping in from the north to shadow the long plains. Then, afoot, without a weapon save the bowie knife hanging at the back of my belt, I began my plodding way south. I had already let Della down. She had trusted her life savings to me, trusted me to guide her and her sister to Steubenville and a new life. I had done nothing to justify her faith in me.

That didn't mean I wasn't going to keep trying, no matter what it cost.

The day dragged on as I staggered forward throughout the afternoon, the land growing darker as the clouds porched over the land. I saw no hoofprints, no wagon-wheel ruts, no sign of habitation. The buffalo had passed on; the only living thing I saw was a badger I startled in passing. We gave each other wide berth.

Behind me, to the north, I heard the ominous rumble of distant thunder. My ribs ached, my legs were growing leaden, and I was shivering in my cotton shirt and short leather jacket. My buffalo coat had been tied behind the saddle on the black horse's back.

Isolation became a heavy weight, and the

wind was so cutting cold that it nearly numbed the fire in my broken rib. The sky went black although it was hours before sundown and the snow began to drift down in wind-tossed flakes which gathered into waves of obscuring swirls and then to heavy clumps. I was going to freeze to death. It came on me with sudden realization. I was on the open prairie without shelter, without warm clothing. My boots were already ankle-deep in new snow – black snow, wind-drifted snow.

Then, for a moment I believed that I saw the tracks of a heavy wagon, and I turned my face into the biting wind and followed them, but the darkness and the falling snow erased them. My reality became only swirling coldness, dark skies and pummeling wind.

I nearly fell over the sad heap in my progress. I stopped, pressing my hat to my skull, bent low and recognized the hummock for what it was. A human form, inert, smothered beneath new-fallen snow. Some obscure instinct told me that it was the body of a woman that I had found – or perhaps it was the slimness of the cold blue protruding fingers which had clawed at the snow in a vain attempt to rise. I thought, 'They have killed Della for her little purse of gold.'

I was only half right. Pawing away at the snow I found the hem of a skirt, a woman's long boot. I touched the flesh and found it warm and began to dig more furiously. It was a woman, but not Della. I sat her up in my arms and looked into the colorless face of Regina Adair. I slapped her face – hard – and did it again until her blue eyes blinked open, stared at me in stunned confusion and then heated with anger.

Her left hand reached out and dug through the snow for a weapon I recognized as Henry Coughlin's side-hammer Sharps .45-70 rifle. His initials were carved deeply into the walnut stock. I twisted the gun out of her weak grasp before she could create any mischief with it.

'I hate you,' I heard the young woman

whisper, and I swept her up into my arms and started for the coulee bottom where the wind at least would be cut by the twenty-foot high banks, and the driving snow might prove less furious in its assault. I started down the slope through the willow brush, slipped, half-fell and then skidded headlong to the snowy ground, tumbling over Regina's body as we cart-wheeled through the leafless willow and sumac.

Cursing, I picked her up again, shouldering her in a fireman's carry. She kicked her feet in protest, but there was more anger than strength in it. I continued on. Not far ahead I had seen a smudge of darkness against the white banks of the coulee. I took it for a cave, of which there were many, and proved to be right. I splashed across the snaking, shallow rill in the coulee bottom and clambered up the sandy bank beyond to enter the shallowest of caves, no more than twelve feet deep with a ceiling rising no more than that, and, panting for breath, crouched and laid the woman down against the cold gravel floor of the hollow.

Regina reached up for me, but I saw her intent and yanked the Sharps rifle away.

'Don't fight with me,' I said hoarsely. 'You may not like it, but I'm the one who's going to keep you alive.'

She sat up, glared at me and then fell back against the ground, the fight out of her. I scraped together what driftwood there was littering the cave floor. Some of it was already half-charred. Someone, Indians perhaps, had used this tiny shelter before. The walls were smoke-streaked and one corner of the floor was leveled out, seemingly by human hands.

I gathered the wood together, crouched and struck a match from the waterproof cylinder we all carried in those times – only a madman would attempt life on the plains without a means of making fire. I am many things, but not quite that mad.

The fire started slowly, a wisp, a curlicue of smoke, a pathetic, hopeful little lick of reddish-gold flame and then the wood caught and held, as I crouched near to the bushel-basket of fire; it was enough to shake the ice from trembling bones. Exhausted, I sagged beside it and watched the young woman across the fire from me. I wanted to ask her questions, but it was not the time. I wished I had a blanket to cover her with, but I had none.

We were abandoned by events and isolated in a fierce wilderness. The storm brooded, rumbled and slashed at the skies with terrible lightning. I felt alone, impotent and my unease gradually was turning to fear. I picked up Henry Coughlin's rough-used rifle and checked it over carefully. I had the rifle and my bowie knife still. It wasn't much, but it was a comfort. I didn't know what to expect now – from Tom DeFord or Brian Adair, or from the two men on their trail: Lazarus and Barry; but the first man to threaten me or the little blond girl sleeping deeply beside the fire was going to pay a terrible price if it came down to it. Henry's old buffalo gun could tear a terrible hole through a man. And if all that was left after the ammunition was expended turned out to be my razor-edged bowie ... well, a knife is a weapon you don't miss with in close quarters.

I could see the constant snow beyond the mouth of the cave. I watched it fall in sheets, in blankets, in squalls. From time to time I heard the small woman murmur in her troubled sleep, clenching her hands into tiny fists. It was cold, very cold, but the smoky fire was warm if I sat near enough to it and with the buffalo gun across my lap, I found my head nodding heavily and sometime before dawn my chin sagged onto my chest and I could no longer fight off the comfort of sleep.

When I awoke again, the sky was bright and the big bore of the .45-70 was staring me in the face.

FIVE

The fierceness in the blond girl's eyes was startling. Her hair was unpinned, trailing across her shoulders. I was struck again by how small her hands seemed. Her slender finger crooked over the curved steel of the Sharps rifle's trigger looked sturdy enough to tug it back, however. She stood in dark silhouette against the sparkling blue-white glare of the morning beyond the cave mouth. Her lip did not tremble, her grip on the gun did not waver.

'I'm leaving now,' Regina said. 'If you have any sense, you won't try to follow me, because I will shoot you.'

She was near enough that it was easy for me to end the stand-off. I swept out a hand and knocked her feet from under her. She sat down hard and I wrenched the big

Sharps from her hands, carefully lowering the hammer. She sat glaring at me, a strand of hair in her eyes, her fists tightly clenched.

'I don't like you,' she hissed.

'I'd already gotten that idea,' I answered. I sat there, the rifle across my lap, staring back at her. 'Just where is it you think you're going, Regina – and how do you plan to get there?'

'I just ... after my sister, of course! To find Della.' Her voice was still firm, but a note of doubt had crept into it. I nodded.

'I don't think you have an idea in the world what you mean to do,' I said, 'and I know you have no idea how to go about it.'

'I'd be away from you at least!' she said hotly. I sighed through my teeth and clambered to my feet, holding my ribs with one hand.

'What is it you dislike about me so much?' I asked, trying to keep my voice neutral.

'What you did to my sister! What all the men like you did to Della.'

'You don't know what you're talking

about. Della is a friend of mine. Nothing more.'

'I don't believe you.' That note of doubt was gone from her voice. She was convinced that I had led Della down the wrong trail in life.

'Let's drop all that, Gina,' I said.

'Don't call me that! Only my friends and family call me that!'

I was looking out at the long land, flat and white and endless, nearly featureless until, far to the south the hills began to rise and fold as the long trail neared the outskirts of Steubenville.

'We have to find Della. You're right there. You didn't tell me how you came to have Henry Coughlin's rifle.'

'Back there,' she said nodding vaguely. 'When we stopped to rest the horses. I wanted to walk out by myself. Henry insisted I take his rifle for protection.'

I nodded. That sounded like Henry. Slowly Regina got to her feet to stand with but not close to me, staring out at the empty land. A cloud of snowbirds rose in unison from the flats across the coulee and exploded into the sky, probably startled by a stalking coyote or bobcat. There were certainly no horses, no men out there to frighten them into flight.

'Where do you think they have taken Della?' Regina asked in a slightly softened voice. 'And who has done it?'

'I was hoping you could tell me,' I said, frowning at her, but she shook her head.

'I told you – I was out by myself...' she blushed ever so faintly. 'I heard three shots. Two different guns.' At my curious look she flared up again, 'I'm not that stupid! I know the difference between a rifle and a pistol shot.'

'I didn't say a word. Which were these?'

'One was a pistol shot, the other two were both rifles, but one of them was a much heavier weapon – like a .50 Sharps or maybe a .56 Spencer.'

I smiled with reluctant admiration. The girl did know a few things about weapons, then. Probably learned from her brother who was certain to know much about them – including how to use them with deadly precision.

'What kind of rifle was your brother carrying?' I asked.

'You saw it. A Winchester, like yours. But the rifles I heard didn't have the sharp crack of a Winchester or of a Henry repeater ... why do you ask?' she asked, her eyes narrowing suspiciously.

'I was just trying to put a mental picture together of what might have happened back there. Did you see anyone on the ground?'

'Mister, I took to my heels, skirts flying. I was down into the coulee with that Sharps at the ready in seconds.'

I looked at her, not smiling this time. The girl had sense. And I was beginning to consider that I might have been closer to trouble facing the muzzle of that old buffalo rifle with it in her hands than I'd considered.

'We've got to find them,' Regina said, not harshly, but definitely.

'We will. They must have stopped somewhere during the storm, so I doubt they're
more than a few miles ahead of us. I don't
think they'll be heading to Steubenville now.
Do you know of another place? Did your
brother mention any?'

'I don't know this country, Miles,' she
replied, using my name for the first time I
could recall. 'Why is it you keep asking
questions about Brian, anyway. You can't
think he...?' She didn't finish her question.

I decided that I had better tell her what I'd
been told by Lazarus and Barry and so I
did, as calmly as possible. I could see her
fury rising as I repeated the conversation. At
one point she spun in a half circle, throwing
her arms into the air in frustration. She then
took a step toward me and glared up
furiously.

'They are liars! Whoever they were. I
happen to know that story, mister. It's one
reason Brian decided that we should come
west. He had heard the gossip too many
times.' She looked away and thumped her

fist against her thigh. 'Now it's followed him out here!'

She went on defiantly, 'My brother is a good man who lost his arm fighting for his country. He would do anything for me, anything for Della. You don't know Brian Adair.'

I didn't. I had to admit that. Truth or fiction, the stories didn't matter at that very moment. We were going to have to start walking out of there before the weather took another turn.

We proceeded.

The snow glare was blinding in its brilliance. We slid and fumbled our way down the coulee bank and clambered up the far side. I was guessing the wagon's direction, but my guess was based on this thinking – that wagon was not going to be able cross that ravine at this point. It was simply too deep and wide. Therefore, they would be forced to continue south toward Steubenville – which I doubted they would wish to reach if real mischief had been done – or turned toward the east. There were a handful of little hamlets very widely scattered around this section of the Dakotas, usually where there were river or crossings, but I could not guess which of them was familiar to DeFord, to Lazarus and Barry or to Brian.

And which of them was now in command? Who had been shot at back along the trail? I could not guess and so I plodded on through the crystal-white day, the snow crackling under my boots, leading the small blond girl in her divided skirt and fringed buckskin jacket.

We found Henry Coughlin about two miles on.

I couldn't be sure at first that it was a man. Flat against the ground, half-covered by drifted snow, I saw a hint of color, a dark blue patch that proved to be Henry's scarf. I went to my knees to uncover him, placing the rifle aside. Regina for once was struck dumb. Shocked, she stood back, her fingers to her lips.

'It's Henry, isn't it?' she asked, almost

hopefully. Maybe she had feared that it was her brother lying there in the snow.

I sat Henry Coughlin up. He was stiff and as cold as if he were dead, but his eyes opened as I breathed on his face and rubbed his hands.

'Miles,' he said in a voice as faint as a muffled breeze.

'It's me, Henry. What happened?'

Blinking the snow from his eyelashes, he shuddered, then began to tremble violently. Little wonder after spending a night in the open. He kept trying to talk, but his teeth chattered so that I couldn't understand him.

'I never told them, Miles,' he said, gripping my collar with his clawlike hand.

'I knew you wouldn't,' I answered. I wasn't sure what he meant but the answer seemed to calm him a little.

'I never even told Della,' he said, more frantically, but more weakly. I knew then that he meant the location of the gold under the floorboards of the wagon.

'That doesn't matter right now, Henry,' I

told him, continuing to rub his hands.

'Sure it does. Della has to have it. I need it because when she builds her house, I'll have a place to live out my days.'

His teeth continued to chatter; his lips were numb and swollen. It had taken him a long minute to frame those few sentences. 'What happened?' I asked again. Regina, I saw from the corner of my eye had edged nearer so that she could understand his weak voice.

'They came on us ... four of 'em...'

Four? Then it could not have been Lazarus and Barry – unless they had other searchers with them that I had been unaware of. Henry coughed, a long, pain-wracked deep-chest cough, convulsing his features. 'They got me pretty good, I guess,' Henry said.

'Where are you hit, Henry?' I asked, beginning to unbutton his sheepskin coat. 'Where'd they get you?'

He sagged back against my arm and looked up at me with eyes that seemed to be smiling but did not blink. I lowered him gently to the cold earth and stood slowly. It didn't matter any more where he had been wounded. One of them had been a killing shot. I wiped my brow with the back of my wrist, angrily snatched up the rifle from the snow and hovered over him, not praying exactly, but mourning the passing of a man and his lonely dream of finding a simple place to live out his days in comfort.

'He's dead,' Regina said. I didn't answer. 'We couldn't have done anything for him anyway. Couldn't have taken him with us.'

I was ready to shout an angry word at her, but looking at her face I saw that she had meant nothing disrespectful. My own voice trembled slightly; I had to put a growl behind my words to feign hardness. 'We can't leave him here. The wild things will be at him.'

Then I handed her the rifle and shouldered Henry's body. I carried him forward as the cold wind began to gust into my face once again. I took him down into the coulee and laid him in a shallow hollow. Then, clambering up the snow-dusted bank I began kicking at the sandy soil until the earth began to shift and cave down over the earthly remains of Henry Coughlin.

I slipped down the bank again, marched to Regina and snatched the rifle out of her hands. She looked at me as if I had hurt her. Her blue eyes were wide and bewildered, her yellow hair drifting across her face.

'Come on,' I muttered, maintaining a gruffness to cover my own sorrow.

We walked on as the sun rose and the wind continued to stiffen. There were more stacked thunderclouds to the north, but they didn't appear to be imminently menacing. The snow which had been granular, crackling underfoot, now began to melt into slush. The cold mud underneath sucked at our boots, making our progress still more difficult.

'Miles!'

We had come perhaps a mile from where we had buried Henry. Now Regina grabbed my arm and pointed to the east, her eyes fixed on the moving distant figures. Squinting against the snow glare, I could make them out too. It was a line of about twenty Indians, Cheyenne at my guess. Traveling southward, they were nearly in the tracks of the buffalo herd we had seen earlier. Their faces were not painted for war, nor were their horses decorated for battle. They were a small solitary group of nomads fleeing the winter, following the buffalo as their ancestors had done from time immemorial.

'They don't have any interest in us,' I told Regina. 'Let's keep moving.'

'And just ignore them!'

'I didn't say that,' I answered tightly. 'It behooves us to keep an eye on them, but I doubt they want trouble.'

Fearfully she smiled, and for a little while as we started on our way again she unaccountably clung to my arm. The day continued bleak and cold. We saw no horses, wagons, only occasional clumps of broken oak trees, with here and there a lone sycamore. For some reason a flock of crows had briefly followed us, darkening the sky. Regina eyed them unhappily as if they were birds of omen.

'How do you know which way to go?' she asked me, pausing to wipe back her hair and take in a dozen deep breaths. 'Everything looks the same out here!'

'No,' I told her. 'Not at all.' I had to point it out to her, but when I did she understood. Earlier the snow had sheathed all of the land in anonymity. Now, as it slowly melted it had begun naturally to sink into the lower-lying ground while it lasted longer on higher. I pointed out to her what I had been following. Before the snow had fallen, a heavy wagon had cut grooves into the soft earth. With the snow melting, these tracks appeared again, showing themselves as long bluish southbound ruts.

'What's off in that direction?' she asked, squinting into the vast distances. I shook my head.

'I don't know. Some small settlement, maybe even an outlaw camp. But that's the direction they've taken.'

'We'll never catch up with them!' Regina complained.

'Maybe not. But, those horses aren't having an easy time of it either, drawing that wagon through this half-frozen mud.'

'But if we do. What then?'

I didn't respond. I didn't know what then. I didn't know how many men I was going up against. I didn't even know who I faced. None of them were friends of mine, that was for sure. But I had promised Della. I had taken on this job and I would fight it out to the last if need be.

I only wished that I didn't also have that small blue-eyed girl in tow.

We trudged on, the woman a few steps behind me. Sometimes, seeing that she was lagging, I slowed my pace. But for the most part she kept up with me, her face grim but determined. Our shadows were already long before us, crooked wraiths darting here and there across the blue snow when I heard her gasp and call to me in a whisper.

'There's a house!'

I was about to respond that there could be no house standing alone on the wide prairie when I saw the low form of a soddy built near to a twisted stand of tall oak trees. What's more, smoke rose from the crude structure. I narrowed my eyes as we stood shoulder to shoulder, looking that way. Still from the smokehole, curlicues of gray smoke weaved their way skyward and we knew the place to be inhabited.

There was no wagon to be seen, no men standing watch. I hesitated to approach the mysterious building which I took to be an abandoned stage station taken over by squatters. For no man could raise crops on this desolate earth or run cattle here in unfenced Indian territory.

'They may have food,' Regina said hopefully.

'We have to risk it,' I said after a moment's consideration. 'Whoever's in there may have seen Della's wagon pass.'

I didn't like it, but we slogged on through the deep mud toward the shanty which had no windows, of course, but only rifle slits cut out of the sod for fending off Indian attacks. What forlorn hope of freedom or wish for land could have led to someone building this sad little shelter on the open prairie?

Nearing the soddy, I cocked the rifle and slowed my pace. No one stirred, nothing moved but the slimmest branches high in the reaches of the broken black oak trees. Regina grabbed my arm suddenly.

'Look!'

I did so and my astonishment deepened. Standing tied to an upright post sunk into the sodden earth was my black horse, Dodger. He was unmistakable, even at a distance with that single white ear and the splash of white on his flank. He was still saddled, and as we approached with caution, he lifted his head, pricked his ears and strained at the tether holding him.

'Be careful,' I said to Regina. 'We don't

know who might be holed up in there.'

I had no sooner said those words than the front door of the soddy was flung open and a bulky, squat man, hatless and bowlegged, stepped out of the hovel to face us, a double-twelve shotgun in his hands. We stared at each other for a long while. Then I lowered my rifle and hoisted a hand.

'Hello the house! All right to approach you?'

'Come ahead,' he shouted back after a short pause. I guessed that the curious sight of a woman out in this wild country indicated to the property owner that we were not raiders.

Cautiously we walked toward him. He stood on the threshold of the sod house, his eyes narrowed. His shotgun was now held loosely, not threateningly, in the crook of his arm. The breeze shifted his sparse hair across a nearly bald dome. His tiny eyes watched with interest, but no apparent hostility. I could understand why a man alone on the prairie would be ever cautious and took no offense at it. I did have to wonder, though, if anyone else was in the house, hiding.

'Name's Carlton,' he said in a rather thin voice as we drew within ten feet of him. 'Welcome to you.'

I introduced myself and Regina, then told him, 'You're wondering why we're afoot out here. Well,' I inclined my head. 'that's my horse.'

'I guess you can prove that,' Carlton said uneasily.

'His name's Dodger. If you untie him, he'll come when I whistle. He's branded "JJ" for the Jackson Jewel Ranch of Wyoming on the right shoulder. If you'll look under the saddle skirt you'll find my initials "M.D" burned into the leather. If you'll look on the flap of that buffalo coat tied up behind, you'll see the same initials marked there.'

Carlton's face sagged into unhappiness. 'I knew it,' he said sadly. 'I never do have no luck. I found the black wandering, reins trailing and thought I'd come into some cash money.'

'You didn't see where it came from?' Regina asked eagerly, but the old plainsman just shook his head.

'Seen no one around?' I chipped in.

'No, son. Just your horse looking for a place to belong. What you tell me is true. I know that. I already looked under the saddle skirt where a man normally burns his initials. Figured someone had been attacked by the Indians or killed by robbers out there.'

Carlton looked so miserable that I had to offer: 'I'd be happy to give you a few dollars for catching him up.'

I still had some money left from what Della had given me to take care of the stable bill and the purchase of the Conestoga at Jocko's stable in Deadwood. Carlton brightened at my words and smiled for the first time.

'I thank you,' he said. 'Would you two care for some coffee – well chicory, actually. It's the best I can do.'

'I'd be grateful for anything warm,' I told him. 'Regina?'

'In a minute,' she said.

I didn't question her, for her voice had grown cold again. I never knew what the woman was thinking and likely never would. I shrugged and followed Carlton into the soddy. Like most of these prairie affairs, slapped together from cut chunks of sod, it was muddy and dank. The packed-earth floor was pooled with water. A smoky fire built from buffalo chips sent rank-smelling smoke upward toward a crumbling smoke-hole. It was funny, I thought. In spring and summer a soddy could be almost magically charming with bright new grass and flowers, like black-eyed Susans and daisies sprouting across their roofs, but with the coming of the fall rain and winter snow, with mud constantly dripping through a sagging earthen roof, many a prairie woman had been driven near to madness trying to keep their little nests clean. Still, with no timber to be had on the wide plains, the soddies were ubiquitous and folks looking for land, for a simple place of their own, continued to throw them up from Kansas to Dakota.

We sat at a puncheon table, uneven and shaky on its thick legs.

'What were you figuring?' Carlton asked me, folding his brawny forearms on the table.

'Sir, I have a total of thirteen dollars in my poke. I am offering you ten dollars for the return of my horse, for your trouble in catching him up.'

'Sir,' he replied with a broad, nearly toothless grin. 'I said I was having a bad run of luck, but I have not seen ten silver dollars for six months. I accept gratefully.'

That settled, we talked for a few minutes. The open door showed the long dreary plains, the sunlight brilliant on the new, fast-fading snow, a clutch of crows sparring and hopping against the dark earth as if it were cold against their feet, the long wavering shadows of the oak trees as the wind nipped at them. Sharing steaming cups of chicory coffee I answered his conversation as well as I could, knowing that he probably had visitors no more than twice a year, if that frequently. The Indians were on his mind, as any reasonable man's would be out there.

'Yes, we saw a small party of Cheyenne,' I told him. 'But they were following the buffalo herd, wearing neither paint nor feathers.'

'Hope that's the last of them for the year,' Carlton said over the chipped rim of his mug. 'Not that I don't do my best to get along with them – even have a few friends among them – if that's the right word. But last fall I had some young bucks slip onto my property and steal off with my two hogs. Do you know what it takes to find a hog out here!'

He had a dreamy look on his face as if imagining the smoked ham he might have had, the bacon, chops and hocks-and-beans he might have feasted on throughout the coming winter. But he was sifting the ten silver dollars I had given him through his fingers and his smile returned gradually. That was a lot of hard money to come across out on the lonesome prairie.

So far as Carlton knew, the nearest town to the south-east was a collection of shanties called Waycross where the rougher elements held sway. There was no rule of law, but only of the gun. I rose, thanking him and started toward the door, planting my hat.

Outside, then, I heard a small creaking sound and looked toward the door, seeing nothing. A moment later there was a series of soft clumping sounds, fading away bit by bit. Was someone approaching... or? I snatched up my rifle and we rushed to the door as one, looking across the empty yard.

Dolefully Canton said, 'Mister, I think you just lost your horse again.'

SIX

I've been angrier, but I can't remember when. The girl had climbed aboard Dodger and hied him out of the yard, leaving me afoot, hungry and tired. I did find my buffalo skin coat thrown into the mud and shouldered into it, unable to dredge up much gratitude for the small favor Regina might have thought she was doing me.

In the doorway of the soddy, Canton watched me for a minute, then shaking his head as if saying, 'What else can you expect from a woman?' he went inside, closed the door and left me to my unhappy fate.

With the sun already tilting toward the eastern horizon it was easy enough to follow Dodger's hoofprints, imprinted deep in the muck beneath the patchy snow. I trudged on, unsurprised when after a mile or so, my horse's tracks merged with those of the southward-bound wagon. The wind had risen again, cold as ice on the back of my neck, and the inconstant clouds continued to gather, to break and shift across the fading colors of the sky.

The dusk was now darkening all around me into indistinct purples. I began to slow my march, following the tracks uncertainly. I had given up any idea of reaching safe haven on that night, resigning myself to a frigid night alone on the prairie when something caused my head to lift.

I smelled smoke.

The land was damp, the mud doughy and deep. It was dark enough that I had no shadow. I had lost the tracks of my horse and the wagon alike, but somewhere ahead of me – not far if my senses could be trusted – a fire offering warmth and companionship was burning. I knew it could be an enemy camp, of course, but the chill in my bones prodded me at least to survey the situation.

I don't know if you could say it was better

than I had hoped for, but certainly it was more expansive. For after another quarter of a mile I spotted the jumbled shantytown I took to be Waycross. Tiny shacks, a few tipis, two adobe brick buildings low, flat and unremarkable, and the glint of lanternlight. I didn't care if it was an outlaw town or a collection of thieves, killers and thugs living alone on the prairie, far from any arm of the law. There would be food there – and warmth.

I trudged on with a new sense of purpose. The poorest sanctuary was preferable to the night I had envisioned on the open range. I was a man with a good rifle and two silver dollars. I was the wealthiest I had ever been in my life.

I walked the deep-rutted muddy streets of the dismal, scattered town, weary and chill. I knocked on the door of a tiny hut, seemingly built from the remnants of the abandoned wagons of overland pioneers, but no one would open the door to me.

Slogging on through the ankle-deep mud I

heard the tinny jangle of a banjo and someone's shout of joy. I was near, then, to what passed for civilization out here. Meaning, I had found a saloon. For where men chose to settle on the broad plains, there was no more than an eye's blink before the first purveyor of liquor set up shop.

I found the source of the celebrations with little effort. Lights blazed, the ceiling was so low that a man could easily touch it, reaching up through the cloud of rank tobacco smoke. A rough crew lined itself along the bar, hats tilted back, drinking-glasses raised in salute to Bacchus. Every single man wore a belted gun, some two and even three, and there were rifles tilted against the bar and strewn across the badly planked floor.

They looked at me, one and all, measuring me without seeming to as I entered and closed the chipped, green-painted door behind me. The warmth of the dilapidated haunt was nearly overwhelming. I peeled off my buffalo coat and tossed it into the corner, as seemed to be the custom judging by the pile of furs strewn there. I watched the local residents as carefully as they watched me. For when you enter a strange house, whether foreign or simply unfamiliar, it is valuable to a stranger to measure the local habits.

Cautiously, I stepped to the very end of the bar, placing the Sharps rifle beside me on the floor as the others had done and ordered a whiskey I did not need or want, but which was indicated to be their customary drink. After a few minutes they ceased to take notice of me. I continued to scan the faces around me. Hooking my elbows on the bar I studied the scattered tables. There was not a face there I knew.

Not Tom DeFord's nor Brian Adair's. Nor did I see Barry or Lazarus, no one familiar to me from Deadwood. Where then, had they all gotten to?

A big-shouldered, badly scarred man, as thick through the chest as an oak tree, wedged himself in beside me. He was drunk and wanted to fight someone, anyone. I knew his type and slipped away before a challenge could be issued.

I saw a slender youth with a broom in his hand standing at the back of the saloon and crossed the splintered floor to talk to him. For, dwelling on my problem, I'd come to a possible solution.

'Can you tell me where the stable is?' I asked him.

'Which one?' he seemed half bright but friendly.

'Any of them,' I said. 'I need to put my horse up. And,' I added, 'I'm just about to starve to death. Where can I get a decent steak?'

Haltingly, the man gave me inexact directions which included a lot of raving over Mother Finch's broiled steaks served with hot buttered cornbread and beans. I exited the saloon as easily as possible, my boots as soft against the floor as moccasins. I knew that these men engaged in private conversations were up to no good and didn't care to have a stranger among them. As Carlton had hinted, I believed I had stumbled upon an outlaw town.

That caused me to wonder if DeFord, Brian Adair and perhaps the others had known that all along and chosen this destination as a safe haven. So far as I knew there was not an army post within a hundred miles, and certainly no lawman bold enough or foolish enough to enter this violent stronghold. What did that auger for Della and Regina? Was Brian strong enough to hold the others off? Was he even involved in this plan, or as Regina believed, simply a man viciously maligned?

At the first stable I had no luck, but entering the hay-and-manure-scented second structure, I saw a white ear twitching above the gate of a stall and then Dodger's head lift to eye me as if I had gone crazy, abandoning him as I had. I started that way.

A skeleton of a man with a huge old Colt Walker revolver appeared from another stall, his hand shaking as he aimed the heavy weapon at me. His eyes, frosted over with white eyebrows, blinked rapidly. His voice, though thin, was controlled.

'Just stay away from these horses. I don't brook any thievery.'

'And properly,' I said, lifting my hands. 'But if that black pony doesn't have a "JJ" brand on his right front shoulder, then you can shoot me for a horse thief.'

Uncertainly the stablehand said, 'A little girl...'

'A little lady with big blue eyes and golden hair, no taller than my shoulder, wearing a divided buckskin riding skirt and white blouse, brought that horse in.'

He lowered the pistol and shrugged weakly.

'You know her then.'

'Mister,' I told him. 'That was my wife. She runs off all the time. I just can't keep her to home.' I felt no compunctions about the lie. It was a lot easier for him to understand, told that way.

The stableman ran a hand over his balding head and asked worriedly, 'Well, what shall we do about this?'

'I'm taking my horse,' I answered. 'What do I owe you?'

The man shrugged miserably. 'He ain't even had time to cool down yet. Gimme a dollar and we'll call it square.'

I did so gladly, since that left me with a couple of silver dollars to call my own. If not enough to purchase one of Mother Finch's steaks with buttered cornbread and beans, it was enough to allow me to tuck something into my nagging stomach.

I saddled Dodger again and slipped his bridle on. Giving him the bit, I got another of those looks that dogs, horses, most animals give us when they are convinced that the entire human race is crazy. Leading him back out into the street I was set upon again.

I was not going to take it this time. I'm not a huge man, but I have spent my life hiking the long hills, chopping wood and scything hay. I'm strong enough to take care of myself when the odds aren't overwhelming, and I have some warning. The two men I encountered in the muddy street came at me recklessly with fists flying. My rifle was already sheathed under the black horse's saddle, and I still had not come by a new handgun, but that did not matter. I was furious and tired of being attacked by every stranger on the prairie.

The first man was bulky but clumsy. I could see him – his silhouette really – by the moonlight behind him and as he tried to club me with a meaty right fist I stepped to one side and jabbed my left into his face twice. His head was jolted back and I saw blood, showing black, stream from a broken nose.

The second man was even wilder in his assault. He tried to hit me with overhand windmill punches as if he would drive me into the ground. There was no science involved in his fighting technique, and little in mine, I suppose. But I stepped inside his flailing arms, dug my left fist into his belly just below the liver and chopped a right hand into his jaw. He stepped back, but I would not let him escape.

I delivered an uppercut that clacked his teeth together and then weighed in with both fists to his body, furious in my attack. I don't know what the final result might have been if they had regrouped and come at me methodically, but it didn't come to that.

I heard the near roar of a .44 revolver, saw the flash of reddish-yellow fire from its muzzle and leaped back, my hand going to the twelve-inch bowie knife at the back of my belt. My two attackers scattered and ran and then there was only a lone figure there, a moon shadow of a man as I crouched, holding my knife low.

He laughed.

'Didn't anyone ever teach you not to bring a knife to a gunfight?'

His voice was familiar, his figure vaguely so, but I did not recognize him until he had holstered his Colt and taken a few more steps toward me. Then I could see that his left sleeve was pinned up and that the one-armed man facing me was Brian Adair.

Uncertain about his motives I only muttered, 'Thanks, they might have taken me.'

'You gave a good account of yourself,' Brian said, tilting his hat back. I wondered why he was there, why he had come to my aid, but did not ask. I still knew nothing about this man and his motives except what I had been told by strangers.

'Who were they?' I asked. 'Could you make out their faces?'

'Sure,' Della's brother said. 'Barry Shore and Lazarus Thorne. I've known them for a while. Quite a while,' he added bitterly.

Reflecting on what I had seen of them, I realized that Brian was right. 'That's the second time they've jumped me.' I found myself holding my broken rib. 'What is it that they want, Brian?'

'Why, Miles,' he answered coolly, 'I imagine that it's the gold, wouldn't you?'

I led Dodger by the reins as we slipped away from that ramshackle, unfriendly town, talking to Brian Adair as we went. The moon was brighter now. Rime coated the muddy earth, shimmering in its eerie glow.

'I had decided that you didn't care for me much, Brian,' I said as we followed our shadows up a broad, deserted alleyway.

'You'll have to forgive me,' he said. 'I'm as prone as anyone to let first impressions cloud my judgement. If you'll remember how I found you with my sister...'

'There was nothing to that,' I said hastily. Brian waved a hand in the air.

'No. I realize that now. Della and I had time for a long talk on the wagon. It's all forgotten now, and I hope forgiven.'

I didn't answer. I could almost feel his frown in the darkness. Well, what did I *yet* know of Brian Adair?

'Sorry,' Adair said unexpectedly. 'I can't expect you to completely trust a man you've only just met. Maybe this will help a little.' Then I felt something cool and heavy thrust into my hand. It was Brian's .45 Peace-maker. I started to object, but he told me,

'I've another brace of them in my goods in the wagon.'

I holstered the weapon with few qualms. I have to admit it did make me feel a little more comfortable.

'Where is the wagon?' I asked him as we walked on, 'and why did you stop here at all?'

'We stopped in a small oak grove up ahead. You can just make it out,' he said, pointing. 'The horses needed forage, of course, but I decided Waycross was too rough for Della, though she's used to rough men.'

'Why Waycross?' I asked.

'DeFord knows we're headed to Steubenville, doesn't he?' Brian explained carefully as if I had taken one too many blows to the head. Perhaps I had. 'I was trying to lose him.'

'Also,' he said, 'we had to pull up somewhere near enough so that you and Regina could catch up. I knew Regina was alive – about you, we were not sure.'

'What happened back there?' I asked as we

neared the oak grove where Brian had left the wagon. 'Regina said you were attacked.'

Brian's answer was almost indifferent. 'A few men opened up at us with rifles, trying to take the horses down, I think. They scattered when I drew my Colt,' he said contemptuously.

'Who did you take them to be?' I enquired.

'Drifters, opportunists who had somehow heard about Della's gold. It was no secret in Deadwood.'

That was so, I knew.

'Not Tom DeFord, though?'

Brian's voice was grim as we entered the deep shadows of the oak grove. 'No, not him. Do you know DeFord, Miles?'

'Yes.' My voice became equally savage. 'I know him too well.'

'Then you know he would not have fled once he had his mind set on his objective. No, not him.' Brian said more soberly, 'I only regret that a stray bullet caught Henry Coughlin. Regina told me that you came upon him and he didn't make it.'

My heart gave a little leap. I had sup-
pressed my urge to ask Brian about his
younger sister. I needed to know that she
was safe, but had been fearful to ask. She
had found her family then. She was all right.

Brian seemed to sense my joy. He said,
'Yes, yes. She is fine. She put Dodger up in
the stable, knowing you would come after
him ... if not after her,' he said slyly. I did
not answer.

Brian continued, 'She and Della are coiled
up in the wagon. I felt I owed it to you to go
looking for you after ... after the things I
accused you of. So here we are then!' he
finished triumphantly.

Except we weren't anywhere at all.

The wagon we had been expecting to find
there wasn't there. The team of horses was
gone. Della was absent from the ghostly,
star-shadowed oak grove.

Regina was gone into the bitter cold of the
night.

SEVEN

'Where could they have taken the women?'
I asked Brian Adair as we poked around in
the moon-shadowed oak grove, searching
through the strewn finery and women's
things that had been ransacked from Della's
upturned trunk in a search for the missing
gold.

'I don't know this area any better than you
do,' the one-armed man told me. He had
removed his hat and now stood holding it in
front of him like a man at a funeral service.
'Somewhere they can hold Della until she
agrees to hand over the money, I suppose.'

'She doesn't know where it is!' I said. I
regretted my decision not to tell Della now.
If they tried to coerce her, torture Della or
even Regina to force her to talk, she
couldn't even save herself by revealing the

location of the gold.

I looked skyward. The moon was nearly full and bright as a silver coin. I thought we had a chance of tracking the bandits and the stolen wagon by its light although it would be slow going.

'Let's see if we can pick up their trail,' I said, swinging into the saddle.

Brian Adair hesitated. Looking up at me, he said, 'I'll only slow you down. Go on ahead. I'll follow on foot.'

'Dodger's capable of carrying double. Climb up behind.'

Still the man hesitated and slowly things that had been puzzling me began to come clear in my mind. Why Adair had been in town. Why and how the groups of men were connected. What everyone's motives were.

I did not like the conclusions I had come to, but at least – finally – I believed I understood. My voice was gruff as I told him, 'Climb up behind me. We're going after your sisters.' I stretched out my hand and freed one stirrup to assist him and he silently swung up behind me.

The moon silvered the rime, Dodger's shadow stretched out ahead of us. The night was growing very cold, but it was a windless, silent chill. Any fresh snowfall would have defeated our quest before we had begun. I cut the wagon's tracks not a hundred yards from the oak grove. They were plain, arrow-straight. Had I been alone I knew that I could have caught up with a lumbering wagon and heavy dray team in nearly no time. Even carrying double, Dodger was much quicker than our quarry and I knew the black horse to be tireless.

I still had not eaten. I was almost ashamed to find myself thinking of food, but my body was remonstrating with me fiercely. I let my stomach groan, complain and seemingly shrink and guided the big horse on through the night.

I had to ask, 'It was Henry Coughlin who fired his pistol at the bandits, wasn't it? That's why he was shot.'

Brian didn't answer and I knew that I was

right. Two rifles. One handgun, Regina had told me. The handgun was Henry's because he had given his rifle to Regina. Brian Adair had never fired a shot.

The one-armed man was simply ... a coward. Even with the lives of his sisters involved, he had panicked, perhaps even hidden. That was the reason he had come into Waycross – to avoid his hunters. Barry and Lazarus.

Hating myself, I confronted him. I could not see his face, of course, as he clung to me with his one good arm and Dodger plunged on through the night, but I could nearly feel the pain it must have reflected as I demanded to – finally – know all of the truth.

'Lazarus and Barry were telling the truth, weren't they?' I asked.

There was no answer.

'You knew that these men from your past were out to kill you. You also knew that Della was coming into a good deal of money. You ran across Tom DeFord again and told him of your situation. You begged him to defend you, and in return promised him a share of Della's gold – perhaps all of it – if he would only protect you from Barry and Lazarus. The men who knew you were a coward and a snitch in Andersonville Prison.'

Still the one-armed man did not answer. 'Did Tom DeFord laugh at you, Brian? Did he remind you again that you were a coward and that only by virtue of his protection and that of the other prison guards did you manage to survive the war?'

'I hate DeFord,' was his only answer, and I knew by that simple statement that I had guessed correctly. I could see their meeting in my mind; I could see the fierce and merciless Tom DeFord mocking the weakness in Brian. Adair would have pleaded, perhaps sobbed and DeFord would have laughed again, promising in the end to protect Brian for a cut of Della's hard-earned fortune.

It was after we had traveled perhaps another mile that Brian Adair spoke to me again. My concentration had been on the wagon tracks, on the hoofprints of the outriders' horses, watching to assure myself that none had swung out to circle onto the backtrail. It was a surprise, therefore, when his low, whispering voice said, 'Barry and Lazarus ... they had put out the word that they were going to shoot my other arm off.'

I understood the depths of his terror then. To be a man with one arm was debilitating, but there were many war veterans in the same condition. To be a man without arms – unable to feed yourself, perform the smallest personal functions...

My pity ebbed and then turned to anger. My voice was too harsh as I demanded, 'What of your sisters! Don't you know what kind of man Tom DeFord is? What he's capable of?' For I had never forgotten that young Blackfoot woman. A day did not go by that I did not think of her and the sneering confidence on Tom DeFord's face on that long-ago day.

And now we were talking about Della and Regina!

'Is it DeFord that has them?' I asked urgently.

'Yes,' was Brian's feeble response.

'You simply ran away?' I asked. I was incredulous: no one could be so heartless, so cowardly.

His explanation was frantic. 'They couldn't find the gold. I saw DeFord slap Della to the ground. They were tearing everything apart. I knew that if he didn't discover the money he would leave me to Lazarus and Barry. Maybe kill me himself! For God's sake, Miles! You must understand. I slipped away and ran into Waycross, thinking I could get your horse – Regina had told us where she left it. I could have gotten away. I came upon you in the alleyway. I fired into the air out of panic, thinking that they had found me again!'

I didn't speak. I was incapable of speech. I thought I heard sobbing, but I did not care. I had thought I had an ally to carry on with, now I knew that Brian Adair was only an obstacle in my search for his sisters. I could have elbowed him off the horse's back and traveled on more quickly, with fewer encumbrances, but I did not. I guided the indefatigable Dodger on through the silver-black night, desperate to find the two women before a worse fate could befall them.

It was midnight, I think, when I heard the muffled voice against the back of my buffalo coat say, 'Do the charitable thing, Miles. Have the mercy to ... just kill me now.'

The moon began to lower its head and the vast land to darken. I could tell by the way he moved that Dodger was tiring so I instructed Brian Adair to swing down and I followed him to the cold earth. We spoke.

'Adair, you've got to tell me the truth, all of it, if we're going to save your sisters.'

He nodded mutely. I gripped his shoulder and shook it roughly.

'How many men was DeFord riding with? How did he ever catch up with you?'

Numbly Adair told me, 'There were four of them – you can see why I didn't try to fight them off.'

'No, I can't,' I said angrily. 'Was it easier to just run away like you did at the battle of Bull Run?'

'Who told you that lie?' he demanded, showing the first hot emotions of the long night.

'Who do you think? Barry and Lazarus.'

'They weren't there! It's calumny, I tell you. Something that spread around the prison camp.'

'We'll let that pass, then,' I said. After all I wasn't there either. I had only said that to raise a spark of manhood in this defeated man. There must have been a time when he had been a warrior – no one survives years of brutal war and remains a complete coward. Maybe it was the cumulative shock of the war, the weariness of rising each morning to pitched battle. I would not ever know; I only knew that I needed his help now. Two against four is a much better number than a single man attempting it alone.

It was cold, bitter cold, yet there was perspiration on Brian's forehead and his eyes shunted about nervously. 'Is it Barry and Lazarus you're looking for?' I asked, and his head gave the faintest of nods. 'They'll never find us on this dark night.' Then I unholstered the Colt revolver he had lent me and said, 'You'll need this, Brian.'

'How did DeFord know how to find you?' I asked him.

'We had talked over a plan. He knew Waycross well. He was among the rough crowd there,' he said with only a shadow of shame. 'We discussed, I mean, that Barry and Lazarus had somehow gotten onto my trail and that he would side with me against those devils if I would see that he got Della's little fortune from selling her saloon. It was all going to look like a robbery. Della would never know, nor Regina. Then,' he shrugged, 'I was going to get half of her money and so I would be able to take care of both of them.'

'You can't have been so sure of DeFord!' I said in astonishment. 'You forget – I know the man as well as you do.'

'I know...' he said miserably. 'But Barry and Lazarus – you must see! They have vowed to kill me after taking off my other arm. I had no choice but to deal with DeFord.'

'And give your sisters into his possession?' I said with disgust. Brian grabbed my arm. His grip was surprisingly strong.

'I'd do nothing to harm Regina and Della. It's just that DeFord got angry when Della wouldn't tell him where the gold was. He ... began to threaten me with the same sort of threat Barry and Lazarus had made.'

'And so you took to your heels, leaving the women with him.' I was so angry that my lips barely moved as I spoke. In those times, in that place, you have to understand, there were two sorts of men despised more than killers and robbers: liars and cowards. I am not sure which of these two was the more despised in the Dakota country. A man could trust neither. The one you could not do honest business with, the other you could not count on in a fight. These traits were of paramount importance in a lawless land.

I stilled my anger – it was not serving my purpose. 'Do you know where DeFord might be headed?'

'I know,' Brian Adair said hesitantly, his eyes dew-bright in the starshine. The moon was a fading memory in the east. I heard a prairie wolf baying at the dying apparition. 'It's a tiny place called Cripple Creek.' He murmured the last words as if they had terrible significance to him.

'We're on the right trail, then?'

'As near as I can guess. I haven't traveled the plains like you have.'

My experience did me little good. These little communities cropped up, flourished and died away to ghost towns in a matter of a few years, leaving you to wonder why anyone had ever thought to build there. I can name you half a hundred such deserted towns in Dakota Territory alone, old mining camps, settlements that had been promised a railroad spur, so many vanished towns and lost dreams...

I judged Dodger to be rested enough to continue. The saddle creaked beneath my weight as I mounted and Brian Adair groaned as I pulled him up behind me, knowing now that there was no way he could escape the debt due to the ghosts of his past.

I should have had sympathy for him, I suppose, but my thoughts were only on the hardworking Della who had done her best to make a living and prosper in a hard-bitten land. And on Regina–

The little blue-eyed girl who had shown nothing but hatred for me, despising my very name. I tried to tell myself that I would ride on into danger for any woman needing my help, but there was more to it. I could not lie to my heart. If Regina hated me still, yet I believed that I was very close to being in love with her.

Not that I knew what love was supposed to feel like. I was a long-riding, lonesome sort of man, never much in the company of women – who were few enough out here on the long plains. Nor did I have anything to offer Regina even if she might consider that I was not an object of scorn – and that seemed doubtful.

But even a lonesome man has to have his dreams.

'I see something,' Brian Adair said and I slowed Dodger, halting him easily. Adair was right. The dawn was breaking and there was a streaky orange glow across the horizon in front of us, and silhouetted against that dully glowing backdrop I could make out half a dozen structures. From one of these, smoke curlicued into the crisp morning sky. The last stars were fading. We began to see the morning birds. Doves winged across the sky, cutting quick Vs. Quail and partridges emerged from the sagebrush and crowded sumac to feed, startled when they found us waiting there so that they hid themselves away again. Far away I saw a small herd of antelope watching us, their heads lifted alertly.

'Should we wait?' Brian Adair asked me uneasily.

'For what?'

I kneed Dodger and the big black started toward the clump of buildings ahead of us.

What I meant was – what was there to wait for? Help? From where? Besides, dawning is the time that criminals are least alert. And I would not wait for them to pursue more devilment with Della and Regina being held hostage. DeFord was bound to grow angrier, thinking that Della was lying about knowing where the gold was.

And he was known for his savage treatment of women.

I saw as we neared the tiny outpost that only three buildings stood there, long narrow pole-and-sod buildings. What their original purpose had been I could not discern. This was not farmland, ranchland, mining country. Perhaps once a group of weary settlers had found this place and thought, 'No more. This is far enough to travel these endless plains.'

There were two leafless sycamores standing on a low knoll behind the huts. These offered little concealment, but there I swung down from Dodger and went flat on my belly to study the layout as best I could. Brian stretched out beside me. I could feel his nervousness, and gave credence to the possibility that wild animals can scent fear. His legs trembled and there was perspiration on his brow in the chill of the morning.

'What do we do?' he asked.

'Take it to them. There's no sense in letting them rise and shake themselves awake.'

'I don't see the wagon,' he whispered in a ragged voice.

Nor did I. Did that mean that the Conestoga was hidden, that the women in fact were not here, or that they had abandoned it along the trail as being to slow and cumbersome?

'No matter,' I said. 'We have to find out and do what we can.' The man still trembled beside me and I said sharply, 'Brian, pull yourself together. I know you are familiar with weapons and their use. The war was a long time ago, but you cannot have forgotten that much.' His eyes widened and then narrowed as I flung words at him that hurt as much as a slap on the face, 'These are your sisters. Be a man! If you were to lose your other arm it wouldn't be as bad as having "coward" etched on your tombstone.'

We started on down toward the encampment through the dawn-daubed morning.

EIGHT

Leaving Dodger in the scant shelter of the sycamore trees, we worked our way down the knoll, the frozen grass crackling beneath our boots. I saw no sentries posted, and wondered at that before I realized that DeFord would have no fear of us. Why should he? Brian Adair he had marked as a coward. He must have known that Regina had left me afoot miles behind.

Still I frowned as we paused briefly behind the windowless back wall of one of the pole and sod long-houses. Where were their horses? Where were the women? Had I made too many assumptions? We would just have to find out.

Taking a deep, calming breath, I motioned to Brian to remain behind me a few paces as we rounded the corner of the building and I approached the front door. I saw one sign that all was not as I assumed, but that I was on the right trail. Simple as it seems, I spotted the horse-droppings near the hitch-rail and knew them to be fresh. It bolstered my flagging confidence at least a little. Someone was within, or had recently been.

Then I was stumped. Did I try to knock on the door and risk being shot through it, try to shoulder my way inside, or use guile which is far from my strong suit? I reasoned that they would be expecting no one who was not part of the gang to find them and decided that bluffing was my best option.

I stepped onto the porch and banged on the door with the stock of the Sharps rifle.

'Hey!' I bellowed. 'What's going on here! No one awake? Let me in, damnit!'

If it weren't for instinct I wouldn't be here to tell you about what happened next, because as soon as I had demanded that the door be opened it was – in a hurry. I saw a grinning, bearded face and glimpsed the menacing twin muzzles of a shotgun lifting toward my head. I also, distantly it seemed, heard a scream.

I flung an arm up, deflecting the outlaw's weapon and rolled into his thighs, taking him down to the plank floor where we tangled ourselves in a confused pile. From the tail of my eye I saw a second man, also bearded, leap for his holstered revolver which was hanging on a wall peg.

I was a dead man. There was no way I could wrestle with the man with the shotgun and defend myself against the second gunman at the same time.

I cried out a bitter curse and struggled to free myself, but I found myself in the sights of the second man's blue-steel Colt revolver. I could see his eye squinting at me, the slight amused twist to his lips. Then from behind me I heard the thunder of another pistol, saw the gunman stagger back, fire into the floor and slide down the wall to sit there lifelessly.

The distraction gave me a fragment of a second to club the man with the shotgun with my right hand, drive my fist a second time into the hinge of his jaw and rip the weapon from his hands before he could do any damage with it.

I rose panting, saw Brian Adair framed in the doorway, his Colt still curling smoke from its muzzle and I half-collapsed onto a nearby leather-strap chair, my Sharps rifle trained on the outlaw on the floor.

Regina shrieked with relief, ran to her brother and threw herself against him. Brian was trembling, which was understandable. I had a twitch or two in my own limbs as I stood and walked to the man who had wielded the shotgun, kicked the weapon away and yanked him to his feet.

I had one moment to turn and nod my thanks to Brian. Then I returned my attention to the thug with the shotgun, hurling him back toward a roughly made cot where he landed in a sprawl. I could barely speak as I asked Regina, 'Did they touch you?'

'No,' the little blond girl told me as she continued to cling to her brother. 'They knew that if they did, they would have to deal with Brian.'

She was defiant and angry. I was only vaguely disappointed, as a man who has seen his thunder stolen from him always feels. There was no time for these petty thoughts, however.

'Where's Della?' I asked.

'Make him tell you,' she said, waving a hand at the rough-looking man on the cot.

'No one told me,' he said, rubbing his chin with the back of his wrist. 'They just took off, leaving us to watch the little girl.'

'DeFord, you mean?'

'Who else?' The gunhand turned his head and spat blood onto the floor.

'They had me in the back room,' Regina said, 'but I heard a part of it. The man – DeFord – said that if the gold had been deposited, they wouldn't hurt Della. Or me.'

'I don't understand,' Adair said in confusion. I thought I did. 'Steubenville, that's where they've gone isn't it?' I asked the thug on the cot. He didn't answer which was as good as an affirmative response. Sullenly he turned his eyes down. Brian still looked puzzled. I illuminated him.

'Della is a clever woman. She, herself, doesn't know where the gold is, but telling that story to DeFord would only bring disbelief. Then he would try to beat it out of her – and out of Regina, assuming that her sister might know.'

'How does that take her to Steubenville?' Adair asked. He was as angry and frustrated as when I had first met him.

'Knowing Della, she would be quick to come up with an explanation,' I believed. 'She must have told DeFord that she had arranged to have the gold shipped to Steubenville in a Wells Fargo strongbox. It makes sense, don't you see? She'd explain to DeFord that people in Deadwood knew that she was selling the Eagle's Lair and didn't want to risk transporting it herself.

'Then,' I speculated, 'she would have made up some story about having Mc-

Culloch – anybody – making arrangements with the stage company to have the gold shipped to Steubenville, since everyone also knew that was where she was planning to settle.'

'It makes sense,' Brian said slowly.

'Of course it does.' If, unlike me, no one knew that Della had not had the time to make those sorts of arrangements on the night we pulled out of Deadwood.

'What will she try to do now?' Regina wondered, her eyes wide.

'Bluff as long as she can. She's probably near to panic. She can't even try to draw attention to herself in Steubenville for fear they will harm you, Regina. You were the hostage, after all.'

Brian was nodding silently. His eyes met mine. 'So what do we do now, Miles?'

'Get to Steubenville as quickly as possible.'

'On one horse?'

'There were two men here,' I pointed out. 'They have horses picketed out somewhere.'

I turned my attention back to the bearded man. 'You want to tell us where, or do you want to join your friend there in Hades?'

The man's uncertainty was short-lived. Maybe I didn't have a killing look about me, but there was no mistaking the savage glint in the eyes of Brian Adair. The outlaw looked once at his dead friend and told us what we wanted to know, 'Over behind the broke-down building next door. Mister, could you leave me one of the ponies?'

'Not likely.'

'DeFord will kill me,' he said, burying his bearded face in his thick hands.

'I wouldn't worry about him,' Brian Adair said coldly. 'DeFord won't be coming back.'

The sun was still only a flat-topped, streaked ball of crimson peering over the far Rocky Mountains when we hit the long trail toward Steubenville. We flogged our horses with our reins, believing that with or without the Conestoga wagon DeFord would be traveling at an easy pace with no sense of urgency, not knowing that there was anyone trailing behind. We would catch up before long.

I don't know what the others were thinking, but my thoughts were only with Della, that calm, brave lady who had worked her life to gain some small amount of wealth that she could share with her brother and sister – and they had effectually turned their backs on her, scorned her for her way of life.

I watched Regina's slender back as she rode ahead on one of our newly-acquired mounts – a thick-chested blue roan. I had come to feel that there was something deep and fine in her heart, but I could not open her up to find it ... and it might have been merely the romantic fantasizing of a lonely man.

Brian Adair was even more of a puzzle. He was a coward, yet he had acted with bravery back at the outpost.

Were the two of them more intent on Della's little fortune than anything else? I hated to think so.

We slowed the horses as the morning sun turned yellow and shrank in the long silver-blue sky. I could feel Dodger faltering beneath me. I patted his neck. I had never abused him and he had the will always to give me all he had. I muttered an apology. Understanding, or not, he twitched his white ear in my direction.

I don't know if the others had seen them or not, but innate caution had prompted me always to watch the backtrail. There were two men on horseback behind us on the silver-frosted grass of the long plains: far distant, quietly menacing silhouettes. I was pretty sure I recognized them even at that distance. I did not know if they would bother me or harm Regina.

But I knew, given the chance, that Barry and Lazarus would certainly kill Brian Adair.

That seemed to be their mission in life now, to track down all of those men who had betrayed them or abused them in Andersonville Prison. DeFord was also on their killing list. I wondered how many others they might have shot down – perhaps men trying to rebuild their lives, men who had only been caught up in the shifting tides of war, pawns in the barbarities of the great up-heaval. Only Barry and Lazarus knew that, of course. A second, quite dreadful thought occurred to me: were there others like them roaming the West. Fifty, a hundred seeking redress from their long ago enemies, real or supposed?

I slowed Dodger a little more. He was beginning to tire badly. Ahead now, like a squat collection of insects I could see a settlement. We were nearing Steubenville.

The land here began to rise slightly and fold up upon itself so that we began to pass through modestly formed hills. The oaks and the scattered sycamore trees also became more abundant. The grass, I noticed, was no longer simply buffalo grass, but thickened by blue gramma, much better fodder for livestock. A tiny rill glinted in the morning sunlight, showing silver. I could see why

Steubenville – unlike some of the other settlements we had seen recently – had drawn pioneers to it.

I turned in the saddle, glancing back. The rising ground had become a vista of concealment for our trackers. They had vanished from my line of sight.

Now wearing two revolvers taken from the badmen, I felt more secure, but only a little. We had two men ahead of us in Steubenville – Brian had said that there were four attackers in DeFord's party, and we had accounted for only two of them so far. Behind us were another two men, and from what I had seen of them they were no less violent in their zealousness than DeFord was in his greed.

Barry and Lazarus might or might not kill me. They would certainly try to execute both Brian and DeFord. I was in the middle of it all now, and I did not like it.

'Here we are!' I heard Brian call out, and glancing up I could see that we were nearly into Steubenville.

'Hold up!' I called to him.

Regina looked angrily at me across her shoulder. 'They have my sister! There's no time to waste.'

'We don't know where they are,' I said, taking hold of her roan's bridle. I thought for a moment that she would strike at my face, but she held back. Brian circled uncertainly on his little gray pony before pulling up beside me. I told him, 'Nothing at all will happen until the Wells Fargo office opens and they discover that Della has been running a bluff. I don't know what time that will be, but the sun's just barely risen. We have time to formulate a plan, Brian. It's better than just rushing into town and starting a shooting war.'

The former soldier nodded his understanding. Impatient as we all were to rescue Della from the outlaws, riding headlong into the main street of Steubenville while the town still slept made no sense.

'What do you propose?' the one-armed man asked me. He was quite calm now.

159

Even Regina, after her burst of impatience seemed to understand the need for calm. Our horses stood together, nudging one another's heads.

'The place to take them is outside the Wells Fargo office, before they can enter the building and Della's bluff must run out. We have to locate it first, leave our horses hidden away. A stable, if we can find one. Regina can stay there until … until it's over.'

'I can fight,' Regina said gamely.

'I won't have it,' I answered. I still could not make out this little blond girl. She had grown feisty again, and I half believed that she would fight it out if it came to that.

'You know that I can shoot,' she said sharply. 'If you won't let me walk up to the express office, at least let me have one of your guns. I'll take the Sharps,' she declared.

I still didn't like it, but as she had pointed out, I was now carrying two Colts and Henry Coughlin's .45-70 Sharps. If I needed that much firepower, I had no chance anyway. I nodded and dutifully unsheathed the long rifle, handing it to her.

'Keep an eye out for the wagon,' I told them. 'It won't be easy to hide. It may be that they're holding Della in it.'

I didn't tell them that that was where the gold was hidden. I still wasn't totally sure of Brian's motives – nor of Regina's, I thought grimly as we started on. Could their purpose be mercenary? My idea concerning the wagon was that if worse came to worst I would give up the gold to DeFord for Della's safety. She, herself, probably would have not wished me to, but Della was my friend, a lady I would do anything for. I wandered through these uncertain thoughts as we started our mounts on again, down the gently sloping knolls toward Steubenville.

'Anything else on your mind, Miles?' Brian Adair asked as Regina pulled briefly ahead of us, her blue roan's hoofs singing through the long grass. 'Something you're not telling me?'

'Yes,' I answered softly. 'I'm afraid so. You will have to watch your back at all times ...

161

because they are back there, and they want your hide.'

He smiled lopsidedly and replied, 'I know that. I saw them a few miles back.' There was a resoluteness in his voice that had not been there a few hours earlier. Perhaps it was thoughts of his sister, perhaps the realization that eventually comes to every man – that he could not live forever no matter how he tried to protect himself in this dangerous world.

'What's a damned arm worth anyway?' he murmured, looking back toward the north where the two vultures ranged.

NINE

Steubenville was a pleasant area, gently-sculptured land studded with scattered oaks and in one far valley a small growth of Douglas fir trees. The sun had risen clear and pretty, yet there seemed to be a pall across the land. I wondered if this was only something I was carrying in my mind, fearful of the gunsmoke to come and the danger to the two women I cared about most in the world – the one who trusted me as a friend and her younger sister who looked at me as she'd look at a cowflop in her flower garden.

'There's a stable,' I told Brian in a low voice. The town had not yet awakened, and I wished to make no unnecessary sounds to announce our presence. Of the covered wagon, I had seen nothing, nor had the others. 'Let's approach it from the back. Get

163

off the main street.'

Of a freight office I had also seen nothing, but if we could find a stableman around the premises, he was certain to know where it was.

'Have you seen them?' Brian asked in a quiet voice, and I shook my head. Regina glanced at us closely, not knowing about the danger from Barry and Lazarus trailing behind. Was it time to tell her? Probably not. They were not savages like DeFord, simply men focused on their single killing objective.

'What are you two keeping from me?' she asked in that hot little way she had. Neither of us answered. Why heap more concerns upon her? She was brave and resolute. But there were signs that it was all getting to be more than she could take. When she swung down from the blue roan her legs were trembling. She flared a look at me as if daring me to comment. She stood there sturdily with the rifle in her hands as I entered the shadows of the stable to look for a man to care for the horses.

The man I found was drunk, stupid and ugly. He had a strip of thin graying hair on his head and jug-handle ears, a surly expression and broken teeth. None of that mattered to me; we are all only what we can be. What I needed to know most was where the Wells Fargo office was and when it opened. He told me.

I still had a pair of silver dollars in my pocket, and he was happy to accept one. He suddenly seemed less surly, and of course now knew how to come by his morning 'wake-up' drink of whiskey.

'Half a block,' I said to Brian, pointing in the direction the stablehand had indicated.

'I still want to go,' Regina said with sharp petulance.

'You still can't,' I said firmly and Brian backed me up.

'No, Regina,' her brother said. 'I won't have it. Della's in a lot of trouble. I don't wish to have to worry about you as well.'

Reluctantly, but with what seemed to be a whisper of relief, Regina nodded and agreed. Brian and I started away. To my surprise, Regina grabbed my jacket sleeve and whispered fiercely into my ear:

'Take care of him, Miles Donovan. Take care of both of them!' She paused, turned from me and added, in the smallest of voices, 'And take care of yourself.'

The last time I saw Regina she was perched on a nail barrel, the Sharps rifle across her knees, watching the stablehand hurriedly unsaddle and curry the ponies – presumably so he could make it to the door of the saloon as soon as it was swung open. There was concern in her eyes, but I judged it to be for Brian and Della and not for me. Our friendship had not progressed far enough for me to believe that she cared if I lived or died, so long as I did my job.

'Let's find out first what time the freight office opens,' I suggested to Brian as we walked the main street in the chill of morning. I had asked the stablehand, but he had never had dealings with them and did not know.

The streets of Steubenville were deadly silent which did not surprise me. The trades-people were still rising. The drinkers and gamblers, the night-people, were exhausted and sound asleep. The small ranchers and dirt farmers would be hard at it in their fields or on the range. It not being the week-end, there was no influx of shoppers.

We passed a small round man in a neat town suit and Brian stopped him to ask for the time. Glancing at his gold watch he told us, 6:45.

The little man glanced at us curiously as we continued on our way past several closed shops, a saddlery, a dry goods store, our boots clicking on the planks of the board-walk. I had my hat low against the morning glare of the sun. Brian seemed oblivious to it.

'Did you see them?' he asked, as we passed between two rows of buildings. I only nodded.

Two men sat their horses in a crossing alley. Barry and Lazarus. I could imagine what their conversation was at that moment.

We eventually found the Wells Fargo office. On its plate-glass window, the office hours were painted in gilt. '7 a.m. to 5 p.m. except by appointment.'

That didn't give us long to make preparations, since if my logic was correct, Tom DeFord and his fellow bandit would be escorting Della to the freight office the moment it opened, eager for the gold shipment they expected to be waiting for them. And what of Della? She would be terrified by now, having played her last card, not having any way of knowing that Brian and I were there.

What of the gold itself? *Where* was the Conestoga wagon? Had the fools burned it? It was still in my mind to give up the money if there was no other way to save Della's life, but I seemed to have lost that option.

'What are you thinking about, Miles?' Brian Adair asked me as we slipped into a narrow alley to pause in its cool shade while the sun rose higher. A scrawny, yellow alley-dog scooted away at our appearance. I leaned my back against the plank wall of the Wells Fargo office.

'About the value of gold. How worthless it really is,' I told him.

'Not so dissimilar from my own thoughts,' Brian replied, tilting back his hat. 'I was pleased to find that Della had a few dollars saved. Hell of a time a one-armed man has finding honest work. But the gold doesn't mean anything now – except that Della will have something when she needs it.' He half-smiled at me. 'To tell you the truth, Miles, I thought at first that you were playing this game for the sake of her little fortune.'

'I know that,' I said, yawning despite my-self. The yellow dog had returned to look at us, cock its head and bolt again.

Brian went on. 'Then I saw the way they were looking at you when you didn't know they were looking. I could see the admir-ation there, and I knew.'

'The way *they* were looking at me?' I said in surprise.

'Sure,' Brian said. He grinned for the first time since I had known him. 'Both of them, Miles. They both care for you.'

Well, that was news to me. Della and I had always been good friends, but if Regina cared about me much she was most secretive about it. We heard a small click and the opening of a door on rusty hinges. Our eyes flickered that way.

'Sounds like the Wells Fargo man is opening up,' Brian Adair said. 'How do we play it?'

'When they show up,' I told him, 'I'll brace down Tom DeFord. Watch my back. Lazarus and Barry are out there.'

'They're my problem.'

'We're in this together now, Brian.'

'Yes,' he said tightly, 'I guess we are.'

We waited. Minutes crept by. As the day warmed, bluebottle flies emerged from their night hiding places to hover, humming in the still air. I caught a sound, gestured to Brian for stillness, listened more intently. Then I was sure. Heavy boots on the plankwalk, and mingled with them the lighter sounds of a woman's step. I unholstered my Colts. Brian drew his revolver. We were going to have to bring a little bit of hell into this peaceful Dakota morning.

My hat was still pulled low as I stepped out of the alley onto the main street. I saw DeFord and his bearded cohort – Della between them, gripped roughly by her arms. I saw her eyes lift and flicker through stages of recognition, hope, fear. Then DeFord recognized me and he reached for his weapon.

The other man was slow – he had never seen me before, didn't expect any sudden thunder on this bright morning. I had already flicked up one of my Colt .44s, meaning to throw down on DeFord, but he stepped behind Della and fired wildly. The second man offered himself as a clumsy target and I took him instead. The spinning slug from my .44 sent him reeling back against the hitch-rail and he toppled backward into the muddy street.

Far away someone shrieked. I threw myself to one side to avoid DeFord's fire. The red-headed man fired twice, sending splinters from the side of the building outward in a spray of wood. Behind me Brian yelled, but I did not take my attention from DeFord. He was backing away now, his arm clenched tightly around Della's waist.

From inside the freight office a slender man with a handlebar mustache emerged with a determined expression and a shotgun in his hands. Maybe he believed a robbery was in progress. And now behind me there was more gunfire, and I had to roll away and come to one knee to face the two onrushing horsemen.

Lazarus and Barry had Brian in their sights, and, as I watched, one of them gunned down the one-armed man. Barry's bay horse was nearly on top of me. I heard him shout out, 'Keep out of this. It's not your fight.'

I thought it was. I leaped to one side and fired off-handedly, tagging Barry through the shoulder. He flopped like a rag doll from his big horse's back.

Brian was down. Lazarus fired another wild shot and then fell from his own mount. Brian must have gotten him with a shot I didn't see. A crowd of people was beginning to gather. From up the Street a little blond girl with a big rifle in her hands was running toward the scene, screaming. I saw a hatless, potbellied man with a silver star emerge from a restaurant.

I went to Brian, sprawled against the ground, reaching him just as Regina reached us.

'I'll make it,' Brian said with weak determination. Regina threw her rifle aside and took her brother's head on her skirted lap. The town lawman was striding toward us. He looked unwilling to join the trouble, uncertain and confused.

Della and DeFord were gone.

'You explain it to the law,' I said, rising. Brian nodded grimly; Regina didn't understand.

'DeFord's still got Della,' I told her before

I took to my heels.

Dodger has always thought I was crazy. Now, I thought, he knew it, as I ran to the stable, caught up that white-eared pony of mine and rode him out of Steubenville without saddle or bridle. Gripping his mane I guided him with my knees, Indian-fashion. He didn't understand why I was doing this, but Dodger had always been a well-trained and faithful creature, he carried me forward, at speed, without hesitation.

I took the alley behind the stable and circled the town, reasoning that if DeFord was running, he would be trying to make his way back to the settlement where he had left his gang. Emerging from the town I began to work my way in an arc, hoping that I could find some sign of wagon-wheel ruts. The Conestoga would be an encumbrance, and Dodger could bring me up on their heels in no time.

I did find the heavy wagon. It was abandoned in a gully where clotted live oak trees and manzanita brush nearly hid it from view. I slowed Dodger and approached the wagon with my right-hand gun drawn. A cursory search showed me that DeFord and Della were gone. DeFord was a lot of things, but no one had ever called him a fool. He knew now that I was on his trail. He must have cut a horse from the leather and taken that, or – more likely – he had had his own pony tied on behind the Conestoga, planning all along on a quick getaway once the robbery was done.

The bottom of the gully was white sand and gravel. I could find no clear imprints of hoofprints, try though I might. The day was suddenly warm in that breathless ravine. I was sweating with fear. Fear for Della.

I had not forgotten the savagery of DeFord on that long ago day when he had assaulted that nameless Blackfoot Indian woman. DeFord was without compunctions, and now he was furious with me, the failure of his plan, with Della whom he must still believe knew where the gold could be had. He had seen one of his fellow bandits killed, must have known that if we had tracked him this far the other members of his gang had not fared well either.

He knew I was coming.

I could not cut his sign in the sand of the wash. I guided Dodger this way and that, searching almost desperately. Gnats swarmed about my head, the Dakota skies began to roof over with heavy clouds.

I saw then – or thought I did – a stone nicked by a steel-shod hoof, turned slightly aside by the striking blow. I walked Dodger onward, looking to all sides of the brushy ravine. I saw a shallow sandy ramp to my right and started that way, toward the long flats, convinced viscerally that this was the way DeFord would have gone.

If I was wrong, Della and the badman would be far away in another direction before I could catch up to them. Dodger made his way heavily up the incline, the sand hock-deep, and broke onto the open prairie.

I glanced behind me once to assure myself that no officer of the law or interfering townspeople who could not have understood the situation were following me. There was only the quiet land and one high-sailing golden eagle against the long sky.

I sat the big black pony, turning him one way and then the other uncertainly then lined out eastward, following instinct once again. DeFord would be heading back to his hideout, had to be. I had to slow Dodger more than I would have liked, searching the ground constantly for hoof-prints. I could find nothing at all against the gramma-grass strewn earth.

And then I did!

Between two brown clumps of long grass I saw clearly one single imprint made by a horseshoe. I read it for fresh sign, certainly cut this morning. And who else was on the prairie to have marked it there but DeFord? I lifted Dodger into a canter. He was comfortable with this long, easy-loping, ground-devouring stride, and even without a saddle he was easy to sit as he settled in to the gait.

I trusted the horse to watch for obstacles in

our way, clumps of rocks, fallen timber, snags, because my eyes remained riveted on the long horizon, my eyes searching for the vaguest of shadows, a hint of color. The wind was beginning to rise once more and the cloud-shadows moved swiftly across the land, staining it darkly. I silently cursed. Matters were bad enough. If it began to thunder and storm, my search might prove futile.

Or prove to be too late for Della.

With an eye to the skies, I hurried on. Dodger had not had proper rest in days, and again I could feel him faltering between my knees, but he was a heavily muscled, noble animal of aristocratic breeding and he ran on. I, knowing that the horse would run itself to death for its master, felt pained and cruel. But, weighing the animal's welfare against Della's life left me no choice.

We rode on.

It was a long minute before I realized that what I had feared was beginning. A spatter of rain against my cheek and a rising howling sound accompanying the gusts of wind.

If the storm came in heavily I could no longer hope to find any tracks. If it snowed I would be lost in the swirling drive of the snowfall. I began to believe that I could not go on for much longer. Dodger seemed to be at the edge of his resources.

And then I saw them.

I stung the big stallion with my spurs. I used them only on rare, desperate occasions, but I touched Dodger's flanks with them now and he understood, dredging up some last burst of speed from out of his flagging resources, and I closed ground on Tom DeFord even as he heard our thudding approach, turned his head, recognized my intent and drew his handgun.

TEN

DeFord's first shot went so wild that he might have been aiming at the sky. There is nothing more difficult than firing with accuracy from a running horse. His second was much nearer. DeFord had been a fighting man all his life and had honed his skills well.

I leaned low over Dodger's withers, unable to fire back because Della was with the man, seated behind him on the back of the big gray horse DeFord was mounted on. Not only could I not fire back, but the gray appeared – unsurprisingly – to be much fresher than Dodger. Not only could I not fight back, but it was obvious that I was not gaining ground on the outlaw.

I saw – once – Della's dark eyes, hopeful, fearful, pleading, but I could not close the gap between myself and the fleeing gunman. Never have I felt more frustrated. DeFord slowed his pony just a little and fired back across his shoulder. This shot sang past me far too close for comfort. I tried desperately to conjure some strategy, but I had none. I had entered this mad race toward death without clear strategy and with uneven odds. Now I and maybe Della would have to pay the price.

And then she jumped!

I watched through the fine rain as she kicked herself free of the horse. With one hand on the reins and the other clenching his six-gun, DeFord could do nothing to prevent it. Della tumbled to the ground, landing on elbows, knees, shoulder and skull, skirts flying.

I shot DeFord's gray horse out from under him.

I had wanted the man and not his brave animal, but as I have said when firing from a running horse your aim is not precise. I didn't have the time to feel sorry for the animal. I was driving down on DeFord, wanting to finish the job, but Dodger could do no more. I knew it; he knew it. His knees just sort of buckled and then locked up, and he glanced wildly back at me, his eyes flashing a sorrowful look as if he felt shame and remorse.

I kicked off his back before he could founder and roll on me which seemed a real possibility.

I stumbled as I hit the ground, put out my left hand to brace myself and rose from the damp grass of the plains. DeFord was on his knees, stunned it seemed, from his own topple. I walked to him, and he pulled the trigger of his Colt twice more, kicking up damp earth beside my boots. I was looking into his eyes when the outlaw cursed me and said, 'Miles Donovan, you interfering son of bitch.' He lifted his revolver again, clenching it in both hands in the silver mesh of the falling of the rain, and I shot him dead.

Della was sobbing when I found her and

scooped her up in my arms. 'Now, Miles,' she asked, 'can I please go home?'

The days fell into a quiet, comfortable pattern.

The law in Steubenville, knowing full well who Tom DeFord was, had no charges brought up against any of us. Brian Adair recovered from his wound without serious complications. Della began to build her little house up on the piney hills with a lot of help from the townsmen. I wasn't much more help than Brian was with that work.

I had purchased a neat little high-stepping three-year-old palomino gelding to ride. Dodger had pretty much broken down, lost his wind on the day of the chase. Now and then the black pony would follow along in unhappy eagerness from behind the corral fences if he saw me on the young palomino.

It was Della that gave me the idea: now and then I would catch up Dodger and saddle him, slip him his bit and just walk him around the yard, though I didn't mount him, and that somehow seemed to make him feel useful again.

From time to time Brian and I would sit near the fireplace in the new house and talk. He would light his pipe, and though I had never smoked, watching the blue layers of tobacco smoke rise gave me a kind of restful feeling.

It was weeks before he finally got around to asking me. He leaned forward after glancing around to see that the women were not listening and asked me, 'Miles, did you ever tell the two of them – Della and Regina – the truth about my Andersonville Prison years?'

'Brian,' I said, 'what would that profit anyone?'

The days grew colder but the weather held clear. When Della approached me from the house she was wearing a striped shawl around her shoulders. Her dark hair was free in the morning sunlight. She stood beside me as I meditatively watched the palomino frisking in the meadow. She must have

185

known what I was thinking.

'You don't need to travel on, Miles.'

I turned, resting my elbows on the top rail of the corral. 'A man's got to be doing something, Della. I can't just be sitting around like this.'

'You know I can offer you four walls and a roof.'

'You don't understand me,' I said, shaking my head. 'I'm not old Henry Coughlin. He needed a place to pass his days. Me, I still need to prove up somewhere.'

'You've already done more than that,' Della said, clutching her shawl more tightly around her shoulders. She placed a hand on mine. 'Would you stay on as ranch manager?'

I smiled only inwardly. I knew she was sincere. I also knew that Della owned forty acres, mostly forest land. What was there to manage? Even if she did need someone, Brian Adair was more suited for a job like that than a rambling man like me.

'I'll be leaving Dodger with you if it's all right,' I said. 'The old boy can't travel any more. I'll be sending back what I can for his feed bill and such.' Della lowered her head nodding, knowing that my mind was made up.

Around us the tall dark pines swayed in the rising wind, their scent heavy and sweet. Della patted my hand and said, 'All right, Miles. Do what you must, but I think you should talk to the others first.'

'Brian and I have had our talk,' I said.

'That's not what I meant,' Della replied. She shifted her eyes and I saw that she was looking at the small blond girl standing in a tiny shadow near the new stable.

'Your sister and I never got along that well anyway,' I said, my voice coming out strangely muffled.

Della's hand went to my shoulder. She smiled up at me. 'At least do her the courtesy.'

'I guess I had better,' I answered.

Della kissed her finger and touched it to my cheek. Turning, she started back up the path toward her new house. Regina remained standing before the new barn, her hands folded together. The rising wind rattled a few pinecones down around me. I was reluctant to move toward Regina. Why? It seemed that my legs were incapable of motion. Angrily, I reminded myself that I was a man, afraid of neither beast nor man and started that way, my stride longer than natural.

She did not move as I approached her, nor even glance up until I spoke.

'Della thinks I ought to talk to you before I go,' I managed to say.

'Don't you think so too?' she asked and her blue eyes lifted to meet mine.

'Yes, I suppose. You see – the snows are going to be falling again soon, and heavy. I have to be on my way south, Gina ... I mean "Regina" ... I apologize, I know you don't like me to call you that.'

'I told you that only my friends and family were allowed to call me "Gina",' she said. Quite decisively she added, 'Now that we are going to be married I certainly have no objection.'

I fumbled her into my arms and held her tightly, looking past her soft pale hair and gently seeking eyes into the unexpected promise of the wide Dakota skies.

The publishers hope that this book has given you enjoyable reading. Large Print Books are especially designed to be as easy to see and hold as possible. If you wish a complete list of our books please ask at your local library or write directly to:

Dales Large Print Books
Magna House, Long Preston,
Skipton, North Yorkshire.
BD23 4ND

This Large Print Book, for people
who cannot read normal print,
is published under the auspices of
THE ULVERSCROFT FOUNDATION